MORE PRAISE FOR *THE HIDDEN SPIRITUALITY OF MEN*

"Matthew Fox, a one-of-a-kind voice, a wild man   d
emancipating modern men from an overculture t   i's
blood and bones. Fox holds a different vision of   d
filled with spirit."
    — Clarissa Pinkola Estés, PhD, au   *es*
    and weekly columnist for the Nationa   *g*)

"An amazing experience to read and at the same time a powerful cultural critique."
    — *Tikkun*

"Matthew Fox's book raises the [men's] movement to a completely new level."
    — Gary Null, host of *Natural Living with Gary Null*

"I have numerous shelves full of books written specifically for women. What I realized as I began reading *The Hidden Spirituality of Men* is that I don't have any books written for men or about the masculine parts of us all. What about my husband, my son, and my grandson? This book opened my eyes. Caught in my own struggles, I hadn't really considered the male perspective. I hadn't realized that just as the roles of women have been distorted so have those of men."
    — Dr. Tami Brady, TCM Reviews

"Fox shows how the challenges of humanity — environment, conflict, and social justice — are linked to the spiritual crisis faced by Western men. He demonstrates that we can start repairing our relationship with the earth and its citizens by repairing our own relationship with the sacred. *The Hidden Spirituality of Men* is essential reading for men who dream of becoming more effective agents of change, contributors to family and community, and warriors in the struggle to make the world a better place. Fox shows that if we wish to repair a world that faces crises of militarism, injustice, and ecological collapse, we must start with the conflicts and potential within ourselves and work outward from spiritual strength."
    — Rex Weyler, cofounder of Greenpeace International,
    author of *The Jesus Sayings*, and coauthor of *Chop Wood, Carry Water*

"For the past thirty years, Matthew Fox has been blazing new trails in consciousness and theology — and often getting in trouble for it. Now he does it again with *The Hidden Spirituality of Men*, potentially launching a viable and consequential men's spirituality movement. His book could not come at a better time for our world, with its distorted, unsustainable, testosterone-frenzied perceptions of what it means to be a man. His prophetic vision and courageous message both expand how we think of the masculine and elevate it to the level of the sacred."
    — Christian de la Huerta, author of *Coming Out Spiritually*

"Leonard Bernstein, a great fan of Matthew Fox, once said to me, 'It will take another generation before a true men's movement emerges.' In *The Hidden Spirituality of Men*, Matt sounds the call and illuminates the path for every man to step into his spiritual destiny, giving birth to an authentic men's movement of the highest order. Bravo!"
    — Aaron Stern, cofounder (with Leonard Bernstein)
    of the Academy for the Love of Learning, Santa Fe, New Mexico

OTHER TITLES BY MATTHEW FOX

THE HIDDEN SPIRITUALITY OF MEN

Ten Metaphors to Awaken the Sacred Masculine

MATTHEW FOX

New World Library
Novato, California

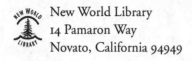

New World Library
14 Pamaron Way
Novato, California 94949

The permission acknowledgments on page 326 are an extension of the copyright page.

Text design by Tona Pearce Myers

Library of Congress Cataloging-in-Publication Data
Fox, Matthew.
  The hidden spirituality of men : ten metaphors to awaken the sacred masculine / Matthew Fox.
      p. cm.
Includes bibliographical references and index.
ISBN 978-1-57731-607-7 (hardcover : alk. paper)
ISBN 978-1-57731-675-6 (paperback : alk. paper)
  1. Men (Christian theology) I. Title.
BT703.5.F69 2008
204'.4081—dc22   2008025398

First paperback printing, March 2009
ISBN 978-1-57731-675-6
Printed in Canada on 100% postconsumer-waste recycled paper

New World Library is a proud member of the Green Press Initiative.

10 9 8 7 6 5 4

This book is dedicated to my (literal) brothers, Tom, Nat, and Mike, who have been my teachers in so many ways and circumstances; and to my father, George Fox, who was the same.

To my special warrior brother, Buck Ghosthorse.

And to my many other (more than literal) brothers the world over with whom I struggle and learn, rejoice and work. I hope we may all wake up together.

CONTENTS

PREFACE: WHY "HIDDEN"?

THE TITLE OF THIS BOOK is meant to be provocative. Is it true that the spiritual life of men is "hidden," even secret? What evidence for this is there? If it's true, why might this be? Also, what are the consequences of this, and is it possible for the spiritual life of men to become more open and accepted by individuals and society?

The great medieval philosopher and mystic Thomas Aquinas observed that there are "various kinds of silences: That of dullness; that of security; that of patience; and that of a quiet heart." We are no doubt silent for all of these reasons at some time in our lives: because we are disinterested or too lazy to speak out; because, for political or social necessity, we swallow our wisdom and gag ourselves; because we are waiting patiently for an opportune moment to speak up; or because we have retreated into a "quiet heart" — attempting, through solitude and meditation, to stop the busy chattering of our monkey minds.

A lot of self-preservation seems to require silence. Consider, for example, men who return from war. Some don't talk about what they've seen and done in combat because they don't want others to have to suffer knowing about those events, and they hope, by keeping these events hidden, that they themselves will not have to relive them. However, more often than not, the events don't stay hidden inside; they create their own noise with nightmares and other unwanted visitations.

Norman Lloyd is a cameraman who spent four years filming the Vietnam War. In his recent documentary *Shakey's Hill*, he revisits a battalion of soldiers that he lived with in the jungles of Cambodia in 1970. At one point, he talks about post-traumatic stress disorder, his own and that of many soldiers, saying: "It's anger, you know. You spend a lot of time alone. I can talk to you, but we'll only go so deep on issues. A lot of things you don't want to talk about."

How much of a man's life — his whole life, including his work and family — becomes filled with symptoms mirroring the post-traumatic stress disorder of war veterans? A war correspondent, Lloyd says, is "in an environment where the people you're with are being killed and wounded. You lose your senses. You don't have room for sensitivity. You become a fairly insensitive person because there's no room for that. This is what happens with PTSD." In reconnecting with his old army acquaintances, Lloyd found that getting the men to talk about Vietnam, even after all these years, wasn't easy. Most of them hadn't even spoken about their combat experiences with their wives and children. "You put stuff in boxes. You've got to to survive." Often, on the day of the interview, the men confessed that they hadn't slept all night. One says: "It's not like there's nothing to hide. It's just that that overwhelming experience comes back." But seeing the film, the men find that good things happen. The film does the talking, and entire families can see what the history of each man's struggle has been.

But do the extreme experiences of war veterans really relate to all men? I asked Christian de la Huerta, author of *Coming Out Spiritually*, if he felt the spirituality of men is hidden or secret. He replied: "It's been repressed, a secret from ourselves." But why? I asked. "Many men have a misunderstanding of masculinity and would categorize anything spiritual as something less than masculine, something feminine. A rejection of an intrinsic part of who we are as men. I would imagine that is more the case with heterosexual men but not exclusively."

We see this is true in the testimony of a male undergraduate, a chemistry and management major, at an English university who one day came across the work of Thomas Berry, author of *The Dream of the Earth* and *The Great Work*. He wrote the following to his professor:

> The deep ecology of Tom Berry was difficult to comprehend at first because it took me out of my "scientific" comfort zone. It required me to connect with my spiritual side and this was not something I have ever had to do before. In all honesty, I greeted Berry's perspectives with initial skepticism for it was not until I began to ponder his ideas in my mind more deeply that I began to connect with *the spiritual side*

I did not know existed within me. This in turn led me to questioning whether or not I truly appreciated the spirituality and the beauty of our planet.... I began to remember those precious occasions when I have marveled at, or simply been in awe of, the wonder nature of our planet — times when I have just sat silently and gazed in amazement at the beauty of a snow-covered Bath landscape, or the beauty of a star-filled night sky. At the time I did not realize the importance or significance in feeling these emotions. Now I understood that these are valuable moments we risk losing forever.

This confession from a young man who is a science and business major is most revealing — and also scary. How many other young men have never connected with a spiritual side they do not know exists within them? And how many, unlike this man, will never be exposed to Thomas Berry or other writers who will challenge them to get connected? How deeply have our schools and our religions truly failed us? Psychologist Marion Woodman observes that "most young men in our culture have no spiritual heritage into which their elders are going to welcome them."

One of the best kept secrets of our culture is that many men are deeply spiritual and care deeply about their spiritual life. It is a *secret*, however, because it is hidden — sometimes, as above, even from the men themselves. Sometimes the hiding is deliberate: I know of a renowned scientist who has a large sweat lodge in his backyard where he and his wife do regular sweats led by Native Americans. They even know the ancient songs in the Lakota language. But no one at the university where he works knows of his spiritual practice. It is hidden from them.

For many men, work itself is often a pursuit of the spiritual, an expression of their spiritual life. Their devotion to their family is the same. For many, spirituality may be expressed as a devotion to their country, a willingness to give all for their country or their family, or even for their "tribe" or gang. Or for their art. Male artists can be their own type of warriors, trusting the universe to provide economically and trusting the muses to feed them their art. And there are political warriors, committing their lives to justice, whether social, ecological, racial, gender, and more. In fact, anyone who gives life their all — be they engineers, doctors, lawyers, taxi drivers, businesspeople, teachers, nurses, writers, mechanics, or carpenters — is announcing his or her *spirituality, which is giving life one's all.* Biophilia. Love of life. Lovers of life. Lovers. That is spirituality.

And yet, so few men would ever call it that. Why have men, to greater and lesser degrees, "hidden" their spiritual lives? The reasons are almost endless, but often each man's reasons interlock in a tight web that keeps spirituality unacknowledged and unexpressed. Here are just a few:

- Because Western culture is still a dualistic patriarchy that values thinking over feeling, material wealth over spiritual, scientific fact over intuitive knowledge, men over women, and heterosexuals over homosexuals.

- Because men are rarely rewarded, and often mocked, for openly expressing their deepest feelings of joy, sensitivity, and pain.

- Because many men carry wounds inside they would rather forget or put aside than admit are there.

- Because modern religions are out of touch with their mystical traditions, whose language and concepts help us cope with our deepest experiences, our "dark nights of the soul."

- Because often spiritual truth and understandings defy language and live in silence, and what is not lassoed by words is considered secret and kept hidden.

- Because men, who are "not supposed to cry," learn to hide their grief as well as their joy.

- Because in times of war, governments do not welcome the authentic, questioning spirituality of warriors, but want the religious obedience of soldiers.

- Because our anthropocentric culture puts more value on human life, needs, and rules than in connecting humbly to the vast cosmos.

- Because men sometimes work so hard that they do not have time or space for exploring their hearts.

- Because, in an attempt to respect the women's movement, some men feel compelled to silence themselves and hide any "unacceptable" maleness.

- Because homophobia robs men of their capacity to relate deeply to other men. Even men who overcome homophobia must often keep this secret in an excessively heterosexist culture.

- Because men sometimes confuse religion and spirituality, and in the process run from their own journey with Spirit.

- Because men lack rites of passage that demarcate movement from boyhood to adulthood, and such rituals that modern religions maintain, such as confirmation and bar mitzvah, fail to do the job.

- Because our culture more often rewards men for their extroverted rather than their introverted sides.
- Because there may be a hiddenness about all spirituality. What is deep is hidden, and a spiritual journey explores the "unnameable" aspects of Divinity, the Godhead behind God.
- Because many men are mystics but lack the vocabulary to name what they experience.
- Because "men learn only through ritual" (Robert Bly) and substantive rituals are hard to come by in modern culture.
- Because men want to hide their shame and aggression or at least hide *from* them.
- Because communication between boys and fathers is often cold or nonexistent in our culture, and too many elders "retire" to the golf course rather than mentor younger generations.
- Because fatherless homes offer few role models for young men to emulate.
- Because an "original sin ideology" makes men doubt their beauty and right to be here, and teachings about God as a punitive Father create a toxic, punitive role model.
- Because men don't know how — and are not trained — to deal with their anger and outrage in healthy ways.
- Because men, like all humans, can be lazy and will avoid the hard work of spiritual exploration if they can.
- Because cynicism, depression, and exhaustion can make soul work seem pointless or overwhelming.

WHAT IS NOT HIDDEN

If, for any of the above reasons, the spiritual life of men remains hidden, what is no secret is that men today are in trouble. And these troubles affect everyone. The warring of our species continues, from Iraq to Sri Lanka, from Lebanon to Somalia; the United States government sells more weaponry worldwide than even entertainment. As this is happening, the rest of creation is suffering at our hands and before our eyes. Global warming is also a *global warning*: a warning that we are not doing well as a species and as a planet. One out of four mammal species is dying out, and where are our leaders? Where are the elders? Where are the men?

In fact, young men are also disappearing. In Baltimore, in the shadow of the nation's capital, 76 percent of young black men are not graduating from high school. It is no secret that failed education frequently leads to incarceration, and as a result, in America today there are more young black men in prison than in college. For many inner city youth, it is more "cool" and more manly to go to jail than to get a degree.

A recent study found that in America boys commit 86 percent of all adolescent suicides. Columnist Joan Ryan, a mother of a boy, wrote an article about this, yet what most alarmed her was the silence it generated:

> Not a single email, phone call or letter about the column mentioned the striking statistic. It occurred to me that if 86 percent of adolescent suicides were girls, there would be a national commission to find out why. There'd be front-page stories and Oprah shows and nonprofit foundations throwing money at sociologists and psychologists to study female self-destruction. My feminist sisters and I would be asking, rightly, "What's wrong with a culture that drives girls, much more than boys, to take their own lives?"
>
> So why aren't we asking what's wrong with a culture that drives boys, much more than girls, to take their own lives?

It is a worldwide phenomenon that three times as many men as women commit suicide. In part, this is because women *fail* at it more often than men; women tend to take pills or cut themselves, while men tend to shoot or hang themselves. However, Ryan believes the issue isn't one of methods, but *shame*, and this goes back a very long way to our days of hunting and gathering.

> Women are socialized to feel little or no shame about being vulnerable or dependent. But for men, seeking help suggests weakness and incompetence. It is antithetical to the traditional male role. Power and control are critically important to men, dating back surely to the day when a man's job was to hunt dangerous prey. In their minds, seeking help means ceding power and control to someone else. It means allowing themselves to be vulnerable.

And Ryan calls on men to relate in new ways with their sons.

> Just as we enlisted fathers to empower their daughters, we need them now to empower their sons.... They learn how to be men from their fathers.... Then maybe we have a chance at changing the centuries of hard-wiring that makes boys and men so much more violent than women — whether toward others or toward themselves.

And maybe more of our sons will live long enough to pass along those lessons to their sons.

Clearly, as with suicide, and as with returning soldiers, the primary issues for men involve both shame and aggression. So how do we deal with them? How does our culture deal with them? Furthermore, what does it mean to enlist fathers to teach their sons what it is to be a man in a time of cultural, ecological, and personal upheaval such as we are passing through today? What are the elements of healthy maleness? What is fresh and what needs to be discarded?

This book is about more than young men committing suicide and young men dropping out of school. This book is about whether our species can survive or not. As one scientist put it, "We are the first species that can choose not to go extinct. But we have to make that choice." Can we change our ways and be sustainable? This includes the ways we feel and act (or don't feel and act) as men — and as women, as parents and grandparents and citizens.

In this book, I hope to provide some answers and some positive models to follow. I will outline ten archetypes that illuminate pathways to spiritual maturity, so that men can put aside the days of hiding and concealment. This book is meant to be *a breaking of secrets. A making known what was hidden.* It is time for men to grow up spiritually. As a species, we can no longer be stuck in our adolescence. We need to explore ancient wisdom and deep teachings about the spiritual life of men, about the Sacred Masculine, and how we touch it and how it touches us.

If it is true that the spiritual life of men is, for many, hidden or concealed, buried or covered up, repressed or forgotten, secret even from ourselves, then great things might follow if we dare to unbury and open up, reveal and unveil, uncover and herald, and speak out loud.

INTRODUCTION:
IN SEARCH OF THE SACRED MASCULINE

RECENTLY I HAD A VERY POWERFUL AND BEAUTIFUL DREAM at a place and on an occasion that was very auspicious. I had arrived at night and in the dark at the top of a mountain at a retreat center named Mount Madonna not far from Santa Cruz, California. The purpose of my visit was to lead a day workshop that was part of a larger conference sponsored by the Institute of Transpersonal Psychology titled "The Divine Feminine and the Sacred Masculine." The night was dark as I stumbled along the rocky terrain, made my way to my room, and prepared for the workshop the next day.

That night I dreamt that I was on a mountain in rocky terrain. It was daytime, and someone came to me and said, "Come look at this." I followed this person over hills and rocky places and arrived at a dirt road where an entire caravan of cars was moving through the mountain. As far as the eye could see, over hill and dale, something like a grand wedding was taking place — it was a wedding day parade with newly married couples in each car as far as the eye could see. Only, lo and behold, in the back seat of each car, as bride and groom, were an elephant and a tiger. They were newlyweds, compassion and passion. A sacred marriage revisited! As one car passed, I saw that the elephant was more or less embracing the tiger, and the tiger had its head out the window and was staring at me. The tiger was beautiful and strong, and in the dream I said, "Look how large the tiger's head is." It was a generous and bountiful occasion. All were happy, the sun was shining, and the four-legged ones, far from going extinct, were intermarrying. Progeny were sure to follow. The return of the Sacred Masculine and the Divine Feminine? The return of the Sacred Marriage of the two? One can hope. It was, in the end, a very hopeful and amazing dream.

I take the dream to mean, among other things, that the elephant represents the divine feminine. It is grand and powerful but also maternal and community-minded. I take the tiger to stand for the sacred masculine — a tiger is a hunter, it is noble and beautiful, and also intelligent (the large head) and cunning. The animals were getting along in the back seat of the car, though the maternal, the elephant, was essentially holding or embracing the tiger, the masculine. I could not see who was driving the car. Probably a human being acting as chauffeur.

Of course, tigers and elephants cannot actually mate, and this dream about the masculine and the feminine should not be taken literally. We carry both masculine and feminine attributes within us, just as the tiger family carries both within it and the elephant family the same.

The caravan in the dream is significant. Middle Eastern philosophy pictures history as a caravan with the ancestors leading, rather than bringing up the rear. We are all part of history and this was an ancestral caravan, one that in the real world is seriously damaged, since tigers and elephants and the entire natural world is suffering at this time in history. Why were the elephant and tiger in the backseat? It's an interesting question, but maybe that is another point of the dream: humans (as chauffeurs) have a responsibility to help preserve these endangered but amazing beings. We are here to serve.

Which takes us back to the essence of the dream — it is time that we gathered our beautiful masculine (tiger) and powerfully feminine (elephant) powers. We need a relationship of equality between the yang and yin powers within ourselves and within our cultural institutions. We are a long way from that situation in our current caravans.

It is widely acknowledged and regarded that the Divine Feminine has made a grand comeback in recent history. This has taken the form of women circles, women scholarship, WomenChurch, women organizing, women leading, women becoming educated and taking their place in science, medicine, politics, business, religion, and more. Far more women go to college today than men. Whether we call her the Goddess, Gaia, God as Mother, the Divine Feminine, the Black Madonna, Tara, Kuan Yin, the Bodhisattva, the Dark Mother, Oshun, Sophia, Wisdom, the Tao, Mary, Kali, or the Lady of Guadalupe, she is making a much-needed and much-heralded return. Indeed, not since the twelfth century has the Goddess been so active in Western Culture. At that time she led the charge to reinvent education and worship, lifestyles and architecture.

But what about the Sacred Masculine? Here we have far less evidence of an awakening. We need to search, we need to dig — *and* we need to let go of images of Male Godliness that are damaging and destructive. What good is it if the goddess returns and men refuse her presence? What good is it if the goddess strives to blossom in both women *and* men, but men offer her no home? What good is it if Sophia wakes women up but not men? This will not do — not in personal relationships and not in cultural institutions, all of which need a healthy gender balance of masculine and feminine, male and female, yin and yang. As Meister Eckhart put it seven centuries ago, "All the names we give to God come from an understanding of ourselves." If men and women, girls and boys, cannot receive a balanced sense of the gender of God (any statement on God is always a metaphor), then it follows that we are not living with a balanced gender sense *of ourselves*.

Of course, not too long ago, a men's movement emerged that seemed to inaugurate the redefining of the Sacred Masculine described above. But for various reasons it has been only partially successful. One reason for this may be that the mass media ridiculed many of the efforts of the movement; another may be that certain representatives of the movement seemed bent on defining masculinity in a crazy macho way — for example, Robert Moore in his book *King, Warrior, Magician, Lover: Rediscovering the Archetypes of the Mature Masculine*, spends far more ink citing General Patton than Gandhi, Jesus, Malcolm X, or Martin Luther King Jr. In an interview with Christian de la Huerta, a leader in the gay spirituality movement and author of *Coming Out Spiritually*, I asked him what he felt about the men's movement. Had it accomplished much so far?

> I haven't been personally impacted by it. I think for the most part the men's movement impacted the straight men's community, so in that sense I think it did a lot of good as far as it could take it. But for some reason it seems to have stalled or petered out, and I'm not sure what that's about.
>
> There is still an acute need to open up men's hearts and spirits. Look at the evolution of humanity, and I would say that men, and straight men in particular, are the rear guard where the majority of the work needs to happen. And it's because of that disconnection with themselves, their bodies and their emotions and with the Divine, that

frustration surfaces and comes out in inappropriate ways, with violence and rape and war.

I asked Christian if he felt men in our society have a distorted view of masculinity. He responded, "Definitely. In a lot of men I find a fear of introspection, a fear of pleasure: they become very stuck in their lives. Disconnected from their bodies; completely repressing the emotions. And that, of course, all comes out in inappropriate and sometimes destructive ways."

I asked Jim Miller, a seventy-two-year-old retired farmer, poet, photographer, and swimmer (he swam the English Channel at sixty-six, and regularly swims to Alcatraz in the San Francisco Bay) what the men's movement meant to him. Miller has been involved with it for over twenty years, beginning with the "Friends of Iron John." He spoke about the positive work the men's movement has done, and all that's left to be done:

> The men's movement has been a powerful thing with Robert Bly and Mendocino men's gatherings over many years. It made me appreciate the gold my father did not give to me. The men in my family were all alcoholics or crazy. The men's movement was very valuable for me in terms of getting my feet on the ground and my legs underneath me and understanding some of the things that men are about, including the feminine pole and the masculine pole — awareness and awakenness. Men have been asleep in our patriarchal theocracies. And they've had a lot of wool pulled over their eyes over a long period of time. And a lot are awakening to their vulnerability and their sensitiveness to Life.

METAPHORS AND ARCHETYPES

My method in this book is to explore ten archetypes or metaphors that I believe speak to a revival of the healthy masculine, indeed the Sacred Masculine. When the Sacred Masculine is combined with the sacred feminine inside each of us, we create the "sacred marriage" of compassion and passion in ourselves, like the marriage of the elephant and the tiger in my dream.

Joseph Jastrab, in his fine book *Sacred Manhood, Sacred Earth: A Vision Quest into the Wilderness of a Man's Heart,* says men lack positive masculine images. "Many of us were looking to the Great Mother for salvation but nobody I knew was seeking right relationship with the Great Father. We all seemed to be reacting against the 'Terrible Father,' the one who sires reason cut off from love, truth hardened into static form, law void of compassion. But there was no mention of any positive masculine alternative."

How important are positive images and ancient metaphors? Daniel Pink, in his provocative study *A Whole New Mind*, describes George Lakoff's idea that the material comforts of life matter much less than "the metaphors you live by — whether, say, you think of your life as a 'journey' or as a 'treadmill.'" For this reason "a large part of self-understanding is the search for appropriate personal metaphors that make sense of our lives." One problem we run up against is that modern Western culture has "excluded metaphor from the domain of reason" — even though "human thought processes are largely metaphorical." The human mind is unique in its capacity for metaphor.

In other words, metaphors, myths, and archetypes empower us, they guide our actions. As psychiatrist Jean Shinoda Bolen observes: "Whenever we recognize ourselves in a myth, it is empowering. A myth that evokes an 'Aha!' helps us stay true to what moves us deeply, to be our authentic selves."

Hopefully the ten archetypes I play with in this book will assist men both to authentic empowerment and to be true to their truest selves. The ten metaphors are the following:

1. Father Sky: The Cosmos Lives!
2. The Green Man
3. Icarus and Daedalus
4. Hunter-Gatherers
5. Spiritual Warriors
6. Masculine Sexuality, Numinous Sexuality
7. Our Cosmic and Animal Bodies
8. The Blue Man
9. Earth Father: The Fatherly Heart
10. Grandfather Sky: The Grandfatherly Heart

Recovering each of these leads not to *one* sacred marriage but to multiple sacred marriages. Whenever we speak metaphorically, it is easy to trip ourselves up on literalism, to forget that an archetype's "gender" does not indicate our gender. Robert Bly and Marion Woodman talk about the "noisy literalism" that often sparks masculine and feminine debates, but "in the great world of metaphor, both masculine and feminine take on rigor and dimension." A male archetype is not about men, nor are female archetypes about women, but all archetypes describe aspects of being human. The ten archetypes I offer are ten stories, ten images, ten ways that men and boys, women and girls can relate to the masculine inside themselves. We slip into literal thinking if we say that a masculine archetype like the Green Man is exclusively for men, and feminine archetypes are exclusively for women. Each of us needs both masculine and feminine archetypes. As Bly puts it, "with its overemphasis on sports and financial success, our culture gives very little help to the feminine side of men. Thus, the masculine in young men may know almost nothing about the feminine, particularly its depth and fierceness."

This book, then, is for women as well as men — it is of course about the men in women's lives, their sons, grandsons, husbands, lovers, coworkers, cocitizens. But it also addresses the metaphorically masculine side of women's souls. As a woman, how healthy are your masculine archetypes? Do you tell yourself stories that respect your own masculinity? How in touch are you with the ten archetypes in this book, and how do you apply them to yourself? Or do you feel your strength and spirit have been compromised by a passive consumer culture? Or that masculinity means violence, domination, and greed?

Metaphors: The Language of the Sacred

When we find ourselves mirrored in certain metaphors, when we drink them in and make them our own, then we begin speaking the soul's language. Metaphor is the proper language for the Sacred, for that which is bigger than our controlled world of words. It is also deeper and more grounding, more primeval, more child-like, and more bodily than the literal. Woodman puts it this way:

> Metaphor is more easily experienced unconsciously than consciously understood because it is the kinetic or bodily dimension of language. It is language bound to its bodily source in the mother's body, language as rhythm, breath, sound. Metaphor is language at the level of infants who are first learning to speak by making words out of sounds and then attaching sound words to persons and things (ma-ma da-da). ... Words at this primitive level had, therefore, a magical power.... Language at this primitive level is the carrier of bodily energy, transformed through sound into psychic energy. Language operating at this energy level, where psyche and soma meet, is what, in essence, metaphor is. Thus, when we were children, we felt metaphor; we didn't care what metaphor meant.

Hopefully, you will find a kind of "magical power" and somatic truth in rediscovering these ten archetypes or metaphors. Only when we make them our own, imbibe them, will we put them to concrete expression in our relationships and cultural institutions, which are so hungry today for new metaphors. Archetypes are meant to be practiced, to be put to good use.

It is interesting that Jesus spoke almost exclusively in metaphor — yet some Christians prefer to interpret what he said literally. Even religious institutions often prefer the literal to the metaphorical. This is why Jesus taught that the Sabbath is for people and not people for the Sabbath. A rebirth of culture and self comes from one's soul and not from institutions.

Webster's defines metaphor as "a figure of speech in which a word or phrase literally denoting one kind of object or idea is used in place of another to suggest a likeness or analogy between them." In this way, the word "God" is always a metaphor. No name for God is God or tells the whole story. Respecting the truth of this, many spiritual traditions do not allow the overuse of the name "God." Jewish people are forbidden to write God's name. Christian theologian Thomas Aquinas says, "We do not know who God is. Only what God is not." Yet Aquinas also proposes, because "God" is such a vast metaphor, that "every creature can be a name for God.... And *no* creature!" The Hindu tradition talks about the "million names for God."

Of course, literalism has its place. The legal system does not deal in metaphors, but in actual evidence of real crimes. Sports contests, too, are decided by the literal — by whether a football player's feet are in bounds or not when he makes a catch, by whether a baseball is hit inside or outside a foul line, by whether a basketball goes in the hoop or bounces off, and so on. Sports and games often depend on the literal to even be played; without hard-and-fast rules, which are decided by referees and umpires, the game would dissolve into chaos. My metaphorical home run would be different than yours, and who would decide who won? Literalism is what makes sports satisfying.

But not life. Life is not about the literal. Here, winning and losing are relative and changeable, and success is achieved by trial and error — where *trial* means try and try again. "Trial" means: Be creative! Try new directions! Use your imagination! Be more than literal. Tap into your powers of metaphor!

Scientists Joel Primack and Nancy Abrams underscore the power of metaphor when they describe metaphors as "mental reframings of reality itself." They see the new cosmology that science is discovering as "a source of new metaphors — and metaphors matter." Research in neuroscience, cognitive psychology, and linguistics has found that metaphors are not just images that help to explain things, but rather they are "the way the human brain understands anything abstract." Metaphors are a kind of sense like hearing or seeing, and

their effect on us is such that "the expansiveness of our metaphors determines
the expansiveness of our reality." Cease thinking in metaphors and you cease
growing.

The Archetypal Sea

While I have spoken of metaphors and archetypes interchangeably, they can
be thought of as different things. Metaphors change, but archetypes are eternal. Each society, each person, each age may develop individual and distinct
metaphors for the same archetypal energy, and conversely, metaphors can stir up
archetypes and archetypal energy. They can elicit archetypes which, as Marion
Woodman points out, are "invisible." An archetype, she writes,

> is an energy field, like that of a magnet, onto which we project images.
> If, metaphorically speaking, the complex is carrying 1,000 volts of en-
> ergy, its core, the archetype, is carrying 100,000 volts. The archetype
> is more than everyday human energy. It is energy that bursts through
> us from some sacred place — demonic, angelic.... It bursts into
> flame from someplace within us, someplace that manifests imagery
> shared by human beings from many cultures and many eras. The im-
> ages change because as cultures change, energies shift and their images
> automatically change, except when people are stuck. An archetypal im-
> age that does not change becomes a stereotype — dead energy.

Living archetypes, in other words, jolt us with energy, so that we ourselves feel
we might "burst into flame." They provide the 100,000 volts that are necessary to make cultural shifts, which today our species needs to do for its own
survival. I know that working on this book has energized me in many ways I
hardly expected.

Archetypes, like stories, make demands on us. They are not neutral. They
are behind all music, all poetry, all stories, all energizing activities. A good artist
is a fisher of archetypes — he or she brings them up from below so that they
"hit us between the eyes," in our sixth chakra, in order to *wake us up* from sleep.
An archetype *rocks* us. They don't arise to entertain, but to guide our actions,
and only in action do we fully realize an archetype — in this case, by choosing to change our images of an outdated masculinity. Bolen reminds us that
"in the inner world, doing is becoming: if we repeat a behavior motivated by
an attitude or a principle enough times, eventually we become what we do."
The authors of the classic work *Green Man* point out that for Jung, "an

archetype will reappear in a new form to redress imbalances in society at a particular time when it is needed. According to this theory, therefore, the Green Man is rising up into our present awareness in order to counterbalance a lack in our attitude to Nature." I think each of the ten archetypes in this book is arising for the same reasons — to redress imbalances in our culture and in our very souls. For the latter flows from the former.

In addition, all archetypes are available to and inside all of us. Each chapter is about *me* and *you* and *us*. And archetypes intermingle. They do not stand alone; they are not sealed in air-tight compartments. In metaphors, and among this book's chapters, they can overlap: for example, the Green Man has a fierceness and a determination that parallels that of the Warrior. The Blue Man, calling in the sky energy, which is blue, has much in common with Father Sky. Icarus, the lost youth, emerges in relationship with his father Daedalus also in the "Fatherly Heart" chapter, and so on. What is important is recognizing when archetypes and metaphors energize us, which is the signal that we've found the adventurous path we need to take.

TALKING WITH MEN ABOUT MEN

Another dimension to my methodology arose very spontaneously during the writing of this book: that is to say, interviews. As I shared some of my ideas with others, I came to realize that many men were filled with concern and with wisdom. They had a lot to say. So I asked them to speak out in this book, and I have sprinkled all or parts of those interviews throughout. I am aware that many men become intensely introverted when asked to talk about their spirituality, yet it is time to speak out and be heard.

The men I spoke with are diverse in age, sexual preference, profession, and ethnicity. They include African Americans, Asian Americans, Mexican and Indigenous Americans, Cuban Americans, and Caucasian Americans. Their ages range from thirty to seventy-two. Some are straight and some are gay. I like the interview mode because it is alive and lively. We hear real people being spontaneous and genuine as they wrestle with intensely personal spiritual issues. The interviews are also invitations to you to *participate* and see yourself in the issues raised in this book.

One of the strong lessons that came through while talking with other men, and in reading for this book, was the role of shame and aggression in the life and psyches of men. I am grateful to psychologist John Conger for his insight

on this seemingly universal situation. It is almost as if shame and aggression
are the "original wounds," to use Otto Rank's phrase, with which men have entered the world. Both are about separation and the price we pay for it. In the
concluding chapter I will summarize the roles that shame and aggression have
played in all of these archetypes, but I invite you to be alert to them as we move
from chapter to chapter, metaphor to metaphor.

For years I have been writing as a male feminist — indeed that was the
number one objection to my theology voiced by the chief inquisitor general
of our day, Cardinal Ratzinger (now the current Pope Benedict XVI), when he
expelled me from the Dominican Order, saying that I was a "feminist theologian." Despite its title, this book is in no way a denial of my previous work;
rather it is a logical extension of it. Where are the men in the awakening our
species needs so badly? Women have been recovering their stories and their archetypes. Where is the healthy masculine in men and in women?

Our culture has latched onto images of God as Male and then defined for
us what male means. Male means winning (being number one in sports, business, politics, academia), going to war ("kill or be killed"), being rational, not
emotional ("boys don't cry"), and embracing homophobia (fear of male affection). Male means domination, lording over others — whether nature, one's
own body, women, or others.

Are these masculine stereotypes true? Do they constitute the sum of maleness? In this book, we will explore ancient and new masculine images that allow men breathing room to be our best and deepest selves: our wild and fierce
selves, our gentle and loving selves, our soaring and mystical selves. Our
prophetic, sharing, earth-loving, cosmic, and expansive selves. Our generative,
creative, compassionate, fatherly, and wise selves. Our heterosexual, bisexual,
and homosexual selves. In short, our true selves.

We men have been allowing others, including corporations, the media, and
politicians, to define our manhood for long enough. Who and where are the
forces defining manhood for us and how are they profiting from this and at
whose expense? Enough is enough!

It is time for us to take our manhood back. And we must do this before
it is too late — before excessive yang energy (which is fire) literally burns the
earth up. The history of the distorted masculine goes back thousands of years
to around 4500 B.C. with the overthrow of matriarchy and the triumph of patriarchy. This led to what Riane Eisler calls the "dominator trance," which reveals itself in empire building and witch burning, in inquisitions and crusades,

in banishing of the goddess and the Divine Feminine, in making a scapegoat of pleasure and sexuality, and in a modern philosophy that promised to "torture mother earth for her secrets," to quote Francis Bacon. The male soul has been profoundly wounded by this history — as has the female soul. Today, the stakes for finding a Sacred Marriage of the Divine Feminine and the Sacred Masculine have never been higher. Our survival hangs in the balance.

When a healthy masculinity returns, both men and women will rejoice. And so too will animals, plants, and future generations not yet born. We will not only be lovers but also the beloved. We will rediscover friendship and the value of alliances over hostilities. Beauty will return. The Goddess will return. And we will know what Julian of Norwich said when she declared that "God is both Mother and Father." We will find God within ourselves and within all of creation. And we will act like we have found God within. Life will become a celebration more than an unending struggle.

Ultimately, men are not "problems to be solved" but deep, impenetrable mysteries. Each one of us carries many stories, many ancestors, many metaphors, and many archetypes in often hidden places. We are diverse. There is no single "man problem." Our unique DNA assures us that each of us came through this long, fourteen-billion-year journey with our own tales to tell and work to do. We are wondrous and surprising and full of creativity. And we are evolving still. We are green *and* blue, warrior *and* hunter, Icarus *and* Daedalus, father *and* son, husband *and* lover, spiritual *and* sensual, free *and* bound. That is the adventure of it all. That is why we need fresh and ancient metaphors to awaken us.

PART I

TEN ARCHETYPES
OF AUTHENTIC MASCULINITY

FATHER SKY: THE COSMOS LIVES!

FATHER SKY IS AN ANCIENT ARCHETYPE for naming the Sacred Masculine or the Divine Masculine. It is found among indigenous peoples, such as Indians of South America, who have a saying: "To be human one must make room in one's heart for the wonders of the universe." This call to relate to the wonders of the universe is found among many religions, including the people of the Bible, the Jews and Christians and Muslims. And certainly this call is found in today's science.

But the modern era (from the seventeenth to twentieth centuries) shut down Father Sky — indeed, it rendered the term practically meaningless. This left the male heart bereft and potentially more violent, for men had no place to invest their sky-sized hearts and souls. D. H. Lawrence sensed this when he wrote: "What a catastrophe, what a maiming of life when it was made a personal, merely personal feeling, taken away from the rising and setting of the sun, and cut off from the magic connection of the solstice and equinox! This is what is the matter with us, we are bleeding at the roots, because we are cut off from the earth and sun and stars, and love is a grinning mockery, because poor blossom, we plucked it from its stem on the tree of life, and expected it to keep on blooming in our civilized vase on the table." What happens when cosmology is replaced by psychology? When cosmic connections are displaced by shopping malls? The heart shrivels. Men's souls shrink. And untold violence goes through their heads.

It was not always this way. Nor does it always have to be this way. Today's postmodern cosmology opens the sky up again to amazing goings-on, and in the process invites men to rediscover Father Sky and the Sacred Masculine.

SKY GODS — THE PREMODERN SKY

For most of human history and in nearly every culture, the sky has been considered an abode for the Divine. Christians sing "Glory to God in the highest" and "you alone are the Most High" in their liturgies. They tell the story of the Transfiguration, when Jesus went to the top of a mountain with three of his friends, and he was shown glorious as they all entered inside a cloud. Christians also tell the story of Jesus "ascending into heaven" after his death and resurrection. Jesus taught his disciples to pray like this: "Our Father who art in heaven. . . ." And for Paul, the first Christian theologian and cosmic mystic, the Christ is the one who unites "everything on earth, under the earth and in the heavens."

In his sermons, the great mystic Meister Eckhart makes consistent and fluid connections between the sky and the earth. He says the heavens "invade the earth, energize it and make it sacred." He says the heavens "are continually running, running into peace" and seek repose. Eckhart recognizes the stretching that the human undergoes in its search for the Divine. For the divine spirit in the human soul "is not easily satisfied. It storms the firmament and scales the heavens trying to reach the Spirit that drives the heavens. Because of this energy everything in the world grows green, flourishes, and busts into leaf. But the spirit is never satisfied. It presses on deeper and deeper into the vortex, further and further into the whirlpool, the primary source in which the spirit has its origin."

The Jewish people tell about Moses encountering God at the top of a mountain, Mount Sinai, and encountering such glory there that he had to cover his face with a veil for the "skin of his face was shining" so. And in Psalm 99 we hear that God "is high above all peoples," a "mighty King, lover of justice and establisher of equity" who spoke to Moses, Aaron, and Samuel "out of the pillar of cloud." The psalmist recommends that we "look up" to the mountain and to the heavens to see God, especially when things are not going so well on earth. As Rabbi Zalman Schachter-Shalomi points out, this is the opposite of the missionary position in sex when men look down. Instead of looking down, men are to look up. To the vastness of God's sky.

Pre-Christian characterizations of Father Sky abound. Among the Aboriginals of Australia in the Dieri country, the sky is understood to be a vast plain inhabited by wild tribes that are the prototype of the Aboriginals themselves. When a drought threatens the people on earth, they call upon their supernatural relatives in the sky to make rain happen to save the peoples on earth. The southeastern tribes of Australia believe in supernatural sky beings called "All-Fathers" or "Sky Beings." The father of them all is Nurrundere, who made all things on the earth, bestowed weapons of war and hunting to humans, and also instituted all rites and ceremonies. Nurrundere took all his children with him and traveled to Wyrrawarre, which is the sky. The sky is his homeland. One connects with the sky god through ceremony: for example, if the tribe kills a wallaby and the wallaby is cooked, the hunters chant as the fire, kindled by women, raises smoke to the sky. As the smoke ascends, the hunters rush in and lift their weapons and branches toward heaven.

Another Australian tribe, the Wiimbaio, believe Nurelli made the trees, animals, and land, and after giving laws to the humans he went up to the sky and is now one of the constellations. Other tribes call the Supreme Being — who once lived on the earth as a Great Man but eventually ascended to the sky — "Our Father" or "Father of All of Us." For the Kulin people, the son of God is Binbeal, the rainbow, who teaches humans the arts of life and social institutions and who ascended to the sky land, from where he oversees the tribe.

Interestingly, among the Aboriginals, there is a special encounter with the "Father," whose voice resembles that of distant thunder, during male puberty rites. Teachings include stories of the creative deeds and anger and disappearance from the earth of the Supreme Being now dwelling on high. He fashioned the ceremonies and made the bull-roarer (located under the foam of the breakers in the ocean), which is the sound representing his own voice and gives the medicine men their powers. When a person dies, this Supreme Being meets and cares for his or her spirit. Thus the spirit, like smoke from the fire, ascends into the heavens and returns to the ancestors there. The ancestors are the stars. It's worth noting that these stories of celestial supreme beings antecede any presence of Western missionaries among the ancient tribes of Australia.

In the Aranda-speaking areas, it was believed that the earth and the sky had always existed and had always been the home of Supernatural Beings. The western Aranda believe that the sky is inhabited by an Emu-footed Great Father who is also the Eternal Youth. He has dog-footed wives and many sons and daughters, and they live on fruits and vegetables in a land that is eternally green and unaffected by droughts. Through it the Milky Way flows like a broad river and the stars are their campfires. All these sky dwellers are as old as the stars and death never touches them. The Great Father of the sky appears as young as his children.

Death happens only on earth, and that occurred because connections were severed between the sky and the earth. A ladder between earth and heaven, or a great tree, was cut down, and so the bridge between earth and heaven was destroyed and death ensued. Immortality and ageless youth belong to the celestial bodies and Sky Beings. Through symbols and ceremonies here on earth entrance is gained to the sacred and life-giving world in the sky.

The Australian Murinbata tribe of western Arnhem Land talk of a pure spirit who lived during the "dream time" named Nogamain, who is a sky-dweller. Some identified him as the man in the moon, others did not. But once when they were asked, "Where does he live?" the tribe raised its arms toward the entire sky and said, "On high." He sends down thunder and lightning and spirit children who are good children.

Across both Polynesia and Micronesia there is a great commonality of belief around a *divinized sky*. The sense of the heavens' enormity is certain to have been experienced by those who sailed long distances under its expanse — and who depended on the stars and night sky to guide them on their perilous journeys. In the Maori traditions of southern Polynesia, the gods operate in the realms of sky, earth, and underworld. Rangi (heaven) and Papa (earth) are the divine ancestral pair from whom humans descend. Among their six children, only the God of Forests, Birds, and Insects can raise his father up to the skies, since he is firmly planted on his mother the earth. In Polynesia, "the greater gods are almost always 'heavenly.'" And in Micronesia also, major deities associated with biocosmic forces are usually from above.

African tribes also often divide the universe into two parts: the visible and the invisible, the heavens or sky and the earth. African scholar John Mbiti writes: "The heavenly part of the universe is the home of the stars, sun, moon, meteorites, sky, the wind and the rain, with all the phenomena connected with them such as thunder and lightning, storms, eclipses of the sun and the moon, 'falling stars,' and so on. It is also thought to be the home of God, although people cannot quite locate where he dwells, other than saying that he lives in 'the sky,' in 'heaven,' or 'beyond the clouds' or they simply say that 'god does not live on the earth like man.'"

While the heavenly part of the universe is the father, many Africans understand the earth to be the mother and refer to her as a living being, "Mother

Earth," "the goddess earth," or "the divinity of the earth." Earth is sacred, and she is honored by ceremonies and other expressions of respect, as are her parts, such as mountains, waterfalls, rocks, forests, trees, birds, animals, and insects.

Many African myths say that at one time in the past the heavens or sky and the earth were united as one. Some myths teach that there was a ladder or rope between the two worlds but that a separation took place. Some say that animals bit the leather rope into two so that one part went up to the sky and the other fell to the ground; some say that it was through man's fault that the two parts of the universe were split. In any case, a severing occurred. (Is that much different from the Garden of Eden story?)

The universe is seen as without edge, just as the earth has no edge. It is eternal. Thus circles are important in ceremonies and rituals, for they symbolize the continuity of the universe and its unendingness. Birth, death, and rebirth rituals also underscore the fact that life is stronger than death.

Native American peoples have a strong sense of the Great Spirit in both its immanent and transcendent presence and its identity as Father Sky. For example, Big Thunder of the Algonquin tribe says: "The Great Spirit is in all things. He is in the air we breathe. The Great Spirit is our Father, but the Earth is our Mother. She nourishes us. . . . That which we put into the ground she returns to us." And Chief Red Cloud of the Lakota prays to a heaven-centered father: "I hope the Great Heavenly Father, who will look down upon us, will give all the tribes His blessing, that we may go forth in peace and live in peace all our days, and that He will look down upon our children and finally lift us far above the earth; and that our Heavenly Father will look upon our children as His children, and that all the tribes may be His children, and as we shake hands to-day upon this broad plain, we may forever live in peace."

Among the ancient Greeks, the Sky Fathers were hardly admirable characters. Zeus evolved. His father Cronus had consumed his seven children out of fear they would take over his power. Zeus swallowed Metis (the goddess of feminine wisdom) to abort a son he feared would take over from him. Says Jean Bolen, "The mythology of the sky gods (Uranus, Cronus, and Zeus) reflect changes in the father archetype."

For Aristotle, it was a combination of the order and the beauty — one might say the elegance — of the sky that moved him to posit a Deity. In a very early book probably put together when he was a student in Athens, Aristotle wrote, "Those who first looked up to the heavens and saw the sun running its courses from its rising to its setting and the well-ordered choral dances of the stars sought after the Craftsman of this very beautiful design and conjectured that it came about not by chance but by the agency of some mightier and incorruptible nature, which was God."

For the premoderns and indigenous peoples everywhere, the sky was alive. It harbored God the Father, among others, and was full of watchful eyes tending to human needs. Not so the God of the modern era.

THE SKY GOD OF THE MODERN ERA

The modern era put the Father God of the living sky to bed and eventually to death. "The death of God" that Nietzsche recognized in the nineteenth century very much corresponded to the death of the sky. From roughly the seventeenth to the early twentieth century, modern science (unlike premodern and postmodern science) taught that the sky was a machine, and if it needed a deity, it was only to oil the machine once in a while. Eventually, that lone duty was taken away from God as well. So we hunkered down, men especially, expecting no help, no insight, no enlightenment from the sky. We took our vast energies for which we were made, all of us being *capax universi* ("capable of the universe") in the words of the premodern philosopher Thomas Aquinas, and we constrained our souls to fit under a mechanical sky and within an industrial world. We substituted the awe of the heavens with the awe of human-made destruction.

Newton taught that the universe is essentially a completed product, like a machine. Our task is to fit in, to obey the machine. There is little creativity in such a universe. Indeed, creativity gave way in the modern era to *compliance*. And obey we did. We fit ourselves into our increasingly mechanized world, and this sophisticated technology took the stone that Cain used to kill Abel and converted it to tanks and gas, to submarines and aircraft carriers, to machine guns and atomic bombs. As our destructive capabilities increased, our reptilian brains went crazy. Violence came to rule the world on unprecedented scales.

Under a secularized sky, despair ruled. Barbara Ehrenreich talks about "an epidemic of depression" that hit the European world in the seventeenth century and culminated in a rash of suicides. An "anxious self" emerged that transformed "the individual into a kind of walled fortress, carefully defended from everyone else." Might this collective autism be what happens when we are cut off from Father Sky? Consider the two modern thinkers John Calvin and

Bertrand Russell. The first was a religious figure who arrived at the dawn of the modern era, and the latter was a philosopher and scientist who arrived near the end of the modern era. Both gave voice to an existential despair that looked around and saw fate as feckless and humans as essentially useless.

John Calvin was a religious reformer of the sixteenth century, and he wrote in *Institution Chretienne*, "No matter where we look, high or low, we can see only a curse that, spreading over all creatures and embracing the earth and the sky, ought to burden our souls with horrible despair." Despite his religious beliefs, John Calvin had no cosmology that could pull him out of this despair. He confesses:

> If God had formed us of the stuff of the sun or the stars, or if he had created any other celestial matter out of which man could have been made, then we might have said that our beginning was honorable... but when someone is made of clay, who pays any attention to him?... [So] who are we? We are all made of mud, and this mud is not just on the hem of our gown, or on the sole of our boots, or in our shoes. We are full of it, we are nothing but mud and filth both inside and outside.

Bertrand Russell, a mid-twentieth-century philosopher and mathematician, echoed Calvin's pessimism in an essay entitled "The Free Man's Worship":

> That Man is the product of causes which had no prevision of the end they were achieving; that his origin, his growth, his hopes and fears, his loves and his beliefs, are but *the outcome of accidental collocations of atoms*; that no fire, no heroes, no intensity of thought and feeling, can preserve an individual life beyond the grave; that all the laborers of the ages, all the devotion, all the inspiration, all the noonday brightness of human genius, are destined to extinction in the vast death of the solar system, and that the whole temple of Man's achievement must inevitably be buried beneath the debris of a universe in ruins — all these things, if not quite beyond dispute, are yet so nearly certain, that no philosophy which rejects them can hope to stand. Only within the scaffolding of these truths, only on the first foundation of unyielding despair, can the soul's habitation henceforth be safely built.

According to Russell, we are but accidental collections of atoms, and this belief persists. More recently, in 1995, scientist Stephen Jay Gould called humans merely "a fortuitous afterthought" on the part of the cosmos in his book *Dinosaur in a Haystack.*

When people believe humans are basically of no particular significance in the universe, this mind-set "reinforces our collective irresponsibility," as astrophysicist Joel Primack and writer Nancy Abrams have wisely pointed out. If we are just afterthoughts and happenstance, what difference do our actions make and how can our choices possibly matter? In addition, the "call to despair" exemplified by Calvin and Russell is profoundly dangerous, as Thomas Aquinas observed in the thirteenth century. He said that despair is the "most dangerous" of all sins because when people are in despair they do not care about others. This might help to explain the widespread passivity and ennui many exhibit in the face of growing social inequalities, ecological disasters, and global warming.

We need a new cosmology to move us beyond self-pity and despair and collective irresponsibility. We need a new understanding of Father Sky and the heavens. And we have one. The universe is far vaster than Newton imagined. And more interesting. And more alive.

FATHER SKY — ALIVE AGAIN!

Today's science has broken sharply with that of the Newtonian or modern era, which believed the sky was inert, dead, a clockwork machine ticking off cold eternal hours. Today's sky is alive and nurturing; it is living, dying, and resurrecting.

For instance, Newton thought that the largest objects in the universe were stars and that they were randomly distributed forever. Instead, superclusters contain tens of thousands of galaxies, and each galaxy contains hundreds of billions of stars, and these are the great superstructures of the universe. New stars are themselves being born every fifteen seconds, while others are dying. And supernovas, galaxies, and human beings join in this great dance. We drink in the universe, which is not static but constantly evolving and unfolding. It is vast and full of drama. It is a spectacle to behold, and behold it we can thanks to science and human creativity and the amazing serendipity of our particular place in time. Today, we *can* study the sky like never before.

THE POSTMODERN SKY

In their book *The View from the Center of the Universe*, Primack and Abrams write that they believe humans are living in a unique and special moment in the history of the universe that makes it possible to know the universe in an intimate way. They say this is "the midpoint of time for our solar system": our sun and planets are about five billion years old and within another six billion years the sun will grow so hot that it will expand and burn Earth to a crisp.

In other words, as opposed to the unchanging constant of the Newtonian universe, our current situation did not exist before and won't last. Primack and Abrams write, "Just as intelligent life on Earth is acquiring the ability to see to the distant reaches of the universe, accelerating expansion is carrying the most distant galaxies away ever faster, and they are disappearing over the cosmic horizon. In short, our visible universe is emptying out: our distant descendants, no matter how advanced their telescopes may be, will never be able to see as many galaxies as we can see now. In this sense, our era is the midpoint of cosmic time." Today represents a "special window of time that can only happen during a relatively brief epoch in the entire history of the universe: late enough that intelligent beings have evolved who have instruments to observe the distant galaxies, but not so late that the galaxies have begun to disappear. Without this period of overlap it might have been impossible for intelligent beings ever to get the chance to figure out the nature of the universe."

But that is not all. They say the size of a human being matters, and it is in fact just right for this task. Primack and Abrams write that the size of a thing "is not arbitrary but crucial to its nature," and we humans are "at the center of all the possible sizes in the universe." Why does size matter? Our size, it turns out, is "the only size that conscious beings like us could be. Smaller creatures would not have enough atoms to be sufficiently complex, while larger ones would suffer from slow communication — which would mean that they would effectively be communities rather than individuals." Human beings are midway between the size of a living cell and the size of Earth. A cell on the tip of my finger is as tiny compared to me as I am compared to planet Earth, while a single atom in that cell is as tiny compared to me as I am compared to the sun. Primack and Abrams call this the "Goldilocks Principle":

> Creatures much smaller than we are could not have sufficient complexity for our kind of intelligence, because they would not be made of a large enough number of atoms. But intelligent creatures could not be much larger than we are, either, because the speed of nerve impulses — and ultimately the speed of light — becomes a serious internal limitation. We are just the right size.... The number of thoughts that

could have traveled back and forth across the vast reaches of our Galaxy in its roughly 10-billion-year lifetime is perhaps the number an average person has every few minutes. The speed of light seems dizzyingly fast to us, but on the scale of the visible universe it is excruciatingly slow and would prevent the parts of any large intelligence from communicating with each other in a reasonable amount of time compared to the age of the universe.

The authors conclude that we humans — contrary to the teachings of modern thinkers like Calvin and Russell and Gould — *are significant to the universe*. We are *special*. Special for our size, special for our intelligence and creativity, and special for the time in which we live — our time on Earth, in the solar system, and in the universe's fourteen billion years. By the "interplay of the complexity of our brains and the age of the universe," and in ways that modern cosmology never could have known, we can now say that "humans are at the center of the universe." Our species only evolved to its present state about a hundred thousand years ago. What this means is that it took Earth almost the entire 4.5 billion years of its existence to produce our kind of intelligent life. We have come on the scene at approximately the midpoint of Earth's lifetime, since in 6 billion years the Earth will be consumed by the heat of an expanding sun. And all of recorded history, which means the past five thousand years, represents only one-millionth of the age of the Earth.

Furthermore, we live in a most interesting corner of the universe because of its density. Where the sun orbits on our galaxy's disc, the density is around a million times the cosmic average. Within the solar system it is about a billion billion times the cosmic average. But on Earth, the densest planet in the solar system, the density is a trillion times higher still. The average density of the Earth is about four times that of the sun.

Our universe is astoundingly creative. In its beginning "there was — and almost everywhere else there still is — nothing but creativity: infinite potential, dense and hot.... Creativity was wildly experimenting with every possibility that quantum uncertainty permits. There were billions of events per second expanding from every sparkpoint for all eternity, unlimited by the speed of light or lack of space."

Furthermore, our universe is very imperfect. Space time in our universe is full of wrinkles. How wonderful is that? "If space time had been perfectly smooth, there would be no galaxies, no stars, no planets, no life, just a thick soup of particles. Life could only have evolved in an 'imperfect' universe." Ours is an imperfect universe, and therefore a home for humans who are, among other things, wildly imperfect.

Another wonder to the universe or the sky as we now know it is this: it is full of darkness. Darkness is everywhere. Actually, what we now call "dark matter" is in fact not dark; rather it is invisible and "totally transparent... a vast cloud of invisible matter fills *and surrounds* each galaxy and each cluster of galaxies." Like huge halos, the dark matter extends to ten times the radius of the disk of visible stars. Stars, gas clouds, satellite galaxies are all immersed inside the dark matter. The dark matter is like a mother, a dark mother, embracing all that is.

Who can read about the new cosmology and not be awed and thunderstruck by the marvel of it all? Who cannot be woken up by this new creation story, our special place in a special universe? As Primack and Abrams say, "We are no longer lost; we have discovered our place in the new order of the universe." Who can deny that Father Sky is *alive* and beckoning us like never before to become alive ourselves? To put life into our work, into our relationships, and into our institutions and communities like never before? If psyche follows cosmos, then clearly cosmos is urging the human psyche today to wake up and throw off the lethargy and depression and despair of the modern era, roll up our sleeves, and get to work. Creative work. The work of the cosmos.

ONE MAN'S TESTIMONY

In his book *Hunting for Hope: A Father's Journeys*, writer Scott Russell Sanders testifies how his soul expands in the presence of the cosmos. "I still hanker for the original world, the one that *makes us* rather than the one we make. I hunger for contact with the shaping power that curves the comet's path and fills the owl's throat with song and fashions every flake of snow and carpets the hills with green. It is a prodigal, awful, magnificent power, forever casting new forms into existence, then tearing them apart and starting over." His very hope comes from the cosmos and its magnificent powers. Sanders recalls a particular moment when, emerging from his car at night, the sky spoke to him in a profound and memorable fashion. "I climbed out of the car with a greeting on my lips, but the sky hushed me. From the black bowl of space countless fiery lights shone down, each one a sun or a swirl of suns the whole brilliant host of them enough to strike me dumb."

He believes that "our deepest religious urge, as D. H. Lawrence wrote, is to bring our lives into 'direct contact with the elemental life of the cosmos, mountain-life, cloud-life, thunder-life, air-life, earth-life, sun-life. To come into immediate felt contact, and so derive energy, powers, and a dark sort of joy.'" No matter how clever our human works, "they will never satisfy this hunger. Only direct experience of Creation will do." We need to open ourselves to the "world we have not made." It is here that Sanders finds his faith. "Faith in what? In our capacity for decent and loving work, in the healing energy of wildness, in the holiness of Creation.... 'Nature is full of genius, full of the divinity so that not a snowflake escapes its fashioning hand,' Thoreau maintains.... That the universe exists at all, that it obeys laws, that those laws have brought forth galaxies and stars and planets and — on one planet, at least — life, and out of life, consciousness, and out of consciousness these words, this breath, is a chain of wonders, I dangle from that chain and hold on tight." Father Sky is returning.

THE DANCE OF FATHER SKY AND MOTHER EARTH

When we talk about "Father Sky" and "Mother Earth," we are not just talking about individual things — trees and soil, air and water, birds and beasts, sun and flowers, fish and fowl, rain and humans. We are talking about a complex energetic dynamic that takes in the cosmos itself. The Earth is thoroughly embedded in the greater matrix of our solar system, of our galaxy, of our cluster of galaxies, and this relationship is by no means static. Everything moves, sometimes whirling at breakneck speeds, including the terra firma we stand on. We whip around the sun, which is in fact the very food we eat, since we eat the plants, and the plants, through photosynthesis, eat the sun. What we call "Father Sky" is both the blue horizon and the very air we breathe — the life blood of our lungs. What is outside, the sky, through our breath we bring inside in a most intimate way. One ounce of air contains a thousand billion trillion atoms. Naturalist Diane Ackerman observes that "with every breath, we inhale millions of molecules of sky, heat them briefly, and then exhale them back into the world.... Air works the bellows of our lungs, and it powers our cells. We say 'light as air,' but there is nothing lightweight about our atmosphere, which weighs 5,000 trillion tons. Only a clench as stubborn as gravity's could hold it to the earth; otherwise it would simply float away and seep into the cornerless expanse of space." Sky means Breath and Spirit therefore. Each breath we take is a piece of the sky, a "piece" of spirit. No wonder meditation practices focus so often on the breath. Such meditation is acknowledging the intimacy and presence of the sky.

Sky and air have a shadow side as well. When air is polluted, our health is jeopardized. This has been shown repeatedly. A recent study in Taipei found that bad or polluted air can trigger cardiovascular disease in young adults. That is how intimate the sky is — healthy sky means healthy people; polluted sky can mean heart risks and other ailments.

Every meal is a cosmic meal; every breath is a cosmic breath; all energy, derived from the sun's energy, is cosmic energy. Cosmos is not an abstraction; cosmos is the very matrix, the placenta, for our earthly existence. Father Sky embraces Mother Earth.

Life on Earth is much affected by the goings-on in the heavens. As scientists Primack and Abrams put it: "The evolution of life cannot be explained without geology and climatology and now even astronomy." A good example of the relationship between Father Sky and Mother Earth is how the layer of ozone was built up in the upper atmosphere every time the Earth was frozen (which occurred several times). "As the ozone layer built up, it increasingly shielded the planet from the sun's harmful ultraviolet radiation. This permitted life to thrive at the top of the ocean — and eventually to come onto land."

In the mid-1990s we discovered planets outside our solar system orbiting nearby stars for the first time. Since then we have found more than 150 planets outside our solar system, and we find more every year. Some stars have one planet but many have multiple planets. Most of these are in the range of 150 light-years from Earth, which is just a tiny fraction of the Milky Way galaxy. As our solar system was being formed during its first billion years of existence, our planets were being bombarded constantly by asteroids and meteorites from space, so much so that pieces of each planet were knocked out and transferred to other planets. Indeed, our moon was formed that way, as a chunk from the Earth. Even today similar activity is taking place: matter is being transferred from Mars to Earth and Venus to Earth — but not at all at the rate that the bombardment occurred early in the solar system. We are seeing the principle of interdependence at work in the solar system and beyond. The Earth is not isolated but part of many other ongoing dynamic relationships.

Primack and Abrams list six ways in which the Earth is special among all the planets. In this naming of specialness, we see a new depth to the ancient archetypes of Mother Earth and Father Sky, whose metaphorical relationship embodies cosmic truth.

1. Twenty-five percent of the extrasolar planets astronomers have found
    so far are "hot Jupiters" or massive gas planets. Since they currently or-
    bit close to their suns, they probably formed at a distance and migrated
    closer. In doing so, they would have run over and destroyed small plan-
    ets like Earth.

2. In our solar system Jupiter has been an ally in assisting Mother Earth.
    "Jupiter's gravity has helped protect Earth from being hit by comets."
    Like a big brother, Jupiter has offered protection from potential at-
    tackers of Earth — just one such attack, a meteorite that landed on
    Earth sixty-five million years ago, wiped out dinosaurs and many other
    species. It changed Earth forever. "If such events were happening much
    more often, life on Earth might not have had enough time between
    extinctions to evolve to intelligent creatures."

    Except for tiny Pluto (recently demoted as not an official "planet"),
    the planets in our solar system have orbits around the sun that are es-
    sentially circular. This is unusual. In the extrasolar planetary systems
    we have found up to now, planets that are the approximate distance
    from their star as Earth is from the sun generally follow elliptical or-
    bits. What if this were the case with Earth? The result would be cat-
    astrophic for Earth's seasons. If the Earth had a more elliptical orbit,
    the whole planet would undergo additional 100-degree swings in
    temperature. If Jupiter's orbit were more elliptical, its motion would
    be so profoundly affected that Earth and Mars might have been
    bounced from the solar system altogether! "Jupiter's circular orbit sta-
    bilizes not only Earth's orbit but our entire solar system." Thank you,
    Jupiter!

3. The distance of Earth from the sun is just right — were it closer to
    the sun, water would evaporate and be lost; were it further from the
    sun, water would be permanently frozen. The way things are, most of
    Earth's water is liquid (and of course some of it is frozen). Earth alone
    among the planets in our solar system has liquid water on its surface
    at this time in history. This capacity for liquid water has been part of
    Earth's existence for its entire history — and is considered an essen-
    tial ingredient for the birthing of intelligent life.

4. Thanks to the relatively thin crust and abundant surface water on
    Earth, geological activity is alive and well. Plate tectonics that move
    continents, new mountain ranges that arise — all this contributes to

recycling of carbon and other elements essential for life. Volcanoes and asteroid and comet impacts brought more water and other chemicals to the Earth.

5. The Moon seems to have been created by an impact between a proto-planet and the Earth early in Earth's existence. How fortuitous was that crash in the sky? The Moon stabilizes the rotation of the Earth and thus stabilizes our climate. Our Moon is unusually large compared to other planets with moons. The largeness of the Moon has kept the tilt of the earth's rotation axis practically constant, at around 23.5 degrees, and this tilt gives us our seasons. When moons are much smaller, they render climate much more variable, as is the case with Mars and its two small moons.

The Moon also affects tides on Earth. When the Moon was closer to the Earth, the Earth was more susceptible to tremendous tides. Gradually, however, the Moon distanced itself from Earth, and the lunar tides and the surface winds together with the Earth's rotation have slowed down. The result? More calm and peace and a more be-nign environment for life. With this calmness, the Earth has ad-vanced long-term complexity in its evolutionary history.

6. We live out in the "galactic suburbs," which is a "galactic habitable zone" within our galaxy. Our sun orbits in the disk of the Milky Way about halfway out from the center. Radiation probably destroyed or prevented life on planets that lie closer to the center. But where we live is far enough away from the nearest supernovas that Earth's atmosphere can protect us from their weakened radiation. Yet if the sun had formed much farther from the center of the Milky Way, there would have been too few supernovas to make enough heavy elements, or star-dust, to form rocky planets like Earth.

All these freshly found scientific facts point to the marvelous relationship be-tween Father Sky and Mother Earth, who provide a solid role model for what relationships can and ought to be. Creative, protective, interactive, surprising — all these dynamics seem mirrored in the activities of Father Sky and Mother Earth, whose fruitful relationship has resulted in the birth of Earth's many crea-tures. Father Sky has never been so meaningful. Geologian Thomas Berry cau-tions: "We will recover our sense of wonder and our sense of the sacred only if we appreciate the universe beyond ourselves as a revelatory experience of that numinous presence whence all things come into being. Indeed, the universe is the primary sacred reality. We become sacred by our participation in this more sublime dimension of the world about us."

Now we need new rituals to celebrate these relationships and implant them deep within our cells and minds and imaginations, arousing reverence and gratitude. Through action, rituals help us to realize our understandings and throw off the empty beliefs that have deadened the sky. We should not underestimate, for example, how the invention of electricity and the migration to cities have impinged on our awareness of Father Sky and our sense of cosmology. In cities, perpetually alight, it is hard if not impossible to make contact with the heavenly light of stars. As Eddie Kneebone, an Australian Aboriginal, has said, in his tradition the daytime is for observing the earth and her creatures, but the nighttime is for connecting to the heavens. With images and fractals from spatial telescopes projected onto screens with the aid of postmodern technologies, whole communities can celebrate anew in ritual and dance the ancient but new stories of the universe and its living sky.

It is especially the young who can and must take in this new cosmology, the new relationship to Father Sky, to make relationships new again. As Primack and Abrams put it: "In many ways the young everywhere have more in common with one another than with the old who live in their country or even in their own house. Young people do not share a single religion or language, but they share an epoch in cosmic and terrestrial history that their elders will never know."

Recently Microsoft introduced a "Worldwide Telescope" website, which combines images and databases from every major telescope and astronomical organization in the world. The service is free. The goal is to appeal to amateur astronomers, teachers, and kids, people who might never get a chance to look at the Milky Way through a telescope. The designer of the virtual telescope is Curtis Wong, who grew up in Los Angeles and never saw the Milky Way until he left the city on a trip as a teenager. "I was totally blown away by how many stars there were," he said. Now Father Sky is available to anyone online. "People have been looking at the sky since it existed, but there's been no way to share that. Anybody can go in to the telescope" he has created, he notes. Surely this postmodern invention opens up Father Sky still more to us all. The wonders of the universe are more and more available to those who care to make room in their hearts and minds for the same.

THE GREEN MAN | 2

IN THEIR CLASSIC WORK *The Green Man: The Archetype of Our Oneness with the Earth*, English photographer Clive Hicks and poet William Anderson teamed up to bring to life this amazing and important archetype. In a time when nature is being degraded — when we are losing topsoil at unprecedented rates, when forests and rainforests are disappearing, the latter forever, when one of four mammals is going extinct — what could be more appropriate and important for men than to rediscover the Green Man within each of us? What could be more useful than this image, which comes from the deep past of *many* human cultures and instructs men on how to recover our oneness with the Earth?

Like any rich archetype, the metaphor of the Green Man cuts through the soul at many levels. And these places are precisely the ones that were largely abandoned in the modern and industrial era, when the entire Western world became bent on "mastering nature" — a favorite term of both Descartes and Francis Bacon, key philosophers for that period. The Green Man is decidedly *not* about mastering nature. Rather, the Green Man is about *relating to nature*, about finding the essence of nature within our own nature — indeed, he is about our generating nature, especially from our fifth chakras, where our words represent the combined wisdom of our hearts and heads (the fourth and sixth chakras, respectively). The Green Man is about wisdom holding sway over mere knowledge. In Native American traditions, plants are the wisest of all living creatures. They have been here the longest, and by inventing photosynthesis, they learned how to eat the sun. By doing so, they make life possible for animals and, as a consequence, humans. Plants could live without us, but we could not live without them; we are indebted to them. The Green Man reminds us of that.

EMERGING FROM FIELDS AND FORESTS

The Green Man is an ancient pagan symbol of our relationship to the plant kingdom. Men become tree-like, and the Green Man sports plants and leaves and boughs growing from his mouth or his beard or his hair. Green Men festivals are celebrated even to this day on village greens in England. Christianity adopted the Green Man in a special way in the twelfth century in France, England, and Germany in particular, and he is found in many cathedrals dating from that and later periods around Europe.

In the Green Man we have an archetype for our relationship to *both* the cosmos and the Earth — to Father Sky and Mother Earth. Plants are born from and connect the two. Plants are, like us, cosmic beings; they guarantee that the sun's generous efforts to pour its energy over the Earth are not in vain. The sun finds ready receptivity in the plants. In addition, in a number of Green Man sculptures, birds perch in the branches and fly between the two worlds of Earth and sky. Birds are messengers from Father Sky.

In the Green Man archetype, plants are not forgotten or taken for granted. They are *praised*, reminding us to renew our relationship with Mother Earth — plants, soil, rain, clouds, trees, flowers, sun, seasons — and to consider all of it a gift, all of it a necessity for our sustainability and existence. Writer Fred Hageneder has gifted us with a deep study of trees in his book *The Spirit of Trees*, which sheds light on the Green Man archetype. He points out that "trees are the most successful life forms on Earth" and the most dominant since they first appeared over three hundred millions years ago. Outside of the oceans themselves, "mixed woodland of self-sown trees untouched and uncultivated by man — and tropical rainforest form the richest ecosystems in existence, providing habitat for the widest variety of species." Furthermore, these communities of trees "are fundamental to weather and climate, for a beneficial water cycle; for the development of minerals; for balancing the electrical charges between the ionosphere and the Earth's surface; and for the maintenance of the Earth's magnetic field as a whole."

What makes up a tree? The body of a tree is mostly filled with sunlight. "Light courses through its structure, navigating vital processes and maintaining

the balance and health of the whole organism.... The tree produces a contin-
uous light show from its very cells."

Trees are like "cosmic antennae" and radiation from supernovas — the
gigantic explosions marking the death of a star — has been shown to influence
tree growth. Scientists studying a 807-year-old juniper tree in Tajikistan found
that the tree's annual rings showed a definite slowing down of tree growth with
each known date of three supernovas. Thus we can say, "every star that dies in
our galaxy is perceived by trees."

Trees have assisted humans from the beginning. Consider how humans first
dwelled in the shelter of the woods in Africa just as apes still do today. When
humans left the woods for the open savannahs and discovered fire, "fire became
the driving force in the development of the human species ... and it was always
trees which supported the human need for fuel." When humans started building shelters and bridges and barns, it was wood we relied upon. "Most of the
stone tools from the Stone Age served to work wood" and this included the
building of the great medieval cities, which were built "mostly in wood." Human writing first occurred on bark and wood tablets.

Sacred groves are a universal phenomenon. "Almost everywhere in the
world the beginnings of social and religious life took place under trees." Every
Greek deity was linked to a particular tree species and worshipped under it, such
as the laurel consecrated to Apollo, the myrtle tree to Aphrodite, the olive to
Athena, and the pine tree to Pan. "What we today label as *gods* were originally
the spirits of trees to whom goodwill and gratitude was bestowed." Says
Hazrat Inayat Khan, "Every leaf of a tree is a page in the Holy Book and contains divine revelation."

Because many of the boughs, leaves, and trees emerging from the Green
Man emerge from his mouth, we know we are looking at an archetype about
our fifth chakra. In previous books, I have noted that the fifth chakra, located
in our throats, is essentially a birth canal. This is particularly true for men; the
fifth chakra is a birth channel. Our throats are meant to give birth to our heart
and head wisdom (from the fourth and sixth chakras), and the Green Man reminds us that the color of the fourth or heart chakra is green! The Green Man
puts compassion and generativity first, and this generativity, this birth canal,
primarily gives birth to green compassion.

Hildegard of Bingen, writing in the twelfth century — which was the time
of the great revival of the goddess and of the Green Man as well — called Christ
a "green man," since he brings wetness and aliveness to the human soul. She

also talked about the Holy Spirit as being "green" because it makes us all fecund. In fact, she taught that the only real sin in life is "drying up," which is a metaphor for denying the Green Man, who wants to flourish in all of us. This is why she counseled abbots and bishops, archbishops and other leaders to "stay wet and green and moist and juicy" — the opposite of drying up. When a woman's birth canal "dries up," she cannot deliver new life. Eckhart used similar imagery when he said that "the seed of God is in us" and that with proper cultivation, just as a pear seed grows into a pear tree, a seed of God "grows into God."

Interestingly, the archetype of the Green Man also respects silence and introspection, which are common traits among farmers and indigenous peoples, those who remain close to the land. In some depictions, the Green Man appears cross-eyed, which is surely meant to symbolize looking inward. A Green Man, like any authentic warrior, does not just focus *outward* but also *within*, to contemplate the world inside. The Green Man is not afraid to get to know himself. Further, though located at the throat, the fifth chakra does not signify constant chatter, or endless talking, but true speech, which emerges from silent contemplation, not noise. Only nervousness finds it necessary to fill the empty spaces and contemplative silence with noise. This too the Green Man honors by depicting for us how rich and deep the roots of nature are, telling us that we need to germinate *under the soil, in the silence of our hearts.* If we are silent, maybe something fruitful will emerge. If we look inward, we will give birth to substance. (The eyes of many Green Men look inward.) Receptivity, introversion, and introspection are necessary to generate life; these attributes lead to a deeper place than extroverted action. It's a space where psyche and cosmos, psyche and Gaia, can connect and bear fruit. Fruit that remains.

Medieval theologians were very taken by the biblical images of Christ as a vine. Many of these are taken from John's Gospel, which is a product of the wisdom literature of Israel and early Christianity. "I am the vine; you are the branches. . . . You will bear fruit, fruit that remains." These and many other passages find a welcome echo in the Green Man archetype.

Twelfth-century images of the Green Man are also interesting because they depict the Green Man in many stages of life — some are young, some middle-aged, some old. Some are lying on the ground and dying like leaves in the fall, returning their spirit to the Earth for recycling. In addition the Green Men are portrayed with diverse moods, ranging from playfulness to awestruck to fierce. There is a fierceness and strength to some of the Green Men, a strong warrior energy. This is reinforced in the boughs of many Green Men, which are reminiscent of antlers. In this way, the Green Man connects to the animal world as well as the plant world. Antlers are tree-like, and men are stags who carry antler-like powers.

The Green Man also says something important and positive about male sexuality. The Green Man is almost always bearded. Most often the beard turns into leaves and branches, and sometimes the leaves and branches depict the beard. A story is being told about facial hair: the generative powers of the male that come at puberty are meant to serve the larger cosmic purpose of generation. They are not to serve the individual ego, or even the ego of the family or nation or tribe, but the overall purposes of nature itself. Male creativity, sexuality, and sensuality emerge from the creativity, sexuality, and sensuality of nature — and are meant to serve it. In this way the power of male sexuality is held in its proper, larger context, not as an expression of individual power, in ego strutting. The Green Man does not repress or sublimate sexuality. He expresses it openly — honoring it, praising it — and yet without aggrandizing or personalizing it. It is a rich sexuality that does not draw attention to itself but embodies the ongoing sexual and creative energy of the universe.

THE GREEN MAN IN THE TWELFTH CENTURY

The Green Man reappeared in a powerful way in Western culture in the twelfth century — the same century that saw the reemergence of the goddess. Indeed, the Green Man accompanied the goddess in European culture. The goddess after all was the inspiration for five hundred churches and hundreds of cathedrals, *every one of them dedicated to Mary, the Goddess of Christianity*, which were built over an amazing 125-year span. The Green Man figures prominently and significantly in churches and cathedrals in Chartres, Dijon, St. Denis, Auxerre, Bamberg, Norwich, Sutton, Vendome, Lichfield, Poitiers, Winchester, Marburg, Lincoln, Exeter, Dijon, Trier, Bourges, Southwell, Rheims, Freiburg in Breisgau, St. Dimitri in Vladimir, and more.

Until the Gothic renaissance and the emergence of the goddess and the Green Man, plants were often depicted in Christian art as symbols of sin and excessive sensuality. One influential ninth-century Christian writer identified the leaf with sin, especially with sexual sin. Sexuality and writhing vegetation, along with naked men and women caught in vegetation, are found depicted on these earlier cathedrals. The old gods like Bacchus or Dionysus and Pan were not appreciated, to put it mildly. Indeed, the devil was often depicted as Pan with hairy legs and goat-like sexual libido.

As Anderson points out, beginning in the late twelfth century, sculptors working in the nave of Notre Dame de Paris began for the first time "to portray definite and recognizable species of plants carved with delight and enjoyment as signs of the goodness of creation." The goodness of creation — original blessing — became the new theology of the time. It echoed the theology of the Song of Songs and of wisdom literature in the Bible in general. It also echoed the spiritual training of the historical Jesus, who came from the tradition that honored the holiness of creation.

Plants were depicted on new cathedrals and churches not just for delight and enjoyment but also as a way to study them. A new intellectual vigor and interest arose at this time around the study of nature. "From this time onwards a new spirit entered Western art: that of exact observation of the visible world. . . . It was to be of the profoundest significance in the development of Western science, based as it is upon observation and classification. The Gothic sculptors became skilled in the accurate delineation of plant forms to a degree far beyond the standard of illustration in the botanical texts of the period." The artists rose to the occasion.

At Chartres, for example, there are a number of Green Men, and the leaves on each are recognizable as particular species: the three Green Man heads on the south portal depict the oak, the acanthus, and the vine. The oak was sacred to the Druids who, it was believed, were the first to build on the sacred site of Chartres; the vine symbolized both Bacchus and Christ; and the acanthus was sacred in the classical and northern traditions as a symbol of rebirth. The Green Man of the oak was the Green Man of the forest, while the Green Man of the vine was the Green Man of agriculture. The oak, as Robert Bly explains, was tied "firmly to religious ritual around the Goddess" throughout the Near East. Diana had an oak grove, and the oak was for the Romans the "golden bough" that gave one access to Hades. The Oak King was the Great Goddess's consort, who ruled by her permission, and the king would station himself every seven years under the oak tree to take on all challengers. If he won, he would be king another seven years; if he lost, he would be killed there, under the oak tree. Furthermore, the mighty oak is the "'axis of life' our connection between earth and heaven."

The acanthus represents plants that cross the boundaries of farm and wilderness, the herbs that flavor, heal, or poison. On the south portal, the Green

Men smile, but on the north portal they are the heads of fresh-faced young men growing out of rays of fig leaves, and their faces are yearning. The fig often stands for the Divine Mother, and one honors the Black Madonna by feeding her figs.

As all these associations indicate, the Green Man represents the internalization of the goddess by men. He is a symbol that the goddess, and the revolution she brings in her wake, is as much for men as women. And a revolution the goddess did bring in the twelfth century. She spearheaded a twelfth-century movement that reinvented education, replacing the monastic school with the university, which originally meant a place to go to find your place in the universe. The goddess had a prominent role as Queen of the Arts and Sciences. She, Lady Wisdom, was to rule over all learning. The goddess also reinvented religion, moving its center from the monastic churches in the countryside to the cathedrals in the newborn cities. These cities, birthed from towns primarily by freed serfs and young people escaping a feudal, land-based culture, begged for new forms of religion, and the cathedral came to mean the *throne* (*cathedra* means "throne" in Latin) where the goddess sits. She does not sit passively but celebrates life; she is a center from which culture flows, which includes justice and compassion for the poor.

In the late nineteenth century, cultural historian Henry Adams had a conversion experience on encountering the goddess at Chartres, Bourges, and other medieval cathedrals. For him the cathedral at Chartres and the goddess it represented expressed the assertion of the supremacy of love over force. Adams felt it "expressed an intensity of conviction never again reached by any passion, whether of religion, of loyalty, of patriotism, or of wealth; perhaps never even paralleled by any single economic effort, except in war." The goddess also stood for compassion, the Buddhist element in Christianity, "for the Mother alone was human, imperfect, and could love; she alone was Favour, Duality, Diversity.... The Mother alone could represent whatever was not Unity; whatever was irregular, exceptional, outlawed; and this was the whole human race." The goddess befriends outlaws. So does the Green Man.

Adams asks the following question of the modern era: "Why were all the Protestant churches cold failures without her help.... Why was the Woman struck out of the Church and ignored in the State? ... If a Unity exists, in which and toward which all energies center, it must explain and include Duality, Diversity, Infinity — Sex!" Thus for Adams the return of the goddess in the twelfth century was no small thing. And this return very much included the

Green Man. The goddess's return in the twenty-first century will also prove to be no small thing.

THE RETURN OF FATHER EARTH

The Green Man is interesting also because it challenges us not to take the genders of "Father Sky" and "Mother Earth" literally. In many respects the Green Man represents the notion of "Father Earth." If one wishes, there is no reason not to swap genders and worship Mother Sky and Father Earth, for these are metaphors. The Green Man reminds men not to live solely in the sky and in their heads. Like a tree, men have permission to reach into the ground, to heed their lower chakras, and grow out of the Earth, arms raised to the sky in worship.

For poet William Anderson, the Green Man symbolizes above all "irrepressible life," and "once he has come into your awareness, you will find him speaking to you wherever you go." Anderson wrote a poem about the Green Man in which he hears the Green Man saying:

> *I am the thought of all plants. . . .*
> *I rise with the sap. . . .*
> *I come with the wind. . . .*
> *I burn with desire. . . .*
> *I am honey of love. . . .*
> *It's off with my head. . . .*
> *I speak through the oak. . . .*
> *I shine with the sun. . . .*
> *I swim with the salmon. . . .*
> *I am crushed for your drink. . . .*
> *I have paid for your pleasure. . . .*
> *I have kept her secret. . . .*
> *I am born in the dark. . . .*

Being much older than Christianity, the Green Man comes and goes in history. Today he is returning for many reasons, but in particular he represents the return of environmental awareness and action. The Green Man is a composite image, and this "composite of leaves and a man's head symbolizes the union of humanity and the vegetable world. He knows and utters the secret laws of Nature."

Anderson asks an important question: "Why is the Green Man returning to our awareness now and what does he want from us?" I believe that one thing the Green Man demands is that *men stand up*. That men become men. Men have been stuck in a daze brought on by modern philosophy, consumerism, and a pseudo-masculine media-promoted identity. The Green Man calls us to stand for love of the Earth and the health of future generations. Stand for the trees and the animals that are being destroyed and with them the sustainability of our own species. Stand for community and compassion rather than individual power and domination. Stand for the children and generations to come.

Jung believed that archetypes reappear in new forms at particular times to redress imbalances in society. The Green Man may be recurring today, then, not just because our relationship with Nature is off balance *but also because our relationship with maleness is off balance*. The Green Man calls to men to wake up and smell the coffee. He calls men to reconnect sexuality with nature, culture with cosmos, and economics with stewardship and moral responsibility.

Anderson believes that it was "extraordinary that the Great Mother and her son, lover, guardian the Green Man should both return in this same period [the twelfth century]. It may be that a similar process is taking place today: just as the rise of feminism has been accompanied, through quite independent lines of research, by the rediscovery of the dominant matriarchal religions of ancient Europe, so it may be that the Green Man is stirring again because in the deep ecology of the spirit he is linked to her as part of the same web of myth." The Green Man relates wisely to the Divine Feminine and the Great Mother and boasts a special relationship to the snake, an ancient symbol for the goddess. Many Green Men are depicted in the company of the snake or of the serpent, who is a snake with wings.

The Green Man honors intelligence. He is "the cosmic man or intelligence underlying creation." After all, he is usually depicted as a human head. In fact, he is more than intelligent, he is wise. It takes intelligence to both study nature and relate wisely to it. It is this rebirth of an interest in nature, in ecosystems, that so characterizes our time. Thus, Green Man returns. That is why also he is sometimes identified with the fool — for wisdom, unlike knowledge, finds room for the role of the fool and the trickster. Folly and wisdom wrestle together.

THE SACRED OR COSMIC TREE

The Green Man also appears as a reminder of the Sacred Tree, which often represents the cosmos. In the Bhagavad Gita the tree represents the universe, as it does in the paintings of Hildegard of Bingen in the twelfth century. In the third century in the West, the Tree of Life was described as the center of the world at Golgotha, with a holy spring from which all nations would drink. Christ said, "I am the true vine," and Christians pictured the symbolism of Dionysus yielding to the Green Man of Christ.

Sacred trees abound in human myths, from the Bodhi Tree under which the Buddha received enlightenment to the Lote Tree beside which the prophet Muhammad saw his second vision of the Archangel Gabriel. Many ancient stories tell how spirits of trees speak and sing to humans. Then there is the tree of the cross that Christians venerate for having fixed the mistakes Adam and Eve made concerning the Tree of Life in the Garden of Eden. Sir James Frazer observes that "the killing of the tree spirit is associated always . . . with a revival or resurrection of him in a more youthful and vigorous form." This may explain why Christian art frequently employs the Green Man in the context of the Passion and Resurrection of Christ, so that he who had overcome Christ on the tree that was the cross should also be overcome by Christ. The earliest known depiction of a Christian Green Man is on a tomb of St. Abre in St. Hilaire-le-Grand about 400 A.D. This and many other images place the Green Man in scenes of death and resurrection, and this underscores the message of rejuvenation and immortality that the tree and the risen Christ represent. It is a resurrection that happens in springtime — along with the plants emerging from their winter hibernation.

In illuminated manuscripts like the Book of Kells, as well as in sculpture, the Celtic Christians often pictured the Green Man. Sometimes he is accompanied by the horned god Cernunnos, the ancient Celtic god of the forests, who was half-man and half-stag, often with antlers growing from his brow (the sixth chakra). Deer, snakes, and other wild animals befriended him, and he underwent death and exile in the underworld. Sometimes his hair is vegetation. There is a clear connection between fertility and the leaf head. The human head was understood to be the seat of inspiration and prophecy, and it promoted fertility and could drive away evil forces. The works of both the Celtic philosopher Scotus Erigenus and Thomas Aquinas acknowledge that plants have souls, and that humans share the soul world of the plants and animals, as well as the spirit souls of angels. Humans are mediators between these worlds.

In many of the tympana of twelfth-century cathedrals, there is a celebration of the Cosmic Christ. Anderson talks of the Christ on the abbey church of St. Pierre at Moissac (carved c. 1130) as being "a powerful, frightening lord or king whose garments are vibrant with cosmic power. The beasts of the evangelists symbolize not only the four gospels but the four elements and the four temperaments of man which are made complete in the human nature of Christ. Their bodies twist with extraordinary energies." A horned Cernunnos is located on Christ's left side. Thus the Cosmic Tree and the Cosmic Christ appear together, and psyche (the temperaments of humans) and cosmos come together. The tree reaches to the sky and its roots reach into the depths of the earth, so the tree is a powerful reminder of the union of Father Sky and Mother Earth — it is the *axis mundi*, the center of the world. As poet and symbolist J. E. Cirlot puts it, "in its most general sense, the symbolism of the tree denotes the life of the cosmos: its consistence, growth, proliferation, generative and re-generative processes. It stands for inexhaustible life." The Green Man partic-ipates in all these powers.

Mircea Eliade equated the *axis mundi* with ancient initiation ceremonies for shamans who "journeyed to the center." Psychologist Eugene Monick points out that the "*axis mundi* as World Tree has its roots in the underworld, its trunk in the present, its foliage in heaven." It draws its energy from many worlds therefore. It is not one-dimensional.

Nor are men one-dimensional. We, like the cosmic tree, connect to the three zones of sky, earth, and underworld. Monick recognizes the *axis mundi* as "the ancient image needed by men today as they experience the disintegra-tion of patriarchal Present Consciousness. Surrender to reemerging matriarchy is not the solution, either cultural or personal. It is regressive and will produce, eventually, a stringent reemergent patriarchal attitude in a vain defense of mas-culine identity....*Axis mundi*, suggesting the rigorous, precarious heroism of the shaman, is just the ticket."

ECOLOGICAL PROPHETS

Ecology *is* functional cosmology, as Thomas Berry insists. We do, like trees, take in the entire cosmos, but in our local neighborhood, the Earth. D. H. Lawrence captures this energy when he writes:

> the whole life-effort of man [is] to get his life into direct contact with the elemental life of the cosmos, mountain-life, cloud-life, thunder-life, air-life, earth-life, sun-life. To come into immediate felt contact, and so derive energy, power and a dark sort of joy. This effort into sheer naked contact, without an intermediary or mediator is the root mean-ing of religion.

The reunion of cosmos and ecos (home) is the order of the day. It is our sur-vival mechanism, as Primack and Abrams point out:

Earth as a planet is integrated into the cosmos, but our current think-ing about it is not, and therein lies the root of many problems: we are out of tune with our planet and our universe. . . . The major threats to human survival today — world environmental degradation, extinction of species, climate destabilization, nuclear war, terrorists with weapons of mass destruction — result from unrestrained use of such new technologies without a cosmology that makes sense of the nature and scale of their power.

The Green Man would make these connections anew.

In the twelfth century the rediscovery of the Cosmic Christ and the Cos-mic Tree was a sign that the "aesthetic revolution" of Gothic architecture was being launched. There was a "confidence and energy" in the air. It was in this atmosphere of hope that the Green Man returned. The monastic establishment was undergoing a reform movement. Black Virgins also emerged "contempo-rary with the revival of the Green Man." Anderson asks whether Osiris, the Egyptian god from whose body sprouts the vegetation of the Nile and whose face became green when he acted as judge in the underworld, might have reap-peared as the Green Man with vegetation pouring out of his mouth? Just as Isis is incorporated as the Black Madonna, was the Green Man incorporating her paramour, Osiris? Some of the depictions of the Black Madonna show her as profoundly calm and serene — and this same serenity is found in many of the Green Men of this period.

At Chartres the Green Man comes into his own, and Anderson talks about the "Triumph of the Green Man in the Gothic Period." Not only the Green Man's leaves but also his face is individually and uniquely carved. Each head has a profound individuality and personality about it. Thus the Green Man comes to life in a remarkable fashion. At Chartres the Green Man is represented at least seventy-two times. Says Anderson, "In their portrayals of the Green Man as a benign and beaming image, they expressed a new attitude to Nature, one in which she is no longer the terrifying enemy of human existence of so much Romanesque sculpture but the kindly ally of man. Here, through the image of the Green Man the moods of Nature become humanized; and the attitudes of man and woman are reflected back to them in the principle of awakening con-sciousness underlying all creation." Nature as a "kindly ally of man" is Gaia. The Green Man brings forth our alliance with the rest of nature, a relation-ship of friendship, not of overbearing usefulness. Today, too, a new attitude to-ward nature is required, one that honors our relationship to it and fosters sustainability.

It is not only medieval Europe that honored the Green Man. When I lectured at the University of Hawaii a year ago, I learned afterward that there is a secret ceremony in the Native Hawaiian tradition that honors the Green Man, who is dressed in a cape of tea leaves. He is respected for living in the forest and catching birds and taking just one feather from each bird and releasing it. The Green Man is recognized as the One who Manages the Forest when not at war. He blends into the forest and is seamless with it. Hawaiians had to hide this ritual when the missionaries came, and so hid the Green Man.

Because the Green Man honors the throat, it also honors prophecy. The prophet (from the Greek words "to speak out") addresses injustice and imbalance. The Green Man in all of us is the prophetic voice, and it requires us to find our voice in order to speak out. Often the Green Man is depicted as fierce and strong, which is also part of the energy of the prophet. We need such energy today in order to sustain our species and live in peace with the rest of nature. And in order to be men again. Thus, we need to develop the spiritual warrior in us all. The Green Man is such a warrior. The Green Man will defend and protect the Earth and her creatures for the sake of future generations.

The Green Man represents creativity and generativity, and so he represents the vocation of the artist. Sometimes the prophetic role of the artist can be ignored in our culture. In contrast, Thein Soe is an artist in Burma's underground art movement and has kept going during the forty-six-year rule of the military junta. The military there have crushed pro-democracy demonstrations and banned most freedom of expression. Says Soe: "We paint what we suffer and what we feel. The majority of this is sadness." Government censors are constantly monitoring his work. Many poets and others have died in prison for telling the truth through their art. One sculptor depicted a sleeping mother with a thorn in her ribcage and a rifle barrel for a spine. The artist smuggled the piece out of Burma and to Thailand where it is on display in a Bangkok gallery. "Artists have a responsibility to their people and country to express what happens. My work is what I have seen and what I have suffered," he says. The censorship is drawing many artists together. Says one: "We are not angry. We are sad. All of these years have been wasted time." These artists in Burma, trying to survive under a controlling political regime, are in their way Green Men at work. Their courage and their commitment to telling the truth (fifth chakra work) are testimony of that.

Two contemporary Green Men in America are Saul Griffith and David Shearer. Saul is a thirty-three-year-old scientist who is president of Makani Power in Alameda, California. "The greatest risk to mankind is that we're losing our environment hand over fist," he says — and he is committed to changing that. He is working to lasso wind power from high in the atmosphere where, scientists say, just 1 percent of the energy could power the entire planet. To help his project succeed, he has formed a partnership with Google.

Speaking of wind power closer to the ground, a recent study has determined that two decades from now Americans could get as much electricity from windmills as from nuclear power plants. Wind energy could generate 20 percent of the nation's electricity by 2030. Wind power of course is clean and renewable — just what a Green Man would envision. It can be achieved without new technological breakthroughs and for less than half a cent per kilowatt hour. The report says: "The United States possesses abundant wind resources. While ambitious, it could be feasible." New powerline systems would be required. Carbon dioxide emissions linked to global warming would be reduced by 825 million metric tons a year when wind takes over from coal and natural gas. "This is the equivalent of taking 140 million cars off the road," said the executive director of the American Wind Energy Association, Randall Swisher. What is needed to make this happen? Green Men. Obviously.

David Shearer is chief scientist at California Envionmental Associates in San Francisco. He likes to spread stories through art and news media about entrepreneurial projects that will change the environment for the better. Shearer says, "Art and science go hand in hand in describing some of the big problems we face on the planet and mirroring and showing solution packages around those problems." A practicing Buddhist, he advised Toyota on how to market the Prius as a green investment. He sees the solution to the Earth crisis as cooperation, conversation, and love. "It gets down to having dialogues across countries, across societies." And he advises, "We need to create exciting, realistic solution packages that capture the imagination. It's just too dire without creating some excitement."

Author Joseph Jastrab observes that "generations of modern men have grown alienated from images of manhood connected to the living Earth and to the Great Mystery." Clearly the Green Man archetype addresses this alienation. Embracing the Green Man creates a new male empowerment, a new warriorhood on behalf of Mother Earth and her creatures. Is this not what is happening today as we talk of "green buildings" and "green politics," of "green business" and Greenpeace, of "green belts around cities" and "green economics"?

Yes, the Green Man is back. Are we ready?

ICARUS AND DAEDALUS $\boxed{3}$

THE ANCIENT GREEK STORY of Icarus and Daedalus is well known. In essence, it is the story of a son, Icarus, who disobeys his father, Daedalus, and gets killed for it, crashing to the earth. We will take a deeper and fuller look at the story here, for it can teach us much about the deep masculine.

Daedalus, the father of Icarus, was a famous architect, engineer, inventor, and master craftsman. (His name in Greek means "cunning artificer.") Plato credits him with having constructed a mechanical statue of the gods that was so lifelike that the statues perspired under the hot Aegean sun and had to be restrained lest they run away. Daedalus is credited with inventing many things, including the axe and the labyrinth. His own parentage is confused, since three women have been named as his mother, and his father was unknown altogether. He was mentor to his nephew, Talos, who displayed considerable skills, such as inventing the saw from observing the spine of a fish. In fact, Talos's skills were so admired that Daedalus became envious, and he murdered the boy by throwing him from the Acropolis in Athens. Tried and convicted for this deed, Daedalus was banished from his home city of Athens and fled to the island of Crete.

DAEDALUS AND THE LABYRINTH

On Crete, Daedalus found work at the court of King Minos and Queen Pasiphae in the magnificent palace of Knossos. He constructed a wooden cow for the queen to hide in to satisfy her lust for a white bull sent by Poseidon. The queen became pregnant and gave birth to the Minotaur. Daedalus was conscripted to build the Labyrinth to contain the hideous monster. Each year the king demanded that fourteen youths from Athens be sacrificed to feed the Minotaur, but eventually a hero appeared, Theseus, who was determined to kill the monster. Ariadne, the daughter of Minos and Pasiphae, fell in love with Theseus and asked Daedalus to assist him in his efforts to kill the beast. Daedalus obliged by giving her a flaxen thread for Theseus to tie to the door of the Labyrinth as he entered. In this way he could escape after killing the monster by following the thread to the entrance of the Labyrinth.

Theseus succeeded in killing the monster. He then escaped Crete after setting fire to the palace, taking Ariadne with him. Minos was furious at the loss of his daughter as well as the killing of the Minotaur, and he shut Daedalus and his son Icarus into the Labyrinth as punishment. Daedalus, having built the Labyrinth, was able to navigate his way out. But since the king had it in for him, he knew he had to escape Crete altogether. How to do this, since Minos controlled the sea around Crete? There was only one way: he and his son had to fly off the island.

TAKING FLIGHT

Years earlier Daedalus had watched the witch Medea take flight in a chariot drawn by fiery dragons; ever since that vision, he had secretly devoted himself to creating a mechanism that would allow him to fly, and he had set up a secret workshop on the cliffs overlooking the sea. There, Daedalus fashioned wings out of eagle feathers glued together with wax, which they would use to escape the island. Daedalus warned Icarus not to fly too close to the sun lest the sun melt the wings, and he warned his son not to fly too close to the sea, which would dampen the wings and weigh them down, causing him to fall. Then, the two of them put on their wings and successfully took flight from the island, but Icarus, exhilarated by the thrill of flying, flew too close to the sun. The wax holding his wings melted from the heat, and Icarus tumbled out of the sky and into the sea, where he drowned. The place where he died is now called the Icarian Sea.

Notice that Daedalus is trying to coach his son to follow the middle path, to avoid too much yang energy (the sun) and too much yin (the sea). His son, maybe due to the adolescent surge of masculine hormones, is overly attracted to yang energy and pays the ultimate price for it.

Flying is necessary — especially for the young. Marion Woodman puts it this way: "Young people do start out with imagination, with enthusiasm. Take away their disciplined outlets and they are birds without wings. Moreover, their frustration at not being able to soar results in rage, which they have no idea how to contain." Doesn't this explain young people, many of them potential leaders and adventurous souls, who cannot find ways to fly from impoverished city streets, and who cannot contain their frustrations, and who find themselves as a result flooding our prisons? But Woodman also warns: "The danger lies in hubris, ascending beyond the human limit by sacrificing instinct to pure spirit, like Icarus flying too close to the sun and falling into a bottomless ocean of unconsciousness. If we think of pure spirit, symbolized by the sun, as masculine, we can see that, released from the feminine the masculine spirit is death. The feminine is what holds the masculine in life."

In the story, Daedalus flew on and arrived safely in Sicily, where he built a temple to Apollo and hung up his wings forever as an offering to the god. Daedalus has come to represent the classic artist, a skilled mature craftsman, while Icarus has come to symbolize the romantic artist, an heir of the classic artist, who works from impulse, passion, and rebelliousness, and whose defiance of formal aesthetic and social conventions can prove to be self-destructive.

A PARABLE OF COMMUNICATION

The familiar telling of this story places all the blame for Icarus's death on himself. Icarus disobeyed his father, or else did not listen closely enough to his advice. Icarus listened to his own inflated ego rather than the sage wisdom of his elder, and so he died, maybe deservedly so. There is some truth to this interpretation of the story, but I am skeptical that this is the only interpretation.

Remember, Daedalus is a seriously flawed father figure; he had murdered his nephew out of envy, which is what led to father and son being banished to Crete in the first place. Daedalus hardly represents the model of a healthy father, adult, or elder. Quite the contrary, Daedalus represents the shadow side of the teacher or parent; he is the elder who cannot abide being outshone and overtaken by the success of youth. How ready was Daedalus to watch his son take wing and fly successfully, to someday fly farther without him? Perhaps the son's reckless flight was a reaction to this paternal envy; Icarus was challenging his father, and self-destructed in the process.

Seen this way, the story becomes less a direct condemnation of the excesses of youth (which is a convenient stance for adults who have grown fearful of winged flight — that is, their mystic self — and envy the bravery of the young). Instead, this story is a tragic parable about the importance of *intergenerational wisdom and intergenerational communication*, without which there will be no wisdom. True communication requires trust, understanding, and the ability to speak the same language. Did Daedalus's envy undermine his son's trust in what he said? Was Daedalus so used to commanding and ordering, and so focused on his own need to escape, that he failed to understand his son's desires and what might happen when he strapped on those wings? Or, as is the case so often today, did a generational divide garble the father's message? Youth today speak so many new languages — from rap to rave, from computers to iPods, from Facebook to MySpace — it is imperative that elders and youth listen to each other and learn each other's languages and references. If each generation doesn't listen and communicate in ways the other hears, tragedy follows. Perhaps Daedalus needed to rap his instruction to his son to get his attention, or to text him, or perhaps Daedalus needed to create a *ritual* of flying, and through repetition and shared experience, Icarus would have internalized the father's warnings about limits and prudence before the stakes became so high.

PUTTING ON WINGS

"Putting on wings" is itself an archetypal image, and it is a powerful one for mysticism. Every youth wants to put on wings and fly, to emerge from the cocoon of childhood and "reach for the stars." This is altogether natural. Adolescents want to soar beyond the known, beyond the parental home, beyond the given and the labyrinths and the prisons of society — to reach for the heavens, to stretch to the sky, to fulfill the emerging adult soul that is truly *capax universi*, capable of the universe. It could be said that Icarus becomes the eagle by putting on an eagle's wings, and among the ancient Greeks (as well as among Native Americans and in the Bible) the eagle was an image of divine wisdom. In South America, it is the condor; in Ireland and Siberia, it is the Great Goose. To fly and soar like the eagle is to journey nearer to Father Sky, to make contact with the divine mind and to leave earthly cares temporarily behind.

Archetypally, in teachings around the world, the bird is symbolic of the soul. Among the Egyptians, the bird had a human head and signified how the soul flies away from the body after death. Greek and Roman art picked up on this idea. Some say that the bird was originally a phallic symbol. The bird singing is often symbolic of love. Birds are, like angels, messengers who bear celestial messages. It is said that when Muhammad went to heaven he found the Tree of Life restoring youth to all who ate of it. The Tree of Life was surrounded by leafy trees on whose boughs perched many birds, brilliantly colored and singing melodiously: These are the souls of the faithful.

Symbolist Cirlot writes that "every winged being is symbolic of spiritualization," and according to Jung, the bird is "a beneficent animal representing spirits or angels, supernatural aid, thoughts and flights of fancy." Pertaining to the element of air, birds represent height and loftiness of spirit. High-flying birds symbolize spiritual longing.

I think it is this longing that is at the heart of the Icarus story. Icarus was so right to put on wings, so right to leave behind the king who hated him and his father, so right to set out on a lofty journey. Every youth is right to do that. But the longing is not enough without grounding. We can soar too high, too fast, too far, too close to the sun. We do need to be grounded and prudent. Wiser people than us should indeed warn us of limits and boundaries.

But it's not enough to simply explain things, to talk at youth, at sons; messages must be delivered in ways that the other can hear. Daedalus failed in this regard. Many elders today and many institutions are also failing our youth in this way. Even worse than Daedalus, who at least spent time and imagination to create wings for his son and himself, many elders today are not making this effort. They are doing the opposite. They are imprisoning the young in a variety of cultural and economic labyrinths: of consumerism, of the cult of the individual, of materialism, of personal and national debt, of war-driven economies. These things do not supply the wings that satisfy the heart's desire to soar close to Father Sky.

The metaphor of flight and fall, ascent and descent, is universal. French writer Gaston Bachelard puts it this way: "Of all metaphors, only those pertaining to height, ascent, depth, descent and fall are axiomatic. Nothing can explain them but they can explain everything." Flying deities abound in the myths of ancient cultures. The gods of ancient Egypt, Minoa, and Mesopotamia were often depicted as having magnificent wings, and the Persian god of gods is depicted in the Palace of Darius I (c. 490 BCE) as being nearly all wings. The ancient Hebrews placed wings on the seraphim and the cherubim on the Ark of the Covenant. To the people of ancient times, flying was the province of the gods; humankind's place was on earth. For a human to don wings was an expression of the desire to become closer to the divine, but it was also seen as arrogant, a mere mortal's attempt to usurp a prerogative of the gods. Icarus and his father are tempting the gods by putting on wings; they are reaching for the edge, stretching to the sky. They pay a price for this effort, too: Icarus with his life; Daedalus with the loss of his son and the grief that follows. Daedalus indicates this grief by hanging up his wings after he reaches land. He would never don them again.

The lesson? All of us pay a price for stretching our humanity, for reaching for the divine, for daring to soar, for developing the mystic and with it the prophet or spiritual warrior within us; for going *beyond*. Psychologist Otto Rank observes that we all "seek to go beyond." Beyond is the horizon that beckons us, that opens up our souls, that puts us in communion with the vast universe and with Father Sky. A good parent helps the young by both fashioning the wings that help them soar and communicating the dangers of flight. To survive, we need wings and a knowledge of how to use them. Success (or perhaps minimizing damage) depends on how well elders and youth learn to communicate, so that sons and daughters rightly outlive their parents.

THE STORY OF PHAËTHON

The story of Phaëthon is a similar young man's misadventure. Phaëthon has an absentee father, and he is ridiculed by his peers for it. He presses his mother to know who his father is, and finally she tells him: "Your father is the Sun." Phaëthon travels to the Sun and confronts his father, who admits that he is indeed his parent. And, like many an absentee parent, the father tries to make things up to his son and gives him too much. He promises Phaëthon he will fulfill any wish, and Phaëthon, lacking wisdom or boundaries, says he wants to fly across the sky in the Sun's chariot (a slightly more dangerous equivalent of asking for the car keys). As psychologist John Conger points out, "his dreams were inflated and unrelated to his earthbound capacities." The result? Phaëthon crashed and died and set the world on fire. Such happens when we are "in a boundless state of imaginings, or the reverse, to be unable to dream, to act like a well-behaved little adult, to face no dangers and never risk pushing beyond our limits."

The sky beckons us, but we also need grounding, which is what a good father or parental figure can provide. But again, notice that faulty intergenerational communication is at the root of this tragedy — Phaëthon and his father were separated for his entire childhood, and his father overindulged his son, probably out of guilt for being absent so long, and proved a poor judge of his son's capabilities by granting his most grandiose desire.

LA TRAVIATA

Another story of miscommunication between father and son is found in Giuseppe Verdi's opera *La Traviata*. With a libretto by Francesco Maria Plave — based on the novel and play by Alexandre Dumas, *La Dame aux Camélias*, — *La Traviata* is the story of a successful young Parisian courtesan, Violetta, who meets Alfredo at one of her gala parties. Alfredo, a young man from Provence, confesses his love for her, and she considers whether to surrender her successful courtesan status for a chance at real love. Meanwhile, however, she is showing signs of consumption, or tuberculosis.

She takes the challenge and makes the plunge. She quits her former life and commits to love. The lovers move out of Paris and live idyllically in her country home. She gives up all thought of returning to the wild life of Paris, but one day a surprise visitor arrives: Alfredo's father, Germont. Germont demands that Violetta end her relationship with his son, who is then away, because her bad reputation is hurting the family's good one, and the wedding planned for Germont's daughter is in danger of being broken off due to the scandal. Violetta pleads and pleads that he not demand this of her, as her and Alfredo's love is so real. But finally she agrees to leave Alfredo at his father's behest.

Alfredo meanwhile is in Paris looking for work or money. He had learned that Violetta was selling her jewelry and property in order to finance their relationship, and he is beginning to grow up and learn that love is not always just being with the beloved. There are bills to pay. When Alfredo returns, Violetta hides a farewell note she has written and pleads with him to love her no matter what transpires between them. She leaves, and later a messenger delivers Violetta's letter to Alfredo, who becomes furious. Germont arrives to console his son, but Alfredo leaves for Paris, where he finds Violetta at a party with another man, the Baron, as her escort.

At the party Alfredo gambles recklessly. Violetta urges him to leave, fearing for his life, and he agrees, but only if she will go with him. Lying to him, she says she no longer loves him, and in his unbridled rage he takes his winnings and throws them at Violetta. Germont berates his son for humiliating a woman in public. The Baron challenges Alfredo to a duel, and Alfredo, filled with self-loathing, storms out.

In the final act Violetta is impoverished, abandoned by her friends, and in the last stages of consumption. Germont writes to her that he and his son have reconciled and will soon come to see her. When they arrive, Alfredo bursts in and utters his profound remorse. Germont enters and begs her to forgive him, realizing the real love Violetta had for his son, having made so deep a sacrifice for his sake. At the last minute Violetta imagines that she is cured and well again, but she dies with the word "joy" on her lips.

This story is something of a mirror opposite to the Icarus story: here, a young man struggles to love, to grow up, to fly on his own, but the profound interference of his well-meaning, overprotective father causes a tragedy. Like Icarus, Alfredo falls; that is, his love fails, it falls from the sky, he tumbles from the soaring ecstasy of life with Violetta. And clearly, his father's interference precipitates that fall. While, through the course of the story, both father and son learn what true love is about, this understanding turns tragic because it arrives too late to save love in its earthly form. Violetta is a victim of their ignorance.

From the start, Germont knows his son loves Violetta. Early on, Germont tells Violetta, "Alfredo thinks of nobody but you — when you were ill, he came every day, inquiring anxiously about you." Germont cannot claim ignorance. He would rather pluck his son's wings than let him risk failure, saying: "I'm the father of that headstrong boy who's rushing to his ruin because of his infatuation for you." He diminishes Alfredo's love (which Alfredo calls "the pulse of the universe") as a mere infatuation. Moreover, to shore up his authority, Germont invokes God for his decisions. "My child," he says to Violetta, "it is God who inspires the words this father speaks." Yet he has sympathy for her plight as well, saying: "Weep, unhappy girl, weep! I see the sacrifice I ask is the greatest one of all; in my own heart I feel your sorrow. Have courage and your generous heart will conquer." At least he shows some awareness of her generosity.

Addressing his son, Germont says: "Become your father's pride and joy again.... It was God who brought me here! You do not know what pain your old father has suffered — what, no response to your father's love?" In order to keep Alfredo home, and safe, Germont invokes shame, God, and self-pity — asking Alfredo to acknowledge his suffering over that which he has caused son and beloved alike.

Violetta, for her part, says explicitly that the death of their relationship will bring about her own death. She demonstrates the connection between the health of mind, body, and spirit, as we do today with holistic medicine; she foresees that the breaking of her spirit will facilitate her consumption, sap her body, and kill her. She sings, "If I parted from Alfredo, my suffering would be so unbearable that I would rather die, why yes, much rather die." And later she says, after going along with Germont's wish, "I shall soon die." As for Alfredo, his inability to fly results in uncontrolled outburst of anger and a desire for revenge, culminating in Alfredo shaming himself and his beloved by throwing his card earnings at Violetta. His father says, "Where is my son? I see him nowhere in you, Alfredo." Germont's machinations, rather than protecting Alfredo, bring out the worst in his son.

In the final scene, as Violetta welcomes father and son to the side of her deathbed, Alfredo asks for forgiveness. "Forget the pain, beloved. Forgive me and my father." He takes responsibility, but he does so appropriately, knowing at last the full context of his father's meddling. Alfredo says, "How much to blame I am, but now, dearest, I know everything."

Germont then offers a "deathbed" conversion — *his* conversion at *her* deathbed. As Violetta lies dying, he begs: "Say no more, don't torture me, remorse seizes my soul. Her every word strikes me like lightning! Rash old fool like I was, only now do I see what I have done! Forgive me for the torment inflicted on your fair heart." Finally, the parent achieves insight.

Part of the prophetic dimension to this opera was its critique of family. The opera was considered scandalous in its day because it proposed that someone in a bad profession (courtesan) could still be a good person. Violetta becomes the shining star in this drama. Furthermore, she is young, only twenty-three years old when she died, so there is a clear attack on adultism by Verdi. Adultism, as I have discussed elsewhere, is the repression of the child in the adult that results in an unconscious hostility toward the young. The young are teaching the old — if they will learn. Violetta is the generous one who sacrifices the one love of her life to rescue the family of her beloved. She even extends the definition of family when she asks her lover's father to hold her tight like he would a daughter.

In the Icarus story, the son died. In *La Traviata*, the son's lover dies. In both cases, the father bears responsibility for the deaths because of faulty communication. But further, in both stories, the fathers are also led astray by their own needs, agendas, and fears: in *La Traviata*, the father undermines his son because he values his own agenda (preserving family honor) over his son's (who would love Violetta in spite of her worldly reputation). Daedalus can't control his jealousy of the younger generation (he kills his nephew), and this drives father and son away from Athens in the first place. In fact, the only reason Icarus needs wings to escape King Monos is because the son can't avoid being caught up in his father's political agenda and palace intrigue. In each of this chapter's stories, the fathers attempt to construct wings for or manage the flight of their sons, but each fail. Each were too wrapped up in their own agendas, and this led to faulty communication and bad instructions, with fatal results.

The Icarus and Daedalus story resonates with archetypal energy because it reflects reality. For instance, a number of years ago, a gay student of mine, who graduated from our master's program, died of AIDS. He was from a large Midwest family, and when he was a young man he opposed the Vietnam War. His father became so angry with him over this he kicked him out of the house and said, "Either come back in a uniform or come back in a coffin." Instead, he became a conscientious objector and a psychiatric nurse. He did many good things in his life, such as starting a radio program for young gays even though his life was threatened for doing so. His death was very special. A nurse reported that "a light hung around the room for twenty-four hours afterward." After his death, his father and I spoke. His father broke down and cried, "He was right about the Vietnam War. He was more morally astute than I was."

Passion in the young is not always wrong, and neither is their moral judgment. Nor is the caution and perspective of elders always right. Both need each other, though. They need to remain open and receptive to the other, unafraid to fly and unafraid to learn.

HUNTER-GATHERERS $\boxed{4}$

FOR 90 PERCENT OF HUMAN HISTORY we were almost exclusively hunter-gatherers. Today, we are farmers, particularly in Western culture. This is literally true — as our food comes almost entirely from farms, and the only hunting or gathering people do is in supermarkets — but we are also farmers by sensibility. We tend, cultivate, and grow. Living in a period of farming and benefiting from farming does *not* mean that we have thrown off our hunter-gatherer genius, the skills and intelligence learned from all those millennia of hunting. One does not shuck off the souls of one's ancestors. Even if we no longer actively use them for day-to-day sustenance and survival, those powers and crafts and skills remain inside, as untapped potential, and they can unconsciously affect us subtly and in unexpected ways. Even as we move into the twenty-first century, we are hunter-gatherers still.

In what ways do the skills and intelligence learned by our hunting ancestors assert themselves in our lives today? Which ways are positive and which negative? And how might men access these skills to benefit our communities and our very survival at this critical time in human history?

TO BE A HUNTER-GATHERER

First, let us take a look at what it means to be a hunter-gatherer. For this, I draw in particular on the excellent study by Jared Diamond, *Guns, Germs, and Steel*. Diamond has a lot to say about the particular intelligence of our hunter-gatherer ancestors. Diamond writes, "Until the end of the last Ice Age, around 11,000 B.C., all peoples on all continents were still hunter-gatherers. . . . For most of the time since the ancestors of modern humans diverged from the ancestors of the living great apes, around 7 million years ago, all humans on Earth fed themselves exclusively by hunting wild animals and gathering wild plants, as the Blackfeet still did in the 19th century."

Notice the universality of this fact: Every one of us comes from hunter-gatherer stock. To be a human is to be a hunter-gatherer. To be a man is to serve the tribe and the survival of the community through the skills of hunting and gathering. This has been the case for about 90,000 of the 100,000 years of our most recent ancestors — and for millions of years before that.

Today, a few societies — such as Native Americans, Aboriginal Australians, and New Guinea peoples — remain partly or entirely dependent on a hunter-gatherer lifestyle. The seeming simplicity of these cultures stand in contrast to the modern agriculture-based world, which along with farming and herding developed complex political organizations and hierarchies and built enormous cities. In many ways hunting-gathering was not conducive to city-building; it has always been largely tribal and done best in small groups. Very little hierarchy is involved, and a kind of egalitarianism rules, since all are hunting or gathering. There is little time for specialization or for settling down to practice specialized trades. Hunter-gatherers often must keep moving, following the game and the seasons.

Diamond lived among hunter-gatherers in New Guinea for many years, and he concludes that moving from a hunter-gatherer lifestyle to one based on farming and industry does not guarantee "progress" or happiness or greater intelligence. "My own impression, from having divided my life between United States cities and New Guinea villages, is that the so-called blessings of civilization are mixed. For example, compared with hunter-gatherers, citizens of modern industrialized states enjoy better medical care, lower risk of death by homicide, and a longer life span, but receive much less social support from friendships and extended families." Could it be that there are things we've forgotten and need to relearn today from hunter-gatherers and the hunter-gatherer lurking within each of us?

I am reminded of a young Jesuit priest I met seventeen years ago when I was in a village in the Amazon rainforest of Brazil. The priest was living on an island with an indigenous tribe; due to the tribe's isolation, it was quite self-sufficient, and its entire culture revolved around the monkey, both for nourishment and for religious ceremonies. He said to me, "I don't know what I am doing there, what I have to teach them." I responded, "But what do they teach you?" Immediately, he replied in French, "*La joie*. They experience more joy in a day than my people do in a lifetime." Joy might be one benefit of paying more attention to the hunter-gatherer inside.

JOY AND RITUAL

One reason joy matters among hunter-gatherer peoples is that ritual matters. As Barbara Ehrenreich observes in *Dancing in the Streets*, ecstatic ritual was part of the "hunter-gatherers of Australia, the horticulturists of Polynesia, the village peoples of India." Europeans called it "savagery," but it often led to trance. Encountering these dances, Westerners learned that "the essence of the Western mind, and particularly the Western male, upper-class mind, was its ability to resist the contagious rhythm of the drums, to wall itself up in a fortress of ego and rationality against the seductive wildness of the world." Among hunter-gatherers, ritual insured a "kind of spiritual merger with the group," and this in turn healed and brought joy. Here is how Ehrenreich envisions life among the hunter-gatherers:

> Go back ten thousand years and you will find humans toiling away at the many mundane activities required for survival: hunting, food gathering, making weapons and garments, beginning to experiment with agriculture. But if you land on the right moonlit night or seasonal turning point, you might also find them engaged in what seems, by comparison, to be a gratuitous waste of energy: dancing in lines or circles, sometimes wearing masks or what appear to be costumes, often waving branches or sticks. Most likely, both sexes would be dancing, each in its separate line or circle. Their faces and bodies might be painted with red ochre.... We can infer these scenes from prehistoric rock art depicting dancing figures which has been discovered in sites in Africa, India, Australia, Italy, Turkey, Israel, Iran, and Egypt, among other places.... Well before people had a written language, and possibly before they took up a settled lifestyle, they danced and understood dancing as an activity important enough to record on stone.

Some of the male figures wear masks in the form of animal heads or abstract designs; other dancers wear what archeologists interpret as "costumes," such as leopard skins. Ritual of a danced and possibly ecstatic nature was central to the lives of our ancestors. And it brought joy with it.

But this sense of community was not only about joy. It was also about defense. "Like primates in the wild today, early humans probably faced off predatory animals collectively — banding together in a tight group, stamping their feet, shouting, and waving sticks or branches. If done in unison, the animal might think it is one very large being and would go away." Hunting too invoked the lessons from dance. Hunting was often done by the entire group, which "advanced against a herd of game animals, shouting, stamping, and waving sticks or torches." Over time, as communal hunting waned and the threat of animal predators declined, the thrill of the human triumph over animals could still be reinvoked as ritual. Aldous Huxley comments: "Ritual dances provide a religious experience. That seems more satisfying and convincing than any other. . . . It is with their muscles that humans most easily obtain knowledge of the divine."

Anthropologist Marshall Sahlins has proposed that hunter-gatherers, because they worked far fewer hours than members of industrial society do, had more leisure time and also ate well. They were an "original affluent society" because they were satisfied with very little in the material sense — a kind of "zen economy." Such a society has time for community and joyful conviviality. This would correspond directly with what an Australian Aboriginal once told me: "In our society we work four hours a day and the rest of the day we make things." Among those things made? Ritual.

INTELLIGENCE

Jared Diamond concludes, after thirty-three years of working with New Guineans in their own societies, that they are more intelligent than his counterparts in Europe or America. He says, "They impressed me as being on the average more intelligent, more alert, more expressive, and more interested in things and people around them than the average European or American is." When he says this, Diamond is not being sentimental or patronizing; he means the New Guineans are actually smarter: they are more alert, which means more awake and more curious and seeking after knowledge — eager even; they are more expressive, which means more in touch with one's creativity and the artist within; they are more interested in things and people, which means more curious, more spontaneous in following one's creativity, and more eager to learn. Who among us would not like to be more intelligent, more alert, more expressive, and more curious? Given this, why would we ever want to hold back our better hunter-gatherer selves?

As Diamond makes clear, the intelligence level of hunter-gatherers needn't ever be questioned. Studies indicate that they were and are "walking encyclopedias of natural history, with individual names (in their local language) for as many as a thousand or more plant and animal species, and with detailed knowledge of those species' biological characteristics, distribution, and potential uses. As people become increasingly dependent on domesticated plants and animals this traditional knowledge gradually loses its value and becomes lost until one arrives at modern supermarket shoppers who could not distinguish a wild grass from a wild pulse."

Why are hunter-gatherers smarter? Diamond feels it's the combined result of the hunter-gatherer lifestyle and the process of natural selection, which would promote genes for intelligence by weeding out those not quite smart enough to survive and overcome obstacles. And what about the hunter-gatherer lifestyle would make them smarter? Though it seems counterintuitive, the lack of an alphabet and writing, which no traditional hunter-gatherers ever developed. The upside of this is that, as a rule, if you can't write things down, you develop a better memory, you do more storytelling, you're a keener listener, and you hone your ability to speak from the heart. You communicate more and better, and develop richer community rituals. Your observational skills can mean life and death, and you tend to live more in the now, since the world around you is the main focus of your attention.

Diamond noticed all this among tribal New Guineans, who lacked something else we in the West take for granted: advanced technology and prefabricated entertainment. Unlike in the West, neither tribal children nor adults spend hour after hour being passively entertained by television and movies (the average American household has its TV set on seven hours per day). New Guineans do not lead passive lives; they spend each day actively problem-solving, interacting with each other and the natural world. Children are thoroughly stimulated and engaged in this communal effort, but even their play is always interactive. Diamond concludes: "In mental ability New Guineans are probably genetically superior to Westerners, and they surely are superior in escaping the devastating developmental disadvantages under which most children in industrialized societies now grow up." It would seem that calling upon our hunter-gatherer instincts would lead to healthier children and, quite likely, make us all smarter.

FROM THE SPEAR TO THE PLOW

When humans moved from hunting-gathering to agriculture, they and society changed. Some of these changes we would consider "positive" and some "negative," but nearly all have led to unintended consequences that now trouble modern life.

For instance, domesticating wild animals and plants resulted in humans having far more food to eat, and this resulted in far greater numbers of human beings. From one acre of land, hunter-gatherers typically can use .1 percent for food, but farmers can convert 90 percent of the biomass into edible calories. "As a result, one acre can feed many more herders and farmers — typically, 10 to 100 times more — than hunter-gatherers." Domesticated animals assist farming by providing fertilizer to enrich the soil, and plowing fields allows for deeper penetration of soil, thus allowing for more plants to be harvested. More food and a sedentary lifestyle allowed for more children. On average, hunter-gatherers space their children four years apart, whereas farmers space theirs at about two years apart. Today, human population growth is outpacing the planet's resources, in part because the natural constraints of our previous hunter-gatherer life are missing.

Agriculture and the ensuing abundance of food had political implications. Humans could now sustain not just larger families but larger communities. Small tribal bands expanded into towns and cities, and managing these ever-larger communities required specialists and hierarchies, a division of labor. Some grew food, while others controlled its distribution, and so bureaucrats were born, along with professional soldiers, clergy, artisans, and more. Despite its benefits, farming is overall harder work than hunting and gathering. Studies show that hunter-gatherers typically have more free time to enjoy life, family, and friends. "Most peasant farmers and herders, who constitute the great majority of the world's actual food producers, aren't necessarily better off than hunter-gatherers. Time budget studies show that they may spend more rather than fewer hours per day at work than hunter-gatherers do." The first farmers, we now know, were less well nourished and suffered from more serious diseases and died at a younger age than hunter-gatherers did.

Indeed, I have long felt that the biblical Garden of Eden story in Genesis is in fact a kind of lament for the "old days" of hunting-gathering when life seemed more idyllic and game and beauty was more abundant in the "garden" (the word "paradise" has roots in the Persian word for "garden"). The fall of Adam and Eve symbolized a fall from the garden of hunting-gathering and into the rigors of farming and city-building. Diamond's observations only encourage my thinking about the Adam and Eve myth. Perhaps the metaphor of the "tree of good and evil" alludes to the decision to eat agricultural products, that is, orchards of fruit. As we've seen above, this decision was fraught with consequences, some favorable (more food, more people); some less so (more hierarchy, more technology, an increased capacity for destruction, overpopulation).

But this is not a moral judgment. As Diamond points out, "there was often not even a conscious choice between food production and hunting-gathering.... Food production *evolved* as a by-product of decisions made without awareness of their consequences." This too would seem to support the warning from Genesis: Beware of knowledge. It can have consequences that are beyond your capacity to deal with. Biting into an apple might bear results you never dreamed of. Be careful what you wish for.

In addition, all kinds of mixed societies developed where hunting-gathering and some kind of land management coexisted, and wandering blended with sedentary living. The cultivation of plants was an evolutionary event, not a revolutionary invention. In the early stages of food production, people simultaneously collected wild foods *and* raised cultivated ones. It is likely that the first farming was in fact a strategy to provide a reserve backup to wild food foraging. Creativity, flexibility, and adaptation are key traits of a hunter-gatherer mind-set, which meant that they were willing to change, but the changes were still gradual. Diamond writes, "Even in the cases of the most rapid independent development of food production from a hunting-gathering lifestyle it took thousands of years to shift from complete dependence on wild foods to a diet with very few wild foods."

Hierarchy was developed most strongly during the agricultural era, according to Ehrenreich. This was often the case with leaders of ritual. Nine thousand years ago, hunter-gatherers lived on a cleared "dance ground" for rituals that included the entire community. Later, with agriculture, rituals were led by members of an elite, most likely men. Two thousand years ago, important rituals were performed only by trained full-time priests. Social hierarchy went "hand in hand with militarism and war" and a certain "hostility to the danced rituals of the archaic past" arose.

Thus, over many thousands of years, human society eventually shifted from being primarily based on hunting-gathering to primarily based on farming, but this was not a conscious decision. Humans did not weigh the advantages and disadvantages of each and make a choice of one over the other. Among these circumstances were evolutionary forces such as the decline of game and animals and the expansion of wild crops fit for domestication. The "agricultural revolution" was birthed in the area of the Fertile Crescent around 11,000 B.C. Yet it was not the special intelligence of the people of the Fertile Crescent, but the unique conflagration of climate, environment, wild plants, and animals that brought about this profound change.

With the domestication of animals came germs that the animals spread, but by living with these animals over eras, Europeans and others developed considerable immunity from those germs. This in turn enabled them to conquer many hunter-gatherer tribes that had not domesticated such animals and had not developed immunities. "Germs thus played decisive roles in the European conquests of Native Americans, Australians, South Africans, and Pacific Islanders," Diamond says.

History demonstrates that the move from hunter-gatherer to farmer was often a smooth transition. It was, after all, hunter-gatherers who became farmers or partial farmers, as the case may be. New Guinea has been populated for forty thousand years, and most of the population today are farmers. Some combine farming and hunting, but there is very little wild game remaining in New Guinea. Yet it seems that the *memory* of hunting and gathering is still very much alive in these people and therefore there are lessons to be learned about the ways and intelligence of our hunter-gathering ancestors. As Diamond explains so well, circumstances played a large role in why certain agriculturally-based societies eventually flourished and "out-competed" hunter-gatherers. But from our vantage today, we might well ask what we lost, and if we made a good bargain. How much smarter, how much more in touch with plants and animals might we be, if we still nourished our hunter-gatherer ways? And can we call on these instincts now to help save the natural world from the overpopulation, overdevelopment, and pollution that have been the consequences of our farm-based lives?

AGGRESSION, THEN AND NOW

Despite his admiration for them, Diamond does not romanticize the tribal people of New Guinea. He makes clear that they suffer high mortality rates from murder, chronic tribal warfare, accidents, and food shortages. In fact, murder and aggression is strongly evident among many hunter-gatherer societies, both then and now. Similarly, aggression is an integral part of the hunter-gatherer archetype, and by engaging this archetype, men can find new and better ways of dealing with their own aggression.

For instance, in ancient New Guinea, war was real, it was fierce, and the losers were often eaten. Cannibalism was an accepted part of life. And yet, despite the cultural shift to agriculture, violence and aggression do not seem to have lessened. When it comes to war, it's hard to see how dropping bombs and napalm are "better" or more "civilized" than cannibalism; they are less personal, perhaps, but even more efficiently deadly, destroying more people. If anything, advanced technology has only amplified aggression, increasing its power and spreading its effects further.

In other words, aggression seems to be an inherent part of life, not merely of a particular archetype. This is something that psychologist John Conger described very eloquently in my interview with him for this book. Describing recent fossil finds, Dr. Conger said:

> Aggression is primitive. It goes down to the very core of our animal evolution, in fact, to the evolution of life itself. Recall that 543 million years ago with the Cambrian explosion something amazing happened: there were only four phyla, and then suddenly in two to four million years an explosion expanded to thirty-eight phyla that have not expanded since. What happened? The development of the eye. Once life could see, it started to eat. Fossils show that these early creatures suddenly developed claws and armor, and if you increase your protein, you develop diversity. Once life could see, it could get a better source of protein by eating each other, and then it developed. You get a certain parallel. That's why aggression is the reason why we diversify, which is not such a nice picture, but it is the essential evolutionary understanding of why we diversify. The whole theme has to do with acquiring a better source of protein.
>
> So there's something about aggression itself that is very central to evolution. What we do with that aggression is the issue. As males we become hunter-gatherers.

Dr. Conger says he sees this evolutionary dynamic of aggression still at work today, though humans are beginning to make some progress.

> How do we understand My Lai or the Holocaust — where in Vienna the Viennese were voting for independent representation, and a few days

later Hitler marches in and everyone is in the streets cheering him, and they are humiliating their friends and neighbors, forcing them to scrub the streets with toothbrushes? How do we explain this incredible and unspeakable behavior as sons of God? There's no way to explain it.

But think of two chimpanzees: they may be altruistic within the group, but they go and kill the babies of other tribes. Basically it's the same as us as hunter-gatherers up to twelve thousand years ago. That's what hunter-gatherers did. They defeated their enemies, and anyone that was not within their tribe they killed. And there was an awful lot of cannibalism. How do we understand it? We actually have improved because we have become less violent insofar as we have developed skills of communication. Language helps. It's actually not as bad; it's better. That's why I say we are made in the image of *God in our becoming*. We aren't there yet.

Tribal hunter-gatherer aggression is certainly alive and well in America's cities. A recent study was done in Oakland, California, where in the past five years 557 people, most of them young black men, have been killed — mostly by young black men. It's notable that much of the aggression is spurred over issues of shame and "respect."

A handful of their killers, speaking from prison, describe an environment where violence is so woven into the culture that murder has become a symbol of manhood.

The inmates say the only difference between these neighborhoods and prison is the absence of walls. The same hierarchies apply — the meanest rise to the top.

How does it begin? With anger. "Without anyone in charge of their moral development, young boys come up with their own rules. When they get in disputes, they don't have the ability to resolve them because no one has ever taught them how to manage anger and stress other than with fists or a gun." There is a kind of "hunt" going on, with boys becoming "prey."

In this world, challenges cannot be left unanswered. A boy who is jumped, robbed or insulted and doesn't respond is labeled "soft," or a "punk" or a "bitch." He becomes prey. Once he is perceived as weak, the attacks keep coming. He loses not only his honor, but his friends and his personal safety, until he fights back and wins — sometimes via homicide.

Their role models are the drug dealers on the corner who have the cars, clothes, girls, money and most of all — respect. "In a dysfunctional environment, it's prestigious to be a gangster, and it inspires you to act the same," said [one] convicted killer. . . . Respect is money, money is power and power is masculinity. Violence defines you as a man.

When gang members speak about the importance of belonging, we know that shame plays a large role in the violence and aggression that is integral to their life.

Inmates told the Chronicle that it was the drug dealers who gave them their first sense of belonging. The gang on the block is the first group that wants them, that pays attention to their whereabouts, that asks what they are doing and what they think about things.

Boys don't think they will live past 25, so they don't live their life as if they will. . . . Only a handful of the killers had legitimate jobs. Criminal records and lack of a high school diploma, no car to get to work, and no support from immediate family ensure that they simply don't fit in to what society sees as employee material.

What can make a difference? The article concluded, "The experts — and the killers — say a mentor might have saved them, anyone from the outside who could have shown them another way to be a man."

This is indeed the challenge. We need to find another way to be a man. Another way to honor our hunter-gatherer instincts without resorting to killing.

One avenue that several men described was martial arts. Through these ancient practices they found a way to tame the ancient aggressor inside and thereby develop a healthy masculinity. Dr. Conger used Korean martial arts in this way, receiving a black belt at the age of sixty-one. I asked him why he did this.

In part it was a father/son thing. It was also important to me personally regarding my own sense of the masculine because in growing up I was somewhat invisible. My father was more distant, and I wasn't given a clear picture about how to be male in the world. There wasn't a lot of room for my aggression and my inner conflict. I grew up avoiding conflict. I was good at staying out of it, though I had a few fights that I enjoyed. I had aggression but no narrative to help me to understand it.

I have come to feel that life *is conflict*, and if you want to have

peace, you will be dead early. So the martial arts intrigued me when
I was teaching English in high school and I started doing karate on the
side. When I came to the West Coast and my sons were hitting middle school, I knew kids really push you, and you push back to find out
who you are. It's not sadistic — they just want to know who you are.
So I wanted my sons to learn martial arts, and one of my boys had met
a teacher who demonstrated in the school. It was a Korean system and
I felt at home in it. Both my sons worked at it — they stopped at the
brown belt but I carried through. I still practice, but I stopped going
because it's such an emotional commitment that I can't do much else.
So I do the forms and practice.

TRIBAL SHAME

Like aggression, shame goes back a very long way. Studies of ancient hunter-
gatherer tribes, such as in New Guinea, make it clear that, along with violence,
shame was and is a primary way of maintaining control. Among tribal peoples,
the ultimate shame — and the ultimate punishment — is to be expelled from the
tribe. That, not capital punishment, is the way the worst offenders against the
community are treated. Expulsion from the tribe is tantamount to death by isolation. Shame, by this definition, is the equivalent of "not belonging," in that
the consequences of bad action lead to separation and expulsion. At this
point, after some tens of thousands of years of this, our DNA might even be
hardwired for shame. No wonder shame plays such a large role in men, leading them so often into aggression.

The modern world is full of tribal groups, so that the weight of tribal expulsion weighs as heavily on us today as ever. One example of an extreme form
of modern tribalism is fundamentalist religion — which is based in the conviction that "we are saved and others are not," that "we are God's friends and others are God's enemies." For fundamentalist religions, belonging is an either/or
proposition — "we are completely right and others are all wrong" — which feeds
their anti-intellectual tendencies. Questioning the tribal mentality risks shame
and expulsion, so members surrender thought and consciousness. They surrender mind and self *in order to belong at any cost*. The quest for belonging becomes
so powerful, and belonging is so narrowly defined and easily threatened, that the
self, compassion, the mind, all gifts from God, are negated and pushed aside.

In contrast, is it not true that authentic prophets risk shame? They too risk being expelled from the community, literally or figuratively, as Jesus observed when he said the "prophet is without honor in his own land." But there is a difference. Do we not, in retrospect usually, admire men who have put their conscience before their comfort, an expanded community ahead of a limited tribal community? Such would be Mahatma Gandhi, or Martin Luther King Jr. or Howard Thurman or Pope John XXIII or Dietrich Bonhoeffer. By definition the prophet (or warrior) goes against the tide, he risks being ostracized and "not belonging" in the effort to redefine what belonging means — to focus attention on the greater good of everyone and create a larger, more expansive community.

MARK NICHOLSON:
THE MEN'S MOVEMENT, SHAME, AND ANGER

Mark Nicholson is a forty-five-year-old therapist who grew up in Birmingham, England, which when he was a child was "very much in the shadow of the First and Second World War." He currently works at the Academy for the Love of Learning in Santa Fe, New Mexico.

Nicholson was first introduced to the men's movement in 1994, when he attended an initiation workshop with Robert Bly and James Hillman. For the past ten years he's been leading workshops in personal development, and for the past two also been leading a men's workshop. There are seven men in the group, and they meet twice a month for three hours, and Nicholson has seen firsthand how important, and rare, this kind of group is for men. We spoke about his perspective on the men's movement, the sources of shame and anger for men today, and on how they deal with them.

FOX: What are your goals in working with the men's movement?

NICHOLSON: I seek to live in a culture where it's okay to acknowledge we have made mistakes. Currently, such a confession is a sign of weakness.

Rilke wrote a wonderful poem about a lame goat that goes down to the river. It is last. But when they return it is first. So the idea of the acknowledgment of places where we are not fully competent — this is what supports our learning. Otherwise we don't acknowledge. That's where I want my work to go eventually, to create environments where we can acknowledge what we've done and not be blamed, shamed for it. Look at South Africa's amazing court investigating the crimes during Apartheid. Acknowledge our capacity for evil. Until we acknowledge that in ourselves, we can't live fully.

FOX: How do you feel about the men's movement today? What shape is it in?

NICHOLSON: I feel in some ways disappointed by what might be called the men's movement in the public eye. One reason is that the whole idea of men being vulnerable together is of course something that gets scapegoated by the culture. Any vulnerability by men gets scapegoated. So it has been really hard for the men's movement to have a place that doesn't get marginalized. It's very hard for men to find places to go to.

When I think of the men's movement now, I think of the less-public expressions of the men's movement. Obviously Bly's work has been the guidepost for it, not the only one of course, but the places where I've been influenced are much more under the radar.

FOX: It's that "hidden" dimension.

NICHOLSON: I think of a group in Monterey which does not have a very big name in self-development but has been hugely influential for men in the Monterey area. It has been hugely supportive of men. I think about the work of Gordon Whelan, president of Esalen, and his work on shame. His attention on shame has helped men to be intimate with each other. This is much less in the public eye than was the earlier phase of the men's movement.

FOX: Tell us more about Whelan's work on shame.

NICHOLSON: Gordon comes out of the world of gestalt — not Fritz Perls's line but Goodman, and he has worked a lot on field dynamics. How is the self something that is constantly being shaped rather than something formed and not in process? So his work on shame really looks at how living in a postmodern culture is an experience of alienation because so many ties that are ours from the past have been lost. We go around with a sense of alienation, and this leaves us in a position of being easily shamed — and especially men because men have gone through experiences of being shamed so intensely from the time we were very young.

FOX: How do you define shame?

NICHOLSON: In Gordon's work shame is the opposite of belonging. Shame is the experience of not belonging. I would go further. I think there is appropriate shame when you commit harm — we need that to regulate our social structures. But the secondary shame is the feeling of not belonging, that who we are is not okay. That is very easily evoked in a culture when what it takes to belong has shifted so dramatically. We tend to get our sense of belonging from a certain status or financial condition. That is unsustainable as a sense of belonging.

FOX: That is striking as a definition because we've been taught we don't belong in the modern era because we live in a machine universe, and we've had to hunker down and cut our souls off from the universe and our souls are shrunk. This takes shame beyond the psychological realm and to a much bigger community and sociological ethos. And that really makes sense. Are women less shamed? Father Sky and Mother Earth — women are closer to the Earth and its processes and men are cut off from Father Sky and its machine parts. Therefore we don't belong.

NICHOLSON: On an essential level women are just that much better at processing their experience of shame, at coming together and talking about their inner experience. As distinct from exterior experiences, which men are more likely to talk about.

FOX: Have you seen this dynamic in workshops you have done, how women are more effective at processing their shame than men are?

NICHOLSON: Carol Gilligan's research of young boys is giving us this extraordinary insight that boys get shamed for their vulnerability at a very young age, right around kindergarten, and that's the time at which they really learn to hold off from expressing their feelings and experience. Girls don't go through that shaming process, so it becomes much, much harder for the men to transcend those experiences of not belonging or not feeling so good because that part has been wiped out very, very young.

FOX: I wonder if this can help explain why homosexual men are often more mature than heterosexual men because they had to deal with that shame and even a geometrically increased proportion of it at an early age — and they either die of it, going the way of addiction, or they go beyond it, beyond the norm of what is shameful and isn't for a male. Would you say there's something to that?

NICHOLSON: I agree. But it's important not to shame heterosexual men for not being where homosexual men are. Heterosexual and homosexual men have been through necessarily different initiations. Homosexual men have had to come out in a culture that scapegoats their sexuality. They've had to deal with that culture in a very upfront way, and they generally find places where they find allies and talk about and work that shame. Like women do.

I don't think heterosexual men have the same opportunities where they can process their shame. They go through a different initiation, which is to find a way to develop the capacity to live in the world without having vulnerability. They develop an armor and ability to move through this world that requires men to exhaust themselves in order to make money. It's a very different skill set and it is exhausting. It's why women initiate two-thirds of breakups, because men don't have a support group to go to.

My men's groups have a mixture of hetero and homosexual men. The heterosexuals are prescreened in a way because the description says we will talk about our lives and draw on support of one another. My experience is that the support that comes from being with other men is not dependent on one's sexual orientation.

FOX: In other words, hetero men are just as capable of it as homosexual men but have had less experience.

NICHOLSON: Exactly. As soon as you put them in the room, they relax.

FOX: Might you say that the homosexuals hold a space, making it easier for heterosexual men?

NICHOLSON: The homosexuals have a patience with heterosexual men. One gay man said: "I never thought I would sit in a room with heterosexual men doing this exercise." And that is true. At the beginning it's not something heterosexual men would feel comfortable doing, but once they have developed their trust, they are ready to go.

FOX: Healing the shame and moving it. What about "trust" — what are your issues and strategies for getting through the shame?

NICHOLSON: Shame in this culture is shameful. You can't point to it and say. "Now we'll heal our shame." That puts people in a certain place. The way I work with it is to do things together whereby we experience things together. We help people really look at the experiences in their lives and how they have been affected by them so that process is not shameful.

For example, I invite people to go and find an object that represents one of the greatest losses in their lives. Come back and have people speak about it. That is a ritual of mourning that enables people to express grief. So often grief itself is shamed. This gives them a sense of belonging that has been lost. Through that a trust builds — "I won't be shamed for the loss. So maybe there are other things I can reveal."

FOX: Getting men in touch with their loss seems very important.

NICHOLSON: Formalizing it and making it clear that the purpose of affect is to give us the opportunity to be initiated into a soul quality. So fear has the opportunity to be transformed into courage; grief into compassion. If we turn away from our grief, it turns to melancholy. Turning to one's feeling gives one the opportunity to develop these essential goals that we are all seeking and we all know we want to live. That normalizes the process.

FOX: Our cosmic masses all have a grieving experience in them. If we keep grief in, it is no longer universal. We make it private, and we are losing out on a lot of energy and rarely are able to convert it into compassion, as you say.

NICHOLSON: This is what healthy religion would look like.

FOX: What about the issue of aggression? How universal is that and what kind of strategies do you work with?

NICHOLSON: Aggression in men is very tricky, because as men we have so much anger about the way in which we have been treated or dismissed or rejected by other men. This whole culture lives within a story of war, and to go to war the culture takes so much away from men. We carry with us so much, not just natural aggression, but carried aggression. In most men a lot of anger has built up that never gets an outlet. Anger is really marginalized in this culture and produces lots of destruction.

You have to be very careful when we are dealing with it that it not get triggered and expressed against the other men in the room. Because it doesn't properly belong to the other men in the room but to *our history*. We have to find ways that some of our anger can be understood as appropriate but also belonging to another part of our life than what is going on in the room. The potential of anger is that it can stand for nonviolent work defending truth. It's very tricky to talk about because the level of vulnerability those men can go into when processing their anger is so great that men can be marginalized working with it. The expression of the anger needs to be protected. An essential piece is that the places not be mocked, and the deep wounds that produce anger be honored for what they are. You must understand the underlying story in this culture. We have to learn how much we live in this story to realize the validity of some of your anger. It's partly creating places where your anger is considered valid.

My favorite example of this is the story Bruce Springsteen tells before he plays "The River." He tells about his relationship with his dad and how bad it was. His father says, "Wait till the army gets hold of you. They'll make a man of you." He goes for his physical and fails. When he comes home three days later, he is terrified to see his father. His dad says: "Where have you been?" Bruce says: "I took my physical and failed." And his father says, "That's good." And there is this beautiful moment of is-ness. The anger has been digested. He is happy with his father's words and can respect his dad. He's not afraid to express his own agony, what he went through in relationship to his dad.

FOX: What would you like to see happening today regarding the inner work of men?

NICHOLSON: The simplest thing is just to be in men's work. I belong to an incredible men's group. All are doing beautiful work in the world and raising kids; we get together twice a month and talk about what's up for us and what's between us and how we are affecting one another. We have the opportunity to explore what's going on with each other. We find that more and more we can bring the truth of some of the experiences of our lives to this group. When I tell other men about this they ask: "Where can I find this?" They feel how I have a place to go and process very tricky experiences I am going through in my life and am not dependent on my partner. There is somewhere else I can go and I don't have to always turn to one person. That's important. I think if men had that kind of support and were talking about their experiences, that would be huge.

Another reason I feel so clear this group is right for all of us is that all of our sons ask us about the group. They care. They are curious. They sense it is important for us — which it is.

HUNTER-GATHERERS AT WORK TODAY

As an archetype, and as part of our ancient heritage, hunter-gatherers have many positive and powerful traits. Among these are keen intelligence, our powers of observation and relating to plants and animals, to the land and to the sky; a sense of egalitarianism and democracy, as opposed to bureaucracy and hierarchy; and a sense of community, family, and extended family. The hunter-gatherer also embodies alertness and wakefulness, seeking and learning, expression and artistic manifestation, creativity, curiosity in others and the world, spontaneity and improvisation, deep listening, good memories, powerful storytelling, the joy of living in the now and living at the edge, and the power of ritual. All these values are passed on to the children, who are thereby more playful and alive. Can we recapture some of these values? How do we employ them in the new context of our postmodern lives? Where can we invest our hunter-gatherer powers in the work we are already doing and in the ways that best serve this time in history? Consider the following applications.

The Hunt for a Mate

Almost universally, both gay and straight men talk about their hunt for a partner. Sexuality and intimacy arouse the hunting instinct. Quite a few hunter-gatherer qualities come into play: this hunt for a mate takes a lot of creativity and keen observation; a lot of alertness and watchfulness, of curiosity and artistic manifestation (What to wear? What to see? What to do? How to woo?). When one is in love, the hunt takes over the hunter as well as the hunted. Storytelling and spontaneity dominate. Egalitarianism is the proper relationship with the beloved. All one's powers and senses get focused. Thomas Aquinas observed back in the Middle Ages that the "lover is not content with superficial knowledge of the beloved, but strives for intimate discovery and even entering into the beloved." Suffice it to say, this is rich territory, and we will be dealing with more about sexuality and love in chapter six.

The Quest for Scientific Understanding and Truth

Scientists are merely hunter-gatherers with a degree and better tools: their goals and actions are nearly the same. Each experiments and observes to learn more about the world, how it works, and how we might work more successfully in it, whether looking at the universe, the microcosmic world, the natural world, or our own species. One excellent example is Nobel-winning physicist Steve Chu, who oversees the Lawrence Berkeley National Laboratory. Chu sees science as our last best defense against climate catastrophe, and he is leading the hunt for new energy sources with the help of a $500 million grant given to the University of Berkeley by BP. He seeks innovative ideas like "solar paint," which would convert the sun's energy into liquid fuel by mimicking plant photosynthesis. He says, "The history of innovation has taught us that, once people stop thinking politically and start thinking from a scientific point of view, surprisingly all the predictions of 'we can't do this' don't seem to come true." Chu feels that science working with business can make great headway in converting light into energy and electricity. Isn't the search for sustainable and clean fuels a profound application of our hunter-gatherer powers? And it links to the Green Man as well.

When NASA's Cassini spacecraft sent back pictures of Titan, the largest moon of the planet Saturn, a journalist wrote: "*As the hunt progressed,* some scientists began adjusting their thinking, wondering if the methane was coming from volcanic eruptions...."

The search for truth and knowledge is a hunt. There are no guarantees we will capture what we seek, but the effort itself arouses our passions and hopes, calling forth all our skills and intelligence.

Journalism: The Hunt for the True Story

If a scientist hunts facts and processes, a good investigative journalist hunts stories. Not just any stories, however, but true ones. They hunt, seeking and sensing, sniffing and following leads, making connections and revealing implications that would otherwise remain hidden.

Consider, for example, this story on war profiteering in the Iraq war. Some one hundred thousand civilian contractors are at work on America's behalf in Iraq, and about half of these provide quasi security work. Blackwater is one of the major contractors, as is KBR, a subsidiary of Vice-President Dick Cheney's former company Halliburton. "As reported by the *Norfolk Virginian-Pilot,* Pentagon auditors are looking at improprieties in a 'four-tiered chain' of security contractors, with Blackwater at the bottom and KBR at the top." Blackwater billed the next firm up the chain $2.3 million. "Now the Pentagon has calculated that by the time KBR got around to billing the government, the tab to the taxpayers...had reached $19.6 million." An audit two years ago by the State Department found Blackwater double-billing for services and including profit in its overhead costs. "Critics of the use of private security contractors call them mercenaries, who operate in a shadowy realm of no-bid contracts and lax control by the Pentagon." The founder of Blackwater is a major Republican campaign contributor.

Consider how this is not a Republican/Democrat story but a story that affects all of us. It took a hardened hunter, a searcher and gatherer of facts who worked his way through the jungles of pseudo-speech and corporate and governmental cover-up to arrive at the truth and to be able to express that truth so that we might hear it. Rhetorical flourishes and flights of political fancy cannot make up for the truth that needs to come out.

The Search for Spiritual Truth

Real theology seeks to hunt and gather truths that our ancestors lived and taught and desire to teach us still. It is a search for those universal, bedrock spiritual truths that individuals and communities need in perilous times. As a writer, I often find myself hunting for good books, exciting ideas, good questions, and intellectual companions. I have walked miles and spent days in libraries tracking lost footnotes and exciting leads. It is hunter-gathering energy. When I wrote *One River, Many Wells: Wisdom Rising from Global Faiths*, about the world's spiritual traditions, I felt myself to be very much a hunter-gatherer. I was hunting myths and stories in religious texts from all the world's faith traditions, and I was amazed at the unanimity I found. Whether indigenous people or Celts, whether East or West, every tradition had something profound and practical to teach us about the sacredness of creation, about meditation, about community, about compassion, about holy imagination, about sexuality, about joy, about spiritual warriorhood, about light, about death, about the feminine, and more.

Whether sifting the archeological record or ancient texts, religious scholars are finding new information and changing our understandings. For instance, the scholars within the Jesus Seminar are trying to recover the real teachings of Jesus and to understand as best we can who he really was as an historical figure and teacher, as well as to gather new information about the mystical metaphor of the Cosmic Christ. Much is happening in women's studies, as we uncover giants of our past who have been neglected or forgotten, such as Hildegard of Bingen, who was a profound musician, healer, and prophet, or Meister Eckhart, whose depth has been rarely if ever exceeded in Western writings.

Gathering Herbs, Seeking Cures

Those seeking cures for human diseases are also hunter-gatherers. The only real difference between then and now is that humans can hunt inside the body and inside cells for healing remedies. For instance, a recent report described how AIDS researchers have "successfully mapped a spot on the surface of HIV that might make the virus especially vulnerable to an assault by antibodies, rejuvenating hopes that science might eventually find a way to stop the epidemic with a vaccine." This high-tech medical search for the right cure, the right vaccine, can rightly be characterized as a hunting and gathering expedition. It calls forth our ancient instincts cultivated over the eons to protect the tribe, to save our family and community, to survive and be sustainable.

Just recently I learned of an amazing find based on a Nobel prize in medicine that involved research on Arginine-derived nitric oxide (ANDO), which keeps blood vessels open, elastic, and functioning well. Louis J. Ignarro, from the University of California at Los Angeles School of Medicine, writes that "one tiny molecule produced by the body may do more than any drug to prevent heart attack and stroke. . . . Nitric oxide helps prevent heart disease and stroke." Dr. Joe Prendergast, who works at the Stanford Medical School, has created an L-Arginine complex and formula that combines with L-citrulline, another amino acid. He has made his product available to many and with significant results. So many searches, so much research is afoot to assist human suffering. All of it carries the stamp of hunter-gatherer energy put to use on behalf of the community.

Putting Bread on the Table: Hunting for Work

We hunt for jobs and for *work*. Whatever a person's particular job, work itself is a very important category in understanding masculine spirituality. Indeed, Robert Bly concludes that the place where men in our culture feel the deepest wounds is in their work.

Almost by definition, the hunter-gatherer archetype is related to work — the work of providing for family and community. This is ancient. We work to eat, to sustain ourselves and our families, to put bread on the table and a roof over our heads. Men feel a primal urge to succeed at this essential task, to satisfy the main purpose of their inner hunter-gatherer. Yet in ancient times the understanding of "family" included the *extended* family of the community. This understanding is often lost in the modern, reductionist, literalist understanding of nuclear family, which would include just one's own immediate wife and children and possibly one's aging parents. One example of this communal extended family is how among Australian Aboriginals young men are initiated into their puberty rituals not by fathers but by adopted uncles of their particular totem. This is something we can learn from our ancestral hunter-gatherers. Shouldn't all work worthy of the name be a work that heals the community and assists its sustainability? Today, we call this our role and work as citizens, that which benefits our broader family. It is our responsibility as fellow inhabitors of our communities and cities and the Earth itself, and it is our duty to those who come after us, our descendants.

Hunting, and Listening for, the Muse

Many of my friends are artists, and I see firsthand how artists are *always on the hunt*. They gather the meaningful symbols and beautiful images that move us and make sense of the world. They satisfy the hunter-gatherer urge to observe, to be in the moment, and to experience joy. I like to hire artists to teach in the alternative education programs I have run for the last thirty years. I have a friend who does rap and makes film. He often has his camera with him and stops to take brief footage of a bird or trees or water falling or a fish. He is always alert and ready for images to show up, images that he can include in his filmmaking. That is how artists move through the world: hunting and gathering the muse, not waiting for her.

I have another friend who is a self-taught architect and builder who loves to renovate homes and other buildings. I like walking down the street with him because he will stop to admire a building, a corner there or a window here, and point out the exquisiteness of the design. He will "steal" ideas from rooms and buildings he visits. He is always alert, always on the prowl, always hunting for ideas.

I have another friend who is a painter whose style is thoroughly original. He does not copy others, but he too observes and gathers. He studies classical paintings and learns from their techniques; he respects and honors the work of the past and incorporates the craft into his own work. While he hunts artworks for their techniques, he also hunts in the streets around him, in his own memories, and in the people he meets for ideas and themes. He is joyful when he is painting, bringing a new gift into the world. Art, especially, is an expression of the joy of being a hunter-gatherer today. Authentic artists hunt, gather, and create not for the ego's sake but for the community's sake, just as our ancient ancestors did.

Searching and Learning as an End in Itself

Let us not forget those who turn their hunter-gatherer instincts inward. This includes those who are searching and foraging for their own identities, for their ancestral wisdom, for their family histories and community histories, as well as for their professional histories and their lineage as human beings, as earth dwellers and stargazers and citizens of the universe. And those who seek out their authentic religious histories as well. Whenever I have researched the medieval mystics — like Hildegard of Bingen, Thomas Aquinas, and Meister Eckhart — and have searched for the Cosmic Christ and Wisdom among my Jewish and Christian ancestors, I have been a spiritual hunter-gatherer. Any search for real spirituality nourishes the soul and one's life. This is as vital as gathering nurturing food, and in the same way that we expand our work to provide nourishment for family *and* community, our personal spiritual path can help light the way for others. In my search, I have also managed to bring back a hermeneutic, a way to interpret the wisdom of the past in light of our spiritual journeying today. The four paths of creation spirituality allow us to do that.

Each of the areas above can be understood as an exercise in *learning*. Learning is an activity of hunting and gathering; it taps into our ancient instincts of alertness, intelligence, and joy. Unfortunately, as I discuss in *The A. W. E. Project: Reinventing Education, Reinventing the Human*, education in our modern world is too often divorced from the joy and wonder and risk and adventure that learning is all about. Reducing education to taking exams — as so much of the "No Child Left Behind" law does — is not the way to solicit hunter-gatherer instincts. In fact, it kills them. It kills adventure and imagination and with these the fun and joy of learning. In our schools, education becomes passive, encouraging and inviting little hunting-gathering. Too often, we manage to separate learning from education, just as contemporary society separates spirituality from religion, justice from law, and stewardship from commerce. This is why I call for a new mode of education that brings about Ancestral Wisdom Education (A.W.E.).

Whenever we are learning, I believe, we are engaged in the same ancient practices as the original hunter-gatherers, who are still alive in our souls. We use our curiosity and intelligence, stalking and seeking, alert and expressive — and using these, we both survive and sustain the world we live in. It is serious work. What we choose to learn about and to explore reveals what it is we are deeply interested in. This reveals our hunter-gatherer self, who, as Diamond observed, is always keenly interested in both things and people.

SPORTS: HUNTER-GATHERERS AT PLAY

Ehrenreich believes that "for most people in the world today, the experience of collective ecstasy is likely to be found, if it is found at all, not in a church or at a concert or rally but at a sports event.... These games now provide what the sports sociologist Allen Guttmann calls 'Saturnalia-like occasions for the uninhibited expression of emotions which are tightly controlled in our ordinary lives.'" In the United States alone, between 1980 and 2003, 101 stadiums were constructed, each with an average capacity of about seventy thousand people. For centuries the tensions over sports ran along lines of class, and by the early twentieth century, spectator sports became "a mass proletarian cult." Today's sports events mirror in many ways the rituals of hunting-gathering times. Feasting, for example, takes place at tailgate parties, and costumes abound with cheese heads, Viking helmets, pig snouts, faces painted in team colors, and more.

In our contemporary world, sports and competition are "safe" and acceptable areas for men to let loose the energies of their ancestral hunter-gatherer. Surely, the ancient hunt for prey was in part a competition — between hunters, between tribes, between man and beast — and the rewards for success were not just a full belly, but adulation and approval, a sense of personal pride. In fact, Jared Diamond in his studies of hunter-gatherers points out that, when choosing prey, "men hunters tend to guide themselves by considerations of prestige." Thus, hunting a giraffe may not be the most practical choice, but if one is bagged, it brings greater admiration to the hunter than if, say, the hunter arrives with a handful of rabbits. Providing delicacies or hard-to-kill animals adds to prestige. We can readily see how this "prestige factor" translates into modern-day sports and competition — in which fishermen try to impress with the biggest fish stories, and while winning is lauded, beating the "best" team by the largest margin elevates the winner's status.

Then, for actual hunter-gatherers, there are the real dangers and adventure of hunting wild game — using weapons that require skill and craft, studying and understanding prey, risking personal injury and even death to kill prey up close. Just as surely, sports engage and hone these same skills: they require alertness and bravery and physical risk, craft and adeptness, observation and intelligence. Like the hunter, the athlete is attuned to his body and needs to keep it in good shape. And like the hunter, there is a goal or prize: the athlete aims to be the fastest, or score the most points, to secure victory. For the professional, winning also results in a better income (and thus food on the table), but for all athletes, the prize of victory brings an emotional satisfaction to fans and community. The rewards are not only personal, but shared with an entire stadium cheering their hearts out, with a city and sometimes a nation. In sport, athletes also tap the hunter-gatherer archetype through teamwork. Isn't that one of the main reasons boys are encouraged to join organized sports in the first place? To learn how to work as a team, to develop a sense of camaraderie and shared purpose, to learn how to cooperate, so that the team is served and succeeds, not just the individual.

In sport, as in hunting, there is also the thrill of surprise and suspense, of unscripted results, of adventure and daring that brings out someone's best. Competition can have that positive effect on the male psyche in particular — it can wake us up from lethargy and passivity and bring out the best in us. We train hard to become stronger, more alert, more skillful, more ready to best our adversary. In many ways, this is a very positive expression of our ancestral hunter-gatherer.

Of course there is a shadow side to modern sports, as there is to every human invention and activity. The first is when our "participation" in sports becomes solely as a spectator. Sometimes we invest more time and money watching sports than playing them. Our culture's obsession with sports combined with modern media makes this all too easy. Is there a minute in a twenty-four-hour day when there is *not* some sport — basketball or football or baseball or golf or ping-pong — showing on TV? Of course not. If we get caught up watching, constantly and obsessively (and sports addictions are real), then we become passive. We become vicarious athletes. When this happens, sports do not improve our physical and mental health, sports do not serve our family and community. Just the opposite happens. Our physical health may suffer, we may neglect our actual jobs, we may neglect our family. In the extreme, though we seem "in the moment" watching sports, we are really cheering our lost youth, our once-athletic selves. We wallow in nostalgia and get caught up in living in the past. And even this past may be a kind of dream or fiction of accomplishments and success that never quite were.

This is not authentic hunter-gathering energy. The hunter who is caught living in the past is dangerous, a danger to himself and his hunting "team." A hunter who is not in good shape physically and mentally is a danger as well. To be a vicarious athlete, a nostalgic fan, is not how we engage our hunter-gatherer.

This is not to say that we can't remember and honor past athletic accomplishments, or cheer on our favorite teams, but we shouldn't let these be a cause for nostalgia (as if the best part of life, its greatest adventure and beauty, cannot be repeated today) or for inaction. As we age, our bodies cannot do what they once did, it's true, but we can still be athletes. We can still engage in sports in all the positive ways the hunter-gatherer archetype exemplifies: as a way to hone our attention and skills, as a way to engage with the world and others — perhaps now as a coach and mentor to boys, rather than an adolescent athlete oneself. This is certainly how our ancestral hunters worked: teaching younger hunters, thereby ensuring their survival, strengthening families, and sustaining our communities.

Another shadow side to sport is our narrow definition and excessive adulation of athletes. It is as if the only athletes worth praising and becoming are those like Tiger Woods, Muhammad Ali, or Michael Jordan. It is as if the only "heroes" or "warriors" it is worth becoming are professional athletes. Yet the lesson of the hunter-gatherer is that all men play a role in community survival. All men must play a daring and intelligent and skillful role. That is a lesson we need to pass on to our young people today. Not all young men will be adept at sports, or even play sports. But success at sports is not as important as participation in sports, and athletics themselves are not the only arena where boys can engage their hunter-gatherer energies. Competition and athleticism are not confined to the ballfield.

A third shadow side to sport is an exaggerated belief in the benefits of competition. Competition, as we have pointed out, has its positive side. It combats laziness and couchpotatoitis, the temptation to merely watch games on TV. When we succumb to this, instead of being hunters, we are the hunted: We are prey for corporations and political forces who prefer us to be passive, unthinking, and uncritical. Who prefer us to be consumers.

However, competition can breed *shame*. This is perhaps the darkest shadow that sports cast today. The competitive urge is primal, it is inherent in the hunter-gatherer archetype, but when taken to extremes, as it so often is today, it can be destructive.

I spoke with psychologist John Conger, and this was his perspective on it:

> I think the demands on us are very intense now. Because on the one hand there is this Odysseus world that is competitive, and you are meant to throw the discus farther than someone else. And if you don't you are not considered a man. There's a lot of pressure in this culture to be very narcissistic. We are not worth anything if we lose. Men are meant to win. Men are meant to get the best grades and become doctors and be successful, whereas if you're a loser, no woman will want you because women want you to be successful so they can have a nest for their children. There is a lot of pressure on men to just look after themselves and be very successful. Then they are attacked for the very same reason — that all they care about is themselves. But what is going on is the *shame* if you don't become a winner. If you are not number one, then you should be in the first 10 percent. Getting to the right college.

Simply put, not all competition is good, and too much is bad. For centuries we have received toxic messages about the "necessity" of competition to survival, such as philosopher Thomas Hobbes saying brutishness is the hallmark of nature and Darwinian "survival of the fittest." In fact, as today's science is learning on a deep scale, cooperation is often a far more effective survival strategy than competition. And in sports, without cooperation within the team and between players, the competition itself becomes impossible.

Instead, we need to remember that the hunter-gatherer archetype emphasizes the importance of cooperation as much as or more than competition. Hunter-gatherers hunted *together* more than solo. Their shared rituals were all about finding community together. One might say that competition is a beginning principle but cooperation is a more mature principle. Unhealthy competition leads to one person succeeding at the expense of others. Healthy competition sustains everyone, and invariably the true focus of healthy competition is oneself: it's an effort to improve one's capacities, to achieve excellence. This is a very wonderful thing, and we should always compete with ourselves and strive for excellence. In an entirely different context, I suspect that this understanding of competition with oneself comes closer to Muhammad's idea of "jihad" than does righteous warring with others. Muhammad himself said that the first meaning of jihad is jihad with oneself.

The principle of competition with others, if left to its devices, very often leads to war. It leads to *overfeeding the reptilian brain*. And that is a very serious matter for our species at this time in history. The reptilian brain is about action/reaction, "fight or flight," win/lose. We need to develop the more recent *mammalian brain*, which is half as old as our reptilian brains, but which is special for bringing compassion to our planet (this may be why in both Hebrew and Arabic the root words for "compassion" and "womb" are identical).

Is there room in competitive sports for compassion and the teaching of compassion? There is, but it is rarely done. Sports too often become an expression of only reptilian brain energy. How can we tell when our enthusiasm for competition is being carried too far? When we cannot control our emotions and become aggressive and violent as a result — such as when an overwrought parent rushes onto the playing field during their child's baseball game to argue a "bad call" and winds up in a physical fight with the umpire or other parents. We regularly hear these kinds of stories, and they are warnings that we have carried our enthusiasm for competition too far and our reptilian brains are in charge.

A good way to reframe sports and competition so that they reflect the true hunter-gatherer energy is to think of them as the *adventure that serves*. What exactly is service? The word "service" comes from the Latin word *servire*, which originally meant to do the work of a slave. That is interesting because, during the Roman Empire, slaves were a bounty in the competitive games of war. They were captured men who were taken back to Rome to serve the upper classes in a variety of ways, including as gladiators to amuse the masses with deadly sport. What I find encouraging is that today the word "serve" does not mean to do the work of a slave. It has been upgraded to mean a loving act of kindness, a helpful gesture, assisting a stranger. For example, let us say you are a teacher. A teacher does not know most of his students. They come to him on the first day of school as strangers who, in effect, ask for his help, for his skills and mentorship. He gives it. He gives it to these strangers. He is serving them. And it may well happen that by the time the semester is over, he and they (or at least some) will have become friends as well.

The same scenario plays out with a counselor or a businessperson or a car mechanic or an actor or a musician. We are constantly sharing our gifts — we are serving others, not out of a slave's obligation, but out of willing compassion. We do this in our work, and in all kinds of ways, but this can also be a way to approach sports. It is an avenue to share and assist and uplift others, to harness the power of our hunter-gatherer energy in the contemporary work world. Whatever we do, so long as our work serves the community and the larger Earth community in some positive fashion we are playing out the hunter-gatherer archetype.

THE ROLE OF THE AUTOMOBILE

Is there a nostalgic connection between cars and our ancient hunter-gatherer souls? Why is it that so many cars or trucks are named after large land mammals and other predators? There are Mustangs, Rams, Vipers, Cobras, and so on. Does driving a car or truck awaken certain hunter-gatherer instincts in men? On one level, our vehicles assist our work of hunting and gathering, getting us to work and to the store, to our paycheck and the bank, and returning us home. It is a vital tool; we must develop skills to drive.

But driving isn't solely goal-oriented. Driving is a process, and surely our hunter-gathering ancestors felt this as well: the goal of the hunt was important, but so was the way the hunt was conducted, the ritual and methods and thrill of the chase. In choosing a vehicle, perhaps we are playing out the ritualized aspect of hunting. We look for a vehicle that will provide us an experience that corresponds in some way to the thrill of the hunt. Of course, much of the time, the power, feel, abilities, and look of our vehicle is an end in itself, not the means to an end. Our "hunt" is for a vehicle that's admired.

This is the world of advertising and illusion, but it holds power because it appeals to something deep in our psyche. Vehicles seem to define us as "masculine," but most often this leads only to a vicarious experience as hunter-gatherers. Any old car might get us to work equally well, but we get sidetracked in feeling that only certain cars are acceptable as expressions of our prowess and skill. With the right car, we are hunter-gatherers again. Or imagine we are. We attend NASCAR events live or by television and identify with the excitement of the race that combines for us both the element of sport — getting to the goal line — and the element of hard-driving pursuit.

HUNTING AND HIKING

What about hunting itself? Wouldn't that be the most direct way to channel one's inner hunter-gatherer, no metaphors involved? Yes and no. First, hunting today is rarely a necessity, it's a choice. It's a recreation or a sport, one that is often reserved for vacations or weekend getaways. And while many certainly eat what they kill or catch, very few people would actually go hungry if they didn't hunt, or if they came home empty-handed; they'd just go to the supermarket. This changes the nature of the activity. The shadow side of hunting is similar to sports: it can become a way to falsely inflate one's ego ("You should see the big buck I bagged"), either through the struggle ("You should have seen the fight this fish put up") or through the experience of domination (killing for the sake of killing). However, hunting also often yields a contemplative experience of being in nature (much like my experience fishing as the sun rose over Lake Mendota in Madison, Wisconsin, as a youth). Many men find that hunting provides a good excuse to return to the woods or to the wilderness or to the waters, where they can have a soul-refreshing experience away from the traffic and busyness and noise of their regular lives. Solitude draws them. Nature and contemplation in nature draw them. But they *pretend* it's about hunting or fishing.

Solitude is a profound thing. Solitude, I am convinced, is what moves us from the reptilian brain (reptiles are experts at solitude, not at bonding) to the compassionate or mammalian brain (mammals being good at kinship and bonding). But to get from there to here one needs to practice solitude, and many men have found hunting or fishing to be a fine cover for what is in fact their favorite and most effective spiritual practice, one that gets them into authentic stillness and quiet and solitude.

Another healthy way to do the same thing is to remove the object of the hunt: to simply enter nature by hiking, running, or going on pilgrimage. A pilgrimage is about backpacking and hiking and encountering nature face-to-face, with the goal to push through and face one's own nature and feel it come alive. Robert Lawrence France is a professor of ecological management and environmental theory at Harvard University, and he has conducted many pilgrimages — such as the Way of Saint James (Santiago de Compostela) and a three-month crossing of Ellesmere Island, a sledding journey in the Canadian High Arctic. His recent book, *Ultreia! Onward! Progress of the Pilgrim*, lays out a philosophy of pilgrimage garnered both from his experiences and those of many others. It tells of the blisters and exhaustion, of the victories, of night skies and rain, of vulnerability, of conversation and of camaraderie, and of primal experiences of soul and spirit. It tells of encounters with plants, flowers, animals, and bees that one misses traveling through life in air-conditioned cars, trains, and airplanes. This is real, not vicarious, hunting and gathering.

I am friends with a thirty-two-year-old high school math teacher who, during summer vacation, likes to backpack through the villages of Thailand, where he spent the first eleven years of his life, having been born and raised in a refugee camp there. His family was from the hills of Laos and had fled the war there. I asked him what he loves most about backpacking. He said, "The freedom. I go where I want, stay as long as I want. No schedule to keep. No timetable to meet." His mother is from the indigenous Hmong people of Laos, so I suspect his sense of freedom while backpacking may relate to the nearness of hunter-gatherers in his lineage. He is also a genius with plants and food and cooking. It comes naturally to him, organically one might say.

BUSINESS

Who can deny that business, the buying and selling of goods, is driven by hunter-gatherer instincts? Whether one is a businessperson looking for a market base or seeking an advertiser to awaken that base or finding a location appropriate to bring in the customer, clearly a hunting-and-gathering strategy is involved at many levels of commerce. And ancient energies are awakened, including the thrill of the hunt and the excitement of the "kill" (that is, the sale) as well as the camaraderie of coworkers and associates who comprise a "team" or community of hunters.

The buyer, too, is running on a hunter-gatherer energy, looking as he or she does for the best deal, the quality product, the latest gizmo, the finest sale, or the best loan. Much of commerce operates on the appeal to our hunter-gatherer instincts.

ADDICTION

Another shadow side of the hunter-gatherer is addiction. Consider how skillfully an alcoholic hunts for liquor. Often against the efforts of friends and loved ones, the alcoholic hunts successfully and finds a way to a bottle. While, this is self-destructive, since the prey hurts the hunter and no prestige follows, nevertheless, a certain goal is achieved, obstacles are overcome, skills honed. One might say that the hunter becomes the hunted in an addictive scenario. In other words, the addict (whether the addiction is drugs, money, power, sex, shopping, or work) feels pursued by the prey, which hunts and haunts the person and will not let go. One must surrender, in this case, in order to take charge of one's life again, to identify healthy prey.

In terms of addiction and the hunter-gatherer archetype, compulsive shopping is particularly pervasive and insidious in present-day culture. It is, in fact, encouraged by our consumer economy, which continually confuses wants with needs. Shopping is, obviously, a form of hunting and gathering, but corporate advertising and marketing can turn this inside out: ads convince us that prestige and success are attached only to certain brands, and so we buy them. But in fact we are the prey the corporate hunters seek, and our need and even addiction to buying makes us easy to catch.

Scott Sanders observes the connection between consumerism and our hunting-gathering ancestors when he writes: "It seems that our evolutionary history has shaped us to equate well-being with increase, to yearn not merely for more offspring but more of everything, more shoes and meat and horsepower and loot. In a hunting and gathering society — the arena in which our ancestors spent all but the last few thousand years — the fruits of an individual's search for more food, better tools, and richer land were brought back and shared with the tribe." He warns us what happens when we don't share: "The constant hankering for more which served hunting and gathering peoples well has become a menace in this age of clever machines and burgeoning populations. Our devotion to perpetual growth now endangers the planet by exhausting resources and accelerating pollution and driving the species to extinction." He thinks we have to get more proactive about curbing our excess: "Biology, I'm afraid, is all on the side of shopping, gluttony, and compulsive growth. If we are to achieve restraint, it will have to come from culture, that shared conversation by which we govern our appetites." While we know that each year the average American consumes roughly thirty times as much of the earth's nonrenewable resources as does the average citizen of India or Mexico, Sanders sees this as a sign of hope: "This very excess is reason for hope, because it means we could cut back dramatically on our consumption of food and fuels, our use of woods and metal, and on the size of our houses and wardrobes, without suffering any deprivation.... Just as we grow fat from eating and drinking too much, so we may grow fit from eating less."

HUNTERS FOR JUSTICE: SPIRITUAL WARRIORS

The hunter-gatherer archetype is based in an essential aspect of human survival: feeding our bodies and those of the community entrusted to us. When, however, we focus our hunter-gatherer energies on larger issues of social justice, we enter the realm of the spiritual warrior. These hunters for justice include Gandhi and Martin Luther King Jr. Oscar Romero and Malcolm X, Buck Ghosthorse, and Jesus. Frequently, hunters for justice challenge their communities, and so they do not always win praise. On the contrary, they may become the hunted. Gandhi, King, Romero, Malcolm X, Jesus, Medgar Evans: they were all gunned down for their search for social justice. During the Civil Rights Movement in the 1960s, the Ku Klux Klan was a hunting organization, as were the Nazis during World War II, and as are many ultra-orthodox fundamentalist religions today. Our medieval ancestors used to say, *Corruptio optimi est pessima*: "Corruption of the best is the worst." These groups corrupt the act of hunting, using it to kill the most noble hunters in our midst.

In the face of such hatred, it takes warrior energy to be a hunter-gatherer for the most precious of human pursuits: justice, freedom, and truth, so that all people may flourish. Accordingly, we consider the warrior archetype in the next chapter.

The hunter-gatherer experience exists so deeply in our memories and psyches that I believe we can say this: When our work includes the hunter-gatherer dimensions of adventure, creativity, joy, community, searching, alertness, spontaneity, and surprise, it is truly human work. When it lacks these dimensions, we need to ask: Is our work sustaining us and our community? A *job* provides a paycheck and economic survival, but the work we are meant to do, which may be the reason we are here on this planet, will provide more. It will always, as it did for our hunter-gatherer ancestors, help serve the larger community, including those who come after us. E. F. Schumacher lamented how so many people have their souls beat up at work, but while we have insurance if one's body is injured, we are not compensated if our souls are abused. Many men are abused at work, some in their bodies, others in their souls. For more on work issues, see my book *The Reinvention of Work*, but here it is enough to see how our hunter-gatherer selves shed light on what does and does not constitute healthy work. Men can use this archetype to heal from the soul abuse that today's economy can deliver so fiercely. Our ancestors, once again, return to heal us. The wisdom of our hunter-gatherer ancestors teaches us much about the ways of healthy and useful work. The hunter-gatherer is in us all.

SPIRITUAL WARRIORS | 5

THE ARCHETYPES OF THE GREEN MAN and the hunter-gatherer lead to that of the spiritual warrior. Thomas Berry talks about the need for "the Great Work." What is this Great Work? It is "the task of moving modern industrial civilization from its present devastating influence on the Earth to a more benign mode of presence." Such a great work will require great spirits, real warriors, and it will require steering our moral outrage and our powers of aggression and competition into more positive directions. The Great Work is "not a role that we have chosen. It is a role given to us, beyond any consultation with ourselves.... We are, as it were, thrown into existence with a challenge and a role that is beyond any personal choice. The nobility of our lives, however, depends upon the manner in which we come to understand and fulfill our assigned role." Noble warriors are called for. The archetype of the spiritual warrior helps to answer in a constructive way two issues raised so far: What to do with male aggression? What to do with competition? How to steer both into healthy directions?

Aggression is in all of us. Whether athlete or preacher, businessperson or taxi driver, aggression will emerge at some point. It's easy to identify the negative ways it expresses itself: as war, as conquest (whether in business or sex), as passivity (aggression turned against oneself: "I can't do that..."), as selfish competition ("I can't win unless you lose"), and more. But what are the healthy ways to engage it? How to turn aggression into nobility, to use Berry's term?

77

To me, the key is understanding the distinction between a warrior and a soldier. They are not the same, and in fact, I have found this distinction taught by every indigenous tribe I have ever studied. A man named Broken Walk, a Vietnam veteran who volunteered to go to war at seventeen, describes this eloquently: "There's a difference between being a soldier and being a warrior. Don't ever get these two confused. When I was in the army I was a soldier. I was a puppet doing whatever anybody told me to do, even if it meant going against what my heart told me was right. I didn't know nothing about being a warrior until I hit the streets and marched alongside my brothers for something I really believed in. When I found something I believed in, a higher power found me. That's it. That's the story." Broken Walk quit being a soldier and became a warrior when he followed his soul's orders, not his officer's; in his case, this meant protesting war and going to jail for it. Chögyam Trungpa talks about the "sad and tender heart of the warrior" and this is very real. The warrior is in touch with his heart — the joy, the sadness, the expansiveness of it.

However, not everyone today understands this distinction. I was shocked to read a very influential men's book by Robert Moore, who completely confuses the two. I believe the confusion of soldier and warrior feeds militarism and the reptilian brain. It's also an expression of homophobia, since I suspect that heterosexism is behind much of the continued ignorance and fear of the real meaning of warriorhood.

The Sufi mystic Hafiz knew the difference between soldier and warrior when he exclaimed in one of his poems that soldiers "were dying all around him in excruciating pain" — for that is what a soldier does, deliver or receive death or excruciating pain. At the same time, Hafiz declares, "You can become a horseman carrying your heart through the world like a life-giving sun, but only if you and God become sweet lovers." The warrior, unlike the soldier, is a lover. The warrior is so much in touch with his heart that he can give it to the world. The warrior loves not only his nearest kin and mate but also the world and God. The warrior relates to God as a lover.

How different is this from right-wing religious depictions of God as judge and not lover? This view of God leads to the distortions of masculinity such as one finds in the Promise Keepers Movement (which we will discuss later in this chapter). The confusion of warrior and soldier feeds unhealthy relationships to not only God but to self and society. It feeds empire building, and the builders of empire would like nothing more than to enlist young men who believe soldiering equals warriorhood. We cannot afford this ignorance and confusion any longer. Nothing could be further from the truth.

PROFESSOR PITT: ON THE MODERN-DAY WARRIOR

Professor Pitt is a thirty-two-year-old African American filmmaker who created a trilogy on the theme of "Kung Fu Meets Hip Hop" called "The Hip Hop Dynasty" and "Hip Hop Dynasty Parts II and III." He is also a rap artist and practitioner of martial arts, and for Pitt, warriorhood is a particularly special and important concept, in both his life and work.

FOX: You use the term "warrior" frequently. When did you first pick up on that term?

PITT: From training in martial arts. But with meditation it is even more of a reference — of being still, of fighting voices in one's head that are irritating me. Or like when meditating, when you get an itch in your nose, you are not supposed to scratch it or move and that decision not to go after the itch is being a warrior, is fighting the physical urge to do that. Usually when I meditate, as soon as you commit to meditating, it's *bam*, in the back of your head, or *bam*, your foot starts throbbing. That's the warrior fight. I got this from my teachers of martial arts and meditation.

FOX: Give me examples of what you call the "warrior fight."

PITT: For me the warrior fight first begins with overcoming yourself and your own demons, your own stuff, which is the hardest. It means to keep going in training, which is fighting yourself. And then externally the true warrior's fight is not to fight physically or to engage in any kind of fight unless it is the last resort. Me, being African American, you run into many situations where people are pushing you to come out physically. For me that's one of the fights — to *not* come out physically, because once we come out physically, everything is already designed to destroy us. We've given them a reason to do what they love doing — locking us up and giving us charges, labeling me in spite of what I do for humanity and the community. The minute I jump into that fighting character all the good stuff I do gets wasted, and they just look and say: "There's that animal again." So that is a big fight with me.

A warrior is being a good man to my wife, 'cause that's always a struggle, the man and woman thing, how to be graceful in how the stuff comes out, to be as graceful as possible.

FOX: Not returning physical for physical, that sounds a lot like the nonviolence strategy of King and Gandhi. Do you see a connection there?

PITT: I don't really agree with Martin Luther King's strategy back then. Every time I watch those movies, I think I would definitely have died back then. If you have nothing to lose and someone is going to beat on you for no reason and guess what, "we're coming to kill you tomorrow" — I believe in Malcolm X on that. If someone is trying to take you off the planet, take them off first. For me, there is so much at stake among African Americans and for me to stay present for my people. I feel like I have the world on my shoulders, and I don't have the right or the time to be wasting my time in negativity like that.

But I've got to give credit to King and Gandhi. They were strong, very strong warriors. They were among the strongest warriors on the planet for what they did. They did not get drowned in the whirlpool of negative physical energy. If they had, we would not know them as the great people that we know them as because one of those instances would have taken them out. That is what evil wants them to do.

FOX: You talk about the "warped warrior" message that society is selling. Elaborate on this.

PITT: I consider the warrior's handbook to be these principles: inner peace, tranquility, love, power, strength, honor, majesty, and respect. I think these are things that all people want. We have to fight for them, no freedom comes free. And I think the warped warrior's handbook is missing lots of those qualities, like honor and inner peace, tranquility — all these are missing. The warped warrior is thinking power, strength, majesty — having money and having a plush lifestyle, a kingly or queenly kind of lifestyle. The warped warrior is somebody who wants to prove to the world that they are the strongest and have all this money and power, and they have no honor among themselves. No happiness. I don't equate having money and power without honor as being happy, because if you have no honor and people around you have no honor, then someone is always plotting to take what you have. And you are thinking there is a plot to take what I have. If the person is without honor, he probably plotted to get his. So it's like an endless circle of mental torture.

Hip-hop is delivering the warped warrior message. So many people are erasing their lives because somebody stepped on their shoes or somebody looked at them the wrong way or bumped into them and spilled their drink or blah, blah, blah. Suddenly in those ten to seventy seconds they get wrapped up in, "I want to prove to the whole world that they can't do that to me and that they can't do that without paying for it." They may even be triumphant in those seventy seconds, but as soon as it's over they realize they got pulled into something that's bigger than them. Now there is karma and justice coming after them. Maybe they killed the person, but whether they killed them or not, there's karma coming back around. Maybe the police don't get you, but these people have family members. The streets talk. Or they go to jail and ruin their lives.

Maybe they're thirteen or fourteen or fifteen, and they're forced to live most of their life in jail over that warped warrior mentality — they had to show the world right then that "Hey! You can't step on my shoe" and their life is lost. And some people go through that life, even while they're in jail, and feel because they've adopted that warped warrior handbook so deep in themselves that they did the right thing. They did what they were supposed to do. They stood up, they showed their gang members or their peers that they couldn't be messed with. Now they're in jail, where they have to face a whole other group of gang members and prove themselves again, and they just get wrapped up in a whirlpool of unhappiness, just pure unhappiness. There's nobody sitting in a jail cell — I don't care how much they stick their chest out — that's happy. I've been in jail — not prison — for three months. Nobody there is happy. The loudest mouth that's acting so cool is probably the most scared character in there.

FOX: Where did you get the positive warrior handbook that you gave out?

PITT: I was writing a song called "My Understanding of Life," and I said it in there: "I meet the man or woman who leads me to the keys to the warrior life for which I seek." That's the question I ask myself. Someone lead me to the keys for the warrior's life that I seek. The royal life that I seek is inner peace, tranquility, love, power, strength, honor, majesty, and respect. That is the question I asked myself: What is the key to a warrior life? After I did that, I thought, "That's serious."

FOX: It applies to more than you. How old were you when you learned this?

PITT: It was just last year.

FOX: Do you see a difference between a warrior and a soldier?

PITT: Oh, 100 percent.

FOX: What's the difference?

PITT: The soldier does what he is told no matter what. And a warrior does what is right, what his heart feels. A warrior should be connected to the universe, should be very reverent and connected to whatever people want to call God. I say "Mom" and "Dad" is God, sun and moon. Some people say "Allah." I say them all, all of them have a feminine counterpart. As long as the warrior is connected to that, they are dealing with what's right. A solider is a piece of a body like a finger or a hand. If I tell my hand to slash someone's throat, it's going to do it; it's not going to think twice. And that's what a soldier is. Anybody who gets involved in the armed forces and thinks they can hold on to their reverentness, they are going to be in a battle because if they say "Go kill your mom," guess what? That's what you gotta do.

FOX: How do you recommend developing warrior energy when you are young? And if you missed that opportunity when you are young, how can you develop it later in life?

PITT: When you're young, through martial arts, and when you are older, through meditation. Meditation is harder for children because they have so much energy. Like with my sons right now, if they come and say, "Hey, Dad, I want to put out albums too," my test to them is that you have to go to these seven days' or several months' meditation thing, so that you can fight yourself, 'cause I'm too distant from inside of your brain to ever really know what's going on. But if I know that you are sitting, I will go there with you. If I know you are there and connecting and sitting down, you've got to face yourself. That's what America's about — distraction — so we never get a chance to face ourselves.

FOX: Do you have examples of people in your life who are mentors or warriors, examples of warriorhood to you?

PITT: All of my teachers, Eddie Deutch and Seefu and models of warriors like Martin Luther King and Malcolm X. People who have gone through having the whole nation being at them — a point that I have not faced yet. I'm not rich yet or in everybody's eye yet. They say when you are poor, everyone is your friend because you're not intimidating to anyone's lifestyle, and once you are of stature with money or power, suddenly the people that were your best friends and always willing to help you are the people that now have to deal with their ego problems, just overall ego problems. And you may be the center of their ego problems, you know what I mean?

FOX: You get a lot of projection.

PITT: Yes! And you know I don't know what that feels like, how Malcolm had various death threats and so forth, but he went up to that podium, you know what I mean? That's a warrior — in his mind, where he was at, his job wasn't done, and he had to keep on going forward no matter what, for the people. Because the people at that time, he knew if he stepped down and disappeared that it would break the heart of the community, and the community needed that heart at that time. I haven't faced that problem yet, and I hope I never do. But look at the world we live in.

So those guys of course, and Jesus — I don't believe all the teachings about his death but I believe all the stories of people persecuting him and stuff like that. A friend of mine says all prophets of the world go through their stoning period, where they have to get their lashes or whatever and nobody sees what they're doing. Prophets are supposed to be messengers from God, but that just means, "I'm sending him or her so I don't have to get involved. Because if I got involved, I might just wipe everybody off the map and start all over."

FOX: It's that bad.

PITT: Yes. The prophet is supposed to come and say what he says, move on, and die. And then the word — what he or she brought — is supposed to carry on and build. I hold myself as one of those people. A lot of people who have taught me things to make me a stronger warrior; they don't step outside to tell people what to do, that is not their role. I've taken that role, taken that burden.

FOX: So do you think warrior and prophet are really the same thing?

PITT: Yup. There are prophets in many degrees, it depends on how deep or high you go. A mother is a prophet when she is telling the kid, "Do not touch that electric wire. If you touch that wire, you're going to die or hurt yourself really, really bad." She may be saving the life of a future prophet. She is saving a life. The prophet goes to many levels.

FOX: Anything else you want to say about the warrior?

PITT: The more of a warrior you become, the less judgmental you become. Because you go through more and more stuff and you realize that all of us have an inner fight — like for me, giving up smoking weed or something like that, the voices never stop. Sometimes I ask, "Wow! Do you ever stop?" It doesn't matter if I'm cool or if I'm not, if the opportunity presents itself, there's a voice inside my head that says, "Go ahead and smoke." Knowing that about myself, I know there's a voice in everybody else's head that's always asking them to do something in the opposite direction. I know you don't win every battle, and if you don't win every battle, then I don't win every battle. You get less judgmental. It seems to me kids judge — and the media is like a big child as far as they try to judge every single thing and make sure everybody else judges with them. Judging comes from nonexperience. The more of the warrior you are, the more humble you become and the more unjudgmental. Everybody is on their own path and has their own time to come to the realizations that they do. When I tell people I'm not smoking, I say, "That's me." I'm not trying to put any judgment on you because you're sitting there smoking and I'm not. Everybody has their own time of evolution.

As a warrior I realize that all cultures uphold their warriors from the past, but today's warrior has to be understanding of other cultures. It's relatively easy to be a warrior in one's own culture, but it is important to recognize warriorhood in a variety of other cultures given how diverse the world is today. Develop perception and understanding before moving forward. Here, too, judgment must often be suspended. For example, I like to look strangers in the eye, but some cultures feel to look a stranger in the eye is to steal their soul. Given the melting pot we find ourselves in, we all need to tread lightly on one another's cultures and ask questions. "In your culture, what is customary? Or what is disrespectful?" Opening a dialogue is so useful because we learn instead of offending one another.

BUCK GHOSTHORSE: A MENTOR WARRIOR

I have had the privilege of knowing some warriors in my life. One of them died recently, and I want to share some thoughts about him and his life and teachings. His name was Buck Ghosthorse, and he grew up on the Rosebud Reservation in South Dakota, in a two-room house that held eleven people. As a boy he was kidnapped by the Mormons, who took him away and instructed him to not speak his native language and forced him to give up his native ceremonies and religion. As a teenager he escaped by joining the marines. He served in Vietnam twice and won a purple heart for his soldiering there. Later, when he was asked about his service in Vietnam, he would say he was proud of some of it and not so proud of other parts of it. On returning to the States he hit the bottle and succumbed to alcohol. But he met a mentor, Wallace Black Elk, who reintroduced him to his Indian ceremonies and language, and that made all the difference. He threw off alcohol, and he went to the University of Florida, where he received a degree in history. He moved to Georgia, where he led many sweat lodges and instructed people in the ways of Native American philosophy. But he had dreams for years that he should work with white people because "they were running things and the earth was in deep trouble."

For a decade, he put off these dreams, but eventually they wore him down. He heard about my Institute in Culture and Creation Spirituality (ICCS), which offered a master's program, that I had just moved from Mundelein College in Chicago to Holy Names College in Oakland, California, and he decided to move out west and join our faculty at ICCS. He taught courses on Native American spirituality and led sweat lodges for faculty, staff, and students. He set the sweat lodge up in a corner of the campus with the help of his students, who were learning the ancient practices. I remember one day stripping down to enter the sweat lodge with a faculty member who taught a course called "Hiking in Nature as Meditation." He said to me, "I must be the only Jew in America stripping down on a Catholic campus to enter a sweat lodge to pray with a Lakota leader." I think he was right.

In sweats and when leading prayers, Buck was both deep and humorous. For him there was no conflict between humor and serious prayer; they went together just fine. Buck worked with us for three years, and then he felt called to go north to the Seattle area to start his own community, which he later moved to Goldendale, Washington. When he left Oakland he surprised me by presenting me with the sacred pipe with which he had led prayers for twenty-four years. I was stunned and moved by so great a gift. He said to me, "When I joined ICCS I did not expect to learning anything from you white Christians. But as I leave I want to tell you, I learned more than I taught you."

While he was in the Seattle area, I had the privilege of undergoing a vision quest under his guidance. It was the beginning of my year of silence that the Vatican imposed on me. In fact, one of the accusations from Cardinal Ratzinger (now Pope Benedict XVI), who was as terrified of creation spirituality as he was of liberation theology, was that I worked too closely with American Indians. Allow me to say that I learned a lot more about prayer from Buck Ghosthorse and his tradition through sweats, vision quests, Sundances, and drumming than I have from stale ecclesial forms of prayer or from modern-day inquisitors. Buck said to me one day: "In our tradition, we believe that fear is the door in the heart that lets evil spirits in. Thus all prayer is a strengthening of the heart to keep fear at bay." I have shared this deep teaching with many people; I would be happy to share it with the Vatican, too, if they would only listen. But to listen you have to give up the fearful notion that you already know everything there is to know.

Last summer, at what turned out to be his last Sundance, he turned over his altar to one of his sons to be leader of the Sundance. He died on a Monday of a heart attack, and his funeral was one of the most profound experiences of my life. Here is what I wrote in my journal after the event:

> They buried him in a marine jacket, hat in one hand and with a marine guard and a gun salute. *And* they buried him in his dancing skirt, red in color, in which he danced so many times and pierced at the dances so often in order that "the people might live."
>
> It was fitting, this bi-native burial, because he was a soldier *and* a warrior having served twice in Vietnam and having received a purple heart for doing so. He also was a drill sergeant at Paris island.
>
> They say the difference between a soldier and a warrior is that the warrior is a lover, the soldier is told to "kill or be killed." Uncle [this was his favorite title] was a lover. And he was loved. Loved by his somewhat cantankerous community of 600+ people and the thousands more whose lives he profoundly affected and helped turn around, often from substance or alcohol addictions to productive and healthy ways of living in the world. He saved lives, literally. He healed — literally. And above all, he got others to save themselves. He empowered others to wake up and smell the coffee (don't know that I ever saw him without a mug in his hand except in prayer sessions). He challenged in his direct way and in his way of humor.
>
> He planted an orchard. His community. And watered it and taught it well, cajoled it, developed it, and ever so wisely he prepared it for his departure and left a healthy and well-trained leadership behind, having passed on his altar to his oldest son at his last Sundance ceremony in 2006.
>
> He honored women and acted from a vision he received to help women heal from abuse at the hands of a patriarchal culture and mind-set.
>
> He was both loyal and generous. He taught us the way to be

generous. His life was a giveaway. He was my friend for twenty-two years. I could call on him for help, and I did so when a brother needed some support and when a nephew needed some intervention. He was a tree bridging sky and soil, heavens and earth. A Green Man, a spiritual warrior, a defender of the people fighting their own demons and others' demons. A welcomer of the divine feminine. A practitioner of "Father Sky" who taught us to look up again with dignity and pride and the strength that community and ceremony bring. He was a good and wise Daedalus instructing his sons in learning ceremonies and practicing healthy warriorhood by strengthening one's own heart.

He was a hunter-gatherer, hunting ancient wisdom from Wallace Black Elk and other teachers and guides, both for his own healing and that of others. He sought wisdom elsewhere as well, even among white Christians. He was not homophobic. I never once heard him utter a word that was disparaging of homosexuals. I remember one incident in which he advised a man not to join up with another man, but the argument was not about men loving men but about the second man being too crazy a guy to commit to.

He had an inner life and profound spiritual practice. He listened to the visions and spirits, who gave him some rough assignments to carry out. He was a reluctant prophet. He was betrayed, he was himself hunted by his own tribe at times. But he persevered. Warriors persevere.

Buck was deeply ecumenical. He did not teach his Lakota ways by demanding that people cease their other (Jewish, Christian, native) ways. He respected other faith traditions — I remember him blessing the altar with his eagle feather at Holy Names Chapel when we were celebrating Mass, and indeed I have a fine photo of it (we both look unbelievably young!). He and a group of Indians smoked people when they came for a special Mass we did in the gymnasium, whose theme was the sacredness of the body, and as it turned out they had to keep at bay screaming right-wing Catholics who wanted to storm the place and wrote to the Vatican that we were showing pictures of naked people at a pagan worship ceremony. Buck told me afterward, "I never met people who would want to interfere with worship." My reply: "Welcome to the world of Christian fundamentalists." As it turned out, however, Buck had to face an analogous struggle when he led ceremonies in Washington and some local Indians tried to disrupt

them. He and his community had to set guards up to protect the
ceremonies and keep them going without interruption. That fight
lasted for several years.

Buck was a *wounded* healer, having journeyed a dark path of
poverty and then kidnapping as a child to the marines and active combat twice in Vietnam and then to the bottle. He accomplished *so much*
on such few resources, if by resources you mean money or power or
influence (in our culture's definitions). *But* if you mean resources of
human spirit when it listens to the prodding of Spirit via dreams and
visions, and if we mean strength of heart, imagination, creativity and
political astuteness, generosity and awakening people's multiple talents
— *then* we can and must say that he was one of the richest and heavily endowed beings on this planet. At his funeral there were 500 persons in attendance and active participation, people from all walks of
life and all races and ages (including tough looking black-jacketed
hombres who arrived on their motorcycles but were as reverent and
respectful — and grief-stricken and grateful — as the rest of us). Buck
touched many varied and distinctive lives with genuine depth.

I can truthfully say that the Catholic Church (whose history I
know very well, perhaps too well) has canonized people as saints who
accomplished far less than Buck accomplished in his lifetime — and
with far more resources at their disposal than Buck possessed. His trust
of Spirit and of visions from Spirit is the very stuff of holiness, of spiritual greatness. What he accomplished not just for individuals but for
his people history will record someday. For now, we all have stories,
and we are busy collecting them from one another. His life bears witness to the nobility of the spiritual depth of the Lakota and indeed indigenous religions everywhere.

Buck sometimes said, "I'm only a dumb Indian." This is like
Hildegard of Bingen writing that she was "only an uneducated and
feeble woman." If Buck was a dumb Indian, then he was dumb like
Jesus, or Buddha, or Lao Tzu or Isaiah or Muhammad or Dorothy Day
or Mother Teresa or Gandhi or Martin Luther King Jr. or Malcolm
X or Howard Thurman. Such dumbness our species needs far more
of at this time. Another word for it is ... wisdom. Wisdom carried by
spiritual warriors.

BHANTE DHARMAWARA, SPIRITUAL WARRIOR

Another spiritual warrior died recently at the age of 109. Bhante Dharmawara was a Buddhist monk who was active up to his final days on earth working as a meditation teacher and healer.

Born in Phnom Penh, Cambodia, Bhante led a privileged youth; he was trained in French schools and studied law and politics at the Sorbonne in Paris. He served as a recruiter for the French army during World War I, enlisting Cambodian volunteers for the Allied cause. He served as a magistrate and advisor in the King's Court of Cambodia, was a judge for seven years, and also a husband and a father of a daughter. He enjoyed life fully as a young man, eating rich foods, smoking, drinking, and more. Yet he was by no means content. About this period, he said, "I was not happy about the workings of government or what I had learned at the school of law. I had money to spend, but I had no satisfaction. There was fear in me."

For some years he was studying Buddhism, and in his mid-thirties he decided to go on a three-month retreat. His wife, with their newborn daughter, was reluctant to see him leave. He never returned. In the monastery he says he "discovered the answer about my life — a most important teaching for me. It was that 'it, I' was the real problem." He found peace there. He joined the forest monks of Thailand, who subsist on one meal per day. He grew his heart in the forest, where he encountered tigers, elephants, wild boars, and snakes. He learned that these wild animals seemed able to determine whether a person was a friend or an enemy just by their sense of smell. Tigers followed him more than once but did not harm him; once he found himself in a herd of wild elephants, who all froze and did nothing as he led his small band of monks away from them. Bhante said that animals could "smell thoughts." If these thoughts were peaceful and loving, the animals would not bother you. If they were negative and fearful, you were considered an enemy.

After seven years in the forest he went to India to study Buddhism in greater depth. He trained in homeopathy and learned to speak at least twelve languages (his teacher spoke fifty-two different languages). He founded the Asoka Mission, which included a monastery and temple meditation center and a healing center — where, among other practices, they celebrated Christmas because he was deeply ecumenical and believed a common thread runs through all true traditions. He was elected president of the World Fellowship of Buddhists and taught in the department of Asian languages at Hindu University in Benares. He was close to Prime Minister Nehru and served as his personal physician. Gandhi was also a friend. He eventually moved to the United States, taught at Georgetown University, and joined a temple in Stockton, California.

He worked extensively as a healer, and one of his teachings is a quote from Buddha: "There is nothing to fear. If there is anything at all to fear, fear only yourself!" His healing sessions emphasized the use of green light. He said: "Light is the source of all life. It contains innumerable colors, both visible and invisible. Green light, in particular, is the most balanced of all the colors; it is also the color of strength and rejuvenation." He saw green as combining earth and sky energies, bringing together the yellow of the sun, which is masculine, with the blue of the Earth, which is feminine. Thus a complete balance. Green characterizes springtime and rejuvenation and is the color of the heart chakra. Sitting under a green light helps calm and reassure both humans and animals, and Bhante also used green light to meditate with.

Bhante often said that "meditation is the highest work we can do on ourselves," an essential way to find inner peace that in turn translates to outer peace. He taught that what we think, what we eat, and what we drink are the three most important elements of living. We are what we think, eat, and drink. Good foods and good thoughts lead to feeling good; bad food and bad thoughts lead to feeling bad.

At the age of 108, he kept to a routine of rising daily at 4:30 A.M., washing, and preparing for morning meditation. Breakfast followed and then healing of patients. A rest, and then lunch and evening meditation. One person who was Bhante's friend and coworker described him this way: "To know Bhante as an elder-teacher is humbling and inspiring. There are no words to properly describe Bhante's warmth, his constant compassion, and his continued attentiveness, even at this grand old age. Bhante is a 'Grandfather to the World,' with his love of life and his love of all of his family, which includes you, even if he has just met you for the first time. He is very ready with a joke and laughter, one of his favorite medicines. There is no heart that doesn't melt in his presence, and people leave him with their minds open to the infinite possibilities that living a life of awareness can bring."

A spiritual warrior indeed. Bhante served and transformed his fear and aggression into such peace-sharing and peace-giving that even the wild animals respected him. And interestingly, green was his healing color. He was a Green Man and spiritual warrior in every sense of the word.

FOUR STEPS TO SPIRITUAL WARRIORHOOD

If the warrior is distinct from the soldier, then there must be distinct ways by which the warrior develops his or her strength. If the warrior is the mystic in action, then let us try the following four steps on for size. They derive from the mystical/prophetic or mystical/warrior journey in the creation spirituality tradition.

The Four Steps

ONE: THE VIA POSITIVA

The Via Positiva is the way of celebrating life. Of seeing the world with its beauty and goodness, its grace and generosity — and being always open to seeing more. This is the way of reverence, respect, and gratitude. It is the way of original blessing, whereby we live out the truth that the universe and life itself, for all their struggle and pain, have birthed us as individuals and as communities with what we need for happiness and for sharing of the joy.

This all spiritual warriors need to undergo many times and in many places and on many occasions and under diverse circumstances.

TWO: THE VIA NEGATIVA

This way goes into the darkness, the wounds, the pain, and also the silence and solitude of existence to find what we have to learn there. It is a way of letting go and letting be, of emptying and being emptied, of moving beyond judgment and beyond control, of sinking and learning to breathe, to sit, to be still, to calm the raging monkey brain, to dwell in silence, to taste nothingness without flinching, and ultimately to focus. It is the way of grieving. Without grief we cannot move on to the next stage, which is one of giving birth.

This all spiritual warriors need to undergo many times and in many places and on many occasions and under diverse circumstances. Eckhart calls the process of letting go "eternal." The warrior faces death and because he has, loves life more passionately.

THREE: THE VIA CREATIVA

Having fallen in love with life often (Via Positiva) and having been emptied and learned to let go and let be numerous times (Via Negativa), the spiritual warrior is ready to give birth. Creativity is the weapon, the sword, of the true spiritual warrior — who is mother as well as father, and who digs deep into a wellspring of wildness that provides the energy for new life, new connections, new images, and new moral imagination by which to change things in a deep, not superficial, way. The true warrior is a cocreator, a worker with Spirit, a worker for Spirit. The warrior's hands are the hands of Spirit at work; the warrior's mind is seized by Spirit precisely in the work of creativity. As Aquinas put it, "the same Spirit that hovered over the waters at the beginning of creation hovers over the mind of the artist at work." Every warrior is an artist, an artist at work for the people that they might live.

FOUR: THE VIA TRANSFORMATIVA

Claims to artistry and to creativity and to cocreation need to be tested. The Spirit requires discernment and testing. The primary test for claims of spirit work is that of justice and of compassion. Does the work I am doing pass the justice test? Does it benefit the poor and not just the powerful? Does it fill gaps between haves and have-nots or make the chasm deeper? Does it contribute to healing and empowerment of the powerless or does it merely reestablish the privileges of the few at the expense of the many?

The prophets always speak on behalf of justice; they are attuned to injustice, which they feel like a kick in the gut. Injustice arouses the passion of anger and the prophet/warrior is in touch with his or her anger and passions. But instead of just responding in a reptilian brain action-reaction mode, the prophet uses the anger as fuel to fire effective and creative ways to enact justice and the healing that justice brings about. And the authentic warrior remains humble, or close to the earth (*humus*, from which "humility" is derived, means "earth" in Latin), and aware that he or she is only an instrument of the work of Spirit. Not a messiah. A prophet is a weak and needy human being like everyone else, fully capable of evil and of mistakes and errors. And needy also for the Via Positiva to be a regular part of one's spiritual practice, a need for filling up and refreshing in the cool waters of peace and joy that life's small moments can bring, even if it is just paying attention gratefully to the gift of a deep breath or a walk. Nevertheless, in all of this the warrior/prophet remains fierce for justice and compassion to happen.

Walking the Warrior Steps

We can see that the warrior not only undergoes these four stages in ever-deepening ways but the warrior becomes them. Look and see. Look at the warrior in yourself, not only as you practice these ways but as you become them. Consider Buck Ghosthorse: notice how beautiful was his strength and his teaching and how his leadership brought beauty out of so many who were themselves deeply wounded. He turned wounded people into wounded healers. Beauty was ever-present at his sweats and prayers, at his Sundances, even at his funeral, as he resurrected the powerful songs and ways of his ancestors and made them live in peoples' souls all over again today. This is the warrior as Via Positiva.

Consider too how the spiritual warrior is a bearer of the Via Negativa. The warrior/prophet invites one into places of darkness, into questions and doubts and challenges and the demands of change. The warrior enters deep places that stir up chaos, not order and control. Think of one who intervenes in a case of addiction or dependency. The act of intervention is not easy or sweet but demanding and life-changing. Buck was such a person; to dance the Sundance in the blazing sun without food or water for days and to pierce one's chest for the sake of the people is not without its struggle and its demands.

To face the truth in ourselves is necessary but not always pleasant. It is not easy to meditate and be still when the brain and body both want to escape, to wallow in the infinite distractions that our culture feeds us. To lounge on our couches watching others live on TV, following the endless gossip surrounding public figures and celebrities — this is easy. But it is not the way of the warrior. The warrior penetrates darkness and learns to live with it, to suck out what it has to teach us. Even if that means tasting nothingness and ashes. The warrior entertains silence and prefers it to noise.

When Thomas Aquinas, the great theologian and defender of the merging of science and spirituality, was writing his last book, his *Summa theologica*, he had finished about two-thirds when he had a mystical experience that caused him to put down his pen, to quit writing and speaking. For a year, the last year of his life, this giant of a thinker and writer said nothing and wrote nothing. He then died with his great work unfinished. This was his unfinished symphony. What he said about his experience was this: "Everything I have written is straw." (And yet what he had written, in a period of twenty-one years, were books of enduringly profound and earth-shattering significance.) We too can say: "All I've written is straw" or "All I've built is straw." "All my loves are straw," "All I've made is straw," "All I've stood for is straw," "All I've believed in is straw."

The tasting of straw, like the tasting of ashes, is a reminder of how small our presence is in the vastness of time and space, in the presence of the universe or even in the history of our species. The warrior — and Aquinas was nothing if not a warrior — acknowledges the straw-likeness of all human accomplishment and becomes at times that straw. Nothingness is real. Black holes and black energy dominate in the universe. Who are we to think we can get through life without drinking it deeply and becoming what we take in? The warrior incarnates nothingness at times. That is just how it is.

Often, to be a warrior, we must let go of our privileged status in life, no matter how hard-won. Putting aside the cloaks of accomplishment, one strips to what Howard Thurman called "the literal substance of oneself before God," and one goes into darkness quite alone and vulnerable. That too is part of the way of the warrior. There are no guarantees that at the other end one will emerge as the same person or fit to play the same role in society ever again. One becomes the Via Negativa. Friends and relationships, achievements and titles, salaries and retirement plans, may all be left aside. We may be asked to live out the principle that, as Eckhart said, "all we have in life is on loan." Life itself is on loan and all our relationships in it. A loan is temporary. The warrior knows about death, does not deny mortality but carries it like a shield, a guard by which to defend self and others. Knowing one's mortality urges one to live fully now and defend what is beautiful now, not tomorrow. The warrior does not wait to live, does not put off living and loving and defending and creating for another day. The loan will come due, so make your opportunity today.

Having learned to let go, the warrior does not harbor resentments or become motivated by revenge to chase after others. Forgiveness, another word for letting go, is learned drip by drip, day by day, not as an act of altruism but as a necessary cleansing of the past, a purification of our souls so we can live and function effectively in the now. The soul does not grow into its potential fullness when it harbors past hurt and turns it over and over. That is the way to grow bitterness, not soul. The warrior is committed to growing the heart and soul, not to freezing it in the puny size it was yesterday or in years past. Here too discipline is needed, even sacrifice, when offering a burnt soul, a soul burnt by the betrayals of life, whether self-induced or not. The warrior learns to live beyond betrayal, neither denying it nor dwelling on it. Beyond betrayal. Beyond the pain of broken love and bleeding relationships and misunderstood communications and unfulfilled yearnings. The warrior has undergone the deep purification of longing that is the lesson learned in the schoolhouse the mystics call the *dark night of the soul.* He or she does not run from the darkness but enters it, overcoming the fear of the dark as well as the fear of the light. The latter — fear of light and love, beauty and grace, a flight from the Via Positiva — can also be an obstacle to the warrior's emergence.

The warrior also becomes the artist and creative being, expressing the creativity and aesthetic bias for beauty that the universe demands in all of its actions, all of its ongoing formation and deformation that we call evolution. The warrior bears ongoing evolution on his or her back, becoming an instrument for evolution, an agent for change and transformation, for the creativity and healing that bring about that evolution. Evolution is not accomplished at the expense of the past but brings the past along, folds it into the new forms, the struggling new seeds of plants or beings, ideas or movements, structures or languages that are yearning to be born. The future germinates from the past. Or as Jesus put it, new wine skins alone can house the new wine, as old wine skins and old forms grow dry and brittle with age or privilege or both.

The warrior carries the new creation in his hands and heart and head. That is why Aquinas teaches that "all cultures in all places" have had their prophets and their warriors. Creativity has always been in demand. Guardians of the dominant culture more often than not stifle creativity, wanting to put it in the back of the bus, in the basement of educational instruction. (For instance, the ironically named "No child left behind" laws are all about exams, which are stifling creativity in children and classrooms and rapidly undermining education rather than reviving it.) Or, consider those hunters of religious orthodoxy who would burn the so-called heretics at the stake or flog or condemn them in public places to dissuade other would-be warriors, to instill fear, to teach the lesson that it is better to sell one's soul than to save it and others' with it.

The warrior incarnates creativity, not for the sake of ego or fame or money, but for community. Creativity was at work when Buck established his community and brought back the Sundance and vision quests and other ceremonies and instructed people in doing them appropriately.

For all these reasons the warrior serves. This service is not coerced, as with a slave, but is offered. The warrior gives and gives generously. And he gives to himself as well as the greater community the gifts of love of life (Via Positiva), of stillness and letting go (Via Negativa), of creativity (Via Creativa) and of justice and compassion (Via Transformativa). Service, as we indicated earlier, is love of strangers. The warrior loves the stranger and finds ways to love the stranger. These ways of love are ways of service. Compassion and Justice both serve the stranger. Thus the warrior walks the talk and dances the trances that have inspired such a calling. The warrior incarnates warriorhood. Healing follows. Celebration follows. More awe and wonder, grace and gratitude result. And creativity — everyone's — flows more freely. And empowerment — everyone's — becomes a regular occurrence in the world. The seeds are planted; the orchard bears fruit. Good fruit. Fruit that remains.

FALSE WARRIORS, FALSE PROPHETS

Jesus warned about "wolves in sheep's clothing" and false prophets. Those who would confuse soldier and warrior, or soldier and prophet, set us up for rank confusion. In many ways, in the United States today, the unholy alliance between right-wing political ideologies and right-wing Christian movements goes beyond confusion and creates a situation that is reminiscent of when Hitler came to power in Nazi Germany with the explicit blessing of the so-called German Christian Church, whose pro-Nazi sympathies were surprisingly uncriticized by many at the time. Dr. James Luther Adams, a former ethics professor at Harvard Divinity School, fled Germany in 1936 after being interrogated by the Gestapo for having supported the Confessing Church led by Dietrich Bonhoeffer. Twenty-five years ago, when Pat Robertson and other radio hosts and televangelists began talking about a new political religion to create a global, Christian empire, Adams warned of the coming rise of American fascism and religion's role in that rise.

Examining the situation in Nazi Germany, Adams was very critical of liberals who talked of dialogue and inclusiveness and lacked the backbone to confront what was really going on: "The power and allure of evil and the cold reality of how the world worked was being ignored by such platitudes." He also criticized prominent research universities and the media in Nazi Germany; he considered these institutions too self-absorbed and compromised by their coziness with government and corporations, so that they were completely unwilling and unable to raise the fundamental moral questions of justice and inequality.

In this context of false prophets I'd like to examine the Promise Keepers, the name for a modern-day Christian men's movement. The founder of Promise Keepers is Dr. Tony Evans, a Dallas minister. He gathers thousands of men at a time, usually in football stadiums, and preaches about creating a Christian state. Borrowing much of his ideology from Rousas Rushdoony, who founded the Reconstructionist movement in 1973, this very strange and right-wing version of Christianity teaches that America should be governed by biblical con-cepts and that "dominion" has been given over the "elect" to rule the Earth and America in particular. This society would, among other things, prescribe the death penalty for adultery, witchcraft, blasphemy, and homosexuality. The fed-eral government should occupy itself with national defense, and education and social welfare should be handled by the churches. Biblical law must replace the secular legal code.

Dominionism found a home not only with Promise Keepers but with in-fluential political figures who were close to Tony Evans, such as George Bush, Tom Delay, Pat Robertson, and Zell Miller. God chooses such people, Evans tells us, to battle the forces of evil embedded in "secular humanism" and to cre-ate a Christian and God-fearing nation. As Pat Robinson has put it, "Our aim is to gain dominion over society." The standard textbook used in many Chris-tian schools and the home schooling movement declares that the Bible calls for "Bible-believing Christians" to take dominion of America. Christ is pictured as an avenger and his message of love, forgiveness, and compassion, as well as his example of defying the Roman empire, is practically forgotten in this surge to create a Christian American Empire. The movement aims to appeal to the lower middle class and to people feeling the economic squeeze. Chris Hedges, Adams's student and a Pulitzer prize–winning journalist, writes: "This image of Christ as warrior is appealing to many within the movement. The loss of manufacturing jobs, lack of affordable healthcare, negligible opportunities for education and poor job security has left many millions of Americans locked out. This ideology is attractive because it offers them the hope of power and revenge. It sanctifies their rage. It stokes the paranoia about the outside world maintained through bizarre conspiracy theories, many on display in Pat Robertson's book *The New World Order* which rants against the United Nations and other international organizations." Hitler too built his movement on the backs of an angry, disenfranchised working class.

The peculiar series of apocalyptic novels called *The Left Behind* series (now in a movie version as well) have sold over 60 million copies in a few years. This should alert people to something serious going on in the souls of Americans these days. And it is not pretty. These books preach holy war and hold up a Christ who eviscerates the flesh of millions of nonbelievers. An angry and vi-olent Messiah will appear after a global nuclear war, which will bring about the second coming. The anti-scientism of the movement is legend; it begins with the refusal to accept the reality of evolution and includes denial of the fact that 8 to 10 percent of any given human population is gay or lesbian. Just days after he took power in 1933, Hitler banned all homosexual and lesbian organizations. The attacks on homosexuals in America, which are splitting many mainline churches, are very real. The specious use of the word "values" is a code word for attacking gays and lesbians, and it distracts from deeper value questions, such as the environment, war and peace, the economy, and racial and gender justice.

Here, too, the right-wing movement is promoting issues of a warped warrior ideology, including a warped message on what it is to be masculine. Gays and liberated women, we are told, are responsible for male confusion. As Hedges puts it, "The cult of masculinity pervades the ideology. Feminism and homosexuality are social forces, believers are told, that have rendered the American male physically and spiritually impotent." Hedges warns that given the fanaticism and rabid ideology of the Christian right, "all debates with the Christian right are useless. We cannot reach this movement. It does not want dialogue. It cares nothing for rational thought and discussion. It is not mollified because John Kerry prays or Jimmy Carter teaches Sunday school." The biggest danger, he believes, is our complacency. One is reminded of the warning from Sinclair Lewis: "Fascism will come to America wrapped in a flag and carrying a cross."

Clearly, the archetype of the spiritual warrior has its shadow side. This is all the more reason to take our commitment seriously and to stand up, in warrior fashion, to forces that would coopt its real meaning, substituting hate for justice and love. Wouldn't it be wonderful, in fact, if true spiritual warriors were to rise en masse to defend the Earth in its current peril and make war against global warming? And also make war with poverty instead of with a projection known as "secularism"? America, the world's largest economy, has one in eight persons (37 million Americans) living in poverty, of whom the greatest number are children — and one in four black persons lives in poverty. Over 46 million citizens have no health insurance. Such facts suggest that there are plenty of battles for real warriors to wage. What are we waiting for?

JOHN CONGER:
ON WARRIORS DON QUIXOTE AND ULYSSES

There are many spiritual warriors in our midst today, and I have written about a few of them, such as Buck Ghosthorse and Bhante Dharmawara. We can recognize and turn to the spiritual warriors in our lives for guidance; they will help lead us to our authentic masculinity and the reemergence of the Divine Masculine, and they will help us develop our own inner warrior. There are also historical persons, like Jesus and Martin Luther King Jr., whom we can turn to for guidance, as well as literary, mythic, or archetypal figures.

I would like to end this discussion of the spiritual warrior by focusing on two literary or mythic warriors: Don Quixote and Odysseus (or Ulysses). In particular, I'd like you to hear what psychologist John Conger has to say about the important role they play in understanding healthy masculinity.

I have always found the farcical figure of Don Quixote to be an important male archetype — for me he is like the prophet Jonah in the Bible, one who pokes fun (although unwittingly) at the whole warrior thing. Just as Wisdom needs to dance with her counterpart, Folly, so the warrior, serious as he or she is, needs to maintain a sense of humor. That is the gift of Quixote. While he does indeed "tilt at windmills," confusing them with wild giants, still he is a reminder for all potential warriors and prophets to laugh at themselves. The difference between a zealot and a prophet or warrior is this capacity for self-deprecating humor, which recognizes one's limits, either of strength or understanding. There are many zealots in today's world— false prophets, false warriors — and they appear scary because of their unyielding beliefs. I believe that one reason for the enduring popularity of Don Quixote is that he helps us see, and identify with, the mistakes and foolishness of literalism, extremism, and obsession. Don Quixote is a literalist — he reads books on chivalry and is obsessed by them. He believes every word in them to be the truth even when they are impossible. In this regard, he provides satiric relief for all literalists, including those who interpret every word of the Bible literally. In fact, all of us, from time to time, share in some of the zealotry and foolishness of Quixote. Is there not a Don Quixote in each of us, just as there is a Christ, a Buddha nature, and a true spiritual warrior? If so, we want to remain open to laughter and paradox. Quixote assists us in that.

Quixote after all is a hunter-gatherer. He hunts out his enemies, real or imagined, whether windmills or knights (disguised in his eyes as priests). He hunts for his Lady, as any authentic and chivalrous knight does. He is busy looking for a fight. And he is constantly defending his *honor*, which is such a male enterprise — to avoid the sting of shame. Quixote becomes our favorite antihero, antiprophet, antiwarrior, anti-hunter-gatherer — and this is good medicine to keep men healthy. John Conger, in particular, speaks to the shame and anger that the figure of Don Quixote addresses in men.

CONGER: Shame has to do with the development of self, protoself, self-awareness, self-consciousness. That's its heart. Aggression and how we deal with it is key to masculinity. The other key is shame. In the days of Don Quixote, how to be a man was about sustaining your honor. *Don Quixote* is a totally sophisticated story that is all about shame in a most ludicrous way. When I teach my introductory class and tell my students they might risk themselves, I tell them that *there is no growth without shame.* Shame is about self-awareness, so you grow and look back at yourself and say, "Oh my God, I did that!" and you feel ashamed. Shame has this double edge — it can attack and destroy the self. You feel so horrible about yourself that you feel you are going crazy; it can destroy your sense of self if your sense of self is weak. Like aggression, it very much needs to be managed as a man.

It is very easy to be humiliated. In the old days, one would have fought a duel. You kept your honor at all costs. But it seems like a very wooden approach for dealing with shame, whereas it is part of growth to find out how to manage your shame. It is extraordinarily hard to be a man because you have to learn how to manage shame and aggression. And not hide it or disclaim it. With aggression, there's a lot of pressure to be a safe male, a male that isn't threatening and doesn't scare anybody. A male like that is a kind of feminine male with a sweater, who isn't going to be a threat to a woman. But the kind of male women like *is* someone who is a little scary, because they are capable of protecting. They are someone a woman can turn to for safety. Safe males tend to turn to women as if they are a mother rather than an equal.

Cervantes, a contemporary of Shakespeare, had an amazingly wild life himself and fought a duel in Spain, and he had to escape the country. He fled to Italy, and there was some point when he was captured by pirates and lived with the Turks; he wrote poetry and more. Don Quixote was a kind of mockery of himself, for he was very sophisticated. But what strikes me about *Don Quixote* was that the narrator is a highly sophisticated, sardonic, terribly amused, cultivated, literary person and becomes like another character in the novel.

As a psychiatrist I study a lot about psychosis, and *Don Quixote* really describes the psychotic break perfectly. A lot of psychosis is very hostile, with a lot of anger in it, and Don Quixote has a flash temper — he immediately distorts everything and is quite angry. He can't be stopped; he is actually quite fierce. So there is this shame that he is desperately trying to avoid. He is defending his honor. An older gentleman with a housekeeper and a twenty-year-old niece living with him, amused, sophisticated, urban Cervantes is describing a whole class of people. It is a shaming picture of living with extreme limita-tion, and in the face of all this, Don Quixote is omnipotent amid limitation. An explosion happens as he reads romance novels and creates this whole delu-sionary world where he is going to become a knight and escape his limitations and give full expression to this omnipotence. He becomes pretty crazy. The whole episodic structure of the novel is built around these encounters with a totally secular world.

How do priests act when Don Quixote meets them? He thinks they're sort of middle class and pompous, well-to-do riding carriages, and so on. And Don Quixote sees them as other knights; one escapes and Quixote beats them pretty badly. They are cowardly. Don Quixote has a brawl with people carrying things, and they put up a real fight. It's a different approach to shame.

And so when you get to Cervantes, you get this amusement about honor and shame. You have a story about a broken man — Don Quixote is broken, he is humiliated, but he refuses to be broken. It's like a noble role he plays; he refuses to be shamed in his noble role, in the act of. And the thing that saves him is his friends. Nothing will convince him. One of his friends dresses up, and it takes several tries as a knight, and if he defeats him, he has to do exactly what he says. So when he does defeat him dressed up as a knight, he tells him he has to go back to his house and stay there. It's only in Don Quixote's death that he awakens to his delusion. Friendship helps him through this crisis.

FOX: How does Jesus deal with shame?

CONGER: Jesus represents the embodiment of shame into the human spirit. It's like God is made present in shame.

FOX: It gives shame a good name.

CONGER: It gives shame a good name, and it makes it part of one's broken-ness rather than one's honor, and this leads to one's development. For me this is a profound psychological progression or development — that it's possible to survive the death of one's ego, and one can have a self that is separate from ego, that self endures and does not die. The soul is what grows our investment in maintaining our honor. So Jesus was this ultimate revolutionary, and the peo-ple who have all the pride and the honor are the Pharisees who give 10 percent honorably and are not being broken and whatever their growth it may not be so substantial. So the rich man comes to Jesus and says, "I've done all these things, followed the laws," and Jesus loves him and says, "Give all you have away and come follow me," and the young man can't. He owns too much.

That's when Jesus says it's harder for a rich man to enter the kingdom of heaven than for a camel to go through the eye of a needle. So there is something about our ego that fights like hell never to be broken, but Jesus offers a profound insight, that there is life after death, psychologically life after being broken. And that's the life of the soul.

FOX: Joseph Jastrab seconds this point when he comments that it is "a troubling notion for many of us — the possibility that we do not gain a warrior's heart through our victories, but through our defeats." How do you feel Jesus dealt with aggression?

CONGER: Very skillfully. I mean he wasn't afraid of it. Consider the money changers incident. He was around aggression all the time; he was being challenged by questions, but he was very Odysseus-like. He is portrayed as someone who knew where the Pharisees are coming from and knows how to answer them in ways that pissed them off. He is not portrayed as someone who wants to die at all, but as someone who does not want to die. But he is doing his work, and he is very upset by the betrayal of his friends.

I think John the Baptist is the real symbol of aggression because he is just in defiance, sort of outside the law; he's not in the cities, off in the wilderness somewhere, sort of a rough guy, and he is saying the kingdom of God is about to come and everything is going to be destroyed. He's taking all the rage that Jews have against the Roman captors and formulating it as a narrative about the end of things. So I think it is a story about very dangerous times.

FOX: Similar to our times, I suppose. What does Odysseus tell us about getting through this?

CONGER: I feel like it is a dangerous world now where changes are taking place. In the book *The World Is Flat*, the author talks about how the last seven years have seen radical changes. How do you have any secure self, any enduring self? And that is sort of the theme of the *Odyssey*. But the *Odyssey* is a world in which gods exist.

I've always loved the *Odyssey*. Because in some ways it's about emotional presence, how to survive in a dangerous world. That's how I experience the world, and the *Odyssey* is all about that. Odysseus is this incredible archetype for the male because in the beginning of the *Odyssey*, Zeus says, "I know who Odysseus is, he is almost one of us." But Odysseus is the ultimately human male because he is trapped on this island with Calypso, who is a goddess who wants him to be her husband and promises he will become immortal, and he does not want it. He has sex with her, but all he can think about is going back to Ithaca to be with his wife, Penelope. As far as he knows his mother and father are still there. It's interesting because it's a world of gods, where humans are on the bottom involved in the gods' whim, but the Odyssey tells us it is so much better to be a human. It looks like it's better to be gods, but the gods cannot experience loss — because they are immortal, they lose the depth of feeling. These gods are petty and jealous and angry, very primal and undeveloped, whereas Odysseus has an internal world that he will not trade in to be immortal and one of the gods. Gods are in love with humans in a strange way, will have sex with them because they are bored. It's tedious to keep living.

FOX: So Ulysses represents what it is to be a man and the relationships of men.

CONGER: In the beginning, the *Odyssey* says Ulysses was never at a loss. He represents masculine confidence. Calypso tells him he can go and Ulysses says, "What's the trick? You might do something terrible to me." She is amused: "Oh, Odysseus, you are so awake and so aware of tricks." Odysseus says, "Swear by the gods" — which she does. He is well traveled and knows the minds of men. This is a model for a highly competent self that can mourn and grieve terrible losses and has pride. The shame he experiences is outside of himself; he struggles to not be shamed and to stay honorable. The shame concerns his family pressures that he cannot affect. It is a fascinating world that he is in because he represented a kind of courage regarding how dangerous and unprepared we are in the world. A kind of fate that spins out of that. Poseidon is pissed off at him because he put out the eye of Polythemus the Cyclops. He made this one mistake, and Cyclops had him locked in a cave and was eating his men one by one. After Odysseus put his eye out, Cyclops said, "Who are you?" "My name is no name. No one." When escaping in his ships, he taunted Cyclops, a lapse of pride that cost him.

And so we have many examples of spiritual warriors in our midst. I have written of only a few. Each has their teaching to impart. Each is a guide to our authentic masculinity and the reemergence of the Divine Masculine. We also have been alerted to the truth of their being false prophets and mistaken spiritual warriors in our midst. This is one more reason for staying alert as warriors do even as we go about developing our own inner warriorhood.

MASCULINE SEXUALITY, NUMINOUS SEXUALITY

THE SECULARIZATION OF THE SKY that occurred in the modern era, which we discussed in chapter one, impacted all levels of masculine awareness and sensibility. This dulling of our cosmic awareness contributed to a secularization of sexuality as well as of the rest of nature. In great part religion succumbed to this forgetfulness of sexual mysticism and settled for playing the role of moralizing sexual scold, acting on behalf of a Peeping Tom kind of deity. Clergy were only too happy to play the role of a punitive and guilt-inducing Father God. Dr. Gunther Weil has put it this way: "Our Western institutional religious tradition has essentially repressed and distorted the sexual instinct and thereby created a variety of personal and social pathologies. In so doing it has also effectively removed sexuality from its spiritual foundations."

The late monk Bede Griffiths got it right when he said, shortly before he died, that sexuality is too important and too powerful not to be ritualized and honored for the sacrament that it is. Many men, and society at large, fail to honor and respect our sexuality and to explore its mystical dimensions, thus failing to celebrate its authentic numinosity. Ancient spiritual traditions East and West can assist us in this important task.

There is a sense of the holy attached to sexuality, which in previous eras actually grounded our appreciation of sex and all it stands for. There is a *numinous* dimension to the male phallus.

How distant are we from this truth? In an important book that can help heal Westerners of sexual ignorance and distrust, called *Taoist Secrets of Love:*

Cultivating Male Sexual Energy, Taoist master Mantak Chia makes the astute observation that "for most people the experience of sex is more powerful than their experience of religion." So often religion seems more bent on controlling sex than on mining it for its spiritual power. Chia comments that "many modern spiritual leaders, whether Christian, Jewish, or Hindu, etc., have forgotten the link in their religious rites connecting sexual power and spirituality.... By accepting sex as sacred, the role of religion will be revitalized in society and made more meaningful in ordinary personal relationships." Chia, operating from ancient Taoist practices passed down in great part by word of mouth, believes that men can reconnect to a powerful source of energy and balance by learning to control their seminal fluids. "The foundation of penis strength is seminal retention.... Life energy is driven down into the testes filling them with extraordinary vitality." If we choose not to do that, we are squandering great potential — "engaging in sexual love with a partner — but without any esoteric practice to cultivate the chi — is an incomplete path to transforming oneself."

ANCIENT SACRED METAPHORS OF SEXUALITY

Sexuality stands for generativity and creativity, for passion, for our desire to have children, for freedom, for ecstasy, for fun, for struggle, for joy, for our communion with another, and even for our communion with God. In all these contexts, sexuality, sex, intercourse, our genitals become transcendent metaphors for desire, connection, and creation.

The Bible dedicated an entire book to this truth (the Song of Songs), while on an island off the coast of Bombay is an ancient Indian temple called the Elephanta Caves. In these caves, carved out of rock, is a giant representation of the great phallus of the Indian god Shiva, the Creator and Destroyer of the world (this phallic symbol is called a lingam). Even today, psychologist Robert Moore writes, "This image is so powerful, so charged with life-force for the faithful, that day and night the cave-temple hums with the comings and goings of thousands of pilgrims and echoes with their songs and chants. The worshipper is caught in a mood of utter fascination by this graphic portrayal of the divine masculine and responds with a hushed 'yes' of recognition." Holy Indian temples in Konarak and Khajuraho also honor sexuality and the art of lovemaking. These are not exercises in titillation but representations of cosmic myth — of how the union of the masculine and the feminine lies at the center of the origin of the universe and, as consciousness itself, in the center of our own beings (located in the second chakra). In these temples, a great joy spreads across the faces of the lovers engaged in acts of love.

Anthropologist Mircea Eliade concluded that the meaning of sexuality is "to reveal to human beings that which is beyond ego — in religious terms, the divine." Eugene Monick points out that, as in the Indian temples, fascination with the phallus serves a higher purpose: "Charm is elemental curiosity, drawing power, a magical capacity to move one from the ordinary to the numinous — the characteristics of a religious experience.... Fascination is an engagement of soul."

At the temple of Angkor in Cambodia, as well as at sacred sites at Preah Khan, there is rich celebration of sacred sexuality, and statues of lingams can be found dating from the seventh century. In Mali, Africa, there are houses built for Muslim religious leaders with phalluses that are an integral part of the architecture of the roof. The same is true of a "young men's house" that "boasts fifty-three phalluses. Usually these houses are the largest and most decorated structures in a village." They function like a combination school and fraternity and are overseen by an adult male who is a kind of jester and trickster who never tells the truth. Eliade points out that "except in the modern world, sexuality has everywhere and always been a hierophany, and the sexual as an integral action and therefore also a means to knowledge." Carl Jung comments, "The phallus is the source of life and libido, the creator and worker of miracles, and as such it was worshipped everywhere."

In cultures the world over, from India to Africa, from the Pacific Islands to Canada, human beings have honored the phallus and its unique powers in temples and in art and sculpture. Even at Chartres Cathedral, there is a statue of a man masturbating with a great smile on his face — the photographer Clive Hicks discovered this statue hidden away at the top of the cathedral and photographed it. But notice how this statue was hidden away. There is far less art that sacralizes sex in the West than in the East. This is no doubt because in Western culture, thanks much to Augustine and Plato, sexuality is considered something less than spiritual. In the West, we prefer linking sex to shame rather than to the sacred.

SEXUALITY AND SHAME: A WESTERN INHERITANCE

How much of male shame is rooted in teachings around sexual shame? Taoist teacher Chia says that in his tradition it is understood that women are more at ease with their sexuality than men, and when men are not grounded in the deepest dimensions of their sexuality — including the spiritual dimension — they feel it necessary to control or dominate women. He also believes that much of the obesity epidemic in the West could be traceable to a lack of sexual grounding because "many people feeling sexual frustration turn to food for gratification. An imbalance in ching (sex) energy ranks as a major cause of obesity — where you are sexually frustrated, food is the easiest substitute."

Riane Eisler, in her important book *Sacred Pleasure: Sex, Myth and the Politics of the Body — New Paths to Power and Love*, offers a substantive analysis of the negative direction sexuality has taken in the West. Augustine and many other church fathers pretty much declared, "as Ranke-Heinemann writes, that 'the locus par excellence of sin is sex.'" It followed that woman is "a constant danger to man," and Christian witch hunts left some towns almost without any female population at all, having killed off thousands (if not millions) of women. Among the losers were Western medicine because this eliminated "invaluable herbal and other healing knowledge that had until then been passed on by pagan priestesses and healers from generation to generation." The church more often than not associated sex not with pleasure "but with eternal punishment and pain." The lesson men learned not only alienated men from women, "thus justifying and maintaining male dominance; it also served to alienate men from their own bodies, their own emotions, and above all from their human need for loving connection." Instead of connection came domination, coercion, and repression and this served political forces. For "it is this control over peoples' bodies that is the ultimate mainstay of dominator social organization." The church often obsesses on sex and distorts spirituality. In the process, like the pornography it condemns, the church "constantly associates sex with violence and domination."

As the examples of Indian temples make clear, it has not always been this way. Even in Europe, studies of prehistoric sites indicate that sexuality was then "associated with the sacred, with religious rites, with the Goddess herself." These "erotic myths and rites were not only expressions of our ancestors' joy and gratitude for the Goddess's gift of life, but also expressions of joy and gratitude for the Goddess's gifts of love and pleasure — particularly for that most intense of physical pleasures, the pleasure of sex."

And yet, eventually sex became associated with male power over women. "Religious authorities taught men that the bodily or carnal is, like woman, of a lower order. So it became man's duty to control and subdue not only woman...but all that is bodily or carnal. All this put men at war with their own bodies. And it also put them at war with women — hence the term 'war of the sexes.'" These teachings fed the "dominator mind." For "the dominator mind making love *is* making war,... and in the end, what the properly socialized macho man is left with is only the 'enjoyment of victory over an opponent — be the opponent another man or a woman,... the association of sex not with mutual pleasure, much less caring, but with violent domination." It is sad to report that "our religious cultural heritage has been 'truly anti-pleasure' and...it has particularly reviled, and even tried to deny, the intense, sometimes ecstatic, pleasures of sex." How much damage has been done to male and female souls alike by this denigration of one of nature's greatest blessings?

Of course, we in the West do honor the phallus as a symbol of the masculine, but we do so in a perverted way; we hush it up, keep it "under wraps," and don't call it by its name. We don't apply it to the wonder and glory of our bodies or of the sacred. Instead, the skyscrapers that house our chieftains and captains of industry and commerce are such phallic idols. Many of our obelisks erected to honor our military victories are such. And our sports stadiums where we play our socially acceptable war games are built like vaginas. Out of prudishness, perhaps, we don't admit the sexuality in these symbols, and instead of temples to Divine Manhood, we get sexually and spiritually neutered shrines to the gods of war and finance, politics and media, sports and businesses, who all play their lethal games without interference of the heart. If the erect penis is, as Moore says, "a symbol of the life-force itself," then maybe one reason we do not honor it as such is that we are less interested in reverencing life than in reverencing our accomplishments of finance, power, war, and profit. Maybe to honor the "life-force itself" would put biophilia too much front and center. Where would all our necrophilia go? Eugene Monick believes that "a man's spirit is his phallic energy; it is spirit that triggers erection; it is spirit that pours forth in ejaculation. Spirit peaks and is gone. Phallos is exhausted. Man tastes a morsel of the end."

The dominator mentality has led to another sexual metaphor, that of "tops" and "bottoms," or what writer David Deida, in his masterful and frank book on male sexuality called *The Way of the Superior Man*, names "sexual polarity." In both heterosexual and homosexual lovemaking, Deida observes that the flow of sexual passion is often missing in modern relationships because, "if you want passion, you need a ravisher and a ravishee; otherwise you just have two buddies who decide to rub genitals in bed." It takes some game playing and imagination to break out of one's role — and the point is that there is no single role to play. We can all — woman with man, man with woman, man with man, woman with woman — break out of our rigid sexual identities and truly *play* at sex. If we don't, our passion dies. Deida writes: "If men and women are clinging to a politically correct sameness even in moments of intimacy, then sexual attraction disappears. I don't mean just the desire for intercourse, but the juice of the entire relationship begins to dry up. The love may still be strong, the friendship may still be strong, but the sexual polarity fades, unless *in moments of intimacy* one partner is willing to play the masculine pole and one partner is willing to play the feminine. You have to animate the masculine and feminine differences if you want to play in the field of sexual passion. . . . You don't need this difference for love, but you do need it for ongoing sexual passion."

THE MANY NAMES OF SEXUALITY

Sexuality goes by many names, most of which center around or are reduced to the act of sex. For some, sex is simply intercourse, penetration, fucking, orgasm, climaxing, and so on. But none of these words and names do the experience or our sexuality justice. They are stuck in literalism, and yet like any mystical experience, our sexuality is beyond words. It is "ineffable" as William James says and mystics like Meister Eckhart testify to. The act of sex is a metaphor for the mystical, all-encompassing nature of love, and this is what sacred representations of the phallus and of lovemaking attempt to remind us.

To expand the concept of the lover and sexuality, here are some other metaphors born from our experience of sexuality to consider and keep in mind. Sexuality is:

Union	Laughter
Communion	Joy
Passion	Ecstasy
Compassion	Emptying
Oneness	Rest
Birthing	Repose
Pleasure	Peace
Pain	Garden
Fulfillment	Delight

Connecting with generations   Promise
   of humans past   Shared Beauty
Connecting with generations   The Sacred Masculine
   of humans future   The Divine Feminine
Wetness   Love
Breath   Healing
Spirit   Reconciliation
Angelic envy   Forgiveness
Forgetfulness   Awe
Remembrance   Wildness
Death   Surrender
Life   Openness
Beginnings   Giving
Now   Ravishment
Ancestors   Play
God, Buddha, the Cosmic Christ   Commitment
Universe   Generativity
Evolution   Creativity
Hope

These are just a few of the metaphors generated by the concept of our sexuality, and to these I'm sure you can add many more of your own. No wonder sexuality enters so many realms of our lives, imaginations, and memories. No wonder sexuality is not easily corralled or locked up. Or forgotten.

People will do the most amazing things for sex. For sex our imaginations run overtime and in overdrive. We are hunter-gatherers for sex. Finding the perfect mate — or at least some mate — drives us to astonishing feats. And sex does amazing things to people. It makes one forget, get lost, remember, surrender, bless, curse, rest, smile, become parents, betray, cheat, be playful, take chances, take risks, get sick, be oneself, hate.

THE LOVER'S REVELATION

Yes, sex itself is indeed a metaphor for revelation. This is the realization awaiting the lover. That is why the Bible devotes an entire book to praising sexual love as a divine theophany, as the Garden of Eden redeemed, as the marriage of God and the human. The *Song of Songs* deserves more attention, for in its deep appreciation of sexuality it recalls teachings from religions around the world that sexuality is special. It is sacred. It is bigger than all of us. Integral to us all. It is a sacred power within that we choose to share with another sacred being. In sexuality the powers of intimacy, intensity, and immensity all come together. Thus sexuality is a mystical experience. Or it can be if we approach it less with ego and more with wonder and gratitude and playfulness.

David Deida observes that a man's relationship to the beauty of women can express itself as "obsession, distraction, *or revelation.*" This echoes Rabbi Abraham Heschel's observation that there are three ways to respond to creation: to exploit it, to enjoy it, or to accept it with awe. Sexuality is a deep part of creation; evolution invented it, we might say. Therefore, sexuality presents itself as 1) an object for exploitation; 2) an object for enjoyment; or 3) a subject for awe. It is the latter that acknowledges its sacred dimension. Spiritual traditions the world over have testified to the deep sacred dimension of sexuality, sexuality as revelation. In the West a fierce battle was fought in the twelfth century over the naming of marriage as a sacrament, and marriage won! The celibate monks lost that battle. Lovemaking is a sacrament, the living presence of the living God in our midst.

Anything as illuminating and light-filling as beauty casts a powerful shadow. The greater the light, the greater the shadow. Shadow sexuality — rape and abuse, power-over and power-under, homophobia, the very depths of the darkness generated by distorted sexuality — actually underscores the authentic power within healthy sexuality and generativity. Remember Matthew Shepard who died slowly through the night alone and roped to a fence enduring the fierce winds of a Wyoming plain — because he was gay. For some girls to be a girl is to be endangered or rendered a second-class citizen or turned into a slave on the market of sexual predators — because of one's sex, one's gender. If we face the truth of our deep attractions, we are capable of converting this energy into serving our mission on Earth. Deida observes, "A man's attraction to women must be converted from attraction to women into attraction through women." In other words, the beauty of anything that strikes us with awe is a doorway to something greater. The Source of all beauty. The Source of all awe and all attraction . . . and all sexuality. The omnipresence of beauty. Beauty everywhere and appreciated.

How do we accomplish this? Deida points out several steps. First is to recognize the fleetingness of beauty, the impermanence of it, the limits of it, and the omnipresence of death. Beauty is immortal but beautiful beings are mortal. "In your worship of women, never forget that they die. . . . Your sensations and feelings are fleeting. . . . Women can attract you, heal you and inspire your gifts but they will never satisfy you absolutely. Never. And you know this." Secondly, Deida advises that we use attractiveness as a "slingshot" that takes us beyond appearances and delivers us "to the source the women only promise." But ultimately, we are happiest when we "are relieved of the need to get anything at all from appearance. Just driving in your car, wanting nothing, watching the trees go by, can be an epiphany of perfection. Deep sleep, orgasm, a day of fishing, looking into an infant's eyes, these occasions can relax you from your search long enough to realize that you already have what you seek, that what appearances promise is a revelation of your own deep and inherently blissful nature."

This experience is called in Buddhism our "deep and inherently blissful nature," what I call "original blessing" and what Meister Eckhart calls "repose," and it is available to us all. All beauty can take us there. Provided we do not cling to the "object" of the beauty or indeed to objects at all. This requires that we not treat the "object" of our lust as an object but as a subject. A subject of our desire is someone we can play with, an equal, one we seek to satisfy, and not someone whose role is merely to satisfy us. Mutuality matters.

Subject-subject relationships thus replace subject-object ones. Much is shared. And when this happens, we journey to the Subject of subjects, whom Buddhists call the Buddha Nature, Judaism calls Wisdom, and Christianity calls the Cosmic Christ. It is that power in nature (including human nature) that binds, as St. Paul said, "everything in the heavens and everything on earth together." Deida puts it this way: "Desire can be a doorway to deep oneness. . . . The revelation of deep oneness is love. Women can seem to bring you to your true nature. Or they can seem to take you away from it. Each moment of appearance and of women may be a distraction, an obsession or a revelation. Notice the distractions — tits, ass, wealth, and fame — and practice the revelation of oneness by feeling through the distractions. . . . Bow down through your woman into the deep." This is mystical language, language of the *unio mystica*. It is wise and appropriate. The Lover seeks ever-deeper layers of love.

Deida wisely encourages us to "feel lust. Feel what it really is, in its totality. Your lust reveals your real desire to unite with the feminine, to penetrate as deeply as possible, to receive her delicious light as radiant food for your masculine soul, and to give her your entirety, losing yourself in the giving, so that you are both liberated beyond your selves in the explosion of your gifts." He also recommends that the sexualizing of one's energy not be restricted to the act of sex alone but that it inform one's relationship to the world itself. "This explosion of giving could be the basis of your life, not just a moment of sexual yielding. When you feel sexual lust or desire for any woman, breathe deeply and allow the feeling of desire to magnify. And allow it to magnify more. Don't let the energy become lodged in your head or genitals, but circulate it throughout your body. Using your breath as the instrument of circulation, bathe every cell in the stimulated energy. Inhale it into your heart, and then feel outward from your heart, feeling the world as if it were your lover."

Joseph Jastrab also connects sexuality and cosmos when he writes that "a mature relationship with Eros is fundamental to the recovery of sacred manhood. By Eros I mean the passion for connection that is immanent to the entire universe. By sacred I mean the felt experience, or em-body-ment, of that connection or union.... A sacred erotic sensibility has to do with establishing a love relationship with the entire universe *through the body*." And why not, since the universe invented sex and sexuality about one billion years ago.

SPERM

Male sexuality includes a unique creation that men produce: sperm. This substance, as we all learned at some point in our adolescence, is a biological necessity for human reproduction. In a lifetime, "the normal male ejaculates enough semen to generate one trillion human lives." What an "immense reservoir of psychic energy" we carry within us, to use Chia's words. The delivery system for sperm is quite amazing and fascinating, as the temples to the phallus in so many parts of the world demonstrate. So the question arises: Is sperm also a metaphor, or is it only a literal gift of our sexuality that we share with another? What is sperm?

I asked this question recently of a group of mostly men and some women. The instructions were to take five to seven minutes to write a simple, spontaneous answer. I was struck by the poetry of the reflections and offer some of them here:

> "Sperm is offered in the love orgasmic echo of the birth movement of the cosmos, chaotic energies dancing their way out into the universe of possibilities of new life unique and implicate in the beginning but never before incarnate, and never to 'come' again."

> "Sperm (half of life) is juicy, smooth, playful, wet cuz sometimes it might need to stick to eggs! Or simply want to adhere to another.

Blessed body booze! Wriggling, leaping, fairy wine valiant warrior seeking welcome Home Sperm... seeking home... penetrate for welcome, Welcome home I say... Welcome home!!!"

"Sperm is life celebrating; it is warm and wet and precious — it longs to be released. It is the culmination of struggle and play. It is both external and internal, life-giving and life-taking. It emerges through will and through imagination. It has scent and taste and texture of its own design."

"Sperm is genetic engine of life
Droplets of divine oceanic water
Raindrops of coital heat
Sweat bullets of eros consummated."

"Sperm is part of the gift men bring in their role of co-creator with the divine. It brings with it history, design, and characteristics that will shape the new life. Without it the 'human species' cannot continue. It is the nectar produced as expression of love, sexual intimacy; it is the male body giving of its self-surrender to the other."

"Sperm is a sexual mystery — essential element of the symphony of life — often being deconstructed, packaged, isolated from the men and maleness producing it — sperm banks, cloning, purposefully single mothers, men who do not understand or value the mystery beyond immediate pleasure, courts and mothers who lack an understanding to value the maleness from whom sperm comes."

"What is Sperm? My contribution to the continued co-creation of the human race; a tangible manifestation of the deep-felt passion for life expressed in celebrating of the self and with another; my link to my genetic and ancestral past; my chance to taste the Divine Orgasm that is Creation and is Creating throughout the Cosmos in and through me.

"The Orgasmic Moment: the Orgasmic Moment is the momentary experience of the Immense and Intense Divine Love of the Creator; so intense, that if it lasted for more than a few moments it would cause a total systemic overload in the human person — to feel so *loved* so *totally* by the Divine One who created us."

One man said he could not put the meaning of sperm into words. Instead he heard music in his head. So I invited him to play the music on a piano, and he did so. It was charged and powerful and beautiful. I also wrote about sperm:

"Sperm is very special. It is not just 'spunk' or 'man juice' or 'cum' — though it is all that. All the liquids we give out have their purpose and their stories to tell: Tears tell us of sorrow and grief and also joy and happiness and being moved; sweat tells us of our efforts physical and intentional; pee tells us of our health and is a story of our capacities to recycle. But what stories does sperm tell us? Sperm tells us of our ancestors. Yes, sperm is where we carry so much of our ancestral memory and inheritance. Sperm is ALL the DNA of our ancestors, mixed and matched from both sides of our families, mom's and dad's ancestors, and mixed with our utter uniqueness. Our sperm is both our ancestor's DNA AND our own unique DNA wrapped into one gushing, wet, powerful, unstoppable, ecstatic, memorable, generative moment. It is what we have to give. Nothing less. Ourselves.

"Now everyone knows the truth of what I say: our sperm becomes our babies, along with of course our woman's egg, a fact of life we did not know as a species until c. 200 years ago. For a long time we thought the sperm did ALL the production of babies. And this is why babies are special and fun and important...and US. But what about those who choose to share their sperm not with the potential mother but with another man. That is very special. To share one's ancestors — one's special lineage — with another of any sex is very special. Not having babies in mind makes it more 'in this moment.' It makes pregnant the MOMENT ITSELF. No waiting for 9 months' gestation. The birth is already happening. The child is there NOW. Look around. Man-to-man sex is about the now. More than man-to-woman sex is. 'Living in the now' is what all mysticism is about. One can meditate and focus on one's breath; but one can also meditate and focus on one's partner's sperm. And the passionate and sometimes noisy giving and receiving of that sperm.

"We give our sperm in great generosity, great thrusting, great desire. And we receive it in the same way. Sperm giving is a mystical act. And sperm receiving too. Like grace before meals, it is a THANK YOU to the universe and to creation. Sperm is truly 14 billion years old, that is, it contains 14 billion years of cosmic history — yet it lands in a particular place and from a particular individual to another particular individual. And wrapped into it is 14 billion years of gestation and birthing coming from the fireball, the galaxies, the supernovas, the stars, the sun, the Earth, the water — coming from 'all our ancestors.' No wonder it means so much and we feel so deeply when we deliver sperm. The delivery of sperm is so memorable a moment, like the delivery of a baby for a heterosexual couple perhaps. A sacred moment. The passing on of the lineage."

Eugene Monick draws further lessons from a reflection on sperm:

> Natural wisdom tells a male that catastrophic consequence is always present, actually or potentially, as in the fate of his sperm.... What the sperm experiences in its life struggle toward ovum is the ground or archetypal pattern for a man's daily struggle for virility. Body awareness that but one sperm will succeed, two million will die, is the raw material of masculine psyche, the fuel for a male's terror of fate.

MALE INFERTILITY: A REFLECTION

When I asked the group above "What is sperm?" one man found the exercise very difficult because he suffers from male infertility — his sperm cannot conceive a child. Afterward, David was willing and courageous enough to talk with me about his difficulty, and his situation is a powerful example of how literalism can cripple our lives and of how metaphor can free us from literalism and unlock our full potential. When we embrace the archetype of the Lover, we become not just lovers but Lovers who are able to step over any of life's roadblocks to create, generate, love, and nurture.

Infertility, it turns out, is a problem shared by one in eight Canadian couples. Thirty percent are due to a male factor, thirty percent to female, and thirty percent are "unexplained," with no clear cause. David and his wife eventually learned that their infertility troubles were due to a male factor, and this led to years of soul searching, for each of them individually and as a couple. In response to my question about sperm, David said: "The notion of 'sperm' is a complicated and grief-bearing subject for those couples who cannot conceive due to infertility. I think the men who suffer male factor infertility simply suffer in silence, or cloak it in matter-of-factness. Or frame it as a shared reality within the couple relationship. Still, there is loss and grief for the couple in general and the man in particular."

David's story is a reminder for couples with healthy sperm and eggs to *not take it for granted*. If you are fertile, be grateful. But more than that, nearly all men experience grief around their sexuality at some point because of some issue. David's story is a brave and beautiful example for any couple wrestling with infertility, but it also helps all men see how grief and loss connected with their sexuality can be reframed in healthy and life-giving ways.

With his permission, here is the story David wrote to me:

In our case, the situation is male factor infertility. We had been trying to have children for a number of years without success. What we learned is that infertility is a quiet not-often-talked about medical problem, which family physicians don't like to talk about either. When I approached my family physician (where I was living at the time) and indicated that we were having difficulty conceiving, his answer was, "Go home and love your wife more." Needless to say, not helpful or even appropriate. No further investigation followed.

When we arrived in High River, we connected with a family doctor who "fast-tracked" the investigation, and it wasn't more than a couple of days before we had conclusive evidence that as a couple we were not going to have any children. That news came on Halloween, when we were faced with more than a hundred trick-or-treaters. We would go to the door, hand out the candy, go back to the sofa, and grab a Kleenex and cry — again and again.

We were then referred to the fertility clinic in Calgary. After a long wait our appointment came, and at that meeting we were presented with two options. One was ICSI (intra cytoplasmic sperm injection), where a single sperm is injected into the egg and then planted in the womb through IVF (in vitro fertilization). The procedure costs thousands of dollars, involves risk, is very invasive, and in our case not likely a good choice. Plus, if we were to conceive a male child, the child may end up in the same boat as me, because the specialist felt there was a genetic cause to the infertility itself. Two, donor insemination, where an anonymous donor's sperm is artificially inseminated.

We also investigated adoption. Again, private adoption is very costly, public adoption is very lengthy — we were already in our late thirties, and international adoption was financially out of the question for us living on pastor's salaries.

After a great deal of consideration, we settled on donor insemination

— a form of "early adoption." Susan became pregnant quite quickly, and we were on the way to becoming parents.

At the time, the process was like a roller coaster. I had to get my head and heart around the decisions we were making. I had to reframe my relationship between biology and parenting. While there would be no biological connection between me and my children, I had to think through and feel through the notion of the father relationship and trust that this, in fact, is the most significant connection of the two. Of course, it is. But at the time, the prospect of raising a donor child was totally unfamiliar territory and *not* the social status quo.

During the later stages of our pregnancy, the Canadian federal government was proposing legislation on NRTs (new reproductive technologies) that included a piece requiring that donors no longer be compensated. At the time, male donors were financially compensated (minimally) for their time and for the discomfort of lab procedures, which were in place in order to ward off any genetics or diseases that may be unsafe for the mom and/or the child. As a couple, we took a position against the government because we believed that if financial compensation was dropped, so would the number of donors. We wrote the government and ended up being invited to witness before a House of Commons committee in Ottawa. We were given five minutes. We read from a carefully prepared statement, arguing that donors needed to be compensated in order to ensure enough donors. We were heard well. The Members of Parliament approached us after the hearing, and I think they learned more from those five minutes than from many of the lobbyists that had appeared earlier. Unfortunately, an election was called soon after, and all the work on that bill was dropped.

We now have two amazing boys. We have been open with them from the beginning regarding their origin, and I am amazed at the mystery of it all. While I sometimes wish for the more conventional model of conceiving, because I grieve that possibility and will never know it, I realize that I would not have the boys I have and that my love for them could never be surpassed. They are my sons, and I could imagine it no other way.

Recently, I was called to do an interview with a class of undergrads in the Maritimes around the ethics of NRTs and speak directly from my experience. It felt good, and I think it reframed the notion of "fathering" and parenting for the students.

So, in response to your reflections on "sperm" the other day, I really feel that infertility causes us to reframe the notion of cosmic biology, progeny, and generativity. I cannot pass on my genes and otherwise ensure that the universe carries on. But in a much broader way, the contribution that I make is equally amazing. First, I had to be very clear and intentional that I wanted to parent because the sometimes accidental but most often conventional means was not available to us as a couple. Second, in partnership, we as a couple have had to be very clear about how we are contributing to the cosmos and how our wisdom in parenting and living is as equally and powerfully generative. And third, the whole experience has called out of me the wonderings about how my values, actions, and personal mission in the world contribute to the overall community and cosmos of which I am a part.

SEXUAL DIVERSITY AND THE LOVER

Science tells us that the invention of sexuality in the universe, which occurred about one billion years ago, had the effect of increasing novelty and diversity at astounding new rates and proportions. Sex and the act of two beings creating a third is all about diversity; it introduces and produces genetic diversity. This is clear from the variety of characteristics one encounters in just one family: different eye colors, hair colors, and so on. But it's not just biological diversity: we are all "born with" different personalities, smiles, temperaments, and interests. All this is evidence of the scientific fact that sexuality produces variation and multiplicity.

Gender, sexual attraction, gender roles, and even gender preference are part of this diversity. Sexuality, as an archetype of universal creativity, is not a machine that manufactures clones; nature never makes two humans completely alike (even twins have different fingerprints), and it constantly experiments. It is ironic that those who claim that heterosexual sex is the only "normal" expression of sexuality are in fact disputed by the universe itself: life brims with diversity. The universe is biased in favor of diversity. The universal urge for diversity does not extend to everything else except sexuality. It extends across the board, to everything, including homosexuals and transgendered persons. Humanity has to open its mind to these realities.

Recently the Anglican archbishop of Nigeria, who is leading a chorus of other bishops to banish gay blessings and gay clergy from the Anglican church, said that homosexuality is not found among other species. This is a frequent claim, and it is simply wrong. He and other like-minded clerics ought to read more than scriptural texts. They should read scientists who have studied creation and have found that so far 464 other species have been observed with homosexual populations. The Anglican archbishop of Nigeria exemplifies a religious ideology that the "word of God" is all found in a book (which, one presumes, keeps illiterate persons from participating in the "word of God"), and that clerics must preach solely from that book, the Bible. They ignore the Bible that is Nature. (It was common practice in premodern Christianity to acknowledge Nature as revelation. Meister Eckhart said, "every creature is a word of God and a book about God.")

Yet, the modern world is also showing signs of considerable progress in its awareness and acceptance of sexual diversity. Countries like Spain, Canada, Belgium, and others are offering gay marriage, while other countries, like the United States, are openly debating the issues of equal rights for gay couples. Even as I was writing this book, a court in Massachusetts rejected a case brought by fundamentalist parents who objected to children being told in school that gay relationships exist. The court ruled that public schools are "entitled to teach anything that is reasonably related to the goals of preparing students to become engaged and productive citizens in our democracy." And, "diversity is a hallmark of our nation.... The Constitution does not permit them [parents] to prescribe what those children will be taught [in public schools]." And the Supreme Court of California recently ruled that denying gay and lesbian persons the right to marry is an offense against the Constitution because it denies equal rights to all citizens.

It is especially true today that among young adults there is greater acceptance of sexual diversity. Thanks to the bravery of many gay people coming out of the closet over the last decades, often at considerable risk and cost, young people today know that they go to high school with gay people; they know relatives who are gay; and they know professional athletes, politicians, actors, musicians, artists, and other public figures who are gay. Young adults are learning the vital lesson that the diversity of sexuality is part of the picture of being human. But clearly, much more needs to happen. Societywide, homophobia remains very strong, and it still sometimes leads to violence, humiliation, and even murder (as with the killing of Matthew Shepard).

HONORING, AND LEARNING FROM,
THE GIFTS OF HOMOSEXUALITY

It really is quite astounding to me that nature is so committed to sexual diversity and homosexuality. Studies have shown that about 8–10 percent of any given human population is gay or lesbian, and most of these persons are born from heterosexual parents. What are the odds of this happening randomly? Why does nature insist on homosexuality as an ordinary and persistent sexual diversity? There must be a reason or reasons. My own guess is that homosexuals offer humanity certain vital gifts that society would be foolish to refuse. Here is a list of four:

1. *The gift of creativity.* No one can look at the work of homosexuals and not be struck by the inordinate amount of creativity that homosexual individuals and communities provide to society. This creativity is evident in the arts as well as the sciences, and it extends to the exercise of sexual practice itself.

2. *A flexible perspective on gender provides a kind of bridge between men and women.* Heterosexuals in particular can become stuck in their society-created gender roles, and homosexuals remind everyone that sexuality exists in the realm of *metaphor* and not literalism. When one's sexual role is not determined by one's body parts, life, imagination, and passion come alive. David Deida observes that "the gay and lesbian community is acutely aware that the sexual polarity is independent of gender. But you still need two poles for a passionate play of sexuality to persist in a relationship: masculine and feminine, top and bottom, butch and femme — whatever you want to call these reciprocal poles of sexual play." Gays and lesbians have much to teach the straight world about sexuality and about restoring passion to relationships.

3. *Humor.* By definition, role-playing does not take things literally. To see gender as a "role" moves us beyond the ego, and it creates a space for fun and humor in sexual play. So often, sexuality becomes burdened with shame, guilt, fear, or self-consciousness, and so it becomes too serious. But healthy spirituality is unselfconscious (as Eckhart pointed out), and so too is healthy sexuality. Yes, sexuality can lead to children, and the Lover becomes the Father (or the Parent), and that is a serious thing with serious responsibilities. But sexuality itself is about process as much as procreation, and the Lover does more than

create babies. Sex can be funny, clownish, humorous, and full of laughter. An Inuit saying is that to make love is to make laughter happen. Within homosexual and transgender communities, sexuality and gender roles are sources of humor and play. This is a very important teaching. Don't take sexuality and gender literally. It is too important for that and too much fun for that.

4. *Spirituality*. There is a long history in many cultures of homosexuals as spiritual leaders. Many years ago, a Native American woman took me aside and said to me that it is well known among Native Americans that gay persons have always been the spiritual directors to their great chiefs. Homosexuals, it seems, don't just bridge male and female worlds, but human and spiritual worlds. A homophobic society deprives itself of a deeper spirituality. This same woman (who was also a Catholic sister) said: "When I give retreats to gay groups, it is always a deeper experience than just giving a retreat to a mixed and mostly heterosexual crowd."

Many Native American cultures recognize that a gay person (called a *berdache* or *winkte*) holds special spiritual powers: of healing, of leading some ceremonies, and of seeing into the future. Lame Deer, a Lakota shaman, says such a person "has a gift of prophecy and that he himself could predict the weather.... If nature puts a burden on a man by making him different, it also gives him a power." Michael One Feather, a gay Indian who grew up on a South Dakota reservation, tells his story this way: "I didn't know about [the *winkte's*] spiritual role until I took an American Indian studies class in high school. The teacher said that *winktes* were holy people who should be respected. A long time ago they went on the warpath with the warriors and took care of them and nursed them." Much of the animus against the Indians exhibited by the original Spanish conquistadors was an animus against homosexuality, which was quite open among the Mayans. The missionaries chimed in with their hatred along with the conquistadors. Ceremonies that honored berdaches were forbidden in the strongest language when the colonizers took over.

Traditionalist Indians may criticize gay people not for their sexual behavior but because they are not fulfilling their spiritual role in the community. One Indian woman whose uncle is *winkte* says: "People who don't respect their Indian traditions criticize gays, but it was part of Indian culture. It makes me mad when I hear someone insult *winktes*. A lot of the younger gays, though, don't fulfill their spiritual role as *winktes*, and that's sad too."

For all these reasons I am convinced that there can be no authentic masculine spirituality without exorcising homophobia. In the face of a frequently homophobic society, it takes a spiritual warrior to do so. But every man must refuse to hide and dare to stand up for their homosexual brothers and sisters, uncles and aunts, fathers and mothers, children and nephews, nieces and coworkers. The gay liberation movement is everyone's movement, just as Martin Luther King Jr. taught when he said that justice denied anyone is justice denied us all.

It is one thing for heterosexuals to tolerate gays, to accept that they have a right to exist. It is something else to admit that *one has something to learn from gays*, to honor their experience as personally valuable. This is similar to overcoming racism, where one first acknowledges and respects other races or ethnicities, and then comes to see that the "other" or outsider has provided them with unique, enlightening, and even essential truths. The time is come for heterosexual men to listen to the stories and ways and spiritualities of homosexual men. In this way, the diversity that the universe proposes will be respected, and the Lover in each man will have access to the full breadth of his love and creativity.

What can homosexual men and heterosexual men working together give birth to? We can take the lost and wasted energy of homophobia and recycle it into community awakenings in so many fields. The fear behind homophobia holds men back, and fear and love are hardly compatible. Fear makes one shrink and become defensive; love expands and connects.

In the realm of lovemaking, what heterosexual man isn't interested in accessing more of the four gifts of homosexuality I list above: creativity, role-playing flexibility, humor, and spirituality? Eros wants all that for us. Overcoming homophobia is a way for heterosexual men to become not just better lovers but spiritual and cultural healers. Overcoming homophobia provides gifts for everyone, since it also helps heal the shame, abuse, and marginalization that many homosexual men have experienced, both as boys and as men. It also provides a liberation for gay men and women, and resolving homophobia can heal generational differences. No matter what our parents and grandparents might have believed, we are the parents and grandparents of the next generations, nearly one in ten of whom will be gay. Healing our homophobia helps heal them before they even arrive.

Recently a newspaper article quoted a heterosexual man who was told by a very attractive woman, "I thought you were gay." About this, the man replied, "I was flattered. Gay men are as a rule smarter, in better shape, and more alive than the heterosexual men I know." Over the years a number of women I know have told me they kept falling in love with gay men (not knowing they were gay) because gay men understood women so much better and they projected a more attractive interest in life and the arts and their own bodies. As these stories give evidence, a healthy, attractive masculinity and spirituality is more than sexual preference and gender identity, and this is something heterosexual men can learn from homosexuals.

SEXUALITY AS SACRED

Poet Gary Snyder defines the sacred this way: "*Sacred* refers to that which helps take us (not only human beings) out of our little selves into the whole mountains-and-rivers mandala universe.... The wilderness as a temple is only a beginning." I believe that ultimately we will never understand sexuality in all its wonderful diversity without placing it in this context of the "mandala universe," the context of the Sacred. This is surely why we have an entire book in the Bible dedicated to the theophany, the God-experience, the God-revelation that sexuality can be. To see sexuality as sacred — everyone's, not just one's own, but surely beginning with one's own — supports our efforts to see every person and indeed every being as sacred, and thus not to be abused, used, or objectified. It is to see another (both human and more than human) as connected to us, yearning to love us, to kiss us, and to make laughter and babies (both metaphorical and literal) together. It is to act on what Baudelaire observed more than a century ago: "We walk through forests of physical things that are also spiritual things that look on us with affectionate looks." The world is sexual, the world is affectionate, the world wants our love, and the world bestows its love and affection on us. We can fall in love with hills and trees, flowers and rivers, birds and animals as well as with people. It is all erotic. It is all sexual. Trust yourself. Fall in love again. And take that reawakening to your partner and start your love life over again.

After all, a mandala universe is a healing universe. Some men believe, if they commit to their sexual beingness, that they will go overboard with their sexuality. Frankly, such men flatter themselves. I think most men err in the opposite direction — they hold in the holiness and awesomeness of their sexuality and sexual energy. I believe, beyond being heterosexual, homosexual, or bi-sexual, that we are pansexual. Ultimately, embracing the archetype of the lover means recovering our pansexuality, which nurtures and feeds all our relation-ships, including our humanly sexual ones.

Sexuality is sacred because it is bigger than all of us. That is also why it is irrepressible, funny, fun, amazing, surprising, generative, serious, playful, mys-tical, and unpredictable. It is one area in our relationship with the cosmos and with Father Sky that has never fully succumbed to anthropocentric mastering and control. Sexuality thrusts us into a relationship with the cosmos. Which is a big part of its appeal. A big part of our staying alive. A big part of the joy of living.

7

OUR COSMIC AND ANIMAL BODIES

WHEN WE HONOR THE GREEN MAN ARCHETYPE, we honor what we hold in common with the plant and vegetative world. When we honor our powers of lovemaking, we honor our sexuality, our creative and generative nature. In this chapter, we will celebrate the body itself. It, too, is a metaphor. Some religions have considered the body fallen, as sinfully separate from God. Other philosophies characterize our bodies as prisons of consciousness, from which it is impossible to escape. The ancient Upanishads of India speak wisely of the proper attitude toward our bodies when they declare: "To darkness are they doomed who worship only the body and to greater darkness they who worship only the spirit.... They who worship both the body and the spirit, by the body overcome death, and by the spirit achieve immortality."

THE AMAZING HUMAN BODY

Our bodies link directly to Father Sky. This is just one of the profound lessons emerging from today's cosmology. Science has now demonstrated that our bodies are formed of the "stuff of the stars" (a teaching John Calvin begged to hear five hundred years ago): 60 percent of the atoms of our bodies are hydrogen and helium atoms, which were birthed in the original fireball 13.7 billion years ago. The other 40 percent of our bodies' atoms were birthed in supernova explosions about 5 billion years ago. We are made of ancient stuff — yet it has all come together to fashion the workable, beautiful, useable instrument that is our body.

Our bodies are truly amazing. One human body — yours or mine — contains a hundred times more cells than there are stars in the galaxy. We are composed of 100 trillion cells and two hundred different kinds of cells. All 100 trillion cells communicate with each other like an orchestra to produce one whole sound — our body. If the DNA in our body's cells were uncoiled and laid end to end, it would reach to the moon and back a hundred thousand times! Our heart weighs only half a pound, but daily it works the equivalent of lifting a ton from the ground up to the top of a five-story building. Our blood vessels, if laid end to end, would encircle the Earth more than two times — they are 60,000 miles long. Our kidneys clean and reclean forty gallons of blood per day, while they maintain an exact proportion of water and chemical balance in the blood. Our bodies are home to six hundred bones. Our bones are four times stronger than steel or reinforced concrete, yet they are very lightweight and grow back when they are broken. Our skin and brain develop from exactly the same primitive cells, thus we could say the skin is the outer surface of the brain, or the brain is the deepest layer of the skin.

Touch is the oldest of the senses and the most urgent. If a hungry lion is touching a paw on your backside, you want to know about it as soon as possible. Smell was the second of our senses, and indeed our cerebral hemispheres were originally buds from the olfactory stalks. Thus we think because we smelled. If we spread our lungs out, they would fill a tennis court and their purpose is to bring oxygen into contact with blood. As naturalist Diane Ackerman says, "With every breath we inhale millions of molecules of sky, heat them briefly, and then exhale them back into the world." This is cosmology at its most intimate. Our skin is not only the largest organ of our body but also key to sexual attraction. One square inch of human skin contains 19 million cells, 625 sweat glands, 90 oil glands, 65 hairs, 19 blood vessels, 19,000 sensory cells, and more than 20 million microscopic animals. The three tiniest bones in our body are in our ears. It is thanks to them that we can hear sounds. Skin is an extension of our ear, so we actually hear with our whole bodies. Our larynx lies deep in our throat, which gives us a unique capacity for speech and singing. Scientist Arne Wyller calls the human eye "the supreme seeing device created by Nature." The human retina contains 100 million rods and cones.

However, the human brain, composed of one trillion cells, outshines the other organs. Wyller compares the human brain to the collective linking of 100 million microcomputers. Most synapses in the brains of mammals are chemical, while those in most invertebrates are electrical. The mammalian brain is the "fastest-developing organ in evolutionary history," having tripled in size over the past four million years. As Wyller puts it: "With the development of the human brain, we have moved into the area of Nature's grandest design scheme. In the creation of the human animal 2 billion years of primitive cell development and 800 million years of multicellular life form development culminate — though with a spectacular brain development (the cerebral cortex) that took only a few million years." Each second, more than 100,000 chemical reactions take place in the brain. The brain produces more than fifty psychoactive drugs that affect memory, intelligence, sedation, and aggression.

Who can say that our bodies are anything except amazing? We need to "accept them with awe" as Heschel taught. We need never to take them for granted. Often, we only truly appreciate them when they fail us — when we suffer an injury or a disease. Only then do we recognize the wonder of how our body works so wonderfully well. Consider: we couldn't run, jump, walk, swim, skate, climb, embrace, kiss, wrestle, make love, eat, sing, dance, paint, sleep, write, or think without our body. All we do we do with our body. And that includes pray and communicate with the divine: body and Soul, body and consciousness, go hand in glove.

BODY AS SHADOW

How much are we in touch with the wonder of our bodies? How much do we respect our bodies? As a culture, the United States is obsessed with how bodies look, but it still does not take very good care of them.

National health officials have said that America is in a "public health crisis." According to Dr. James Marks, senior vice president at the Robert Wood Johns Foundation, it is estimated that 32 percent of Americans currently are obese (obesity being defined as being 20–25 percent over the ideal weight for one's height). In part, this is the result of the sugars and transfats in processed foods and the hormones pumped into the animals that we eat, but lack of exercise is also a big factor. The poor are especially beset with this problem, since "the cheapest foods are the worst for you," says Dr. Marks. The five poorest states are all in the top ten for obesity rates. As a society we also deny healthcare to 30 percent of our citizens.

Why are we, individually and as a society, not honoring our bodies?

Bioenergetics expert and psychiatrist John Conger says that in modern society we have become so distant from our original animal selves that "the body *is* the shadow." He continues:

> The victory of an overrationalized life is promoted at the expense of the more primitive and natural vitality. For those who can read the body, it holds the record of our rejected side, revealing what we dare not speak, expressing our current and past fears. The body as shadow is predominantly the body as "character," the body as bound energy that is unrecognized and untapped, unacknowledged and unavailable.

Humans are animals, and talking about our bodies means recognizing and acknowledging our connection to the *animal world*. The hunter-gatherer in us, as we saw in chapter four, is at home with animals, but are we still at home with our animal nature? Is that the shadow, the fear and the suspicion behind the neglect of our bodies? Jung felt it was, and this is how he describes our relationship to the animal bodies we carry:

> The body is the original animal condition; we are all animals in the body, and so we should have animal psychology in order to be able to live in it.... Since we have a body it is indispensable that we exist also as an animal, and each time we invent a new increase of consciousness we have to put a new link in the chain that binds us to the animal, till finally it will become so long that the complications will surely ensue.

Jung invokes an old symbol of an eagle flying high in the air, and from his body a chain connects to a toad creeping along on the earth. In part, we are dealing with a theological issue, the pessimistic teaching of original sin. For if the body is our "original animal condition," and we believe we are originally sinful, then our bodies carry blame and shame. Conger observes this pessimism in Western consciousness, which especially affects our sexuality: "Unfortunately, in the unfolding drama of Western culture, the mind of man has become divorced from his body. Sexuality, in particular, has been linked with an undesirable animal element, a demonic force that corrupts man's true spiritual nature.... Western culture has denied the value of sexuality." But if we are born into the world as original blessings, then our bodies are a blessing and not a sinful "package." We have every right to explore, test, wonder at, reverence, and give thanks for our bodies and all they can do.

If fear of sexuality relates directly to concepts of sin, our "overrationalized life" is not just a religious issue. It applies to our entire secular work world. How engaged are our bodies in our work? Does our profession "respect" the body? Conger believes, speaking of his own profession, that "psychology has been in danger of becoming body-phobic. We forget the foundations. Our elevator doesn't go all the way to the bottom floor." Surely our educational programs from childhood through professional schools rarely engage and respect the body. Carl Jung put it this way: "It has forever been the aspiration of mankind to fly like a bird, to become a wind, a breath; and it can be done but it is paid for by the loss of the body, or the loss of humanity which is the same thing." To lose our bodiliness is to lose our humanity and our sense of community. As humans we are united by our bodies. We all have bodies in common.

Scott Sanders believes that much of our addictive behavior derives from a vain effort to recover our senses. He observes: "Much of the world we have made starves our senses. As we insulate ourselves from wildness, retreating farther and farther inside our boxes, love loses piquancy, variety, delight. So we gamble or drink or jolt ourselves with drugs; we jump from airplanes with parachutes strapped to our backs, or jump from bridges with elastic ropes tied to our ankles; we ride mechanical bucking bulls in bars or drive fast cars or shoot guns, hunting for a lost thrill. We cruise the malls on the lookout for something, anything, to fill the void. Bored with surroundings that we have so thoroughly tamed, we flee into video games, films, pulp novels, shopping channels, the Internet. But all of those efforts eventually pall. As the novelty wears off, once more our senses go numb, so we crank up the speed, the volume, the voltage."

OUR SACRED BODIES

Many spiritual traditions honor the body as a temple; this is an ancient, enduring association. Recently, I participated in a Lakota sweat lodge in which the Lakota elder instructed us to treat our bodies as if they were temples. St. Paul, the first Christian theologian, used it in his letter to the believers in the city of Corinth, and he did so at a time when many Corinthians were selling their bodies for money.

But what is the meaning of this metaphor? What is a temple, and how should we treat our bodies like one? According to the dictionary, a temple is a "holy dwelling, a place where something holy or divine is thought to dwell." The Latin word *templum* meant a space marked out for observation of auguries. It is probably related to the word *tempus*, meaning "time," because a temple is a place of special times, of suspended or mystical time (a place where time is suspended or lost). *Temple* can mean an "edifice for religious exercises" or a "place devoted to a special purpose."

Surely our bodies echo these various meanings of temple. They are holy dwellings, spaces marked out for observations (if not auguries), places where we undergo special times (even suspended and mystical times), and places devoted to special purposes. A temple is also a "meeting place." Surely our bodies are meeting places. That is what makes them great, awesome, and sacred. Our bodies are where the cosmos and our conscious self meet, for as we noted, our bodies contain atoms from the cosmos itself, atoms cooked in the original fireball 14 million years ago, atoms cooked in supernova explosions 4.5 million years ago. Our bodies also contain the DNA of our ancestors, *all* of them, so each one is a meeting place for the entire human race. Our bodies are marvelous, and therefore miraculous, since the principal meaning of "miraculous" is that which makes us marvel, that which inspires awe. Every body is worthy of our awe and wonder and marveling — yours and mine and everyone we encounter. Do we meditate on this, on the holiness of our bodies?

Also, our bodies are "meeting places" for our chakras, and each chakra is itself a "meeting place" — that is, an *intersection* (the literal meaning of "chakra"), a place where powers come together. We shall explore the chakras later in this chapter, for they help us understand the sacred powers and wonders of our bodies.

A temple is not merely a meeting place, however, or else it would be no different than a market. A temple is also sacred. But what is the "sacred"? As Gary Snyder said, the sacred "helps take us out of our little selves into the whole mountains-and-rivers mandala universe." Do our bodies take us into the "mandala universe," into the cosmos? Of course they do. We think and feel with our bodies; we imagine and dream with our bodies. We eat, and when we do, we are eating the cosmos, eating the plants that have eaten the sun. We create new life with our bodies, and we literally take our bodies into space. Surely all this qualifies as taking us out of our little selves into the big universe.

Considering this, we can treat everything we do as a living and ongoing meditation on our connection to the cosmos. We can befriend, love, care for, and feed our bodies in ways that honor Spirit and cosmos. By keeping ourselves healthy we are actively and directly keeping the universe healthy. It also follows that we are meant to admire the beauty of our bodies — and everyone's body is beautiful, everyone's body is sacred. Community is enhanced by beauty, and beauty calls us to admire it; as Aquinas said, "All beauty yearns to be conspicuous." Young people like to strut their beauty. Why not? We all need beauty in our lives. The challenge for us today is to recognize all human bodies as beautiful, to recognize all of them as displays of love and Spirit, as expressions of inner beauty. Temples were not built to be homely, but to inspire with majesty, and so we can wonder at the awesome majesty of every human body and behold its beauty.

In *The Practice of the Wild*, Gary Snyder identifies the sacred with the wild, and this truth is altogether appropriate and applicable to the metaphor of our bodies as sacred temples. Our bodies are indeed wild — they are wild in their design and wild in their execution; that is, they accomplish wild things together with the wild imaginations that we all carry inside us. But they also seek peace and repose. Our bodies find a dialectic, learn to dance between wildness and repose, just like nature balances the busyness of the day with the tranquility of night's darkness. Sleep prepares our bodies for still more wild things the coming day.

Snyder elaborates on wildness, the sacred, and the body: "Our bodies are wild. The involuntary quick turn of the head at a shout, the vertigo at looking off a precipice, the heart-in-the-throat in a moment of danger, the catch of the breath, the quiet moments relaxing, staring, reflecting — all universal responses of this mammal body.... The body does not require the intercession of some conscious intellect to make it breathe, to keep the heart beating. It is to a great extent self-regulating, it is a life of its own.... The body is, so to speak, in the mind. They are both wild." This is similar to medieval mystics who reminded us that the body is in the soul, not the soul in the body. Our bodies are instruments of our souls; they go where our souls ask them to go. They dance when our souls feel like dancing; they mourn when our souls feel like grieving; they skip lightly when our souls are uplifted. Yes, our body/soul relationship is what Aquinas called a "communio admirabilis," a *wonderful communion.* And the communion for each and every one of us is both wild and sacred. Writer Scott Sanders celebrates the body's wildness this way: "We are wild. Through our bodies, through the ever-flowing channels of our senses, and most vividly through sex, we participate in the energy of Creation. That energy wells up in us like a perennial spring, urging us to ramble and play, to poke about and learn, to seek a mate, join body to body, and carry on with the story."

When humans construct temples, mosques, and cathedrals, they seek to make them not just immensely beautiful — they put their best efforts and often use their best talent and materials to accomplish something uniquely special and "over the top." They seek to create a place filled with a beauty that touches Divine Beauty; it is the beauty of space and emptiness and architecture, and it is the beauty of objects and ceremony and community. Consider the Taj Mahal in India; Chartres Cathedral in France; Stonehenge in England; Knossos in Crete; the Jewish Temple of old in Jerusalem; the pyramids in Mesoamerica; St. John the Divine in New York City; Gaudi's La Sagrada Familia Cathedral in Barcelona; the Sacre Coeur in Paris. Temples are always intended to be *centers of the cosmos*, and in a way they are — insofar as their beauty centers the energies and intentions of individuals and communities. In this way the human heart and the cosmos become united and peace follows.

Hinduism describes this in the Upanishads: "In the center of the castle of Brahman, our own body, there is a small shrine in the form of a lotus-flower, and within can be found a small space. We should find who dwells there, and we should want to know him." Who dwells there? "The little space within the heart is as great as this vast universe. The heavens and the earth are there, and the sun, and the moon, and the stars; fire and lightning and winds are there; and all that now is and all that is not: for the whole universe is in him and he dwells within our heart." Notice that in this worldview our own body is the center of the castle of the Godhead or Brahman. And there comes together in our hearts the universe and the Godhead. A holy temple indeed!

The Native American Black Elk describes a similar awareness: "The heart is a sanctuary at the center of which there is a little place, wherein the Great Spirit dwells, and this is the Eye. This is the Eye of the Great Spirit by which he sees all things, and through which we see him." Here we learn what peace means because "the first peace, which is the most important, is that which comes within the souls of men when they realize their relationship, their oneness, with the universe and all its powers, and when they realize that at the center of the universe dwells Wakan-Tanka, and that this center is really everywhere, it is within each of us. This is the real peace, and the others are but reflections of this." From this temple that houses the "eye" of the Great Spirit within us derives all peace. We operate out of this temple, putting our peace into the world around us.

Christian mystics such as Julian of Norwich also celebrate the body as a sacred Temple and Divine home. Julian writes that the human soul is a "beautiful city" and "in the midst of that city sits our Lord Jesus, God and one of us ... beautifully he sits, peacefully and restfully in the Soul, his most familiar home and endless dwelling." God joins us together because "God is the means whereby our substance and our sensuality are kept together so as to never be apart." There is a "beautiful oneing that was made by God between the body and the soul," and Christ sits in the center of our being. "Our sensuality is the beautiful city in which our Lord Jesus sits and in which He is enclosed."

Yet one more way we do, and can, treat our bodies as temples is through decoration. We dress our temples like we dress our bodies, and we dress up our bodies when we enter temples. Consider the beauty of the handmade and feathered Native American costumes at a powwow dance; consider the beauty of the vestments of Christian priests; consider the stunning regalia of African elders or Bali women on their way to ceremonies. We dress up for church. Our bodies take on the beauty of the cosmos and its multiple gifts to us. I remember being in the island of Bali when women wearing long white dresses that touched the ground were holding their children in hand, also dressed in white, on their way to a ritual ceremony and with baskets of multicolored fruits balanced on their heads. In the middle of the rain! And all were clean and unhurried and just plain beautiful.

We decorate our bodies, pierce them, tattoo them, paint them, and dress them up to be as beautiful as the plumage of birds or the skin of the snake or the colors of flowers. Beauty is wild; it is not tame, not domesticated. And our bodies participate in this wild beauty. Thank God!

Temples illuminate and are illuminated. A kind of brightness accompanies beauty, and Sanders recognizes this when he writes: "Our bodies are bright like Blake's tiger, burning with the energy of Creation. They are also bright with curiosity, like the toddling child in the subway car eager to explore the territory. And they are bright with intelligence. All on their own, they mend and grow, balance and persevere; they yearn to reproduce themselves and many succeed, passing on through their genes a skein of discoveries. Like all wildness, the body's way is orderly, elegant, complex and old. It is also fresh, constantly renewing itself, drawing strength from bottomless springs." We all knew this in our youth. We lived in our bodies. And this knowledge fed our holy curiosity. "We all once dwelt in our bodies with such frank delight. We ran our hands over everything within reach. We sniffed and tasted. We studied buttons and pebbles and bugs as if they were jewels. We turned our cheeks to the wind. We gaped at birds kiting in the sky and froth dancing on water and sunlight flashing through leaves. . . . Any child is a reminder that the rivers of our senses once ran clear. . . . We are still curious and marveling animals. No matter how much we camouflage or medicate them, our bodies remain wild, bright sparks from the great encompassing wildness perfectly made for savoring and exploring this sensuous planet."

There are limits to equating the body with a temple, however. As with any metaphor, one should not be overly attached to it or reduce it to literalism. John Conger identifies a weakness in seeing the body as temple. "The problem is that it's a kind of idealization. In a temple you don't touch things. It's meant to house things and I think there is that aspect — Dionysus as a life-size mask that constellates within it a spirit — the body constellates the presence of spirit in it. But Jung talked about body and psyche as two sides of the same coin, kind of interface or mix that we can't dissect."

JOHN CONGER: THE MANY LANGUAGES OF THE BODY

John Conger is a psychiatrist and student and practitioner of bioenergetics and Korean martial arts, and he teaches that the body has six preverbal languages. His thinking echoes the stories of Native Americans who say that at one time humans talked with animals and communicated with them in a common language. In our interview, I pursued this question of the body's prelinguistic communication, and this was his response:

> I have done training for graduate students in the vocabulary of the body. It was 120,000 years ago that we developed the gene for speech, when the larynx finally falls down and we can begin to talk. Before then there was a lot of communication going on however — communication is fundamental to all life. We are just prejudiced toward language because it's sort of like the technological digital revolution — it's so amazing that it transforms everything, and so we tend to forget about the other ways of communicating.
>
> But the body has all these brains — the three brains of reptilian, mammal, and cortex. Evolution does not throw away what works. The verbal language we finally developed includes bodily *gestures*. The body is always speaking, and when I am working with people around the body, I watch them — they are surprised at how much I know about them from observing their bodies. People are so amazed: "How did you know that?"
>
> Communication is primarily nonverbal. A contemporary of Freud said that all the most precious moments are preverbal; all intimate and complex experiences are this way. Many times when we talk we have

to go past the words to an intuitive understanding of what is behind the word itself.

So I teach people there are at least seven different languages. The first is the instinct. Then there is sensorimotor — for great athletes like Michael Jordan, the information doesn't go to his cortex and back again. There's a kind of a genius in the sensorimotor evolution of vocabulary. For some, whose vocabulary is mainly words, their sensorimotor vocabulary is very limited. Then there is the language of innate patterns recognized by psychology. Then there is the artistry of senses; painters, for example, make complex imagery that is its own complex language. Musicians also go into streaks of creativity that are amazing and elaborate. Then there's the whole development from sign to symbol, drawing a symbol as a metaphor. And finally there is verbal language. I tell students they can use six languages but not the seventh because people like to escape from the body into the verbal.

FOOD — HOLY AND COSMIC

We must eat to live, and this elemental aspect of life seems to mark a clear separation between Spirit and flesh. Or does it? In this context, what does food mean to our bodies? Is eating base survival, or something more?

As we've noted, today's cosmology makes clear that humans are made out of the atoms of ancient stars, and all we eat is too. Thus, science and ancient spiritual teachings reach the same conclusion: food is holy. Food is far more than fuel. Food is just one part of the mysterious cycle of life, death, and rebirth. What we call "food" was once alive, as plant or animal (or star), and it allows us to live, and for this reason, eating has always called forth gratitude. That is why the spiritual practice of saying grace is so universal and so ancient.

As Gary Snyder says, "Everyone who ever lived took the lives of other animals, pulled plants, plucked fruit, and ate. Primary people have had their own ways of trying to understand the precept of nonharming. They knew that taking life required gratitude and care. There is no death that is not somebody's food, no life that is not somebody's death." Many religions, including Christianity, have connected the eating of food and the ingesting of the Holy One in the same ritual. As Snyder observes, "The archaic religion is to kill god and eat him. Or her." Food is a sacrament, a sign of our holy relationship with all that is and all that is behind all that is. We too are food. We are food for upcoming generations. We are meant to be eaten. That is what "sacrifice" means, to offer ourselves as food for others. Literally, after death our bodies are buried in the Earth to become food for plants and other creatures, and eventually feeding humans again.

The sacred dimension of food is harder to see and appreciate when our meat arrives precut and wrapped on styrofoam; when we simply buy packaged bread, but never sow the seeds, harvest the grain, and bake it ourselves. Though we may feel distant from the sacredness of food, it remains. The eating of food is a holy act, and it honors our body to either grow food with care or to encourage and support those who do. Organic farming in its many dimensions is part of the way we honor our bodies and cleanse the body politic. As Snyder observes, "A subsistence economy is a Sacramental economy because it has faced up to one of the critical problems of life and death: the taking of life for food." Since we all eat and are eaten, with only time distinguishing one from the other, it behooves us to be both grateful and reverent and respectful toward food and toward our bodies, which will feed future generations. Surely, the health of the food we eat is a measure of our own health, and this reverberates through time. In this way, when our time to be the eaten arrives, we will have given our best and hope to be received with gratitude, reverence, and respect also. Karma begets karma, after all.

What and how we eat is an essential way to love our bodies and cherish these cosmic temples, but there is a companion activity: exercise. We honor our bodies by keeping fit, by training and working out. Like most things in life, the intention we bring to exercising determines our experience and its value. When we exercise out of vanity, we are not so much honoring our body as trying to control it, to shape it in an attractive way to gain admiration for our ego. Or, we might work out for the many practical benefits. It certainly helps us feel better; it increases energy, fights disease, improves our mood, alleviates depression, and relieves stress.

However, like eating, exercise can become more if we want it to, a prayer itself, an act of praise for the marvel-filled bodies we have been blessed with. Exercise is a means to honor the beautiful temple of our bodies by keeping it fit and functioning, by keeping it healthy and clean. In this way, we praise Creator and creation both, and we honor our communities, which benefit from our physical health. Think of this the next time you work out. When our intention is to honor the temple of our body, exercise can become a profound experience. The physical effort becomes a generous gift to God, to our ancestors, and to our descendants. For we praise them all by honoring the gift of our bodies and staying healthy and beautiful. When approached in this way, eating and exercise become a form of living prayer.

THE CHAKRAS: REDISCOVERING OUR SACRED BODIES

Ever since Plato and St. Augustine, much of Western thought has been haunted by the dualism of spirit versus matter and body versus soul. However, Eastern thought has not shared this prejudice, and in the East the human body is regarded with far less regret and with a deeper level of curiosity. One manifestation of this is the Eastern tradition of the chakras. This teaching says that our bodies contain energy or power centers, called chakras, and that if we allow these centers their proper role and strength in our lives, we ourselves will be strong and healthy spiritually as well as physically. Various traditions interpret and understand the chakras differently; some say there are seven, or nine, or even sixteen. I find the chakras an illuminating way to explore our relationship with the temples that are our bodies, and here I offer my understanding of them, which has been drawn from various sources over the years.

The First Chakra

I recognize seven chakras, and the first is located at our tailbone (called the "sacrum," which means literally the holy bone). The first chakra picks up vibrations and therefore sounds. If our tails were still intact, we would be that much more tuned to the vibrations and sounds of the universe. We now know that all atoms in the universe are giving off sounds or vibrations. All beings are making music. Thus our first chakra connects us to the cosmos, to all the beings and vibrations of the universe. Maybe that is one reason we have lost our tails: if they were intact, it might be just too much input for our sensitive sensory systems. Maybe too this is one reason so many religions honor sound: "In the beginning was the sound" says Hindu scriptures. "In the beginning was the Word" says Christian scriptures. "God spoke" says the Jewish creation story. The Aboriginal peoples of Australia say that God sang each creature into existence.

Where is the religion that does not celebrate the first chakra through chanting, singing, music, drumming, and dance? Dance is critical to the first chakra because sub-chakras exist in our knees and in our feet. To engage the knees and feet in dance on Mother Earth is to trigger and feed the first chakra. It is to connect the Father Sky energy with the Mother Earth energy. It also gets all the chakras moving, since the first chakra is, obviously, first. If we don't get that going, what happens to the other chakras? They get shortchanged and deprived of the energy they need to operate at full capacity.

For men, it is particularly important to exercise this first chakra. Doing so is part of recovering a masculine spirituality. Drumming and dancing are excellent first-chakra activities, as they ground us anew to the Earth.

The Second Chakra

In a previous chapter on lovemaking, we mentioned the second chakra, which is our sexuality. The second chakra is located in the genitals. The East honors our sexuality as a power we have all received not just for our personal pleasure and for our personal relationships but also for the sake of the larger community and the continuation of the family and the tribe. Generativity, creativity, sharing, intimacy, delight, play, propagation of self, family, and species — all these elements find their place in the second chakra.

The Third Chakra

The third chakra is found in our gut, just below the navel. It is here that we center ourselves in such practices as aikido or tai chi. It is here that we ground ourselves. It is also here that we experience anger and moral outrage, such as when we feel "kicked in the stomach" by injustice. Thus the third chakra is very important to bring to life the prophet or spiritual warrior. Compassion begins in the third chakra, with the awareness of injustice and the anger that accompanies it; the full expression of compassion, however, resides in the fourth chakra. Grief too is a third-chakra issue. When we honor deep sorrow and pay attention to our grief, we are respecting the third chakra.

Anger has long gotten a bad rap. Many have been the philosophers who have sold their soul to the status quo and have preached that anger is a sin. Consider the first-century philosopher Philo, who said, "We must keep down our passions just as we keep down the lower classes." At least his motives were clear; controlling anger is the way of the ruling classes, the way of slave masters and empire builders. Compare Augustine, who taught that anger is a capital sin, and contrast that to Aquinas, who taught that nothing great happens without anger.

Anger is not bad; it is necessary. Aggression is a part of life. But how we use it and steer it, whether toward violence or to bolster inner strength, that is paramount. The steps for dealing with third-chakra anger issue are, one, admitting anger; two, finding healthy and nonviolent ways to express it; and three, using it as fuel to energize us in the directions we truly desire and need to go in. How are men doing this in their lives, both personal and societal, at work and at home?

The Fourth Chakra

The fourth chakra is located at the heart and lungs. It is the chakra of compassion, which will be the focus of chapter nine. Notice that it is the *central* chakra — three chakras below hold it up; three chakras above nurture it. It is the chakra of helping hands, of the heart doing good works through the hands — the healing hands that serve the community. Maybe sometimes heart attacks are not just due to too much fat clogging our arteries but to not exercising our compassion enough.

Spiritual warrior Buck Ghosthorse taught me, "Fear is the door in the heart that lets evil spirits in." The heart chakra must be stronger than all the fear that comes our way — that is sold to us by government, the media, or organized religion, which has used "fear of God" as a bludgeon for centuries, when the phrase's true meaning is the "awesomeness of God." Indeed, Thomas Aquinas says we should "fear nothing," except maybe ourselves. But we should never fear God. He also observes that fear is such a powerful human emotion that when it takes over the soul it can "drive all compassion out." Fear is manipulated by religion when it preaches hellfire and damnation to get people to obey. We can make hell on Earth when we actively create fear, but we can make heaven on Earth, too, by spreading compassion. When people are afraid, they shrink up and become defensive. They do not become creative problem-solvers. Our heart chakras need attention, care, and nurturing. They need to be protected from toxic religious or political messages that emphasize fear over love. The two do not readily coexist. "Love drives out fear," John's epistle says, and this is the psychologist's remedy also.

The Fifth Chakra

The fifth chakra honors the power of the throat, the power of speech and of sharing one's wisdom — not for nothing is the throat chakra located between the heart and mind chakras. The throat is a birth canal by which we give birth to our wisdom; through it we find our voice and share it with the world. The very word *prophet* comes from the Greek word *propheto*, to speak out. Of course, if our throats are too full of drink, food, and consumer goodies, we cannot give birth to our wisdom; we cannot give our gift to the community. Today, we call this "consumeritis," which is an update of the old-fashioned sin "gluttony," which comes from the Latin word for throat, *gluttus*. Consumerism can very easily become gluttonous and thus stifle our ability to give birth to wisdom. So keeping our throats clear and open and able to give birth, finding our voice, is an essential part of our spiritual warriorhood, our prophetic calling.

The Sixth Chakra

The sixth chakra honors our mind, the powerful marriage of left and right hemispheres of the brain. It is sometimes called the "brow" chakra because it is located between the eyebrows. This chakra honors our intuitive, mystical side as well as our critical analytic side. Too often men have been narrowly defined by their left brains alone: by their capacity for analysis and for verbalization. That is good and important, to be sure. But our brains have a right hemisphere, a mystical side, a way of seeing and understanding that is more spatial than verbal, more intuitive than rational. That too needs to be nurtured. We men need to give ourselves permission to acknowledge this more mystical side of ourselves, what Otto Rank called the "irrational." As he warns us, "Life itself is irrational." Here lies the work of wonder and awe, the world of the mystical. A healthy sixth chakra boasts a balance of both left- and right-brain thinking; when fully engaged, this develops into what is called the "third eye," which is the marriage of the two sides of our brains. Eckhart said about this eye: "The eye with which I see God is the same eye with which God sees me."

The Seventh Chakra

The seventh and final chakra is located in the top of our heads, near the back where our cowlick is located. This is where monks both Eastern and Western often shave themselves and where Jewish people wear the skullcap. What is the meaning of these ritualistic gestures? The purpose is to honor the serious power of the seventh chakra, which is a culmination of the light energy achieved in all the previous six chakras. These gather at the top of the head, sending their light and warmth into the world to link up with other light beings both living and dead. This chakra connects us to our ancestors, to angels, and to other humans trying to live full and healthy lives. Putting on a skullcap to pray symbolizes that there are times in life when keeping this energy corralled is a good thing. At other times it is appropriate to send the energy and light out.

The seventh chakra needs our attention because it can go awry. Instead of sending our light and energy out to connect to others, we can choose envy. Envy recognizes the goodness in others but *not* in order to link up with it, rather to shoot it down. To destroy it. To compete, make war, and destroy community, rather than bolster it. Men are especially prone to envy and competition, and the wars they inspire, especially when culture nurtures these powers at the expense of other options.

Our Seven-Room Temple

Naming the seven chakras is a rich and practical way to conceptualize our bodies as Temples. We might say the chakras are the altars in our sacred temple, for they are centering places, places where our energies gather and our love and power take root. An altar is a centering device, and our chakras are meeting places in the temple.

Chakras could also be seen as rooms in our holy temple. Each chakra is a sacred door behind which lies beauty and wisdom, grace, love, and empowerment. Think, for example, of the first chakra as the room of sound and vibrations that connects us to the whole, the cosmos, which is humming loudly and inviting us to tune in. The second chakra is the room of generativity, sensual exchange, lovemaking, and the power of birthing and bringing new life into the world. The third chakra is the room of emotional grounding, of standing firm, of sorrowful mourning and of moral outrage and righteous anger. When grounded, we can steer these emotions into acts of nonviolent protest and acts of justice and compassion.

The fourth chakra is the central room, protected and surrounded by three chakras above and below. It is central because the heart dwells there, the furnace for compassion that heats and enlightens the whole body. "The first act of love is melting," observes Thomas Aquinas. Here is found forgiveness as well. The Divine dwells here — in the heart — because Compassion is the Divine Name par excellence. From the fourth room all healing, joy, love, and overcoming of fear emanates.

The fifth chakra is a room housing our voice; it is the throat as the birth canal of our wisdom and passion for justice. This may express itself in words or in art — deeds therefore that flow from your heart and your mind. The sixth chakra is the bridal chamber where the left and right hemispheres of the brain make love; it is the creative birthplace of an authentic intellectual and mystical life. The two sides of the brain work as a couple; they work in tandem to bring divine imagination alive, culminating in the joy that creativity brings.

Finally, the seventh chakra is the room of launching, of sending forth your light and energy — as a coworker, a community builder — to work with all other light beings, from angels to ancestors. In this room, you and all gifted ones commit to realizing a holy and healed world. Thus we recover the body as temple.

RECOVERING BODY AWARENESS:
FOUR PRACTICAL STEPS

As I've said, many of us in the West are not well-connected to our bodies, to our temples. We don't like to think about them or care for them. But this alienates us from our emotions and from our connection to each other and to Spirit. In his book *The Body in Recovery* John Conger offers four ways in which we can reconnect to our bodies and be more fully present in them. I present them here with my own thoughts and suggestions.

Step One: Grounding

The first step is to become grounded. Conger says, "Being ungrounded in this world is dangerous.... To be ungrounded is to be unstable and unsupported by the very earth we walk on. We have no foundation. We are lightweights disconnected from our feeling and unrelated to others." An exercise to become more grounded is to imagine yourself as a tree with roots penetrating deep into the earth. Let another push you when you are imagining yourself as a tree, and you will find considerable strength. That visualization grounds us. Or consider the difference between these three stances: First is a child's stance, wherein one is innocent and unprotected — such a person can easily be pushed over. Then there is a defensive stance, with feet wide apart, but such a person is overly confrontational. The third stance is the "inner stance," wherein one is lined up with oneself and allowing maximum energy to flow up from the ground and into the limbs and trunk and back to the earth again.

Step Two: Boundaries

Once we have learned to be grounded, we are ready for creating boundaries. Conger writes, "Boundaries give us protection. They also tell people where they are intruding. They give people something to bump up against, to identify who we are on a social interactive level, and people really like to bump up against us to find out who we are."

Social space is one thing, and intimate space is another. This is where boundaries come in, learning to discern the difference. Intimate space usually extends out one or two feet from our body. One exercise to experience this is to stand some distance apart from another person, with plenty of "neutral space" between you, and invite another to walk toward you slowly until you feel uncomfortable. Ask that person, "How does this feel?" and look them in the eye. Look for fear. Do not step closer; do not violate the boundary. Then switch roles. Gradually, a sense of healthy boundaries will become more apparent. Conger says, "Without a clear no, we cannot have a clear yes.... To keep the world at arm's length, to push people away with our arms, is a critical aspect of our healthy development.... By learning our boundaries, we can then truly welcome others in."

Step Three: Breathing

Breathing is another way we honor and bring the body alive in us. Conger observes: "Over time, our full breath has been reduced, our ribs grown inflexible, the pulse dimmed, our sea of energy thrown into an enforced and chilling calm. With diaphragm tightened, our breath no longer reaches down to our genitals, no longer connects the upper and lower body. How have we suppressed our life energy?" Many meditation practices teach us to honor our breath, to count our breaths, or to deliberately breathe in especially deep ways. Sports, too, including running, swimming, and hiking, require us to breathe deeper.

Christian de la Huerta conducts workshops in deep breathing that have had significant effects on people. In an interview, he described his work this way:

> It's a type of yoga and breathing that's been done in the East for thousands of years. It was discovered in the West in the San Francisco Bay Area about thirty-five years ago. It's very simple, a type of breathing you do for about an hour; you breathe in a certain way, a circular connected pattern of breathing. My background is psychology; my dad is a psychiatrist. For most garden-type neurotics who are not actively hallucinating and not completely out of touch, I would recommend breath work over therapy because it works so fast and it heals so quickly and so profoundly. This isn't a substitute for a therapeutic

relationship, which can be very beneficial. But this heals at every level — physically, emotionally, mentally, spiritually — and it sometimes bypasses sitting on someone's couch for ten years rehashing the same old crap. I see such dramatic change, such dramatic healing, sometimes after just one session.

For example, a physical one. I had a guy who all his life had not heard as well out of one ear as the other. During the breathing session he heard something pop, and he woke up the next morning and he could hear fine with that one ear. I had another woman who was lying down breathing and heard the facilitator snap his fingers; that triggered a memory when she was five years old. She had been in an upset with her father, went away on her bicycle, fell and broke her nose, and was black and blue for three weeks. She hadn't thought about this for forty years. She looked in the mirror the next day at forty-five and saw her face was black and blue. This shows the power of these memories stored in our bodies — and the importance of healing them.

Another guy came and in one session became so clear about the lack of integrity in living his life that two weeks later I found out he confessed to his girlfriend that he had been cheating on her. He changed his diet, became a vegetarian, and really cleaned up his life from just one session.

In addition to all the healing effects and benefits, what is available from this breathing practice is profoundly ecstatic and some of the most profound spiritual experiences I've had have been in this context. Sometimes in a group you'll have people reporting a visitation from a dead relative or loved one, angelic visitations, people to whom the Christ appears or the Buddha appears, that kind of thing. Truly profound and very humbling process.

I can add that I have participated in some of Christian's workshops and had such profound experiences, such as one time I traveled with my deceased dog and close companion, Tristan, through the sky and heavens.

Step Four: Feeling

Conger explains that with grounding, boundaries, and authentic breathing established, one is ready to entertain a full range of emotions again. "Breathing fully into our chest and belly releases emotion," and emotion has often been cut off or denied in our lives. So important is feeling to our existence that when people, such as murderers, lack normal feeling it shocks us greatly. "The deficits of feeling face us with a humanity that is monstrous, that we consider inhuman." A good parent will "promote feelings, allowing access to their full range." Unfortunately, socialization can cut us off from feelings, as in school and often at home we are told to "behave." Conger writes, "Our socialization demands of us the containment of aggression. In our rush for approval, we may split off hostile feelings, living with little awareness of our shadow. We lose access to a great range of feelings and live in emotional poverty. Instead of being direct, our anger seeps out in convoluted or twisted ways." Passive-aggression may mark our modus operandi in the world.

What do we do about this emotional poverty? Conger recommends exercises in kicking and hitting. They provide the "opportunity to become kinesthetically and psychologically aware of repressed aggression. With effort we may open up feeling tied up in tissue, lost to unconsciousness." To do this, kick or hit a pillow, bed, or foam cube, or use a bat or tennis racket to hit with. While doing so observe what "inner movies" appear in your mind. Move around or just hit or kick in place. Kicking can link upper and lower body. Or stomp on the ground. Stomping is something we may have done in childhood to protest or to express our anger. I have been at rituals where stomping was encouraged.

To be at home in one's body is to be at home everywhere. Embodiment is about being at home. It is about *being present, being here*, and wanting to be here. It may have everything to do with Jesus's instruction that "the kingdom of God *is* among you (and within you)." Being fully present in the now and in the body go together. This in turn overcomes fear and anxiety. Body and soul reunite. What we believe in becomes embodied in the work of our bodies. As Jung put it, "The difference we make between the psyche and the body is artificial. It is done for the sake of a better understanding. In reality, there is nothing but a living body. That is the fact; and psyche is as much a living body as body is living psyche: it is just the same."

A POEM FOR OUR BODIES

Dostoyevsky wrote a poem in *The Brothers Karamazov* about loving all of creation that I reproduce in my book *One River, Many Wells*. I like that poem very much, and it inspired me to write a similar poem about our bodies that I'd like to share.

Love all your body,
Your cells, your organs, your senses, and your powers.
Love your liver,
Love your kidneys,
Love your intestines,
Love your genitals,
Love your lungs,
Love your spleen,
Love your gallbladder,
Love your bones,
Love your heart,
Love your ears and your hearing,
Love your eyes and your seeing,
Love your nose and your smelling,
Love your mouth and your tasting,
Love your skin and touching,
Love your speaking,
Love your muscles,
Love your brain,
Love your imagination,
Love your mind,
Love your feet,
Love your toes,
Love your ankles,
Love your elbows,
Love your neck,
Love your hands and your fingers,
Love your back and your shoulders,
Love your chest and your stomach,
Love your whole body.
If you love your body
You will perceive the Divine mystery
Who dwells therein
Once you perceive it
You will comprehend it better every day.
And you will come at last
To love every other body

With an all-embracing love.
And you will know community
And you will know compassion,
Which, as Meister Eckhart says,
"begins at home with your own body and your own soul."

MORE THAN ONE BODY

Typically, we think of ourselves as having only one body, but in fact we hold many bodies within our large and ever-expanding souls. Part of honoring our body is recognizing that incarnation is a many-splendored thing.

We have *physical* bodies — that is clear. But we also hold the universe within us. Our bodies are made of the stuff of the universe — the carbon, hydrogen, helium, nitrogen, sulfur, magnesium, and more that have filled the universe for some 4.5 to 13 billion years. Thus it can be said with scientific accuracy that we hold a *cosmic* body within us. Far from this being an abstract idea, our cosmic bodies are fed daily with cosmic food, the sunlight converted to plant life, converted to animal life, and so on. We eat cosmic food to keep our cosmic and physical bodies healthy.

Our physical body could also be considered an *Earth* body. Our bodies are in many ways the bodies of Mother Earth, of her soil and her nutrients, her flowers and her trees, her grains and grasses, her animals and fowl. The clay of the Earth is so much like the clay of our bodies. And one day we will return to the Earth; the great mother who fed us in our lifetime will swallow us up at the end and feed other beings with our physical, Earth bodies. No wonder we are instructed to dance on the earth *now*, while we are alive, to celebrate and thank the Earth by exercising our knees, our feet, our heart, our lungs, our sweat. And to defend the Earth when it is badly treated. All this is a thank you for Mother Earth and her love of our bodies, and our love of our bodies.

We also possess a *divine* body. Incarnation is for real. Divinity makes itself flesh in us. We are, as Rabbi Heschel teaches, the "hands of God," so that God can work compassion through us. "God needs us," he insists, exactly for that purpose. Either we bring compassion alive in history and to this planet or we fail. The teaching of Christianity, that God became incarnate in Jesus, is often badly misunderstood and badly taught. Its full meaning is that God becomes incarnate, takes on flesh, in *all of us*. Or at least tries to. Are we open to such extravagance? Are we generous enough to say, "Yes. Come in. Use me, my soul and my body, for your healing, celebrative, and transformative work." Divinity finds an "image and likeness" in each of us. That is why we are so many and so diverse. Because Divinity is so rich and diverse and needs *many images* to even begin to express itself. Divinity expresses itself in our creativity and in our works of compassion in particular.

Throughout our lifetimes, our bodies keep changing. Our bodies keep time, embody time. As Conger puts it: "We have a baby body, a child body, a teen-age body, a young adult body, a middle-aged and old body, a very old body and we tie these bodies together in photo albums. We laugh as we recognize our-selves and family members with and without hair and glasses. 'You were such a cute kid,' we say. From our childhood to our old age our various bodies may be dramatically different and yet, hold something recognizable of us as con-tinuous being, a thread of nature stringing the beads of body. With all our body's differences, it is inspiring to see our nature emerging from each change of form."

All these dimensions of body are ours: to be human is to be a physical body, a cosmic body, an Earth body, a divine body. Fully present, fully incarnated. The human body is part and parcel of the cosmic body and the Earth body — indeed, if Gaia gets sick (which global warming tells us is clearly happening), our bodies will get sick. We depend on Gaia, the Earth body, for the health of our own bodies. We are in an interrelationship with her. We are in no way sep-arate from Earth any more than we are separate from other bodies, whether hu-mans, plants, or animals. We are one body. Paul, ever the mystic, called it the "mystical body of Christ." One body. The Universe in its vastness and ourselves as local microcosms of the macrocosms. Hinduism also talks about the universe as One Man and Buddhism talks about the Buddha Nature of all being. Macro-cosm, microcosm, large body, visible body.

No wonder Meister Eckhart says: "The soul loves the body." The thirteenth-century mystic Mechtild of Magdeburg says:

Do not disdain your body.
For the soul is just as safe in its body as in the kingdom of heaven —
    though not so certain.
It is just as daring — but not so strong.
Just as powerful — but not so constant.
Just as loving — but not so joyful.
Just as gentle — but not so rich.
Just as holy — but not yet so sinless.
Just as content — but not so complete.

It is a great privilege to be *in one's body* — in a particular body at this particular time on this particular blessed planet, whether you are male or female, whether black, brown, red, tan, white, or something else. Do not squander this moment, this opportunity and time. Ask: How can I serve while in this body? This male (or female) body? This twenty-year-old, forty-year-old, or sixty-five-year-old body? This Canadian or Chinese or African or Celtic or American body? This loving, hating; angry, peaceful; happy, sad; imperfect, perfect; funny, serious body? This twenty-first-century body? How can I serve with this body? For the body serves the soul. The body follows the soul's lead. The body goes along with the soul's visions, with the soul's longing. What is our soul longing for? The body and the soul, as Aquinas taught, together form a "communio admirabilis," a wonderful communion.

It is part of the task of the spiritual warrior today to deconstruct the negative teaching about the body that still informs Western culture. This dualism, that began with Plato, that separated matter and spirit, praising the latter and denigrating the former. (Augustine, for example, said "spirit is whatever is not matter.") All healthy warriors have to stand up to this dangerous teaching. Such teaching results in the kind of hatred or indifference that humans now hold against the Earth and our bodies, and against women and animals.

We have a huge ally in this struggle to reinstate the holiness of our bodies and of matter in general. That ally is science. The late physicist David Bohm defined matter as "frozen light." Whether frozen light or just very slowly moving light, matter is something special. We now know that for every molecule of light that is matter in the universe, there are a billion particles of light that are not matter! This means that we who are light incarnate, or light embedded in matter, are *rare* — we are one in a billion! Rejoice! Celebrate! Be amazed! Be grateful! And stand up to all forces and powers that would put matter down and put the body down. The body is a marvel. The body is a miracle, a wondrous event. *You* and everyone you encounter are miracles and wondrous events. Celebrate your temple: nourish it, love it, admire it. And keep your temple clean, which, after all, is the first stage in any spiritual practice.

By defining our bodies as specially organized *light*, David Bohm is employing what may be the oldest and the most universal of all metaphors for God: light. Divinity is honored as light in the ancient tombs of the Egyptian dead; and Buddha is "always shining, always emitting light," and he admonishes us to be "lamps unto yourselves"; and the Christ's words that "I am the light," and Jesus tells us not to "hide your light under a bushel"; and the Hindu's celebration of Brahman as light: "The cosmic waters glow. I am Light! The light glows. I am Brahman!" In this ancient tradition, light is both around us and within us, both transcendent and immanent. "There is a Light that shines above this heaven, above all worlds, above everything that exists in the highest worlds beyond which there are no higher — this is the Light that shines within man."

The oldest creation story in the Jewish Bible honors God as "clothed in majesty and glory, wrapped in a robe of light!" (Psalm 104) and Moses experienced God in a *burning* bush.

Of course, given today's science, we know that *every bush is a burning bush*. Just as every body is a burning body. Matter includes photons or light waves that are present in all things. Science helps to democratize the experience of the burning bush, the experience of the Divine presence as light.

Temples invariably play with light and darkness. So do our bodies. We need to welcome the light that manifests in and through our bodies, in and through all the special organs that adorn them and special altars (chakras) that embellish them. We are indeed illuminated beings who live alongside other illuminated beings. As Hildegard of Bingen put it: "I, the fiery life of divine wisdom, I ignite the beauty of the plains, I sparkle the waters, I burn in the sun, and the moon, and the stars."

Surely our bodies are temples, for it is here that we perform our holy actions of deep living, whether those actions are breathing, eating, sleeping, making love, singing, talking, praying, meditating, laughing, or going to the bathroom (an action Julian of Norwich attributes to the Creator). All is con-templing, making temple happen, bringing the temple to light.

THE BLUE MAN | 8

IN HIS SPIRITUAL AUTOBIOGRAPHY *Play of Consciousness*, the great Indian saint Swami Muktananda describes his experience of the *Blue Pearl* and the *Blue Man* in considerable detail. He talks of the "blue light of love" that exists in "everybody's heart." In the West, the twelfth-century seer and reformer, musician, and scientist Hildegard of Bingen also experienced a "man in sapphire blue." Let us consider the Blue Man and see what light he sheds on healthy manhood.

VISIONS OF BLUE: SWAMI MUKTANANDA

Swami Muktananda tells us that one day he was in a joyful meditation, and he was praying to the goddess Kundalini, who was east, west, north, south; in his ears, eyes, mouth, nose, throat, arms, chest, back, stomach. He prayed, "O mother Guru! O father Guru! You are in my thighs, you are in my legs, you are in my feet. O my Baba! You are in me, I am in you. And you are in any difference there may be between my form and yours." Truly a prayer of pantheism, God in us and us in God. The meditation began with a red aura, "then the white flame, the black light, and the Blue Pearl followed one after the other. My heart was filled with joy."

The Blue Pearl grew and morphed into the shape of an egg and then into a human shape. "The egg grew and grew until it had assumed the shape of a man. Suddenly divine radiance burst forth from it. For a moment I lost consciousness." Coming back, he beheld the egg-shaped Blue Pearl standing before him "in the form of a man. Its brightness lessened. I saw within it a Blue Person. What a beautiful form He had! His blueness shone and scintillated [with] the blue rays of pure Consciousness.... His body was composed of infinite rays of Consciousness.... He was the true form of my Mother, the playful, divine Kundalini. He stood before me, shimmering and resplendent in His divinity." His whole body was blue. And beautiful. The Blue Man spoke and said, "See everything from everywhere.... I have eyes everywhere.... I become the body in all bodies, and yet I am different from the body." Lifting his hand in a gesture of blessing, he left Muktananda "utterly amazed. As I watched, the blue egg, which had grown to a height of six feet, now began to shrink. It became smaller and smaller until it was once more... my blue light, the Blue Pearl."

Who was this visitor? Muktananda said, "The Blue Person, who grants the realization of God with form. He is also called the supreme unmanifest Being.... What I had seen was the Blue Pearl; it was Shiva, the Blue Lord."

Swami Kripananda has called the Blue Pearl a "scintillating blue dot" or the "'cosmic creative drop,' for it is state of the gathered-up power of Consciousness that is about to create the universe. The Blue Pearl 'sprouts' into three pearls" which provide "the source of all sound vibration.... The entire universe of vibrating sound is evolved from the Blue Pearl." How like is this teaching of a pregnant blue dot to today's cosmic creation story wherein all of creation began as a pin prick that birthed the original fireball and all that would follow?

What resulted in this visitation for Muktananda? He finally believed that "God is in me." He is in each of us, yet "He is unattached to it. He is the nourisher of all. He is the sustainer of every cell." He is the recipient of all our gifts. He dwells in all things.

> This Supreme Being appears to be different in different people, races, actions, names, forms, countries, and times, but He is undifferentiated. He lives as human being in a human being, as bird in a bird, as cow in a cow, as horse in a horse, as man in a man, and as woman in a woman. What else can I say? He becomes all things and is yet unique. He gives His strength to all created things. Like a mother He protects and sustains them and then gathers them all into Himself. He is the supreme light of all lights; all lights take their brightness from Him. There is no darkness about Him.

THE BLUE MAN AND HILDEGARD OF BINGEN

In the twelfth century, Hildegard of Bingen also had a powerful encounter with a man in sapphire blue while meditating in her monastic chapel in the heart of the Rhineland area of Germany. "A most quiet light and in it burning with flashing fire the form of a man in sapphire blue." This is how she recounted that vision:

> I saw a very bright light, and inside it there was a person who was the color of sapphire. This person was completely surrounded by a very pleasant fire of reddish color. The very bright light completely surrounded this fire of reddish color, and at the same time this fire completely surrounded the light. Both the fire and the light surrounded the person, existing as one light with one force of potentiality. Then I heard the living light speak to me.

What was spoken to Hildegard were "secret words flowing from [God], the living one." While she does not repeat the words in detail, she declares that the discourse she writes down "will help understand the mysteries of God, so that you may discreetly distinguish and know the fullness which has never been seen from its beginning." Like Muktananda, thanks to her vision she understands the Christ or Blue Man is in all things and the overall message bestowed is Love.

Interestingly, like Muktananda, she talks in this section about a "pearl" — and it is humanity. "God's own great work and most precious pearl, namely human beings whom God formed from the slime of the earth and breathed life into." Previously, like Muktananda, Hildegard had also seen a vision of the universe as an egg. She painted that vision and wrote about its deeper meaning. Christ is "the son of justice having the lightning of burning love and existing with such glory that every creature becomes illuminated by the brightness of his light." He bends "compassionately in the direction of the poverty of the human race."

In her reflection on the Blue Man vision, Hildegard recognizes that God is light in its Trinitarian manifestations. The Creator is a "living light"; the Son is a "flash of light"; the Spirit is "fire." She painted her vision of the "blue Christ," who is a revelation of the compassion of God. Through this form the "maternal love of the embracing God" arrives to inspire people to respond to the suffering of others through service and generosity. We become that Blue Man; we become the compassionate Christ; we become the radiance of God. "The compassion of the grace of God will make humans light up like the sun," she declares.

In Hildegard's mandala painting of this vision, the Blue Man is extending his hands outward. This depicts the archetypal gesture for compassion, in which we take the energy of the heart chakra and put it into our hands, put it to work.

She speaks of how human hands offer the "tangibleness" that provides either a dwelling in which one is held or a way to defend what one cherishes. By naming these two uses of the hands and arms, she is saying much about the "Fatherly Heart," a heart that embraces and a heart that defends. She ascribes that "tangibleness" to the Christ element in God, the "Word who was able to be touched and grasped after being born from the Virgin." Other sides to Divinity include the "moist greenness [that] signifies God, who never becomes dry nor is limited in virtue." And the reddish fire "signifies the Holy Spirit [who] is the attendant and the illuminator of the hearts of faithful people."

Hildegard elaborates on her vision of Divinity when she ascribes to it three "causes," namely Sound, Goodness, and Breath. "A word has sound so that it may be heard, it has goodness so that it may be understood and it has breathing so that it may be completed. In the sound, notice God who makes all things public with indescribable power. In the goodness, notice the Word who was born wondrously. And in the breathing, truly notice the Holy Spirit who glows pleasantly in God and in the Word." Divinity possesses three powers that fire holds, namely, "shining brightness, purplish life and burning fire. It has shining brightness so that it may shine forth, purplish life so that it may flourish, and burning fire so that it may be ablaze." Without these three, "no flame can be found"; nothing lives.

Her mandala also celebrates the "fiery ropes" of the universe that bind all things together. The power of the macrocosm (universe) and microcosm (human) blend, psyche and cosmos come together. Blue is the dominant color. We all possess this "man in sapphire blue" within us. It is our capacity for healing. It is the healing power of Christ within us all.

BLUE THREADS, BLUE VOICES

Blue is the color of the fifth chakra, the chakra that lies in the throat between our heart and our mind chakras. With the fifth chakra, we put the best of our hearts and minds into the world to serve and heal the world. The prophets (or spiritual warriors) were all champions of the fifth chakra; indeed, the word *prophet* means to "speak out." The throat or fifth chakra is where so much healing (or pain) is spread in the world. What do we do with our powers of voice and throat? Are we healing or are we hurting others? Do we create or do we destroy? All these questions are raised in the context of the Blue Man and the blue universe that Hildegard paints for us.

Blue plays a symbolic role in many religious traditions. It symbolizes the infinite and the great because it corresponds to the color of sky, sea, and vastness. Eastern Orthodox churches often sport a dome that symbolizes the heavens, and invariably it is painted blue. Blue is the color of Mary's cloak, the mother of the Christ, the Christ-bearer. In the Torah the Israelites were ordered to put fringes on their garments with a twisted thread of blue woven within them. A rabbinic tradition teaches that blue is the color of God's glory. We are instructed to meditate on sapphire, which is a likeness of the throne of God, according to Ezekiel; this is a very special meditation on the "Chariot of Yahweh" that contemporary scholars believe John the Baptist taught Jesus, and that Jesus in turn taught his disciples. The man in that chariot is surrounded by fire. Indeed, the Hebrew word for "glory" (*kavod*) means "blue" in Arabic. Many vessels in the Ark of the Covenant were covered with blue cloth when they were moved from place to place. In Hinduism, Krishna is depicted as blue, and Lord Shiva has a blue color on his neck that symbolizes how he took poison to save the world from destruction.

Psychologically speaking, it is said that blue signifies distance, love, peace, and happiness. Light blue calms, cools, and soothes. Such a tranquilizing effect generates a sense of well being and creates an ambience of love, peace, and sexuality.

Of course there is a dark side to "blue." To sing "the blues" is to sing from the depths and infinite reaches of our sad and broken hearts. When we are "down," we are "blue." A wound can make us "black and blue," and a dead body might turn blue. In Iran, blue is the color of mourning. Furthermore, cold turns the body blue, so that ice is often depicted as blue. An icy heart is a blue heart. Pharaoh is said to have had a cold and hard heart. Just as blue fire represents a deeper heat than orange or red, so frozen blue represents a greater sin than fire: Dante says the deepest rung of hell is not fire but *ice*. An icy heart is the exact opposite of a compassionate heart. The Tibetans picture Satanic creatures in blue probably for the same reasons.

These shadow sides to the color blue serve to remind us of the *depths* that blue signifies. Blue names the expansiveness of the human heart — not only for beauty but also for pain. Not only are the sky and ocean both blue and deep, but so are our hearts, and the sun shines in them equally deeply. And also when darkness overtakes the heart, it is a blue event, an icy and deadly thing. Thanatos (love of death) takes over from biophilia (love of life).

EMBRACING THE BLUE MAN

The Blue Man that Swami Muktananda encountered has a very strong parallel in the West and in Hildegard's experience of Christ as light. In the teachings of the Cosmic Christ, Christ is a "light of lights," the "light in all things," and the "light of the world" that "darkness cannot overcome."

Swami Muktananda was healed of his fear of death by his encounter with the Blue Man. That is no small thing; as Otto Rank observes, it is our fear of death that most drives us to smother life and not live it fully. All spiritual teachers agree with what Jesus taught: that love drives out fear. Fear of enemies and fear of death. Without this love, fear of death drives us to build fortresses to hold off death and create immortality. Necrophilia replaces biophilia when our hearts fear death more than they love life. Says Muktananda: "Once I had seen that sphere of unmanifest Light I lost all fear. This is the state of liberation from individual existence. Since then my courage has increased a great deal, and I no longer know any fear. . . . The place of fear within me has been destroyed."

Something else changed in him. He came to realize more and more fully the truth that "I am Shiva." (For a Christian, this might be translated as "I am Christ.") Muktananda writes: "The rapture of bliss was steadily increasing. All those memories of the form of the supreme Blue being, of His blessing, of His living within me, of my identification with Him, of 'I am He' — all rang within me." How different is this from St. Paul saying, "I no longer live but it is Christ who lives within me." The same experience, I would propose. It's an encounter with the fullness of being that is available to us all.

Muktananda connects his psyche to the cosmos. "Every day my conviction became stronger: 'He is truly my inner Self whose light is spread throughout the entire universe.' Although I could not see it directly, I saw my inner Self as the blue Person. . . . I was gaining the realization that the Blue One was my own self, the One who lives within all, pervades the entire universe and sets it in motion, who is One-without-a-second, nondual and undifferentiated, and yet is always at play, becoming many from one and one from many. He is Shri Krishna, the eternal blue of Consciousness." How like Hildegard is the Swami's description of his experience of the Blue Man. For Hildegard also sees the man in sapphire blue residing in all of us and furnishing the energy for all our works.

The Blue Man effects consciousness at play, that is, creativity. Out of it all things are born and come into being. Muktananda continues,

> As I gazed at the tiny Blue Pearl, I saw it expand, spreading its radiance in all directions so that the whole sky and earth were illuminated

by it. It was now no longer a Pearl but had become shining, blazing, infinite Light.... The Light pervaded everywhere in the form of the universe. I saw the earth being born and expanding from the Light of Consciousness, just as one can see smoke rising from a fire.... Just as a seed becomes a tree, with branches, leaves, flowers, and fruit, so within Her own being Chiti becomes animals, birds, germs, insects, gods, demons, men, and women. I could see this radiance of Consciousness, resplendent and utterly beautiful, silently pulsing as supreme ecstasy within me, outside me, above me, below me.

"Chiti" is the power of universal consciousness and represents the creative aspect of God portrayed as the universal Mother. She also stands for "the beauty of the whole world." In other words, Muktananda is saying, creativity is everywhere. Birthing is everywhere. The artist within marries the Artist without. We all participate in divine creation. We are cocreators. Creating with God. Playing with God. Consciousness is playing everywhere in the world. Just like Wisdom herself, who in the Western Scriptures "plays everywhere" before the creation of the world.

So overwhelming was this meditation on the Blue Pearl and the Blue Man for Swami Muktananda that it became the center of his entire meditation from that time on. He knew this represented the fulfillment of his spiritual journey; similarly, Hildegard writes that her Blue Man vision represented a "completeness." This is one reason for all men today to embrace the Blue Man: we need goals, and he represents completion. That may be one reason we love watching sports; every game has a clear goal and a definite end. There is satisfaction, even in defeat, to have clearly defined winners and losers. The Blue Man offers a "spiritual goal line," an end to spiritual searching and fear of death, and it's a goal that is within the reach of all of us. The end of this game results in no losers, only winners. The Blue Man is thoroughly democratic. We can all experience the Blue Man, the Blue Krishna, the Blue Christ. Muktananda reports: "As I passed inside the Blue Pearl, I once again saw the universe spreading out in all directions. I looked round everywhere and saw in all men and women — young and old, high and low, in each and every one — that same Blue Pearl that I had seen in myself. I saw that this was the inner self within everyone's sahasrara [or seventh chakra], and with this full realization my meditation stopped." Peace and equanimity followed.

The Blue Man never really left Muktananda. Rather, from that time on, whenever he met anyone, first he saw the Blue Man in that person. "I see first the blue light and then the person. Whenever I see anything, I see first the beautiful subtle rays of Consciousness, and then the thing itself. . . . My eyes have been bathed with the lotion of the blue light, and I have been granted divine vision."

OUR EXPANDING CONSCIOUSNESS

The Blue Man represents our expanding consciousness, and this is critical today for our survival as a species. And our consciousness *is expanding* today — scientific discovery is expanding our consciousness, so that we understand how interconnected and interdependent humans are to each other and to the Earth. Global warming expands our consciousness. Even the HIV epidemic, nuclear proliferation, and the obscene gaps in wealth worldwide expand our consciousness. They are all "wake-up calls," invitations to deepen our awareness and seek justice and healing.

For instance, when science tells us that the human species originated in Africa, and all peoples originally migrated from there, we are invited to embrace the Blue Man, to expand our consciousness, and understand the complete *relativity* of our racial and ethnic and religious differences. As we learn about our planet's uniqueness in the universe, and about its fragility and suffering — all this can expand our consciousness and open our hearts to the *compassionate action* that Hildegard wrote about. For her, the Man in Sapphire Blue represents consciousness put to the service of compassion.

The Blue Man can be found everywhere we turn and whenever we seek to learn and expand our minds — whether we look at sexuality, diversity, economic justice, war, or the deep ecumenism and wisdom found among all religious traditions. All learning nourishes and feeds our consciousness and expands it. Are we up to it? Are we embodying the Blue Man in each of us?

Thomas Berry has spent a lifetime understanding the new science and its meaning to human beings and our work in the world. In his book *The Great Work*, he says simply, "While the universe celebrates itself in every mode of being, the human being might be identified as that being in whom the universe celebrates itself . . . in a special mode of conscious self-awareness." Our awareness is a conscious awareness *and* it is a celebrative awareness. Part of our awareness is waking up to the beauty all around us. Berry says, "To bear the burden and responsibility of human intelligence [the human] needed a magnificent world of beauty in order to give us the meaning we would need. . . . We are genetically coded to exist in a world of beauty. Your first experience is a communion experience: how *wonderful* this is!" To grow in consciousness is to grow in one's appreciation of beauty. It is to explode with gratitude and reverence. Is there ever such a thing as too much gratitude? Or too much reverence? Or too much beauty, for that matter?

The Blue Man, representing the cosmic color blue, brings Father Sky down to Earth, just as Jesus and others have prayed: "Your will be done on earth as it is in the heavens."

BLUE UNIVERSE

The sky seems to be blue, and the ocean, reflecting the sky, is blue. Thus, blue represents the universe, the far reaches of our world. While one might even say that Father Sky is blue, the sky is actually devoid of color. It just seems to be blue. Muktananda, in his book *From the Finite to the Infinite*, says the same is true of the self, which is blue yet lacks "any color, any shape, or any form.... The One which has no form, the One which is nothing, manifests as this universe. The sky has nothing, but it is blue."

When humans first left the Earth and its sky and entered space, they turned around and took pictures of our planet, which forcefully reminded us that Earth is not just a green planet but a *blue* planet. Our oceans constitute 80 percent of the Earth's surface, and water is what makes life possible. Our planet is blue in the most beautiful and yet precarious of ways. Gaia is blue. Indeed, blue precedes the green. Without water there are no plants; without plants, no animals. Blue is our mother. Blue therefore unites sky and sea, cosmos and Earth, Father Sky and Mother Earth.

So too with us. Muktananda says, "The blue light is in everyone's heart. The supreme Principle is the color of blue light. There is no color in the sky, in the ether, still the sky appears to be blue...consciousness is the color of blue." It is not that things are perceived as blue so much as they reveal themselves as blue. Just as the natural color of the sky and of water is blue, so "the innermost light of God is blue." Of course blue also signifies a very great heat — a blue flame, hotter than orange or yellow flame, is within us all.

Muktananda compares the light of the Blue Pearl to the biblical teaching of the Kingdom of God and to the mustard seed. "The light of this Pearl is so brilliant that it is sufficient for an entire cosmos. In the Bible it is said that the effulgent kingdom of heaven is within you, and that is completely true. One seer says, 'O Lord, we see You as pure light that blazes in the form of a flame.'" The Blue Pearl dwells within us, and when one realizes this, then one's "entire being becomes transmuted. He does not experience himself as a perishable being but as divine. The Blue Pearl has such potency that it transforms you completely." The Blue Pearl is the innermost body of the inner Self or soul, and "even though it looks so tiny, it is infinite." Eventually the Blue Pearl explodes, and that is good, too, as one merges with God. Meister Eckhart called this experience "breakthrough," and he tells us that in this experience he learned that "God and I are one."

THE BLUE MAN IS AN ARTIST

The Blue Man unleashes untold creativity. And when we are in the grip of creativity we are being visited by the Blue Man. We frequently say that creative inspiration hits us "out of the blue," but typically this is the result of much effort. We struggle to expand our consciousness, and then in a flash, consciousness expands, and the ever-creative Blue Man helps us bring it to life in the world. For instance, Einstein's great equation of energy and matter ($E = MC^2$) hit him out of the blue while he was getting on a bus. But of course Einstein had already spent years working on his theory without finding the solution. Focusing often opens us up for the infusion of insight.

Indeed, to be immersed in creativity (as to be immersed in the Holy Spirit) is to swim in the rapid rivers of creative energy. These are the very rivers that the universe is made of. Muktananda says, "In reality the universe is a divine sport; it is the playful pastime of Consciousness, the blossoming of Chiti Shakti.... For a man who sees this, the world is nothing but a play of God's energy. For him there is no bondage and no liberation. The veil of duality, which made him see differences, had been torn.... In Her creative aspect, Chiti shines forth in the external world as the body of the whole universe." How like this is to the teaching of Paul that Christ is the mystical body of the universe. But a creative body, a cocreating body, cocreating with us. In its immanent aspect, "it creates the world," says Muktananda. Yes, in the Christ all things get created and recreated, say the Christian scriptures. The universe is not separate from us. We are playing in it and it in us.

Everyone is an artist — every man is an artist — bent on giving his gift to the world. These may be artistic gifts of music, painting, or film, or they may be artistic gifts of physics, medicine, business, farming, building, repairing, counseling, teaching, parenting, or friendship. All is creativity at work. Blue Men participate, and in this participation there lies true satisfaction, true "victory." This is not a victory of individual "success" but of meaning and compassion and service.

When we become the Blue Man, when we take in the Blue Man, we become artists and cocreators. Or to put it differently, all authentic creating and giving is the work of the Blue Man in us. To meet the Blue Man is to meet the basic power of the Universe, a power of playful creativity, the power of Wisdom at work and play in the universe. Men are not whole without it. Our work is not whole without it. With it, we are in a world bigger than our own. We become instruments of forces bigger than those we can ourselves control or manipulate. With it, we can sing and dance and tap into our own wildness. We can give our gift to the world, our work to the ages, our labor to the universe, our blessing to the community. No wonder the Blue Man is blue. For a peace settles in when such gifts are given. A satisfaction greater than any other. A "joy that the world cannot give," as Jesus put it. That was Muktananda's experience, and Hildegarde's and Paul's. And it can be ours.

It's worth remembering here that true creativity does not emerge from men and the masculine alone. It takes a union. It takes a marriage of male and female to birth new life. In part two, we will consider the sacred marriages that true creativity requires. It is the marriage of the Male and the Female, of Masculine and Feminine energies. Of Shiva and Shakti. This is how Shri Shankaracharya put it: "Shiva can create only when He is united with Shakti. Without Shakti, He cannot stir. For this reason, how can an ordinary person bow down to You to praise You, O Mother, who is worshiped by the deities of creation, preservation, and destruction?"

As the phrase "out of the blue" implies, creativity is often something that finds us, that we recognize around us and are amazed by. It's not always something we do. We all underwent this experience as children. For example, Joseph Jastrab, who taught in a wilderness survival school, tells the story of how, when he was seven years old, he found a rock and broke it open and "found a tiny cavern inside lined with glittering quartz crystals. It was as if I had stumbled on a jewel mine, hidden millions of years waiting for me to find it. In an instant, my entire body shook with joy. I had opened a rock and discovered a living, radiating presence inside! I had opened up to an aliveness I had not felt before. I rushed to share this discovery with others. In a way, I was crying out, 'Look at this miracle, look at this joy, look at me and confirm these things are true!' Yet no one to whom I turned saw the divine revelation that I could see. And no one was able to reflect my joy with the intensity that my child's heart demanded."

How good are men in our culture at seeing creativity in the world, including within themselves? Do they recognize the "divine revelations" of the Blue Man? Deida puts forth an important observation when he reminds us that "the purpose of sexual desire is creation. Reproduction is but the biological aspect of creation. As a man, you probably have much more to give the world than your children." In how many ways are we creative? Do we bring our creativity to work? If not, what other ways do we find to express ourselves creatively?

Navajo artist David Palladin endured a terrifying four-year ordeal in a Nazi concentration camp, where he was tortured mercilessly and left to die and from which he emerged a paraplegic in a comatose state. However, according to his elders, this experience provided his initiation as a shaman, and later Palladin lamented how few people in Western culture understand their creativity. "We are all artists," he declared. "If you can talk, you are an artist." An artist translates his or her thoughts, feelings, experiences, and dreams into meaningful expression, into passionate beliefs and compassionate deeds. The "artist" is often narrowly defined as someone who creates only with words, colors, music, dance, and so on. But as with Palladin, the primary work of the artist is one's own life. Too few men recognize themselves as creative and as artists; too few recognize living as creative artistry.

The older I get the more I realize that *life itself is improvisational*. We plan as best we can, but just as often life decisions get made on the fly — about jobs, where to live, partners, parenting, and so on. Who ever lives the script they first write for themselves? As Joseph Campbell put it, "Most of us do not live the life we had intended." What does this mean? That life is an improvisation, created in the moment, expressing the moment, as with any art. We are all artists. Our life itself becomes a deep expression of who we are, what we care about, what our values are. It is our great work. To survive and thrive, in ways small and large, we depend on our imaginations. We call on our wellsprings of creativity to give what we have to the world, to our families, to future generations.

I feel very deeply that our species will not survive if we do not call forth the depths of our creativity at this time (which is something I also address in my book *Creativity: Where the Divine and the Human Meet*). Men (and women) must welcome the creativity of the Blue Man. Sadly, in the modern era, creativity has often been considered less important than obedience, and the arts reserved for "professionals." We let ourselves become estranged from our creativity, disowning it whenever we say, "I can't paint. I'm not creative." This surrender of our creativity is nothing less than a surrender of our humanity. A surrender of our powers of begetting and conceiving; a surrender of our powers as fathers and as mothers. When we surrender our creativity, we become dead inside, and our culture dies. "Pessimism comes from a repression of creativity," noted psychologist Otto Rank over seventy years ago. He is right. Scientific studies have demonstrated that creative work of any kind releases chemicals in our brain that overcome sadness and depression and stress. Creativity keeps us alive and joyful, just as the Chandogya Upanishads say: "Where there is creating, there is progress. Where there is no creating, there is no progress. Know the nature of creating. Where there is joy, there is creating. Know the nature of joy. Where there is the Infinite, there is joy." Joy, the Infinite, creating, progress — they all go together.

Among indigenous peoples, art and artists are so integral to and integrated into the community that few indigenous languages even have a word for "art" or "artist." An artist is a citizen, and a citizen is an artist. That is taken for granted. Art is simply the beautiful way in which we give our gifts to the community — and a living community requires many and varied gifts, many and varied expressions of creativity. "Art is the only language wild enough to articulate vision," comments Joseph Jastrab. This is why Jastrab expects every man in his male retreat experiences to "return claiming himself as artist."

Indeed, how will we solve any of the great problems facing us today *except through human ingenuity and creativity?* Global warming, overpopulation, unemployment, world hunger, AIDS — whether the issues are moral or technological, personal or global, creativity is the only way out of our deepest dilemmas. The great prophets — such as Mahatma Gandhi, Martin Luther King Jr., Jesus, Muhammad — they were all *social artists.* Every prophet is a social artist: one who awakens the collective mind to a better way to do things. They show the way by courage and by imagination to move in new directions, awakening the moral imagination of others.

Do we buy into the limiting belief that only some people are prophets, like only some people are artists? Rabbi Heschel says that there lies in the recesses of every human being a prophet. All men (and women) are meant to be prophets, to speak out against injustice in its many forms and to act on behalf of justice. All men are prophets, artists, and spiritual warriors; all men are Blue Men, expanding consciousness, espousing justice, defending their hearts, expressing compassion, artistically improvising in their daily lives.

COMPASSION AND CREATIVITY

The spiritual traditions of the world agree that compassion is the ultimate expression of our better selves, of human morality. The Dalai Lama teaches that "we can reject everything else: religion, ideology, all received wisdom. But we cannot escape the necessity of love and compassion." And Jesus said, drawing from his Jewish ancestors: "Be you compassionate as your Creator in heaven is compassionate." The most frequently used name for Allah in the Koran is "the compassionate one." Ramakrishna, speaking from the Hindu traditions, says: "The presence of God is felt not only when you shut your eyes; God can also be seen when one looks around. Service to the hungry, poor, sick, and ignorant, in the proper spirit is as effective as any other spiritual discipline."

The Blue Man who honors his powers of compassion is also honoring his powers of creativity. For there can be no compassion without creativity. One must be as "cunning as snakes and wise as doves" if one is to offer alternatives to the dominant way of doing things. Moral imagination cannot simply be learned; it must be lived through practice and courage. If we all have the Blue Man of Compassion within us, we can be certain we also have the Blue Man of Creativity within us. That is one reason Hildegard's vision of the Blue Man boasts such prominent *hands*. With our hands we caress. We hold. We make and repair things. Human hands with their thumbs are unique instruments. Hands get things done. We talk with our hands, heal with our hands. The fifth chakra finds its logical outlet in the hands, which localize what is otherwise expansive and infinite. Hands take in cosmic powers and apply them locally, hand to hand. That is why we shake hands when we meet another person. My history interlocks with your history. Shaking hands and meeting eyes assures mutuality. Power-over gives way to power-with.

Creativity is a major factor in turning aggression into something positive. The Inuit peoples, when they sense a war coming between tribes, hold a poetry contest to find the best poet from the tribes. He who wins the contest wins the war for his tribe. War over. Done. This is something William James called for a hundred years ago — the "moral equivalent of war." Michelangelo, while painting the Sistine Chapel, was accosted by a particular cardinal who convinced the pope to force the artist to put loincloths on his figures. Michelangelo had the last word, however, when he painted the cardinal in hell, where he sits to this day.

Gandhi and King were Blue Men; they channeled the moral outrage of their communities against empire and injustice. Social protest became social art, creativity with a purpose, and their artistry changed history. Gandhi's march to the sea was compassionate creative artistry: he fought the British Empire without hurting anyone. He waged war without returning harm for harm. Martin Luther King Jr. did this, too, turning protests into theater and ritual, filling the jails, allowing one to convert anger into art.

Converting anger into compassion is an internal, as well as an external, struggle, and the Blue Man offers his creativity here, too. Consider Muhammad's idea that jihad is war with your own demons. Or consider the desert fathers, who were first young men who went into the desert to go AWOL when the church married the empire. They too ended up wrestling with other demons — their own inner ones — and not those aroused by empires making war in their name. Even Gandhi said, "I have to struggle with myself."

How do we access the Blue Man? How do we find him when we need him? By meditating and seeking solitude. When roused, our reptilian brains want to lash out. Solitude provides a space for compassion and creativity to enter and find imaginative solutions. Every man, woman, and child has to learn solitude. Being alone is calming. The Bible also teaches this: "I will call you into the wilderness and there speak to you heart to heart."

Our culture is very afraid of solitude. We fill silence with noise, with TV twenty-four hours a day. The Blue Man could shout and not be heard. What did Gandhi do when he struggled with himself? He spent hours at a spinning wheel — spinning cotton into thread. This humble, simple, repetitive practice, steeped in his culture, refreshed him and reconnected him with his compassionate creativity. Men have to find a form of meditation that works for them in their lives. The particular form doesn't matter. Consider Thich Nhat Hanh, who through meditation let go of the resentment and bitterness in his heart over the war that for so long tore up his country. A sign of holiness is going through life without bitterness, which comes from holding anger in. Thich Nhat Hanh channeled his anger into creativity, creating communities. This takes lots of work and leaves no time left over for anger. This is partly the purpose of dancing in the Cosmic Mass I and others created. When you dance for hours at a time, you give your all, you're pooped, and little energy remains for anger, for going to war. This is even more true of a practice like Sundancing.

Meditation instructs us to calm ourselves. In an article entitled "Zen and the Art of Lawyering," we are introduced to Mary Mocine, a former litigator who is also a Zen priest. Mocine has chosen to teach meditation to burned-out attorneys. "I speak two kinds of language — law practice and Zen practice," she says. Studies show that lawyers suffer higher rates of chronic stress and depression than other professions. "Top American law schools including UC Berkeley, Stanford and Harvard, are sponsoring seminars in 'mindfulness meditation.'" Today 15 million Americans are practicing some kind of meditation. Farke Tikoen, a fifty-one-year-old lawyer in practice for twenty-three years, tells this story: "I was a scorched-earth litigator. My way was the right way. There was no negotiation." His life was unraveling with business problems and a painful divorce when a friend invited him to a meditation group. "It was magical. It slowed me down, made me stop and listen." Jan Lecklikner, a San Francisco public defender, had a similar story to tell: "In my first five years of practice in the criminal justice system, I was the angry, hate-everybody kind of practitioner. It finally got through to me that I wasn't going to last long in that frame of mind." When a serious illness struck, she began meditation.

A recent study prepared for the U.S. Department of Health and Human Services found that meditation reduces heart rate, blood pressure, and cholesterol, while increasing verbal creativity. A 2005 study at the University of Wisconsin with Tibetan monks concluded, "Mental training through meditation can change the inner workings of the brains." Monks who practice meditation demonstrate an extraordinary capacity for focus, memory, learning, and consciousness. "Brain activity was especially high in the prefrontal cortex, which is associated with positive emotions." In other words, meditation led to greater happiness. One lawyer who took meditation workshops said, "You can still be a warrior, but because you're at peace with yourself and you're centered, you're not coming from rage or fear or anger. I'm a work in progress. It's exciting." The Blue Man is arising even in legal offices. Beware. They may never be the same again.

Creativity also helps to heal shame. We are naturally proud of what we produce: parents of their children, poets of their poems, artists their drawings, businesspeople their business. Creativity helps to dispel shame and put it on the run. It brings one's pride back.

COMPASSION IN ACTION

A current example of compassion in action is the work of a former student of mine, Dr. Bernard Armadei. Bernard is an engineer and teacher. A few years ago, after returning from studies with us at the University of Creation Spirituality and from visiting poor countries of the world, he launched Engineers

Without Borders. This organization now has ten thousand members across the United States, spread across 235 chapters and working on 250 projects in forty-three countries. These projects range from solar-generated irrigation systems to green homes and purification systems. Bernard has put his creativity and compassion together. As an engineer, he is blessed with concrete skills, and in doing what he has done he is helping to redefine engineering altogether. A different kind of young person is entering engineering schools today. He wrote the following to me:

> It is amazing what the power of compassion in action can do. I had no plan to start anything, and it all happened by itself under the right divine and angelic guidance. It is so beautiful to see the smiles of the students and professionals when they work in a community. We see more smiles in one day in a village in Africa than we see in an entire year in New York City.... As you know, as wonder kids of 15 billion years of evolution, we are all wealthy; the issue is to remember it. Many people in developing countries seem to remember that. They have more wisdom than many of our political, religious, economic, and educational leaders.... I still encounter some bumps on the road (especially from my Ph.D. colleagues), but that is nothing. I am now exploring the Sufi tradition and it is so gentle and beautiful. The Beloved is in all the eyes of the children I have met in several countries in Africa, in Nepal, in India, and in Rwanda, where I have been lately. They remind me of my own divinity and uniqueness as a child of the Divine.

There is so much that a consciously aware and skilled man can do. Who knows the limits?

It is telling that Bernard, in all his travels in the developing world, encountered so much joy there. For where there is joy, there is consciousness, and where there is consciousness, there is joy. Indeed, Thomas Aquinas teaches that "God is supremely joyful and therefore supremely conscious," and "Joy is the human's noblest act." To increase consciousness is to increase joy, and the joy in turn sparks the creativity to spread joy and relieve suffering. Compassion then is born not only of suffering but of joy. And compassion returns joy to the world.

We are badly in need of rituals that awaken the joy latent in all of us and get it moving again. Over the past ten years in developing the Cosmic Mass ritual — which employs the insights of the rave community and combines dance together with images and video — I have become convinced that today's consciousness and technology can assist us greatly in bringing joy alive. And with joy come the energy and strength to carry compassion into action. Good ritual carries good myths into the hearts, cells, and bodies of the community and from there into action.

Consider this teaching from the indigenous Huichol people of Mexico:

> Grandfather Fire is the original light, the original wisdom, the universe's own memory. In the beginning he took the raw energy of creation and transformed it into vision by creating colors and images and into sound by singing. In this way he gave us human knowledge, and we are forever grateful. Grandfather Fire is alive in every flame and spark, and fire is to be treated as an honored being.

In ritual we dance the raw energy of creation with colors and images and music and singing. Gratitude is awakened, and gratitude is an ultimate level of consciousness.

Among the chakras, the third chakra, which pertains to anger, is yellow, and the fourth chakra, relating to compassion, is green. Since anger and compassion together make the prophetic voice, it could be said that yellow and green together produce *blue*, that is, the blue of the fifth chakra and of the prophet. The Blue Man spreads blue into the world.

BECOME THE BLUE MAN

The Blue Man represents the expanded consciousness and the creative compassion we are all capable of. He is an artist at life, recognizing beauty and justice and creating it. We are being tested in a special way today. Because of news both good and terrifying, a global consciousness arises, asking us to expand our minds and hearts. We are interconnected and interdependent in ways we have never experienced before, even as the collective impact of our human society threatens the Earth's health. We must use our powers of creativity, which increase when consciousness increases, to engage and solve the many problems facing us at this important time in history. We must take our expanded consciousness into all our relationships. The purpose of the Blue Man is to empower our hands so that real compassion takes place, the real work of the Divine in our lives. The Blue Man helps us to overcome our fear of death and to let go of our fear-inspired frenzy. Creativity can convert anger and moral outrage into appropriate expressions of protest, so that we build and not simply tear down. Gandhi, Martin Luther King Jr., Jesus, Michelangelo, and many other men have demonstrated the Blue Man in action.

Blue unites sky and earth, Father Sky and Mother Gaia, and it comes together in us, the marriage of heaven and earth. The ancient *I Ching* advises (Hexagram 48, "the Well"): "However men may differ in disposition and in education, the foundations of human nature are the same in everyone. And every human being can draw in the course of his education from the inexhaustible well-spring of the divine in man's nature." The Blue Man has tasted the divine in the self and in all things and returns for more, returns to assist the healing that Divinity requires of us. When we become the Blue Man, we become the compassionate hands of God putting into practice our compassionate hearts.

EARTH FATHER:
THE FATHERLY HEART

WE ARE ALL FATHERS, whether literally or metaphorically, for we are all passing on messages daily to the young about what life is about, what values are worth pursuing, and what directions we can and ought not take in life. How are we doing?

Yes, we are all fathers, but what kind of fathers are we? Are we prepared for the responsibility? What is the role of "heart" in our fatherhood practices? Have we resolved and forgiven mistakes of our fathers so we could 1) learn from them, and 2) move on, and 3) become our own kind of father? If not, why not? Are we addicted to bad fathering, to the promises of control that fascism both political and religious promise above all else? Can we wear our fatherly hearts with joy and playfulness? How many of the problems in the world today are caused by negative fatherly powers, fatherhood with no heart? By mind and authority that is heartless?

FATHERHOOD IN NATURE

In his book *The Evolution of Fatherhood: A Celebration of Animal and Human Families*, Jeffrey Moussaieff Masson unveils much about fatherhood in nature. He observes that we live with a "popular belief that in almost all primates, indeed, in almost all mammals, the males are at best uninvolved fathers, contributing nothing to their offspring but their sperm; at worst, they supposedly kill their young." He offers evidence of the opposite and laments the fact that the "more benevolent animal fathers — penguins, wolves, sea horses, marmosets, beavers — are . . . almost never invoked for the lessons we can learn from them."

Among fathers in the animal kingdom we learn that animal parents "do all they can to secure the safety of their young. . . . When I look at animal fathers protecting their children, risking their lives for them, I see no reason to believe that they don't feel something akin to what I feel." Masson tells the amazing story of the heroism of emperor penguin fathers who stay "with their eggs through the all but unbearable winter, fasting, balancing the precious egg on their feet, barely moving, hardly sleeping until their mate returned from her time at sea." Does this generosity mirror anything in human fathers?

> When I visit the playground on a weekend and see all the fathers, many looking bored no doubt, but still there when they could be someplace else, I am struck by how children come into our lives and simply demand that we give them immediate priority — and we respond. There are many pleasures more exciting than sitting in a sandbox with a three year old digging holes or sitting at the seashore building castles. More exciting, but in some absolute sense, less fulfilling. There is nothing that feels more remarkably right than being with our children, attending to their small pleasures, observing with satisfaction their joy. We may not be emperor penguins, but our embrace of our children is not totally unlike theirs in these moments of parental devotion. We too feel a devotion to our young that makes us forego ordinary pleasures to ensure that they survive and thrive.

Masson recognizes wolves as

> magnificent fathers. . . . It is in the den, or near the den, that we find the male wolf behaving as a father. The wolf father has hunted for his young (and his mate), he often licks the young, cleaning them thoroughly, he guards the den and protects the cubs inside, and once they are able to follow him, he teaches them how to be wolves. Wolves go through a socialization process, much as humans do. They need to learn rules, they need to learn about hierarchy within the pack, and discover where they fit into it. Most of their learning is facilitated by their father and mother working together. There is no indication that wolf fathers ignore their young or leave their raising to the females.

Even hunting, which many people would regard as the ultimate in-
stinctive activity, must be learned."

Interestingly, it is when we domesticate an animal that fatherhood diminishes. Thus, a dog, for example, is a bad father to its own children but
not to humans. Why is this? For the dog, "*we* are the pack; the human family
replaces the wolf pack.... A male dog is very protective of human children, for
as far as he is concerned, they are the cubs of the pack.... The instinct to father has not been entirely eradicated; it has merely been transferred to another
species.... Wolves make great fathers to wolf cubs; dogs make great fathers to
human cubs."

Masson has found that generally speaking, "among mammals, fatherhood
and monogamy are closely linked." Human fathers have much in common with
wolf fathers. "Human fathers, too, can know the delight of playing with their
young, can lie side by side with an infant and feel the overwhelming contentment that comes with parental love. Some men may think it is 'manly' to chafe
at monogamy and grumble that we were not 'made' to behave in this way, but
that wolf we admire so much at the top of the hill, surveying his world, is about
to descend to his den, where his life-long mate and his children await him. That
is where his satisfaction is to be found. Are we so different?"

The fatherly instinct is alive and well in nature, and Masson believes that
"it is a good thing for human fathers to see the vast diversity of paternal behavior in the natural world. It is good to simply know that it exists, to learn
about it, to honor the people who have brought this kind of knowledge back
from the jungles and forests and oceans of the world." But the best thing of
all is to know that "humans and other animals love their children beyond everything else. I find it somehow comforting, as well as humbling, to see that as
different as we are, I have this in common with wild horses of the sea and
pipefish and Darwin frogs."

Recently I met a new grandmother who told me that her son, who was
present for the birth of his first child, said to her: "I have never loved anything
so fast or so fully as my newborn baby." And the new grandmother added, "I
think that today with more and more fathers being present for the entire birth
process of their children, this will become a more and more regular thing." One
can hope so. Psychologist Jean Bolen, from years of listening to male stories,
believes that the father archetype is changing.

As each new generation of men become fathers, they join others who in the last third of the twentieth century have been present during their women's labor and delivery. These men usually bond with their infant children and are often involved fathers, not emotionally distant or unavailable Sky Fathers.... Some men are becoming Earth Fathers altogether.

THE CRISIS OF EARTH FATHERS

What is an "Earth Father"? In *The Father: Mythology and Changing Roles*, Arthur and Libby Colman describe the Earth Father as a man who interacts with his family on a day-to-day basis. For an Earth Father, his family is his primary focus. Even when he is away from home, his consciousness is with his children: "The earth father takes on the job of providing his children with the basic trust and inner security with which to grow up and out of the family towards independence and a unique identity." Bolen observes that in her practice she has heard "professional men whose position in the world placed them like Zeus on summits wish that they could stay home with the children.... These fathers do not resent their little boys, but love them fiercely.... Thus in contemporary American men, the archetype of the father is changing. Although the patriarchal Sky Father still dominates, one at a time individual men are changing."

A companion metaphor for the Earth Father is the "fatherly heart." Meister Eckhart, the great mystic and social activist of the late thirteenth and early fourteenth century, often speaks of the "paternal and fatherly heart" of God. What does it mean to say God has a fatherly heart? Western culture ought to be developing the "fatherly heart" in its boys and young men, but it does not. In 1998, Morehouse College, an all-male black school in Atlanta, sponsored a conference on "Turning the Corner on Father Absence in Black America." In its report it named a strident individualism and a weakened sense of obligation to family as provoking a worldwide crisis: "Fathers the world over, rich and poor alike, are increasingly disengaging from their children and from the mothers of their children." It acknowledged that 70 percent of African American children are born to unmarried mothers and at least 80 percent of African American children can now expect to spend at least a significant part of their childhood years living apart from their fathers. This kind of "national trend of father absence... is affecting nearly all races and ethnic groups in the United States," it pointed out.

Ron Mincy, a scholar in fatherhood studies, says healing the fatherhood crisis today requires "expanding job placement services for fathers to focus on retention and wage and career growth." Legal, educational, team parenting, substance abuse, physical and mental health services are also needed. In addition, the conference called for "nurturing relationships between fathers and their children, much healing must be done between fathers and mothers, men and women." A crisis in male spirituality is part of the cause of the father crisis and a renewal of male spirituality is part of the medicine that can heal this crisis.

Princeton theologian Cornel West considers the father crisis a crisis in long-term and faithful commitment. He considers three issues in today's crisis of commitment: the first is economic, for without job stability, insecurity and anxiety take over relationships. The second is political, since weak and feeble community support is demoralizing. And the third is personal. Our society is, he says, "losing the art of intimacy, . . . the courage to be vulnerable and to accent longevity in your relationship. We've got market moralities; we want disposable bodies. And so it takes time to be able to really be vulnerable. . . . One of the things about folks in the past, they weren't perfect, but they knew they were in this thing together. . . . You've got to work some things through. That's how intimacy is cultivated." Before discussing what the fatherly heart is, it's just as important to identify what it isn't.

THE FALSE OR SHADOW FATHER

The opposite of a fatherly heart is a distant heart, an absent heart, a cold heart, a heart nowhere to be seen, touched, or communicated with. It is a father not in touch with his heart, a heartless father, a father living out of a superficial, distant place in himself. This is, as Bolen indicates, the shadow side of the Father Sky archetype. In Western culture, the absent father is itself an archetype, a man literally removed from family and community, and it means the West has suffered a longstanding absence of the fatherly heart. Marion Woodman puts it this way in her dialogue with Robert Bly in *The Maiden King*:

> Nothing will change so long as we wait for the absent fathers of government to do something. Their fathers, too, were absent, and most of them have no idea what to do or where to find the vision that would guide them. Nor can we look to the stepmothers, whose mothers and grandmothers too were stepmothers, because somewhere they lost touch with their genuine desire. Without a fundamental love of life

at the center of everything, children learn from infancy that they are being judged. That judgment restricts every desire, thought, action.

The "fundamental love of life at the center of everything" is what is meant by *biophilia*. An authentic "fatherly heart" is in love with life, is a nourisher and supporter of biophilia. The Earth Father loves; he is not a punitive judge. Jesus talks about the fatherly heart when he says:

> If you ask your earthly father for a loaf do you get a stone?
> If you ask your earthly father for a fish do you get a snake?
> If you ask your heavenly father for anything at all will you not get it?

In the West, instead of the "fatherly heart," we see many examples of the authoritarian heart: the punitive heart, the judgmental heart, the angry-all-the-time heart, the distant, cold, abstract, and rational heart. An unfatherly heart is a heart that has never been stretched, a mind that has never been challenged into consciousness. An unfatherly heart is still asleep and unconscious. Robert Bly says that "an 'unconscious father' is a force for tyranny, capitalist domination, and gender warfare. The 'unconscious mother' is a force for psychic heaviness and literal-minded consumerism." Unconsciousness often marries, like meeting like, so unconscious fathers and unconscious mothers often end up raising children together.

Marion Woodman sees the authoritarian father and the petrifying mother in consort.

> The old petrifying mother is like a great lizard lounging in the depths of the unconscious. She wants nothing to change. If the feisty ego attempts to accomplish anything, one flash of her tongue disposes of the childish rebel. Her consort, the rigid authoritarian father, passes the laws that maintain her inertia. Together they rule us with an iron fist and a velvet glove. Mother becomes Mother Church, Mother Welfare State, Mother University, the beloved Alma Mater, defended by Father, who becomes Father Hierarchy, Father Law, Father Status Quo.
>
> The effort of centuries to kill the dragon has ended with the worship of mother in concrete materialism. The sons and daughters of patriarchy are, in fact, mother bound.

Psychologists Gordon Wheeler and Daniel Jones have conducted many workshops with men on "Finding Our Sons." In an insightful article on that topic, they point out the overriding role that shame plays in male consciousness. Amid cultural icons of individualism and heroism (think: John Wayne), it is all the more difficult — indeed shame-inducing — for men to seek help from other men. "The hero — by definition solitary — is thus the pinnacle of the individualistic self ideal for men." Furthermore, the very act of introspection and "self-exploration is highly shame laden because of the shame-charged feelings and desires, mostly centering around dependency needs, we risk finding if we are supported enough to look inside." Yet consider how several of the Green Men sculptures of the twelfth century were looking inward. A Green Man is not afraid of introspection. Contemporary men are taught to be.

There is a social investment in shame and in keeping men from looking inside ourselves for "shame operates to keep social patterns and structures in place that far from protecting men's power actually strip them of most or all real power while blocking or inhibiting the kind of discourse that could lead to the destructuring of those patterns and beliefs." Thus men are "in the closet." Men are hidden even to themselves.

All this weight of shame seriously affects fathering, which invariably "implies a relationship of need or dependency." The authors define fathering as "any nurturing/caretaking relationship with a male in the caretaking role." Good fathering affirms, energizes, and supports the growth of another person and of oneself. They recognize that "all men" are fathers to sons whether they have literal children or not because we father younger men and boys whether consciously or not. Shame is "the sense that this world is not for me, is not my world, there is no place in it for me as I really am." In fact, in a milieu of shame, all dependency is characterized as "infantile, shameful, 'primitive' — *and feminine.*" This dependency phobia interferes with good fathering.

The fatherly heart is so important that we must all learn to embody it, whether male or female, young or old, parents or grandparents. Our human nature requires the fatherly heart to accompany the motherly heart. Both need to be conscious — aware and alert. In this way, the expanded consciousness of the Blue Man plays an important role in developing a fatherly heart. Every Earth Father must also be a Blue Man, an awake, aware, searching, curious lover of children. As loving caretakers, we grow up healthy, and our children grow up healthy, and our Earth and its creatures thrive in health.

One proof of the gross absence of the fatherly heart is the way the Earth and her creatures are being treated today. Another proof is the number of young people filling American prisons. Many of these young men grew up without fathers in the home at all. They have little or no experience of a fatherly heart, one that would love them, guide them, steer them, protect them — even from themselves. When a fatherly heart is missing from one's life, despair sets in, and despair, as Thomas Aquinas observed, is the "most dangerous" of all sins. When we are overwhelmed by despair, there are no limits to violence; if we no longer love ourselves, then the admonition to "love your neighbor as yourself" carries no weight.

At the extreme, the false or shadow father leads to fascism, which typically finds justification in a paternalistic, punitive conception of God. Dr. James Adams, whom I quoted in chapter 5 and who lived through Hitler's fascism, did not use the word lightly when he sensed its rise in contemporary America. "The Nazis," he said, "were not going to return with swastikas and brown shirts. Their ideological inheritors had found a mask for fascism in the pages of the Bible." He recognized a kind of déjà vu in the emergence of the right-wing in America, an effort to dismantle the open society in favor of one controlled from the top by an all-knowing father. A false fatherhood and a sick masculinity lies at the heart of this movement. One dare not underestimate how explosive a cocktail emerges when one mixes a false fatherhood teaching with resentment and aggression and wraps it in religious covering. As I explored in my book on evil, the speeches of Hitler were thoroughly laced with religious language and imagery. He was in many ways a religious preacher — and he played the role of a "spiritual" father.

So, we see that a fatherly heart brings hope, promise, and possibility into one's life, while the lack of a fatherly heart often brings hopelessness and despair and the violence that follows. A fatherly heart gives us wings (as in the Daedalus and Icarus story), providing us with ambition, empowerment, and strength. The fatherly heart also provides boundaries and contains us, grounding us like the Green Man. Robert Bly believes that a good father helps "wean each person from the illusion that it is the sole job of the father to provide food and encouragement always. Saturn's cannibalistic nature is the exact opposite of the Good Father nature that each of us carries inside us in our fantasy." A good father encourages personal and individual responsibility. A fatherly heart does not foster dependency or codependency but healthy individuality.

THE EARTH FATHER:
A COMBINATION OF ALL MASCULINE ARCHETYPES

The Earth Father, or the authentic father with a fatherly heart, incorporates *all* the metaphors and archetypes found in the previous eight chapters of this book.

An authentic father passes on by example and story the amazing news of how the sky lives — that Father Sky is for real. An authentic father is also a Green Man — grounding our consciousness and literally being a caretaker for Mother Earth, working to make sure her creatures, soil, water, air, and forests are healthy. A fatherly heart goes out of its way to foster mutual communication within a family and a community: a communication that flows both ways, listening and speaking, teaching and learning. An Earth Father speaks not one language, but new languages — reaching across cultures and generations, and respecting new ways of speaking and communicating.

An authentic fatherly heart is open to the deep and ancient stories of our hunter-gatherer ancestors: he provides for the survival of the tribe, and he fosters an energetic curiosity of and passionate engagement with the natural world. The Earth Father understands reciprocity. He teaches his sons and daughters how to "hunt" in the world and then how to trust their own hunter-gatherer instincts when they are on their own. The fatherly heart also celebrates and models the spiritual warrior; he is comfortable expressing both joy and grief, and he knows and/or creates the rituals that can hold these emotions in the home and community. In this way, children grow up emotionally whole and aware, safe and expressive. A fatherly heart does his inner work and has gone into grief and loss, into initiations of many kinds, and does not hide this from his children.

A healthy father is not silent about sexuality, its power and its dangers, but discusses it openly and models healthy and responsible sexual expression. A healthy father takes delight in showing his children what a healthy life entails: how to eat healthy, cook for themselves, grow food, exercise properly, and honor the body in all its wonder and amazement.

Finally, a healthy father instructs by example and word how to foster an expansive consciousness and how to respond to life creatively, artistically, compassionately. Creative compassion is a primal value that is critical at this time in history. The Blue Man will not be kept under wraps.

The Earth Father, having incorporated all eight archetypes, is the healthy father, one with a fatherly heart. He exemplifies a healthy, integrated masculinity, and of course, in the real world this process is never complete. We never reach a static place of completion, in which our work is done. Then, eventually, as we face old age and death, our masculine archetypal role shifts again. We must learn how a healthy masculine heart enters "refirement," rather than "retirement," and model that for our children and grandchildren.

Dr. Clarissa Pinkola Estés, author of *Women Who Run with the Wolves*, offers this poem on Father Earth:

FATHER EARTH

There's a two-million year old man
No one knows.
They cut into his rivers
Peeled wide pieces of hide
From his legs
Left scorch marks
On his buttocks.
He did not cry out.
No matter what they did, he held firm.
Now he raises his stabbed hands
and whispers that we can heal him yet.
We begin the bandages,
The rolls of gauze,
The unguents, the gut,
The needle, the grafts.
We slowly, carefully turn his body
Face up,
And under him,
His lifelong lover, the old woman,
Is perfect and unmarked
He has laid upon
His two-million year old woman
All this time, protecting her
With his old back, his old scarred back.
And the soil beneath her
Is black with her tears.

MATT HENRY: A SONGWRITER'S REFLECTIONS

Matt Henry is a songwriter who lives in Australia. He is a friend and former student of mine who with his wife recently welcomed their third child into the world. Not long after that happened, I was thinking and writing about the "fatherly heart," and so I decided to ask him his thoughts about fatherhood.

Matt responded with an essay, which is so eloquent and inspiring that I have reprinted it in full here.

For far too long our concept of God has suffered under the all-too-easy projections we cast toward the divine, based often on our human attempts at fatherhood. It's no wonder that there is such a strong resurgence of enthusiasm for the divine feminine! We are familiar with feeble fatherhood that attracts labels such as "deadbeat dad" or "feckless father." When someone's concept of God is impacted by this sense of paternal relationship, the idea of an absent God is simple to adopt. On the other hand, a judgmental, overbearing fatherhood gives rise to "paternalism," which in turn conjures power-over relationships exemplified by colonialism, feudalism, chauvinism, and so on. Of course, there is a cosmos of possibilities between these end-markers of the spectrum.

The guiding question in this reflection is "Can we consider the paternal heart of the divine, and begin to shape human fatherhood in its image, rather than the other way around?"

Consider the sóng "Because of You" by Kelly Clarkson, David Hodges, and Ben Moody. This song exemplifies an overbearing, fear-entrenching paternity alluded to above, with the song's protagonist saying that she finds it hard to trust anyone — including herself — anymore and that she will not make the same mistakes her father made.

How heartbreaking to be fathered in such a way that the trust of anybody, even oneself, is destroyed! Julian of Norwich makes clear that to be lacking in trust is a cause of weakness in us:

Often
our trust is not full.

We are not certain God hears us
because we consider ourselves
worthless and as nothing.

This is ridiculous
And the cause of our weakness.

The tragedy of the paternal relationship in this song is that the trust is not removed from only that relationship, but from all relationships, including, by extension, the relationship with the divine. And possibly more so since fathers have long been considered analogs of God.

Meister Eckhart decries this kind of loss of trust:

> *Nothing people ever do*
> *is as appropriate*
> *as great trust in God.*
> *With such trust,*
> *God never fails to accomplish great things.*

A second song, "Cat's in the Cradle" by Harry Chapin, goes to the other end of the continuum to ponder the effect of a distant, impotent fatherhood. In this song, the writer relates that his father was never present when he was growing up, and that now that he is a father himself he sees the same pattern repeating itself with his son, who has "grown up just like me."

Both of these songs' lyrics insist that paternity is a power. Of course, these are reasonably stark specimens offered to mark out the field, as it were, but each one unmistakably claims that the paternal relationship shapes the child in potent ways. The "too-strong" and the "too-weak" each wield great power. Paternity bears power in all cases. The question is not whether a paternal heart will be powerful, but in what manner will it bear its power?

Elementary biology reminds us of a couple of important things concerning fatherhood. The first is that it cannot occur in isolation, without somebody's motherhood. The second is that it begins before the birth. Considering the prenatal aspects...I cannot think of any peer of mine who did not attend prenatal classes of some kind with his partner. This is a generational shift toward recognizing the active role of the father during pregnancy. While I imagine some such classes suggest a role that is secondary to and supportive of the mother, the classes I took elevated the father's role to a responsibility that reflects the reality of the biological and spiritual union that brought us to that place. I was effectively not permitted to wait for the birth to begin a paternal relationship; the insistence was that *I too was pregnant.*

One of the practices I engaged in as an expectant father was "praying time." This was suggested to me simply by the pairing of Mother Nature and Father Time heard in many cultures. (It seemed reasonably obvious which role ought to attract my attention.) My practice revolved around nurturing an awareness of the growth of the child in the womb, the development through time from the tiniest of cell clusters into the amazing human person. It occurred to me that so much happens so quickly *in utero* that there was never a time without growth. I prayed time by meditating on this, at times pondering the rich descriptions and images from the books I'd read, other times just wondering; and I prayed time simply by watching a clock:

MATTER OF TIME
by Matt Henry
To our child in the womb

Watching the clock,
Seeing the hands as they spin all around,
Up and down they go
One fast one slow.

I dream as they move
The skinny one is fast and the fat one is slow
And since there are two,
One's me, one's you

It's a matter of time.

Once in a while,
The fast one finds that it's there, being held
By one who knows,
And then let go.
It's a matter of time,
'Til this little hand of yours
Is in this big hand of mine.

At first it'll seem
That you're barely moving while we hardly rest
Making sure each day that you're ok.

And all through our lives,
We'll be dancing around, nearby, far way,
Yet not far apart,
If it's 'round one heart

It's a matter of time,
'Til this little hand of yours
Is in this big hand of mine.

And then, at the end,
Somehow we'll find that life circles around
It's been rearranged,
Our hands have changed

It's a matter of time,
'Til this big hand of yours
Holds this little hand of mine.

Creating this song over the course of the entire pregnancy helped me in preparation not only for the growth of our child until her birth, but also for the constancy of change that comes with a child. Praying time and growth in this way was the prenatal paternal heart at work in me. Its gift to me was preparation for the work of letting go and embracing anew that comes with a child. Prepared, but never ready, of course.

What about the divine paternal heart, considered "prenatally"? St. Paul notes that the whole creation has been "groaning in labor pains until now." Meister Eckhart agrees with Paul, noting that in birthing the Son from all eternity God lies in the maternity bed . . . and that the birth is "God's self-knowledge, which from eternity has sprung from his fatherly heart, wherein lies all his joy." So the way of God's paternal heart is one of participation well before the cutting of any umbilical cord. It is from the beginning, because it is The Beginning.

The paternal heart is a good image at this point, too, since we know that the heartbeat precedes the breath. The heart beats in babies from a time very early in gestation, and the breath begins only at birth. This resonates with ideas of the paternal heart of the divine being akin to the Godhead, since it is always yet-to-be-manifest, whereas the breath of God is more revealed in the creatures of the divine.

Of course, applying linear time to the divine is fraught with difficulties. We used to think of time somehow preceding space (matter). We know now that time itself is part of that creation, we believe now that time was created with space. Time, literally, is of the essence. (I would like to claim that the song title "Matter of Time" was a deliberate play on words, but alas, it only occurred to me in hindsight.) As it stands, Father Time, conceptually derived in part from the Celts' Holly King and Oak King (two sides of the Green Man) apparently has no bragging rights over Mother Nature: they're in it together, from The Beginning.

Eckhart's words (maternity bed... fatherly heart) comfortably dance between the maternal and the paternal, because he recognizes the fullness that comes from both. Brazilian theologian Leonardo Boff fondly calls God a "motherly Father and a fatherly Mother." The paternal heart implies relationship not only with a child but also with the maternal, and together their work is parental.

This is not the place for exploring arguments concerning solitary or same-sex-couple parenthood. Let it suffice to say that every male parent is called upon to be both maternal and paternal, as is every female parent. The first locus of the partnership between a father and a mother must be the motherly fatherness and fatherly motherness within the individual. I cannot fully partner or parent with my wife, the mother of my two daughters, unless I can recognize the maternal within myself.

In the Jewish Kabbalah tradition, both the masculine and feminine are recognised in the very name of God. In the Tetragrammaton (God's name) YHWH (*yod heh vav heh*), the *vav* and the *heh* "represent the male and female forces of providence. The male force is that which acts upon the world, while the female force is that which allows the world to be receptive to God's power." Perhaps Boff (above) said this more simply, but finding this within the very name of God gives a powerful affirmation that cannot be overlooked. Talmudic wisdom asserts that when a man and a woman create a child, it is an expression of the most Godlike thing possible, and in doing so, God becomes their partner. Conceivably, the child is gifted with a measure of the heart of the mother, the heart of the father, and the heart of the divine.

So in saying that a paternal heart is capable of loving a child from the beginning, the beginning in question is not merely the child's physical conception, but, as Eckhart would surely agree, The Beginning. What/who is at The Beginning where the paternal heart beats? "Nothing" (*ayin*) would respond the Kabbalists, and Eckhart, too. The Kabbalists would likewise call it Boundless, and say that it is "negated of every conception." Eckhart would say we need to sink "from negation to negation into the one." The Kabbalists would add: call it "I am becoming."

The *Tao Te Ching* meditates:

> *The Tao is like an empty bowl,*
> *Which in being used can never be filled up.*
> *Fathomless, it seems to be the origin of all things.*
> *It blunts all sharp edges,*
> *It unties all tangles,*
> *It harmonizes all lights,*
> *It unites the world into one whole.*
> *Hidden in the deeps,*
> *Yet it seems to exist for ever.*
> *I do not know whose child it is;*
> *It seems to be the common ancestor of all, the father of all things.*

Among these voices I find a consistent articulation of the primary work of the paternal heart: letting go. (It is uncanny, nevertheless, that the Taoist wisdom hints at some of the practical realities of blunting edges, adjusting the lights, untying tangles.) There is archetypal reality behind the almost clichéd fictional depictions of fathers having immense difficulties in letting a daughter marry or a son grow up and vanquish him (even if the depictions of that often mean something as mundane as the son outplaying his father at basketball). The letting go needs to be guided by images such as the Taoist wisdom above: expansion inwardly, rather than escape outwardly. Or, as Eckhart says, "What is created flows out but remains within."

Divine creativity begins with self-emptying (*kenosis*), the making of room within the divine heart for the other to exist. It is a letting go and sacrifice that is too often overlooked by Christians mesmerized by the also-*kenotic* giving of the crucifixion. Creation and crucifixion are a part of the same *kenosis*. The divine paternal heart models for the human paternal heart, and the modeling says "let go."

Letting go is deliberate choice, not an accident. Theologian Jürgen Moltmann contends that God's creativity derives from a "divine resolve of the will." He draws the distinction between this and an alternative which claims that God's creativity is simply an automatic emanation of God's nature, without the act of will. To say that

God's nature includes absolutely and essentially the will to create in the first place is Moltmann's reconciliation of these possibilities. Where the rubber meets the road, I take from this that the work of the paternal heart cannot be thought of as anything other than deliberate. It is not sufficient to consider my paternal relationships with my daughters to be active simply because the three of us exist. The paternal heart must resolve to be creative.

Letting go as a parent means that when you kiss your child goodnight, you know that a changed person will wake there in the morning. Yet you adored beyond measure the one you kissed goodnight! The letting go is the yielding of heartspace for the child to become. The paternal heart recognizes itself in its child, and the child yearns to recognize itself within the embrace of the paternal heart. This is why it is so important for that heart to let go inwardly, in an expansive way, so that the ever-changing child can feel herself remaining in that heart. To let go instead of to drop means the difference between your heart expanding and your heart breaking. In reality, that can feel like a fine line.

WHILE YOU LET ME
by Matt Henry

I'm sure by now
That I've kissed you
A million times

And I'm going to kiss you while you let me
I'm going to carry you while I can.

Maybe one day
You'll turn away
When I kiss you

So I'm going to kiss you while you let me
I'm going to carry you while I can.
I'm sure by then
I'll have kissed you
A billion times

But I won't be done
There's not enough
For my love

And I'm going to kiss you while you let me
I'm going to carry you while I can.
I'm going to carry you while I can.

As the divine has bestowed on us the "dignity of causality," so must we yield to the growth and self of our child. This is not easy, because there is an instinct which simply does not wish to do anything but kiss and carry them. Yet again, the mystics can teach us that the place where God begins is where clinging to things ends.

I do believe that it's time for us to cease projecting our human attempts at fatherhood onto the divine (both the absent fatherhood and the dominating overpowering images), and to begin instead trusting the mystics and artists who recognize God's paternal heart as something wholly more wonderful. Perhaps from that we can shape our own paternal efforts, rather than creating God in our image.

Fatherhood need not break your heart. What fatherhood gives is a big heart. What it takes is courage.

QUALITIES OF THE PATERNAL HEART

Matt displays great wisdom in his honest reflections of a father and a father-to-be. I am moved by a number of Matt's observations, such as that fatherhood is a power, but the choice as to how we interpret that power and how we use it is ours. I'm struck by the ancient, even mystical presence of the father "from the beginning" and, dare we say, even "before the beginning." (Consider Julian of Norwich: "God has loved us from before the beginning.") The lessons of letting go and of demonstrating love and affection "while we can" means that in some ways fatherhood is a temporary job. Or at least the job description alters radically when one's children leave home, achieve independence, and start their own efforts at fatherhood/motherhood. I also like Matt's rephrasing the fatherly heart as the paternal heart.

Here, then, is what I would list as the central qualities of the fatherly or paternal heart:

1. *Caring.* The fatherly heart cares. Whether that is expressed in kissing or hugging, or in working hard to put bread on the table and to provide shelter and educational opportunities, the caring is expressed in countless ways.

2. *Giving and generous.* The fatherly heart is a giving heart, a generous heart. Children can bring out the best in a man, which is his capacity for giving and for generous giving. This giving is not to be construed as filling a child's playpen with stuff. It is a giving of time and of presence and of sharing of life lessons and life philosophies and values. Many are the scientists, for example, both male and female, whom I have met who told me it was their fathers who first introduced them to a love and joy of nature.

3. *Listening.* The fatherly heart is also receptive; it listens. It does not dictate, does not respond with a reptilian brain of action-reaction response. It is an open, receptive heart, one that acknowledges that people are different, are individuals, and they will experience life differently. We all need listeners in our lives, especially when we are young. A fatherly heart has learned to project less and be at home with emptiness so as to be a good listener.

4. *Looking to the future.* A fatherly heart considers the future. It realizes that a father is mortal and will not be around forever. A fatherly heart provides for the future as well as passes on values that will allow children to live and thrive once the father is not around.

5. *Encouraging.* A fatherly heart is an encouraging heart. It helps develop the courage in children, teaching children how to be strong for the journey, how to survive in a sometimes hostile world, and what real strength is (as opposed to make-believe strength, such as power-over trips of racism or sexism, homophobia or militarism). The spiritual warrior is part of the father's repertoire, and this is taught more by example than by words.

6. *Sees the big picture.* A fatherly heart not only looks to the future and draws lessons from the past but also drinks in Father Sky, the Cosmos, the big picture. It embodies magnanimity ("big soul" in Latin). A fatherly heart is not petty or merely tribal or sectarian; it is not bitter because it does not live in the past or carry anger in the heart but rather finds healthy outlets for anger. Outlets like service and healing. The Blue Man is an integral part of the fatherly heart.

7. *Playful and affectionate.* A fatherly heart is affectionate and playful. A fatherly heart seeks to share a love of life, imagination, and problem-solving. A fatherly heart values the gift of humor and laughter and does not take life overly seriously.

8. *Protecting.* A fatherly heart protects, which is part of caring. Being a father means protecting children from the forces in the world that can destroy or stymie growth, whether greed, assault, sickness, or loneliness. A good father protects.

9. *Instructing.* A father instructs, a father teaches. Humans, unlike most creatures, are born very ignorant. Our DNA, while full of potential freedom, does not dictate to us how to survive, what the rules of the game of life are, how *this culture* or *that institution* operates overtly and covertly. Children need parents for these teachings. They need fathers. Fathers help children find their boundaries, set boundaries, and learn inner discipline.

The fatherly heart extends far beyond literal fatherhood. It must. For one thing, literal fatherhood is not a static, frozen relationship — it evolves, beginning with the son needing the father, then becoming more equal as two adults or friends, and eventually as the aging father needing the son. Furthermore, many men who are not literal fathers are not lacking in a fatherly heart. Fatherhood is analogous. There exist many versions of fatherhood. Often we call them mentors, and they can be uncles, teachers, coaches, ministers, fathers-in-law, and so on. Richard Miles is chief executive officer of Big Brothers Big Sister of the Bay Area, and he tells many stories of how mentors have saved lives. "A mentor does not have to be a Mother Teresa on steroids — just a presence in a kid's life, someone who listens and takes a phone call a couple of times a month. Giving these kids a mentor gives them a message that someone cares about them and in turn, they pick up their game a little bit."

EARTH FATHERS RAISE COMMUNITIES, NOT JUST KIDS

Of course, whether men have their own children or not, or whether they mentor children as extended father figures or not, all men can be Earth Fathers to their community and to the world. The fatherly heart seeks to nurture the Earth, and nurture society, in the largest sense. In fact, demonstrating through active citizenship that Earth Fathers raise communities, as well as kids, is an important aspect of being a healthy parent.

Where can Earth Fathers and authentic spiritual warriors put their efforts? One worthy battle is fighting eco-destruction. Ankara, Turkey, has been hit by a drought so fierce that harvests in the region have dropped up to 30 percent.

In Australia, "The Big Dry" is the worst drought there in at least a hundred years; farms are failing and crops dying. In Morocco, 50 percent less rainfall than normal occurred in 2007, and on the Canary Islands, 86,000 acres were burned during fierce wildfires. Mexico, the state of Georgia, and southern California are suffering from record-breaking dry spells and also wildfires. In the coming years around the globe, water wars may prove to be more bitter than oil wars. Will this result in megafires and mass migrations? Indeed, much of America's current "immigration debate" is really an eco-debate — because humans have to migrate when land turns from green to brown. From peak oil to peak water: Is this the future? Is this not a problem in need of healthy fathers?

As Marion Woodman puts it, "A flawed solar myth ... confers upon the masculine a heroic status, which now threatens us with extinction." Indeed, with global warming in all its manifestations, this "flawed solar myth" is coming home to roost. We are literally burning ourselves up. Too much yang energy. Too much fire. Too little water. Too little coolness. Thus every effort to create a sustainable planet is an investment in healthy fatherhood. To create alternative and clean energy sources, to create better auto gas mileage, to create alternative fuels, to cut electrical and gas usage: all this is the work of a *fatherly heart*, for it insures the health and happiness of our children and grandchildren.

As fathers, do we want our kids fed and healthy? Of course, and so working to fix a healthcare system that does not provide health insurance for over forty million persons, and helping to battle poverty (a recent study found thirty-eight million Americans, 18 percent of them children, live in poverty), are worthy battles.

Fighting a culture of consumerism is another. "The transformation of *Homo sapiens* into *Homo consumerus* takes place in two stages. The first, to borrow a phrase from marketing consultants, is the 'consumerization of the child.'" The purpose is to get consumer addictions into children at an early age, before they can distinguish between what one needs and what one wants. The second stage is infantilization, "the unnatural extension of consumerist adolescence into later stages of life." In this context, the market seeks to set the terms of identity, as in Seiko's slogan, "It's your watch that says the most about who you are." A consumerized child very easily becomes a narcissistic adult, so a battle against consumerism is a well-chosen battle for Earth Fathers. Part of a father's role is to liberate one's children from too much television and advertising. In one year children in the United States spend twice as much time watching television as attending school. Scott Sanders comments on the American consumer ethos this way: "Our economy rewards competition rather than cooperation; aggression rather than compassion, greed rather than generosity, haste rather than care. . . . When a corporate CEO is paid a hundred times as much as a schoolteacher or a factory worker, and when the richest one percent of Americans earn as much as the poorest forty percent, how does one teach a child to believe in equity and justice? When success is measured only by quarterly reports, how does one teach patience?"

Another struggle fathers wage for their children is a struggle to find hope even in times of despair — especially in times of despair. What inspired Sanders's book *Hunting for Hope: A Father's Journeys* was a challenge his teenage son put to him on a camping trip when he said to him, "You're so worried about the fate of the earth you can't enjoy anything. We come to these mountains and you bring the shadows with you. You've got me seeing nothing but darkness." Sanders recalls: "Stunned by the force of his words, I could not speak. If my gloom cast a shadow over Creation for my son, then I had failed him. What remedy could there be for such a betrayal?" Sanders, who is a professor, recognizes that his son is like many other young people today. Indeed, "an epidemic of depression is sweeping through their generation. It is the earth they brood about, the outlook for life. . . . The young people who put their disturbing questions to me have had an ecological education, and a political one as well. They know we are in trouble. Everywhere they look they see ruined landscapes and ravaged communities and broken people. So they are asking me if I believe we have the resource for healing the wounds, for mending the breaks. They are asking me if I live in hope." Healthy fathering is hopeful fathering. A father helps with despair.

There are those who would like to make war itself a perpetual thing. They preach that war somehow renders men heroic and great like nothing else can. It is true that heroism and sacrifice happen in war, but to make an idol of war is both dangerous and menacing. James Madison observed this way back in 1795 when he wrote:

> Of all the enemies to public liberty war is, perhaps, the most to be dreaded, because it comprises and develops the germ of every other. War is the parent of armies; from these proceed debts and taxes; and armies, and debts, and taxes are the known instruments for bringing the many under the domination of the few. In war, too, the

discretionary power of the Executive is extended; its influence in dealing out offices, honors, and emoluments is multiplied; and all the means of seducing the minds, are added to those of subduing the force of the people. The same malignant aspect in republicanism may be traced in the inequality of fortunes, and the opportunities of fraud, growing out of a state of war, and in the degeneracy of manners and of morals engendered by both. No nation could preserve its freedom in the midst of continual warfare.

And so to find peaceful options instead of war is altogether the work of a fatherly heart. What father would want to send a son or daughter deliberately to war, unless war was absolutely the last resort and so, in some deep way, an ethical choice? The very notion of "continual warfare," as Madison warned, carries with it the destruction of freedom.

As Madison also warned, war is often a means by which the few maintain their grip on power, and Earth Fathers can resist this concentration of power, whether in the media, business, or government. Thomas Jefferson alerted us to this kind of paternity when he wrote: "Every government degenerates when trusted to the rulers of the people alone. The people themselves, therefore, are its only safe depositories." And Theodore Roosevelt warned against obsessive obeisance to false fathers: To "announce that there must be no criticism of the president, or that we are to stand by the president, right or wrong, is not only unpatriotic and servile, but is morally treasonable to the American public." To stand up against empire-building is a very healthy battle to wage at this time in history.

Earth Fathers can demonstrate and encourage balance and perspective when it comes to America's national obsession with sports. In the right place and context, in balance, sports have many benefits (as we've seen), but having Super Bowl Sunday become a quasi-liturgical event is not altogether a positive achievement of a culture. How far is this from the "bread and circuses" of the Roman Empire, which were deliberate efforts to privatize one's notion of "family" and distract citizens from criticizing Rome's leaders? On a more personal level, healthy fathers make sure children understand the physical price professional athletes frequently pay for entertaining the masses. In NFL football, for example, concussions are sometimes shrugged off as part of the game, but studies show that they can result in suicide, advanced Alzheimer's, and other forms of brain trauma. Major league baseball's steroids scandal is another cautionary example of how individual athletes sometimes throw away their health, and lives, for a game.

Masson reports that he has "never spoken to a father of grown children who did not wish he had spent more time with his children when they were young. If he could change one thing, it would be that one." It is in our evolution to care for and feed our partners and children, to love and protect them and to stay with them and not abandon them. "Children need from us warmth (the human body), comfort (touch, the sounds of soothing speech), protection (from other animals or humans who mean them harm), food, cleaning, shelter, clothing, education, and medical attentions. This is not so daunting if you think that we evolved to be this way." We also evolved to "be in the natural environment, in an outdoor habitat.... No wonder children get bored when they are confined indoors. They have an *innate* preference for the trees and hills and grasses of the savanna.... Research has shown that babies are happiest when they are carried while the parents are walking at a speed of three to four miles per hour."

Scott Sanders reports that "I cannot turn off my fathering mind." No one can do so. As Masson puts it, "fatherhood is not a state that one comes in and out of, as in 'I *was* a father but now I am a free man.' We do not get through and then get over fatherhood. It is, on the contrary, the greatest joy and the greatest expression of love of which the human male is capable." One thing unique about human fatherhood is this: "We appear to be the only species that can consciously choose how involved we want to be as fathers."

A fatherly heart exemplifies the larger context of the father role — an Earth Father's children are not only his literal children. As citizens we are all fathers by the choices we make in our roles as voters, citizens, employees, churchgoers, volunteers. Many parents do a better job at one-on-one parenting than they do in their larger role of *community parenting*. The term "family" can readily become a solely *private* term — indeed, fascism in its many guises always wants this. In this way the political system rarely gets criticized.

This may be the "silver lining" and the "good news" in the ecological crisis of our time: it moves us beyond the personal and local meaning of "family" and "father" to the much larger context of community itself. Crisis may serve as an occasion for us to *wake up* and *get up* off our couches and get *creative* and reinvent the way we live and work on the planet so that humanity and all beings may live. Green Men, spiritual warriors, indeed! We all, whether literal parents or "community elders," instruct others by our example (as much as by words); actions teach and make the "fatherly heart" visible in the world. Actions provide a model of the "fatherly heart" for the young to emulate and imitate. An Earth Father incarnates.

10

GRANDFATHER SKY:
THE GRANDFATHERLY HEART

NOT ONLY IS THERE A FATHERLY HEART that needs attention and development. There is also a *grandfatherly heart* that needs attention and development. We might say that the fatherly heart expands into the grandfatherly heart, that Father Sky expands into Grandfather Sky: it is the fatherly heart doubled or even the fatherly heart squared. This occurs as we become freed from the daily burdens of work and career and from the duties of raising children. As when we were young, our time is more our own, and our heart, purer and less disturbed perhaps, can focus more on what matters. On what remains.

Elders are often neglected in US society, which tends to value people for their consuming power ("I buy therefore I am"). Although our culture occasionally acknowledges elders for their past contributions, it rarely listens to them about today's problems. It almost never includes them or seeks their gifts, which they have spent a lifetime developing. Older men, of grandfatherly and great-grandfatherly age, have a tremendous amount to share with younger generations. Time and experience, laughter and a certain detachment from everyday life — all that brings forth wisdom to be shared between the oldest and the youngest in society. But this wisdom does not spring forth of its own accord: for elders to play the role of Grandfather Sky, they have to *stay alive* and *stay in love with life.* They need to continue to care, to give, to listen, to look to the future, to encourage, to see the big picture, to be playful, and to protect. Elders are teachers about the deeper aspects of life itself. And the young need their wisdom, love of life, and humor.

A recent study has found that, contrary to many myths, old age in fact is the happiest time for most people. "Eye-opening research...found the happiest Americans are the oldest and older adults are more socially active than the stereotype of the lonely senior suggest,...the two go hand-in-hand — being social can help keep away the blues." Older people have generally learned to be more content with what they have than younger adults, and their network of social connecting includes socializing with neighbors, attending religious services, volunteering, and going to group meetings. The study interviewed twenty-eight thousand people aged eighteen to eighty-eight from 1972 to 2004. The study appears in the April 2008 *American Sociological Review*. "Contentment as far as I'm concerned comes with old age," said one senior, "because you accept things the way they are. You know that nothing is perfect." Seniors have, among other things, happiness to share with the young.

The intergenerational wisdom I speak of cannot happen if all generations of men, from youngest to oldest, don't meet together. We need to create more opportunities for such gatherings, more intergenerational rituals, in particular because this teaching and sharing is by no means a one-way street. The young have much to give their elders: meaning and purpose, beauty and spontaneity, questions and challenges, new stories to link with old stories, new languages and music, and an enthusiastic embrace of life. These things can inspire elders, even as elders teach and temper the young.

In these critical times, when the world is undergoing astounding transformations, elders are more important than ever. They can be caretakers and guides, as well as wise critics of greed and human selfishness, which wound our communities, all beings, and Mother Earth. Circles of grandfathers and elders need to join with circles of youth and young men to chant and sing and also to discuss the important matters of our day. These discussions cannot be left to the media or to politicians, who so often sacrifice honest talk and long-term goals for short-term self-interest and greed. Such gatherings of elders and youth could prove to be a far more profound educational experience than most of what we call education today. And far cheaper to accomplish, and far more fun.

DON'T ENTER RETIREMENT, ENTER REFIREMENT

All this can happen when we expand the meaning of *father* and *grandfather* beyond the literal to its broader application. When I pray with Native Americans,

I am moved by their use of the terms "Grandfather Sky" and "Grandmother Earth." Inherent in these names for Divinity is deep respect for elders. We rarely hear such language in Western forms of worship.

In a very rich and deeply felt study of eldership, *From Age-ing to Sage-ing*, Rabbi Zalman Schachter-Shalomi develops a profound and practical understanding of the grandfatherly heart. He tells his own story of how, as he approached the age of sixty, he fell into a state of depression. Then he took a vision quest, a spiritual retreat in the wilderness, and learned deeper things. Instead of becoming depressed about his advancing years, he found he was being "initiated as an elder. . . . I instinctively began harvesting my life, a process that involved bringing one's earthly journey to a successful completion, enjoying the contributions one has made, and passing on a legacy to the future. To initiate the process, I asked myself, 'If I had to die now, what would I most regret not having done? What remains incomplete in my life?'"

These are important questions, and more men than ever are asking them, since more and more people are living to an advanced age. A hundred years ago about 4 percent of Americans were over sixty-five, whereas today it is about 18 percent. During recorded history, only about 10 percent of people lived to be sixty-five, but today about 80 percent of Americans will live to that age and beyond. What will we do with our later years, our "retirement" years? How will men spend their time once they leave the "daily grind"?

First, I believe we must retire the word "retirement." It conjures images of unfocused leisure, of spending days on golf courses or lounging on the couch watching TV. I think a better word is "refirement." Once, the need to put bread on the table for our family and others fired us up. It drove us to work for decades. Where is the fire in the belly, in the gut, now? We can still contribute in special, important, and unique ways, but they will be different ways. Even as "fatherly" fires die, new fires are rekindled in the grandfatherly heart. Schachter calls this *saging*, a "new model of late-life development, . . . a process that enables older people to become spiritually radiant, physically vital, and socially responsible 'elders of the tribe.'" Schachter believes that "extended longevity calls for the development of extended consciousness to help offset the physical and social diminishments of old age." Indeed, he calls this idea "the principal thesis of this book," namely "that extended longevity calls for extended consciousness." Thus, in the archetypal terms we've been discussing, the expanded consciousness of the Blue Man is an inherent attribute of Grandfather Sky, whose gaze takes in not only the entire vastness of life and the

cosmos, but now the inevitable end as well. Schachter quotes psychologist Gay
Luce, who maintains that elderhood "is a time to discover inner richness for
self-development and spiritual growth. It is also a time of transition and preparation for dying, which is at least as important as preparation for a career or family. Out of this time of inner growth come our sages, healers, prophets, and
models for the generation to follow."

Our capacity for meditation and contemplative soaring, for fuller use of
our third brain (our neocortex), may just be beginning to flourish at this time
in our lives. Hopefully these are skills we can develop and pass on to younger
generations. There may be a special role for the right hemisphere or mystical
brain to play in our later years. This is one way that wisdom arrives, after all.
The late Christian monk Bede Griffiths told me on more than one occasion
that a stroke he underwent in his seventies "killed whatever was left of my left
brain" and made him a much purer mystic. Ram Dass has told similar stories
after his stroke, how that experience made him a more peaceful and generous
human being.

Obviously, one's physical capabilities diminish with old age, but creativity does not have to. Some of the world's greatest artistic masterpieces were
created by "old men." Michelangelo completed the "Last Judgment" on the
wall of the Sistine Chapel when he was sixty-six years old. It was radically con-
troversial because it was full of nude men — so much so that within ten years
other artists were hired to put loincloths on all the naked figures. Giuseppe
Verdi composed operas while in his seventies and eighties. Picasso kept painting into his nineties — indeed, I remember being moved to tears as I stood in
front of his final painting, a portrait of himself as an old man in a chair, at the
Picasso Museum in Paris. Picasso was blunt and head-on; in the last gift of his
life, Picasso did not hide anything of his inner feelings, including grief at leav-
ing. Also in his nineties, Arthur Rubenstein still played the piano and wrote
his beautiful autobiography. Pablo Casals taught and played the cello and wrote
well into his late years. Goethe wrote *Faust* when he was eighty. Given all
this, elderhood can clearly compensate for physical diminishment with creative
flowering.

But creativity is not just about what we do or make. It is also about the
way we view the world. Do we see it, and ourselves, as tired and old, as an object to be managed, or as beauty to be wondered at? As we grow older, this last
perspective often takes on whole new meanings, as the time for living and appreciation draws to a close. In this context, appreciation of life becomes part

of the creative act as well; all art is a give-and-take process. After all, the creativity of a Picasso, Mozart, or Casals is nothing without others to appreciate and be moved by their painting and music. The expanded consciousness of the Blue Man includes our ability to appreciate the beauty and creativity of life all around us.

I recall one time when my father, who was then sick with brain cancer, was visiting my youngest sister. It was time to leave and go to the airport, and he was nowhere to be found. After much hunting, my sister found him in the backyard, which had a beautiful vista. My father was just standing, admiring beauty. "It's hard to leave behind, isn't it?" my sister said to him as she gently moved him to the waiting car. "Yes it is," he replied. An appreciation of life's beauty deepens, rather than diminishes, with old age. It becomes all the more important, linking past with future, a present-moment connection that never grows old.

I speak from experience. Time and again I find myself overwhelmed by the beauty of sun hitting a wood pillar in my house — I am awed by how every season the sun hits the wood differently, or by a piece of music, or by a vigorous young mind, or by a beautiful young body at play. As John Weir Perry puts it, "In our later years, we feel connected to the world through bonds of tenderness and empathy. Life becomes more poetic. The ordinary objects that surround us — trees, houses, clouds, animals — shimmer with metaphoric insight, revealing depths of meaning that normally elude our practical minds. We may relate to a tree in the backyard as the Tree of Life that is rooted in eternal life or truth." Recently I ran into a friend I had not seen in years, the photographer Courtney Milnes. Years ago, Milnes made a pilgrimage around the world to photograph all the sacred sites. On his mystical pilgrimage, he took my book *The Coming of the Cosmic Christ*, and afterward he produced a stunning book of his images. But at our recent encounter, he said to me, "I now stay more at home and have taken over 30,000 pictures of the pond in my backyard. It is just as sacred as any of those sacred sites I traveled so far to see."

FACING DEATH

One of the defining attributes of the grandfatherly heart is the expanded consciousness that comes from facing death directly. To do so, we must also face our fear of death. Death means the end of our life, but fear of death keeps us from living life fully while we are alive. Ultimately, our love of life can get us over both thresholds, so that we recognize the seamlessness of death and life — all life gets recycled. Why not ours? Death is integral to life. Not only do animals and plants, all "living beings," live, die, and resurrect in some form, but galaxies, stars, and supernovas do, too. Thankfully, the spiritual side of death, and the denial of death, has been addressed for many years now, such as by author Ernest Becker and by Dr. Elisabeth Kübler-Ross. Through their work, many individuals are able to face death more honestly and in the process to live more fully right up to the end. The hospice movement has contributed substantially to this as well, with its recognition that death is not necessarily something to resist at all costs with every available medical device. Death is our consciousness moving on to another plane of existence.

All religions and spiritual traditions teach of the mystery as well as the wonder of death, though they name death and the afterlife differently: during the goddess era it was "regeneration," but the East now calls it "reincarnation" and the West "resurrection." Meister Eckhart said that at death "life dies but being goes on." At death we return to the Godhead from whence we flowed at birth and from where no one will have missed us in our absence. The Sufi mystic Hafiz declares, "God has written a thousand promises all over your heart that say Life, life, life is far too sacred to ever end." The Mesoamerican poet Nezahualcoyotl explores death and its aftermath with these words:

Thus we are,
We are mortal,
Men through and through,
We all will have to go away,
We all will have to die on earth.

But looking within he finds more than the fear of death or the victory of death.

Within myself I discover this:
Indeed, I shall never die,
Indeed, I shall never disappear.
There where there is no death,
There where death is overcome,
Let me go there.

And, once again, it is in our gifts of beauty that we live on in some form.

My flowers will not come to an end,
My songs will not come to an end,

I, the singer, raise them up;
They are scattered, they are bestowed.

John of the Cross wrote about "dying before dying," and we all need to do this to help overcome fear of death. We need to recognize and name how many times we have already managed to let go in our lives — as Eckhart said, life is an *eternal* act of letting go. The letting go we do at death is just one more, though of uniquely special consequence.

To face death, and therefore to see our lives in its context, deepens our lives. Life deepens when death draws closer. Those who have escaped death often talk of seeing simple things they never noticed before — like wildflowers or a person's smile — in a whole new, magical, grace-filled light. Death raises the important questions: What do we really intend to do with our one, unrepeatable, life? Whom shall we love? Whom shall we serve? These deep questions are elicited by the presence and awareness of death and of mortality.

In a secular culture, who keeps these questions alive? Elders. All of us need to ask them, but elders have a special role to play in passing this deeper awareness on to the young. In the West's materialistic culture, anything related to death is typically denied in a kind of "live, drink, and be merry because tomorrow you disappear" philosophy. Elders, nearer to death than others, typically embrace and remain conscious of its lessons. The ancient Mesoamerican practice that has evolved into today's "Day of the Dead" ritual is a deep reminder that he lives fullest who lives in the context of death. Because life is brief, it is valuable. Because life is brief, it is all the more precious. Let us not waste it.

MENTORING: SHARING OUR GRANDFATHERLY HEART

Tribal hunter-gatherers in particular, those whose genetic code we all still carry with us, developed deep ways to respect the role of elders in the community. As Schachter puts it, "Native Americans think of their elders as wisdomkeepers whose contemplative skills help safeguard tribal survival." Schachter believes that we have, especially with the industrial society, lost our connection to these ancient ways. Elders often feel isolated and cut off from younger generations, and youths often find themselves in rebellion against parents — and distanced from the grandparents. The elders "have not been schooled in the high art of enjoying our achievements." This is an art to be recovered.

An example of healthy grandfatherhood was bequeathed to me by my mentor, the late French Dominican Father M. D. Chenu, who died at age ninety-five on the same day that Nelson Mandela was released from prison (a perfectly chosen moment, I would say, since Chenu was the grandfather of liberation theology). When Chenu was eighty-eight, a journalist who had interviewed him remarked afterward, "This is the youngest man I have ever interviewed." Chenu stayed young; his mind was ever-supple. He never played ego games when he was teaching or in his writing. In class I never once heard him put down or "one-up" a young thinker. Quite the opposite: He would continually encourage his students, like the time he told us, in the middle of the strikes and riots that were shutting all of Paris down in 1968, "go out and join the revolution. Don't come back next week, but come back in two weeks and tell me what you have contributed. We have been studying history, but here is your chance to make it." He was seventy-six at the time.

The last time I saw Chenu he was eighty-eight and on his way to Chartres to debate the bishop on *savoir* ("knowledge") versus *pouvoir* ("power") in the church. Chenu's soul "was as young as the day it was created," to borrow a phrase from Meister Eckhart. Indeed, Eckhart said, "I am younger today than I was yesterday, and if I am not younger tomorrow than I am today, I would be ashamed of myself." What Eckhart and Chenu both demonstrate is that youth is a state of soul, and if one has decently nurtured one's soul, one can maintain its pristine joyfulness and spontaneity. For me one of the signs of a healthy older person is the presence of this child-like youthfulness.

Deepak Chopra writes in *Ageless Body, Timeless Mind* that "the decline of vigor in old age is largely the result of people *expecting* to decline; they have unwittingly implanted a self-defeating intention in the form of a strong belief, and the mind-body connection automatically carries out this intention." If we can influence our mind with negative thoughts, surely the opposite is true also: we can, by intending to stay young, keep our mind-body healthier and younger. That is part of the purpose of mentoring also: older people should *choose* to hang out with younger people and *choose* to learn from younger people. I have seen both kinds of elder in my life: those who dominate the young, either ignoring them or putting them down as inferiors — such men are themselves very old, goat-like, and unfun to be around. For they are not growing; they are stuck. And I have seen the second kind, those who choose the company of the young to learn as well as to teach; to stay young as well as to offer what wisdom they have. No matter how old, in the best sense, these men die young.

Today, the young speak new languages and communicate in ways that were unknown a generation ago: in terms of the Internet and wireless technology in particular. Think Internet. Think iPods. Think MySpace. Think YouTube and so much more. We are between eras — call them the pre-modern and post-modern worlds — and elders are particularly challenged to bridge this communication divide. Elders may wish to teach, but they need the young to teach them their new languages, so perhaps more than ever before, elders need to become students of the young. New art forms are emerging, including rap, raves, break dancing, personal video filmmaking, and more. Far from rendering old stories and abiding spiritual wisdom obsolete, these languages offer interesting new contexts for sharing them — and it is essential that this happen. Healing, vital connections must be forged between young and old today if our planet is to survive.

Society used to provide more direct one-on-one opportunities for this, and elders mentored about more than philosophical questions; they provided practical, applied wisdom for living successfully in all respects. Our modern version of a school-based education arose in the dusty wake of the Industrial Revolution, but can a holistic education ever be mass-produced? In centuries prior, youngsters usually learned by apprenticing with an older man or, in the case of a monastery, by apprenticing and living with older men; youth learned not just the skills of their trade, but also how to be in the world. As Schachter points out, "beginning with the Industrial Revolution, mentoring became institutionalized and bureaucratized as factory-like schools began teaching young people the specialized skills needed in industrial society." Furthermore, until this time rabbinical students did not study in seminaries but were trained through direct apprenticeships with practicing rabbis. In the monastic era of Christianity the young men were trained not just in writing or reading but in chant, in working in the fields, and in self-discipline (such as through fasting, dietary restrictions, early rising, enduring the elements, and more).

A particularly poignant story was recently told of actor Ed Harris who was approached by Logan and Noah Miller, twenty-nine-year-old twins who had a dream: to make a movie about their father who died at fifty-nine in the Marin County jail. He was a roofer and carpenter who slept in his truck. The two had never made a movie before, but after some heavy courting, Harris responded positively to their dream. About their film, *Touching Home*, Logan says, "We wanted to show in the movie that our father would still try to make the best out of a bad situation. You could never just disown him, because he was such a beautiful person." He had a drinking problem, however. "When he was sober, it was fun. You make the best of it. . . . You're just hopin' that he doesn't drink." Their father was a Korean War veteran who had seen fierce battles there. Harris agreeing to play the part helped to bring financing to the project. Said Noah, "Our father died penniless in jail, and a movie star has resurrected him." A fine example of youth and elders linking up as teammates.

Young and old are meant to learn together and to teach each other. The young can teach (or re-teach) a love of life, a joy at living, a less purposeful existence. And hopefully the old can teach the wisdom they've gained from surviving the trials and limits that are an inevitable part of life. Limits are exactly what youth so often dismiss and fail to honor.

John Conger addresses this in our interview when he says:

> The issue is that when you are young, it's okay to be narcissistic. But when you're older, it's kind of ugly. So when you're older, you have to deal with losses, and you have to deal with mistakes and look back at your past. It's harder as an older man to process what you lose. In this culture you're not really taught how to deal with your feelings and to talk about them the way women do; and to talk about relationships. And so you end up leading a path with some wreckage in it as an older man, and you need to deal with your shame and to talk about your feelings and deal with brokenness and communication. Because in the first part of life, you are taught to be omnipotent and without limitation. But life teaches us limitation. So being a man once you get older, you have to have the humility to deal with the limitations. And discover that you can only become a vice president. Or that you're a good doctor but not a great doctor. Or a good researcher but not a brilliant researcher.

Limits speak to us. Time is limited. Our body in its current form exhibits more limits and reminds us that our time is running out. This can increase our desire to leave a gift behind for the young.

The need for elders, and the excitement of being an elder, never diminishes. I remember when, twenty years ago, the late monk Bede Griffiths was preparing to die. He felt his work was essentially finished on this Earth. He had invested his life in an ashram in southern India, where he trained many young men to integrate both Christian and Hindu spiritual practices. But a surprising event happened to him. One day a young British scientist, a graduate of Cambridge University, wandered into his ashram: Rupert Sheldrake. The two men struck up a deep and lasting friendship — one that among other things extended Bede's life on Earth considerably. Bede, ever intellectually as well as spiritually curious, was taken with Rupert's stories about the discoveries of today's sciences, and Rupert was keen on developing a spiritual practice from his own Western tradition, a tradition he felt he had had to abandon when he came East and studied yoga and other ancient ways. The two were balm for each other's souls, and history was changed because they instructed one another. That is how good mentoring works. Elder and youth both blossom, both learn, and both teach.

True elder mentoring, in Schachter's eyes, requires five elements: The first is listening with a great openness of heart. The second is not imposing but evoking your student's innate knowing ("education" after all comes from *educere*, to lead out). Third is to be your searching and tentative and very human self — not be a know-it-all or play a role to impress the other person. The fourth is to call forth that person's uniqueness. Finally, the last element is the awareness that a mentor relationship is not forever. As young men grow into adults, they do not need a mentor relationship so much as friendship, and that is another relationship altogether.

JIM MILLER: COYOTE WISDOM

Seventy-two-year-old Jim Miller identifies himself as a "retired farmer, investor, photographer, poet, a bit of a coyote crazy, and been a swimmer all my life." In my interview with Jim, I was struck by how many of the themes of this book came together in his reflections on his life, his mistakes, his learnings, and his vision. The role of body and sexuality, of land (Green Man), and of consciousness (Blue Man) all play prominent roles in his philosophy of life, and they are equally important for being an elder. So, I've decided to end this chapter with his wonderful example of an enthusiastic old "coyote."

FOX: Tell me more about the role of swimming in your life.

MILLER: I enjoyed it enormously as something to play with; I learned to swim in my parents' fish pond; always loved water. Grandmother would take us to the beach in the summer; I was a surfer in college, swimming team. At forty, my godmother said: "You've got to make changes," and I did it, went back to swimming. I was a type-A personality, and my body was not keeping up with my ego, so I calmed down. I love the open water. It's a meditation. I edited a book around swimming called *The Wet Poet's Society: Anthology of Swimmers'*

Poetry and Art. At sixty-five or sixty-six I swam the English Channel on a re-lay team. It was wonderful, water was very clear. The Catalina Channel was a very long swim; I started at 5 A.M. and again at 11 and a *huge* pod of dolphins came and swam with me. I swam around Manhattan twice, and to Alcatraz and back many times. It's been a medicine, a healing, a meditation for me. Swim-ming is like sex; it's a matter of elongating and riding a wave.

FOX: How big a role does shame plan in men's issues?

MILLER: Huge! Huge! I was loaded with shame until I had a weekend with Dr. Shapiro who directed EMDR, the Rapid Eye Movement Therapy. She's taken it to Turkey and Oklahoma. She's amazing. The toxic shame of my mother permeated everything in my life — shame of my body, of my sexual-ity, of my ideas. Shame has affected many, many men. It's very hard to see, not something you easily identify. It has to come from the experiential level of the body — shame is seated in the body.

FOX: What other strategies do you have for getting men through shame?

MILLER: Validating men. Listening to how men feel, knowing tomorrow in-terpretations will be different as they seep in and percolate and work around it, and as they become more empowered by the fact that one has shame and can get rid of it and see how one is empowered by it. The love and affection men can have for one another gets one through shame also. There is a spiri-tual connection. I have had that experience with different men over the past fifteen to twenty years, and it's been very powerful.

FOX: Regarding the body connection to shame, does your swimming help in that regard?

MILLER: Yes. Swimming comes from the hips. All energy begins in the pelvic area. Yesterday my little granddaughter turned two years of age. I told her mother she should become a ballet dancer — she was moving her hips like to-tal body at work, no shame at all. That's the beauty of children all over the world regardless of creed, color, culture. Every child is born with the same iden-tical language — Buddhist, Christian, pagan, atheist, it doesn't matter. It's all ...love. The body comes into the world shamelessly, and we armor it in the name of civilization, culture, education, religion. The body holds the shame and it permeates. It's not easy to lift it up. The roots are embedded like a fungus.

Swimming helps and breath work and realizing how armored my body is. My armor is part of the shame — "I'm not worthy, not good enough, not strong enough." I was never seen for who I am, so I had to turn myself inside out to become something my parents wanted or to get crumbs of love off the table. The embodiment is important. Life is an inside job. The puer/puella in our culture does not encourage the inside work.

A lot of children today are a lot more attuned to their bodies and their sexuality than in my generation, because we had to become something to appeal to our parents. We had to do something to get their attention and approval. The twelve-step program is so powerful for me because you give up your power in order to get love. Twist yourself and become something other than your true self, and your authentic self shrivels. As I've said in a poem, it was so drastic that I had to move next door. It's very schizophrenic. I ask my cleaning lady: Which house is she cleaning?

FOX: Do men have more of a problem with shame than women?

MILLER: In my mother's generation, there were limits of education, right to property and money, voice and political power for women. Now women have come out of the box; it is men who have a lot of work to do. Consider conservative Islamics and the pope, who want to take us back to centuries ago and make women truly shackled. Christian right men are scared of freedom. Men have come into their own, and men's freedom is behind bars of shame and control and dysfunction, of having to control everything instead of being free and open and allowing kundalini and the juice to flow and celebrate life.

America is one of the angriest nations in the world. American sexuality is extremely shallow because the anger and the sex mirror each other in terms of the body. The body responds.

FOX: Anger and aggression with men. An issue?

MILLER: Enormous. And it comes back to the body. So many men are circumcised, which is not necessary. Consider that the circumcised skin has lost 80 percent of nerve endings in the penis. Thus a circumcised man only gets 20 percent of the sexual pleasure at orgasm that he should get. You get a tip-of-the-penis climax instead of a whole-body climax. Reich said the best cure for cancer is a full-body orgasm where every cell vibrates. Shame that men put on ourselves to control women. The goal of the three religions of the West has been to control women's sexuality and also men's sexuality. It's the anger that Riane Eisler points out — a great deal of Christian history has been so aggressive. Under its name you have the genocide in America, the Crusades, and more.

FOX: What strategies can combat anger?

MILLER: First is to look at it and confront it. I've done a lot of workshops with men and anger, and it's very vital for men to understand that their power of anger covers their grief, and their grief holds their love. Often men will have considerable insights into their own dynamic of getting into their rage, which we all hold. Look at George Bush with his tight jaw — it's like the pelvis. If your jaw is tight, your pelvis is tight, and this goes back to the child nursing. As the child's jaw moves, the excitation of the body occurs while nursing. It's all connected.

A lot of the anger disconnects us from the pleasure of the body, which is the sacredness of men and women. We must make changes. If not, global warming will wake us up, and we'll have a deep change.

FOX: Someone has defined shame as not belonging. What do you say?

MILLER: Personally, I was shamed and I pulled back, I did not belong. Men do that. They don't participate in the family dynamic because they didn't see it in their family dynamic. Especially in the fifties. What was McCarthy's mother like? It often comes from one's mother. Women were put down for so long, and their anger came out through their children. And it's not just genitals but the love the mother can give through her eyes and body contact and warmth and nonverbal language. As Barbara Walker wrote in her wonderful book *The Crone*, it's the mother who grounds her children in their sexuality. If a mother has been abused, as my mother was, severely abused, then because of her wounds, she is unable to give the gift of pure gold to her children. We're all wounded, men and women.

FOX: What about the father-son relationship?

MILLER: My father pushed me away. His message was that men don't love. Men are fuckers, not lovers. Anger, not sweetness. Men are born with two heads, one little one and one big one, and they let the little one do all the thinking for them. *It's not that*. It's about allowing the heart to open. Every wound the child undergoes in the first two years forms the basis of the character of the adult. Wounds get laid in. My mother was incapable of loving, and I went into an anger mode for two or three years until I finally swallowed it, closed down, and would not love. A fully mothering mother gives light and acceptance and shameless honoring of the body to the child. But if she or the father don't have this, they can't get love across. Love is action and anger is action.

FOX: "Only a fool thinks with his head," say the Hopis.

MILLER: Very true. We get out of our bodies. But take football — it's very violent contact. Men carry a great deal of homophobia. My father was very homophobic, but I think he was bisexual. Hesitation in one's sexuality happens very early. I had painful sexuality because I had no grounding. The men's movement has helped me to see myself as a strong male, and I thought I never could do that.

FOX: What changes do you see the movement undergoing? How is it evolving?

MILLER: I've been to a lot of gatherings around the San Francisco Bay Area. Men are working, men are changing. Some groups are doing remarkable work. Michael Meade with kids and men in Oakland. It's work. Drumming is one way to get men involved with rhythm and learning to get in sync with other men, plus dancing, writing, a lot of creativity. As at UCS — get the creativity going and get men together to feel safe to talk from the heart, rather than being guarded all the time. A lot of men are guarded.

FOX: Vulnerability is a real issue with men because from the time we are young we are taught to hold feelings in.

MILLER: The male "A-frame hug." It keeps the pelvises from touching. Nothing more delicious than to hug a woman with her pelvis up against yours. And a man, too. It's not about delving into sexual energy, but it's so sweet. It's touching.

FOX: How long have you had this appreciation of the body? How long did it take you to recover it?

MILLER: A long, long time. Twenty-five years ago with the discovery of Reich's work *The Murder of Christ* and how Christianity has been so repressive. Music in the twenties, the Depression, World War II, then it blew open in Woodstock and the flower days of San Francisco, opening up against the repression of years of theology — "Don't touch this, that is dirty." We need a good funeral for Calvin, who keeps raising his head from the grave every fifty years and stirs things up, like the Christian right. We live his negativity!

FOX: Maybe a funeral for Augustine, too. Now you are a grandfather. What's the best part of being a grandfather?

MILLER: I'm still learning that. I'm a great puer, and my granddaughter didn't ask me to be a grandfather. She just showed up and said, "Now you're a grandfather." I wasn't ready for that. So I had to begin by getting rid of my puer. My puer skin. It's coming around slowly, acknowledging the fact that I have to let go of some toys of mine I held on to; I needed them but now I don't have to have them. Being a grandfather is a total shift.

FOX: She's changing your life and being?

MILLER: Changing my being and the way I look at things. Mellowing out my deep roots of paranoia. Being able to see more with a clear heart, more of a clear connection to this palace that I have inside. Being able to relate from it rather than from what Chuck Kelly called a very strong head defense toward feeling. We think our way through life, which is what I had to do as a child because my feelings were inoculated. I was not given what I needed, so I had to turn myself inside out, and this is where the defense starts — becoming very clever and thinking things through instead of allowing the dance to occur. My granddaughter dances and her little rear end moves like crazy, like a little hula dancer — she speaks terrible pelvic truth.

FOX: Sounds like you have a lot in common with a little person still evolving and the youngest ones in your life.

MILLER: The day she was born and I held her for the first time, I burst into tears. It took me a while to figure out what was happening. Here she was totally innocent, and holding her reminded me of my losses, the lost vulnerability — I had it but one level of that is so deeply ingrained in the body. I didn't think about it, the tears just started coming. The way she looks at me. She looks right into you. Her eyes are connected to the heart.

I was at a party the other night and a very brilliant guy from Silicon Valley — who's retired, a pilot and a swimmer — could not look me straight in the eye when we spoke. He was always looking off to the side. This told me he was not connected. He is very much into his head. He couldn't look at you because he had to go to his head; if he looked at me directly, we would be open with each other. The body is so subtle, especially old farts who have been carrying this armor for a hundred years — it's not easy to get rid of it.

FOX: Do you agree with my term "refirement" instead of retirement?

MILLER: I like that. It's amazing the number of gray-haired men up where I live on bicycles, older people doing athletic things. When we were teenagers I never saw older people exercising. Only people playing tennis so they would have their gin and tonics afterward. Men have changed! A lot of our male culture has been changed; a lot is yet to come however. What the younger generation is doing and seeing — fifty-year-old men out there exercising and riding their bikes and being healthy. And swimming, too.

FOX: Do you relate to Don Quixote?

MILLER: No. He's a trickster. Don Juan is different. I've seen the Don Juan in me, the carouser, the partier, running. I've been a runner a lot of my life — not athletically, but just running away from the pain, which is way, way in the back. I'm a type-A personality, very compulsive, very professionalistic, very hard driven.

FOX: You were a successful farmer and wine grower. Did you enjoy that work?

MILLER: I loved it. I loved being out in the vines. It was basically another level of therapy. My land and ranch was my therapy. I'm now going through the King Lear drama with my son, who hasn't killed me yet, but he wants the vineyard and the empire, and I'm relegated to a tiny cave in the mountains with a few Persian carpets and a little family silver. That's been hard, very hard, how he has changed.

He has a woman in his life, a wife; he is a father. As a man I have to acknowledge him and bless him, which I did at his wedding. But there's been a lot of angst and pain and change within me, permutation, refermenting, refirement — it's been hard on him and hard on me. I raised him, he was my son, and I can see where a bit of resentment is there — because I used that bond for my needs instead of letting him go. I have a lady friend who has the same relationship of pain with her daughter. Was there ever a story written for women along the same idea as King Lear? Such conflicts are famous. She was talking on the phone the other day, and I could see myself mirrored there.

FOX: How many years were you working in the vineyards?

MILLER: Thirty-five years. Bulldozing, my hands were in the dirt, on the vines. Vine growing includes lots of trestles and straight lines, a metaphor for male controlling, the dysfunctional male — everything was lined up, straight lines and stainless-steel wires going down. Everything had to be straight. Managing things right and clipping things right, all the boxes and hedges were all controlled gardens.

FOX: Did your awakening happen after you let go of the work?

MILLER: One is always working. I want to write a book on "Fifty years of therapy and still going strong," because I know several men who are like Robert

Bly and others in their sixties and seventies still working. It would be a window into how older men must be changing subtly. Therapy is never finished. The men's movement has validated that in men's gatherings in different parts of the country. Awareness and awakeness. Men have been asleep in our patriarchal theocracies. And they've had a lot of wool pulled over their eyes over a long period of time. And a lot are awakening to their vulnerability and their sensitivities to Life rather than to badly suited myths.

FOX: Do you see yourself as an elder?

MILLER: Yes.

FOX: What are the most important qualities of an elder?

MILLER: Wisdom, patience, validating youth, listening to youth, dancing with youth, doing creative artwork with youth — what you're doing with Professor Pitt. That is very, very valuable, including what you did with Cosmic Masses, which were such a spectrum of age, elders, and youth. I think nurturing life and being a nurturer, a husband to the youth, to protect, to instill, to incentivize, to keep the fire of youth alive. There's a group of men called the Inside Circle — incredible what they are doing inside the prisons, getting the men to become awake to their interior life. Some hard-core gangs of youth who could be killed learn how to be a man outside of gangs and within one's own vulnerability. Amazing work the poetry coming out of there, the self-discovery.

There are men in Sacramento going into the prison population and doing a new kind of work. The prison guards and warden love it because they see a change in the prison population. Like the movie you told us about, *Doing Time, Doing Vipassana*, a movie about meditation in prisons in India and in Los Angeles, the energy of the prison shifted — again it's about coming back to the body. So much of American male energy has been so compressed that it comes out in a very inappropriate and destructive pattern, angry destruction as opposed to a way that does not put others down.

FOX: So there is lots of work for elders.

MILLER: Tremendous work for elders! And they are there.

FOX: There are a lot of men who want to be elders but don't know it; they don't feel they have an invitation.

MILLER: No invitation because there's no initiation. And behind that is the need for ritual. The sweat lodges and Sundances — these *old* ancient rituals that instill in the young men who do the dance something of tremendous power.

Not having been there, I can't comment further. It's something the Christian culture does not have. Rituals initiate. Pitt does through music; you have done in your life; Michael Meade does through music. Robert Bly has done marvelous work getting people awake to the songs that are in poetry that are out there — David Whyte, another great poet, that's what our poets are doing.

FOX: Anything else you want to add?

MILLER: I have heard you speak of the term the "sacred masculine." I don't think we have much sacred masculinity in the dominant culture. The "sacred masculine" makes me think of Native American Chief Seattle, who was an amazingly beautiful man. That great farewell speech of his was outstanding — it had to come from sacredness that the man held because he was sacred to his body. And being sacred to your body is the root to honoring the sacredness of culture being.

Have we been honoring women? No. So women are passing their anger back on their children, and this is where generation to generation gets wounded. I think sacredness comes from a deep respect for the body.

The zen way of farming is that you don't put a hole in the ground, but you drop the seed and let the weeds come up around it. So it's a matter of how our whole culture has been one of castrating nature and controlling nature, using nature and obliterating nature.

FOX: Wendell Jackson says we've been doing agriculture wrong for ten thousand years.

MILLER: My son is doing the vineyards in a biodynamic way, very conservative, letting the weeds grow. It's a different way of approaching nature. We don't spray.

I think the lack of sacredness comes from a long, long line of theocracy that has been very abusive. Especially, it is a theology based on the denial of sexuality in order to gain power through virtual control. Sexuality is our connection to God and to the Earth. David Deida's work is brilliant, *The Way of the Superior Man* and *Finding God through Sex*. As Reich says, it's about our connection to our bodies, our body orientation, because if we are connected to our bodies, we are connected to the Earth, as many Indian tribes were. So I think it's the sacredness of the body that needs to be looked at; pagan rituals and pre-Christian rituals brought this in many ways. Your Cosmic Masses were very beautiful because they drew together so many of these various elements into the celebration. The ecstatic side of life.

It hurts to have a priest who denies his sexuality say he is superior because he has denied it! It's through our sexuality and our expression of sexuality that we come close to the cosmic energy that flows through all of life that we are all part of — that the trees and the stones are part of. The cosmic energy is flowing and constantly moving; we are made from it. To deny this is to contribute to the diminution of the deeper level of what sexual energy is all about. Western culture is highly repressive. Our sexual education in our culture has been very repressive, whereas the Native American sees sexuality as positive. The Chinese had its secrets, India its tantras. These are all positive ways of teaching healthy sexuality. The worst word I think in our language was "masturbation," coming from *masturbare*, which means to abuse. Starhawk says: "Throw it out." Self-pleasure is the word, which is basically coming back to the needs of the body. We can self-pleasure ourselves — you won't go blind, you might see a lot! Attachment to our bodies is our attachment to the land.

PART II

SACRED MARRIAGES

THE SACRED MARRIAGE
OF MASCULINE AND FEMININE

I BEGAN THIS BOOK RECALLING A DREAM I had while lecturing on the Sacred Masculine. It was a dream of a great wedding caravan that was honoring the marriage of a very happy masculine tiger and a maternal elephant both riding in the backseat of a wedding car. In part II, we close the book with two chapters on the Sacred Marriage. Taoist teacher Mantak Chia says, "Within every moment there is only the Emptiness of yin receiving the Fullness of yang. This is the eternal marriage of man and woman, of spirit and matter, of Heaven and Earth."

In this chapter, we look at the Sacred Marriage of gender, which is archetypal in each of us, though we too often take these gender roles literally. In the next chapter, we look at how to marry many of the other dualities that so often trouble our sense of self and our modern world. Sacred Marriages are what we need inside us and between us to give birth to a whole, green, vibrant, sustainable, diverse, joyful new world.

After all, what good is it if the Sacred Masculine returns and does not wed with the Divine Feminine? What good is it for the Feminine to resurrect and heal itself, as it has been doing for decades, but find no equal, no mate, no wedding with the healthy Masculine? Love is between equals, as Meister Eckhart put it. Love can only be where there is equality, or where we are busy making equality happen. Marriage between slave and master does not happen; individuals marry to serve each other and the Sacred Marriage itself, not to have one person serve and the other be served. Riane Eisler's term for Sacred Marriage is "partnership"; she believes that we do not need either patriarchy or matriarchy but *partnership*. The implications of this union are immense, for in ancient days it was believed that "a balanced union of female and male is the essential foundation for balance and harmony in all aspects of our world." For Carl Jung the "alchemical marriage" was a marriage of the conscious masculine and the conscious feminine.

As Eugene Monick warns, the Sacred Marriage cannot occur when the male feels diminished or "castrated." He writes, "A castrated man cannot enter into the *hieros gamos*; he will have no masculinity to present to his inner feminine." Speaking metaphorically, "castration means to emasculate," and this the male takes to mean "feminization." This is why the archetypes we have explored in this book are so important: With them, men come to the table empowered. Without them, men feel castrated and have little to offer. Ideally, the journey to understand and realize these ten masculine archetypes is what prepares us for Sacred Marriage, both the marriage of gender discussed here and the other marriages explored in the next chapter.

It's important to remember, particularly when we speak of "Sacred Marriages," that we are talking in metaphorical terms about what takes place in the soul of every one of us, be we male or female, gay or straight. This is not about our actual gender, and these archetypes are in no way restricted by our gender or our gender preference. As men, if we have a healthy Sacred Masculine inside of us, then we are ready to incorporate the Divine Feminine inside of us; once this occurs, we each embody a spiritually fertile Sacred Marriage. For many men, their masculine spirituality is "hidden"; it remains unrecognized and unseen. With proper recognition and honoring of masculine spirituality, we lose any fear of the feminine and hopefully can incorporate all spiritual, social, and personal attributes (free of gender bias) in healthy balance.

Of course this process takes place differently in each of us, and that helps account for the marvelous diversity among us all. But if the marriage does not take place in some form, then we find ourselves in trouble, either as individuals or as communities. Indeed, our whole species is in trouble if we do not celebrate these Sacred Marriages. And the truth is that we *are* in deep trouble as a species today. Considering our current direction, some even find it hard to bet on our sustainability.

FALLING IN LOVE:
RECOGNIZING AND HONORING THE FEMININE

If men are not aware or in touch with their masculine spirituality, then it's easy to see why they might fear being feminized by the Divine Feminine, since they have no spiritual masculine counterpart to offer. In some ways, patriarchal ideologies and hypermacho attitudes are spiritually bankrupt overcompensations for this sense of loss. Men fear losing power, control, or authority, and so they refuse to recognize the rights of women or the wisdom of the feminine. Men have passed these attitudes and beliefs down for generations, and yet men can "wake from the dominator trance," as Riane Eisler puts it.

Part of being a healthy male, a male liberated from hiding his spirituality or his depth, is a recognition and respect for the Divine Feminine. A macho male is not a healthy male. A one-sided male, a chauvinist male who lords over women and who cuts the feminine off from his own psyche, is not a healthy male. Such a person, who frequently believes he is defending male priority, actually does injury to himself. Such a male, one who equates oppression of women with justice, is no warrior at all, but a soldier for patriarchy. At one time, slavery was defended by many as reflecting the natural order, but it was in fact forced and unnatural and led, in America, to bloody civil war. When any society or person or religion denies the Divine Feminine, it leads to similar consequences: it legitimizes the actual abuse of women, and it denigrates and kills the feminine inside boys and men, thereby creating self-mutilating monsters.

Men fall in love with women every day, and many avowedly patriarchal men certainly love their wives. However, their love does not change their beliefs that women have limited roles to play in society, and that the feminine has no role to play in their own souls. A healthy male falls in love with both females and the Divine Feminine. He rejoices when women realize self-awareness, self-esteem, and social equality. A healthy male cares about the *justice* at the heart of the women's rights movement. A healthy male listens to the struggles of women and the wisdom of women. This does not mean that "women are always right because they are women," but it does mean that women have stories to tell that may rightly challenge men whose power has often gone unchallenged. And certainly, a healthy male recognizes that the Divine Feminine, which is so often placed solely on one gender, is an integral part of his own psyche. In society and soul, a balance of women and men, of the masculine and the feminine, is a proper goal for all healthy men. Whenever this happens, the Sacred Marriage of the Divine Feminine and the Sacred Masculine is achieved in ourselves and in the world.

A healthy male learns from women, both by listening to them and by studying their stories and their lives. Much has been written by women and about women in the past forty years. One thinks of the great work by Dr. Clarissa Pinkola Estés, *Women Who Run with the Wolves* — of the work of Adrienne Rich and Riane Eisler, of Rosemary Reuther and Mary Daly, of Mary Ford Grabowsky and Monica Sjoo, of Barbara Mor, Alice Walker, bell hooks, Lucia Birnbaum, Luisah Teish, Starhawk, and countless others.

What, then, in archetypal terms, are some of these Sacred Marriages? There are many, and they go by many names, and in this chapter we will look at three: the marriage of Father Sky and Mother Earth, of the Green Man and the Black Madonna, and of Yin and Yang.

FATHER SKY AND MOTHER EARTH: SACRED MARRIAGE OF THE COSMOS

Sky and Earth are not that far apart. In fact, they meet at the horizon, which actually merges both when seen from a ship over the ocean or shimmering in the desert. What we call the "sky" is the very air we and all beings breathe. By standing on the Earth and breathing, we have *already married* Father Sky and Mother Earth; inside us, they have already "tied the knot." Further, as today's science has made clear, we take in the whole cosmos with each breath; the stuff of our lungs and of our cells and of the air we share with other creatures. With every breath, we take in molecules from other creatures and other humans who lived and breathed over hundreds of thousands of years ago.

In fact, all life is a testament to the marriage of Sky and Earth, which is why they are so often depicted as a sacred couple, giving birth to all beings. From Mother Earth's soil we receive our sustenance — from peaches and apples to carrots and beans, from milk and cheese to chickens and ducks. Her waters refresh and quench our thirst and wash us clean. And Earth provides this not just for us, but for all creatures: lions and elephants, tigers and snakes, whales and dolphins, kangaroos and salmon.

Does Father Sky have anything to do with this fecundity? All this diversity and beauty, grace and greenness? Of course it does! From the Sky comes the sun and the rains that nourish and nurture everything that lives on Earth. The Sky also protects, its ozone layer shields life from deadly cosmic radiation, which would otherwise scorch the Earth. Both are necessary, neither better nor more important than the other. Together, both give the magnificent gift of life.

Today, both are wounded, hurt by their children. The environmental movement frequently speaks of protecting the Earth and honoring Gaia (consort to the Green Man), but it is equally true to say we must protect and heal Father Sky — to wake up and change our ways before it is too late. Global warming begins with damage to Father Sky, which is choked with excessive carbon dioxide, so that the life-giving relationship of Earth and Sky is harmed. Of course, Mother Earth and Father Sky will survive even if their children perish, but what a tragedy that would be. Humans must find a new and radical balance of male and female principles before it is too late — for themselves and other creatures.

Thomas Berry puts it this way:

> A younger generation is growing up with greater awareness of the need for a mutually enhancing mode of human presence to the Earth. ... We see quite clearly that what happens to the nonhuman happens to the human. What happens to the outer world happens to the inner world. If the outer world is diminished in its grandeur, then the emotional, imaginative, intellectual, and spiritual life of the human is diminished or extinguished. Without the soaring birds, the great forests, the sounds and coloration of the insects, the free-flowing streams, the flowering fields, the sight of the clouds by day and the stars at night, we become impoverished in all that makes us human.

David Suzuki, in an appropriately titled book *The Sacred Balance: Rediscovering Our Place in Nature*, comments on Gaia, "the great deity of the early Greeks" known as the "deep-breasted Earth. She was the mother goddess from whom everything else came forth. She created Uranus the starry sky; together they peopled the new-made universe. Gaia was the cosmic creator."

Of course, it never hurts to praise one's mother. Homer wrote a poem to Gaia:

MOTHER EARTH

The mother of us all,
the oldest of all,
hard,
splendid as rock
Whatever there is that is of the land
it is she

who nourishes it,
It is the Earth
that I sing.

And yet, Sky is as alive, and as involved in providing life, as Earth. It is truly a *marriage*, a coming together, a holy union, this commingling of Father Sky and Mother Earth. Indeed, it is a Sacred Marriage and a sacred balance no matter how one defines "sacred." For it is bigger than us, we are its offspring, it is not ours! It happened before we ever arrived; we are its children, its progeny. Sky and Earth are our parents, our ancestors and relatives who went before us, our intimates.

Yet, in our anthropocentric modern world, we have distanced ourselves from this fecund understanding and all its ramifications. Today, the sky is empty, obscured by smog and streetlights, and the Earth is a mechanical factory, a bag of supplies for humans to use. We grow only ourselves with no thought to balance or to the process of life itself. Anthropocentrism, our preoccupation with humanity and its artifacts and achievements, actually threatens to wreck the marriage — worse than a pestering mother-in-law — of Father Sky and Mother Earth. One could argue about the chicken and the egg here — which came first, the neglect of Earth and Sky or the overpowering Human Only agenda — but it hardly matters. The results are the same: boredom, restlessness, and confusion about who we are and where we are — about where we come from and therefore where we are going. We unthinkingly pass this confusion on to each new generation of fathers and mothers.

This can be altered with rites of passage wherein the adults acknowledge in a memorable and ancestral way that puberty matters. Puberty is more than shaving for the first time or having one's first wet dream or one's first period. Puberty is as natural and organic as growing itself. Puberty is a new plateau reached in the history of the universe in its invention of sexuality. At puberty every child becomes physically capable of carrying on our species. What a reason to celebrate! What a reason to remember! At puberty Father Sky *does* remarry Mother Earth because all begetting and all conception is a holy remembrance of the ancestors *as well as* a birthing of generations to come.

Without puberty there would be no weddings, no marriages, no holy unions, and no offspring — no children or grandchildren. There would be little direction for our love. The wedding of Father Sky and Mother Earth reminds us all of this, but only if we allow it to. If we let it seep into our consciousness once again in rituals and chants and science study and Bible study and poetry and drumming and singing, we allow it to remake our lives and the rhythms and celebrations of our lives. Puberty is Father Sky saying to boys: "I have arrived *in you* in a special way. I am now bestowing on you my mysterious and potent powers of Fatherhood. Do not take them lightly. They are a lifelong obligation. Provide breath and sun, rain and water, for all living beings by your work and your creativity."

And puberty is Mother Earth saying to girls: "I bestow on you my rich and abundant powers of Motherhood. Do not take them lightly. They will be with you for the rest of your life. Nurture and nourish, brighten and make colorful, yours and everyone's days as I do on a daily basis."

Our lifetimes can be looked at in light of how Father Sky and Mother Earth are marrying in us. As babies it is simply taken for granted. We assume that the motherly breast fits the baby's mouth — and it does! Motherly care holds and feeds a child and fatherly care directs and protects a child, and in their own ways, both provide nourishment and shelter, teachings and direction, parameters and excitement at learning to live on this planet. As children we wander away from home and into the world of yards and parks, of city streets and lakes to play. Sky and Earth speak to us in their own languages on hot summer days and on blistering winter days, on sap-filled spring days and in cooling autumn days. They also speak to us and work in us through our friends and peers, who challenge and instruct us, and through our schoolteachers, who also challenge and instruct us. Sky and Earth are continually communicating with us. The question is: Are we listening?

As adulthood looms, beginning with puberty, Father Sky and Mother Earth become even more embedded in our very being. The monthly periods of the young girl, the proud erections of the young boy, these are not meant to be embarrassments but holy reminders that we are not in charge. We are recipients of Life's great powers, of the Sky's powers and the Earth's powers — and that some day we too will participate in *their* fatherhood and motherhood. For what we give birth to is not solely *ours* — it is bigger than us, which is what makes it sacred. Further, our fatherhood and motherhood need not be engaged in only literally; considering the current overpopulation of humans across the globe, honoring and finding satisfaction in artistic and other types of procreation instead would help care for the Earth. All who nourish and nurture the young are carrying out their fatherhood and motherhood, and this nourishing may be as diverse as making music or making protest; teaching or planting trees or developing sustainable energy sources.

It is all Father Sky and Mother Earth at work in a marriage that is destined to last at least another 4.5 billion years on this planet. A lasting commitment indeed! A Sacred Marriage indeed!

Praising the Sacred Marriage of Sky and Earth

In the Native American tradition there is great power associated with praying with the Sacred Pipe. The smoking of the Sacred Pipe is, among other things, a ritual that marries Sky and Earth. For the tobacco is a gift of the Earth, a special plant. Smoke is, for a while, "visible spirit," and smoking is an action of the fifth chakra. It is a kind of breathing, inhaling and exhaling the breath (spirit) of the universe. The smoke rises to the sky and becomes invisible like spirit itself.

In a brilliant poem conceived nine centuries ago, St. Francis of Assisi celebrated this Sacred Marriage also. In our times when the Earth and Sky are imperiled by human neglect, it seems right to reflect anew on the depths of this poem.

> Most high, all-powerful, all good Lord!
> All praise is yours, all glory, all honor and all blessing.

Notice how he sings first of *praise*, of goodness (for we praise what is good), and of blessing ("blessing" is the theological word for "goodness"). We pay a great price when we fail to praise, as Rumi points out when he observes:

> Your depression is connected to your insolence
> And refusal to praise. Whoever feels himself walking
> On the path, and refuses to praise — that man or woman
> Steals from others every day — is a shoplifter!

People who do not praise are depressed. Cynicism does that. Our souls need a regular taste of "goodness" to keep going. St. Francis wrote a Poem of Praise, and he continues:

> To you alone, Most High, do they belong,
> No mortal lips are worthy
> To pronounce your name.

Here, St. Francis is hinting at the apophatic Divinity, that side of God that is beyond all names, beyond all human understanding — the Awe of the Divine presence that permeates all things and puts them beyond words.

All praise be yours, my Lord, through all that you have made,
and first my Lord Brother Sun,
Who brings the day; and light you give to us through him.
How beautiful he is, how radiant in all his splendor!
Of you, Most High, he bears the likeness.

The Sun is a brother, is masculine; its yang energy is beautiful, radiant, and splendid — a likeness of Divinity itself. Light after all is the oldest and most universal of the names for the Divine the world over, and St. Francis senses that by his own praise of Brother Sun. The sun is a "lord," of higher position than the "lords and ladies" of medieval times that Francis is subtly criticizing here. Nature is greater than human cultures. Francis displaces anthropocentric pretensions with a sense of Nature's royalty. But the Sun is a brother, not a lording-over master.

   Now St. Francis balances his praise of his brother with that for his sister.
   All praise be yours, my Lord, through sister Moon and Stars;
   In the heavens you have made them bright
   and precious and fair.

Moon is a sister. Together with the stars she brightens up the heavens with a dignity that is both precious and fair. Francis has a living relationship with Father Sky — as all indigenous people do.

   Next St. Francis turns to praising Sister Earth, who is also our Mother.
   All praise be yours, my Lord, through Sister Earth, our mother,
   Who feeds us in her sovereignty and produces
   Various fruits and colored flowers and herbs.

Francis celebrates the children of Mother Earth, who is also our Sister: fruits, flowers, herbs, all produced in variation and feeding us in so many ways. Sister Earth our Mother is also sovereign, she is a ruler in her own right — more to be admired than earthly rulers. Herbs are for healing, and St. Francis also celebrates our human gifts of healing when he pronounces next:

   All praise be yours, my Lord, through those who grant pardon
   For love of you; those who endure sickness and trial.
   Happy those who endure in peace,
   By you, Most High, they will be crowned.

So the lessons of gender balance that Francis intuits, the marriage of Masculine and Feminine, get applied in human behavior. That is the way for pardon and forgiveness between peoples, for endurance of sickness and trials, for true peace, to be born.

And still there is death to deal with, and St. Francis personalizes death also. Death is a sister.

All praise be yours, my Lord, through Sister Death,
From whose embrace no mortal can escape.
Woe to those who die in mortal sin!
Happy those She finds doing your will!
The second death can do no harm to them.

Death does no harm if we are doing the will of God in our lives. Sister Death is universal — none of us escapes it. Rather we are to embrace it as part of the family, the family of Sky and Earth, of Father and Mother. Indeed we can be happy at death when we have drunk deeply of the sacred union of Male and Female — that means that we have learned to praise and bless and give thanks for our lives even when the path is not easy. For earthly death is a "second death" — we have died our first deaths many times over. And we die well when we have lived lives committed to service.

Praise and bless my Lord, and give him thanks,
And serve him with great humility.

Yes, Francis knew well and drank deeply from the well of the Sacred Marriage of Masculine and Feminine. He invites us to do the same.

Recently I received the following communication from a therapist, who provides another example of how this Sacred Marriage can be seen and praised. She writes:

While working with a client, I had an incredible communication with "mother earth." The client was working toward a greater realization of the Divine Masculine energy vibration within her — the ultimate goal of balancing her Divine Masculine with her Divine Feminine. Toward the completion of the session, we were grounding this new vibration to the core of "mother earth" — not an unusual procedure except I could not say "mother earth"! It kept coming out "earth" or "the planet" instead.

All of a sudden I got this rush of gratitude back from "the planet"

— "earth" was so grateful for the Divine Masculine energy. She explained that she too is working toward balancing the Divine Masculine and Divine Feminine, that it is just as difficult for her as it is for us! In fact, some of the tumultuous earth activity has to do with old "machismo" energy she thinks would be well replaced with the Divine Masculine — and she'll take all the help we can give her to help her achieve that balance!

By the end of the session, I was much more comfortable referring to her as "Mother-Father Earth."

THE GREEN MAN AND THE BLACK MADONNA:
SACRED MARRIAGE OF NATURE

In chapter two we celebrated the return of the Green Man. The Green Man honors our relationship to other Earth creatures and the plant world in particular. The Green Man is a spiritual warrior standing up for and defending Mother Earth and her creatures. He also represents the heart chakra, the greening power of compassion, since the color of the heart chakra is green. And he represents holy sexuality, our renewed powers of generativity in all their diverse and manifold manifestations.

But does the Green Man return alone? Does he find a mate? Does a feminine companion also emerge who might make a good marriage, a bonding of equals, friends for life? I propose that the return of the Black Madonna represents such a partner, such a consort. Why?

The first reason is historical. The last time the Black Madonna emerged in force in Western culture was at the very time that the Green Man arrived — the twelfth century, the "only renaissance that worked in the West" (according to Chenu) when the goddess emerged and society reinvented itself. In ages past the Black Madonna not only took root in France but in many cultures. She is found all over Europe — in Sicily, Spain, Switzerland, France, Poland, The Czech Republic — as well as in Turkey, Africa, and the Soviet Union. She is Tara in China and Kali in India. She is named Our Lady of Guadalupe in Mexico (sometimes called the "brown Madonna"). And the Celts knew her as "Hag," or the *cailleach*, the dark feminine who exercises "tough mother love that challenges its children to stop acting in destructive ways.... It is the energy that will bring death to those dreams and fantasies that are not for our highest good."

Who is the Black Madonna and what does she stand for? In her study *Dark Goddess*, Lucia Birnbaum describes how the African goddess Isis "prevailed through the force of love, pity, compassion, and her personal concern for sorrows." She was associated with healing, she was a "compassionate mother," and she represented not only the earth but also water, which "held a sacred quality: holy water, holy rivers, and holy sea." A mistress of medicine, she also signifies nonviolent transformation. The sister of Isis was Ma'at, and together Isis and Ma'at epitomized justice and order in nature. For all these reasons the black goddess seems right for our times.

> The next step toward religious understanding, and a just world, is to bring the dark mother of prehistory and popular history to consciousness and to public knowledge. We need to bring her to consciousness in light of genetic and archeological evidence that verifies that all of us descend from an African dark mother, that we are all peoples of colors of many tribes, many climates, and many diasporas....In our violent times, we need to bring the dark mother to consciousness because she connotes justice with compassion.

Recently, a travel exhibit on the Black Madonna was accompanied with this commentary:

> The Black Madonna is the embodiment of the Divine Feminine, our Earth Goddess and the Mother of all humanity. She represents the fertile womb, black and sacred, and stands as a symbol of transformation and change. The images of the Virgin Mother portrayed as a dark-skinned woman symbolize majesty and power, a love of great strength, powerful, enduring and unbroken.... She is an important symbol in the present-day, redefining darkness as a positive image in contemporary culture. Darkness or blackness is too often associated with the negative. That kind of association is one of the cornerstones of racism.... Darkness represents the internal being and includes pride in one's history and culture, as well as struggle, survival, and achievements.

Woodman agrees when she observes:

> In the dreams of contemporary men and women, there is appearing with increasing frequency the image of a sensual, sexual, earthy Black Madonna. This is not an idealized, chaste, detached Madonna, high

up on a pedestal. This is a Madonna who loves her own body, her own flirtations, her own compassionate presence among human beings. . . . That she is beginning to surface in contemporary dreams suggests that as a race we are at last beginning to find in ourselves a vision of the feminine that has been buried in the unconscious for too long.

In a previous study I listed a number of reasons why the Black Madonna is returning in our time. Among them are the following:

The Black Madonna calls us to the darkness and to depth. Darkness is something we need to get used to again — the "Enlightenment" has deceived us into being afraid of the dark and distant from it. Light switches are illusory. They feed the notion that we can "master nature" (Descartes's false promise) and overcome all darkness with a flick of our finger.

Meister Eckhart observes that "the ground of the soul is dark." Thus to avoid the darkness is to live superficially, cut off from one's ground, one's depth. The Black Madonna invites us into the dark and therefore into our depths. This is what the mystics call the "inside" of things, the essence of things. This is where Divinity lies. It is where the true self lies. It is where illusions are broken apart and the truth lies. Andrew Harvey puts it this way: "The Black Madonna is the transcendent Kali-Mother, the black womb of light out of which all of the worlds are always arising and into which they fall, the presence behind all things, the darkness of love and the loving unknowing into which the child of the Mother goes when his or her illumination is perfect." She calls us to that darkness which is mystery itself. She encourages us to be at home there, in the presence of deep, black, unsolvable mystery. She is, in Harvey's words, "the blackness of divine mystery, that mystery celebrated by the great Apophatic mystics, such as Dionysius Areopagite, who see the divine as forever unknowable, mysterious, beyond all our concepts, hidden from all our senses in a light so dazzling it registers on them as darkness." Eckhart calls God's darkness a "superessential darkness, a mystery behind mystery, a mystery within mystery that no light has penetrated."

To honor darkness is to honor the experience of people of color. Its opposite is racism. The Black Madonna invites us to get over racial stereotypes and racial fears and projections and to go for the dark.

The Black Madonna calls us to cosmology, a sense of the whole of space and time. The cosmos is dark in its depths and the Black Madonna represents the great cosmic Mother on whose lap all creation exists. The universe itself is embraced and mothered by her. She yanks us out of our *anthropocentrism* and back into a state of honoring *all our relations*. She ushers in an era of cosmology, of our relationship to the whole instead of just parts, be they nation parts or ethnic parts or religious parts or private parts. She pulls us out of the Newtonian parts-based relation to self and the world — out of our tribalism — into a relationship to the whole again. Since we are indeed inheriting a new cosmology in our time, a new "Universe Story," the timing of the Black Madonna's return could not be more fortuitous. She brings a blessing of the new cosmology, a sense of the sacred, to the task of educating our species in a new universe story.

Today's science is zeroing in on the "dark side of the universe," as Michael Turner, a cosmologist at the University of Chicago, recently put it in a talk about the mysteries of dark matter and dark energy. The truth is that up to now only 4 percent of the matter and energy of the universe has been found. "The other 96 percent remains elusive — scientists are looking in the farthest reaches of space and deepest depths of Earth to solve the two dark riddles," Turner tells us. Light does not interact with dark matter, so it is very hard to detect, but it does exhibit the tug of gravity.

On the micro level, experiments are underway in deep caves in Minnesota in search of WIMPS, or weakly interactive massive particles. These might answer what is going on at a microcosmic or particle level. At the macrocosmic level, "dark energy" is a kind of invisible force that is antigravity, pushing galactic clusters apart and causing the accelerated expansion of the universe. Turner thinks dark energy is the biggest mystery of all, and physicists predict that it makes up 74 percent of energy density in the universe.

The metaphor of the Black Madonna seems especially apt at this moment of exploring the dark matter and dark energy of the universe. Darkness and matter, both at its micro and macro level, seem to go together.

The Black Madonna calls us down to honor our lower chakras. One of the most dangerous aspects of Western culture is its constant flight upward, its race to the upper chakras (Descartes: "truth is clear and distinct ideas") and its flight from the lower chakras. The Black Madonna takes us *down*, down to the first chakras including our relationship to the whole (first chakra picks up the sound vibrations from the whole cosmos), our sexuality (second chakra), and our anger and moral outrage (third chakra). European culture in the modern era has tried to flee from all these elements, both in religion and in education. The Black Madonna will not tolerate such flights from the earth, flights from the depths.

The Black Madonna honors the Earth and represents ecology and environmental concerns. Mother Earth is named by her very presence. Mother Earth is dark and fecund and busy birthing. So is the Black Madonna. Andrew Harvey says, "The Black Madonna is also the Queen of Nature, the blesser and agent of all rich fertile transformations in external and inner nature, in the outside world and in the psyche." Mother Earth nurtures her children and feeds the world, and the Black Madonna welcomes them home when they die. She recycles all things. The Black Madonna calls us to the environmental revolution, to seeing the world in terms of our interconnectedness with all things; she will not let us stand apart to master or rule over nature (as if we can even when we try). She is an affront to the capitalist exploitation of Earth's resources, including the exploitation of indigenous peoples. The Black Madonna sees the whole and therefore does not countenance the abuse, oppression, or exploitation of the many for the sake of the financial aggrandizement of the few. She stands for justice for the oppressed and lower classes (as distinct from the lawyer classes). She urges us to stand up to those powers that, if they had their way, would exploit her beauty for short-term gain, thereby depriving future generations of that beauty. She is a conservationist, one who conserves beauty and health and diversity.

Furthermore, if Thomas Berry is correct that "ecology is functional cosmology," then to be called to cosmology is to be called to its local expression of ecology. One cannot love the universe and not love the Earth. And vice versa, one cannot love the Earth and ignore its temporal and spatial matrix, the universe.

The Black Madonna calls us to our Divinity, which is also our Creativity. First, our Divinity. Because she is a goddess, the Black Madonna resides in all beings. She is the divine presence inside of creation. She calls us *inside*, into the "kingdom/queendom of God" where we can cocreate with Divinity and feel the rush of Divinity's holy breath or spirit. But to call us to Divinity is to call us to our responsibility to give birth.

If Carl Jung is correct when he says that creativity comes "from the realm of the mothers," then the Black Madonna, who is surely a mother, calls us to creativity. She expects nothing less from us than creativity. Hers is a call to create, a call to ignite the imagination. What but our collective imaginations can succeed in moving us beyond our energy dependence on fossil fuels to an era of self-sustaining energy? What but creativity can reinvent learning so that the joy and wonder and enticement of learning displaces our failing and boring educational systems? What but moral imagination can move us beyond the growing divide between materially impoverished nations and materially sated but spiritually impoverished nations?

The Black Madonna would usher in an era where more and more artists will get good work and thrive on good work and reawaken the human soul by way of moral and political imagination.

The Black Madonna calls us to diversity. There is no imagination without diversity — imagination is about inviting disparate elements into soul and culture so that new combinations can make love together and new beings can be birthed. Because the Black Madonna is *black*, she addresses the fundamental phobia around race and differences of color and culture that come with race and ethnic diversity. Meister Eckhart says, "All the names we give to God come from an understanding of ourselves." To give Divinity the name "Black Madonna" is to honor blackness and all people of color and to also honor the feminine.

Divinity is diverse. Diverse in color and diverse in traditions and diverse in gender. God as Mother, not just Father. God as Birther, not just Begetter. Gender diversity is honored by the Black Madonna, and so too is gender preference. The Black Madonna, the Great Mother, is not homophobic. She welcomes the diversity of sexual preferences that are also part of creation, human and more than human.

John Boswell, in his groundbreaking scholarly work *Christianity, Social Tolerance and Homosexuality* has demonstrated that the twelfth century, that century that birthed the great renaissance and the Black Madonna in France, rejected homophobia. For a period of 125 years — years that were the most creative years in Western civilization — diversity was welcomed at all levels of society. Creativity thrives on diversity.

The Black Madonna calls us to grieve. The Black Madonna is the sorrowful mother, the mother who weeps tears for the suffering in the universe, the suffering in the world, the brokenness of our very vulnerable hearts. In the Christian tradition she holds the dying Christ in her lap, but this Christ represents all beings — it is the Cosmic Christ and not just the historical Jesus that she is embracing. All beings suffer, and the Black Madonna, the Great Mother, knows this and empathizes with us in our pain. She embraces us like a tender mother, for compassion is her special gift to the world. She invites us to enter into our grief and name it and be there to learn what suffering has to teach us. Creativity cannot happen, birthing cannot happen, unless we pay attention to the grieving heart. Only by passing through grief can creativity burst forth anew. Grieving is an emptying, it is making the womb open again for new birth to happen. A culture that would substitute addictions for grieving is a culture that has lost its soul *and its womb*. It will birth nothing but more pain and abuse and misuse of resources. It will be a place where waste reigns and where Divinity itself wastes away unused in the hearts and imaginations of the people. Andrew Harvey writes of how the Black Madonna provides "an immense force of protection, an immense alchemical power of transformation through both grief and joy, and an immense inspiration to compassionate service and action in the world."

To grieve is to enter what John of the Cross in the sixteenth century called the "dark night of the soul." We are instructed not to run from this dark night but to stay there to learn what darkness has to teach us. The Dark Madonna does not run from the darkness of spirit and soul that sometimes encompasses us. Part of being a warrior is sticking around for the lessons to be learned when chaos seems to take over.

The Black Madonna is also "queen of hell," Andrew Harvey says, she is "queen of the underworld, . . . that force of pure suffering mystical love that annihilates evil at its root and engenders the Christ-child in the ground of the soul even as the world burns." She holds both creative and destructive aspects within her, just like Kali does. Kali is a dark, fierce mother who is often depicted with a necklace of skulls encircling her neck. What is this about? This is a warning *not to sentimentalize the feminine*. The Feminine is not to be trivialized or sentimentalized, not to be "feminized" in Ann Douglas's terms, not to be treated as the "proper lady" or as a "kept doll." She must be respected for what she is: strong, powerful, and independent. "Mother Nature" is not always benign; Kali brings death as well as life, destruction along with construction. All creativity is that way: it "tears down and builds up" as the prophet Jeremiah says.

Recently I was jolted awake at 3 A.M. by the rattling of my house — it was an earthquake. I live in the San Francisco Bay Area, where we are reminded regularly that Mother Nature is in charge. But every natural disaster is a reminder: like Hurricane Katrina flooding New Orleans or the tsunami that struck Sri Lanka. The Dark Mother will not be mocked or sentimentalized. She is not "dramatic" in the way of soap opera romance; she is fierce, unrelenting, and beautiful in the way of dark tragedy, which creates even as it ferociously destroys, which loves even in the midst of violence. All this is part of the wedding of the Green Man and the Black Madonna. It is a coming together of strong forces. There is nothing prissy about it. Unlike many contemporary weddings, it is the union of wild energies. At this event, wildness reigns. Attendance is not for the faint of heart.

The Black Madonna calls us to Joy, Celebration, and Dance. The Black Madonna, while she weeps tears for the world as the sorrowful mother, does not wallow in her grief. She does not stay there forever. Rather, she is a joyful mother, a mother happy to have being and to share it with so many other creatures. Celebration of life and its pleasures lie at the core of her being. She expects us to take joy in her many pleasures, joy in her fruits. Sophia or Wisdom in the Scriptures sings to this element of pleasure and eros, deep and passionate love of life and all its gifts.

> *I have exhaled a perfume like cinnamon and acacia,*
> *I have breathed out a scent like choice myrrh....*
> *Approach me, you who desire me,*
> *And take your fill of my fruits,*
> *For memories of me are sweeter than honey,*
> *Inheriting me is sweeter than the honeycomb.*
> *They who eat me will hunger for more,*
> *They who drink me will thirst for more.*
> *Whoever listens to me will never have to blush....*

Celebration is part of compassion. As Meister Eckhart puts it: "What happens to another, be it a joy or a sorrow, happens to me." Celebration is the exercise of our common joy. Praise is the noise that joy makes. Joy, praise, and celebration are intrinsic to community and to the presence of the Black Madonna. She did not birth her Divine Child, by whatever name, in vain. She favors children, life, and eros; she favors biophilia. She is a lover of life par excellence. She expects us, her children, to be the same.

The Black Madonna calls us to our Divinity which is Compassion. Compassion is the best of which our species is capable. It is also the secret name for Divinity. There is no spiritual tradition East or West, North or South, that does not instruct its people in how to be compassionate. "Maat" is the name for justice, harmony, balance, and compassion among African peoples, who after all birthed the Black Madonna first as Isis. The Black Madonna calls us to Maat. To balance, harmony, justice, and compassion. Grieving and celebrating and acting justly are all parts of compassion. In both Arabic and Hebrew, the word for *compassion* comes from the word for "womb." A patriarchal ideology does not teach compassion; it ignores the womb-like energies of our world and our species. If it mentions compassion at all, it trivializes it and renders it sissy. Patriarchy neglects what Meister Eckhart and the Jewish prophets knew and taught: "Compassion means justice." Compassion has a hard side; it is not about sentiment but about relationships of justice and interdependence. Jesus pronounced that he brought a sword as well as peace, and Mary his mother is famous for having declared that the Almighty

> *has routed the proud of heart.*
> *He has pulled down princes from their thrones and exalted the lowly.*
> *The hungry he has filled with good things, the rich sent empty away.*

Compassion knows limits, does not overindulge, does not hoard. Compassion trusts life and the universe ultimately to provide what is necessary for our being. Compassion works hard as a cocreator with the universe to see that a balance and basic fairness is achieved among beings. Compassion is present in the Black Madonna in her very essence for, as Eckhart says, "the first outburst of everything God (and Goddess) does is compassion." To return to compassion *is* to return to the Goddess.

Cultural historian and feminist Henry Adams writes about the role of Mary at Chartres Cathedral in the twelfth century: "The convulsive hold which Mary to this day maintains over human imagination — as you can see at Lourdes — was due much less to her power of saving soul or body than to her sympathy with people who suffered under law — justly or unjustly, by accident or design, by decree of God or by guile of Devil." Adams understood Mary as the "Buddhist element in Christianity," for with her as with Buddha, compassion is the first of all the virtues. "To Kwannon the Compassionate One and to Mary the Mother of God, compassion included the idea of sorrowful contemplation." Only the Great Mother could provide the compassion needed by the sorrowful human condition. Mary was a friend of outlaws; she appealed to the masses who "longed for a power above law — or above the contorted mass of ignorance and absurdity bearing the name of law." This power had to be more than human. It required the Goddess.

The Black Madonna, the goddess, provides the womb of the universe as the cosmic lap where all creatures gather. An ancient hymn dedicated to Isis underscores her cosmic role as sovereign over all of nature and queen of all the gods and goddesses.

I am Nature, the universal Mother, mistress of all the elements, primordial child of time, sovereign of all things spiritual, queen of the dead, queen also of the immortals, the single manifestation of all gods and goddesses that are. My nod governs the shining heights of Heaven, the wholesome sea-breezes, the lamentable silences of the world below.

How like a twelfth-century poem to the Christian goddess Mary is this ancient hymn to Isis. Alan of Lille wrote the following poem about Nature in the twelfth century:

> O child of God and Mother of things,
> Bond of the world, its firm-tied knot,
> Jewel set among things of earth, and mirror to all that passes away
>   Morning star of our sphere;
> Peace, love, power, regimen and strength,
> Order, law, end, pathway, captain and source,
> Life, light, glory, beauty and shape,
>   O Rule of our world!

Interestingly, Alan of Lille speaks of the "Mother of things" as a "firm-tied knot," and the Thet "knot" is an important symbol of Isis. We play in her cosmic lap, we bump up against one another there, and we work for balance, Maat, and justice there.

The Black Madonna is the Throne of Compassion, the Divine lap. That is the meaning of the name "Isis," and Isis is the African goddess who inspired the Black Madonna in Ephesus, Turkey, and throughout Spain, Sicily, and Western Europe. Indeed, certain passages of the Christian Gospels, such as the birth narratives (which are clearly not historical but are stories of the Cosmic Christ), are passages taken from stories about Isis and her son, Horus. Sir Ernest A. Wallis Budge, the late keeper of the Egyptian and Assyrian antiquities at the British Museum, writes:

> The pictures and sculptures wherein she is represented in the act of suckling Horus formed the foundation for the Christian paintings of the Madonna and Child.
>
> Several of the incidents of the wanderings of the Virgin with the Child in Egypt as recorded in the Apochryphal Gospels reflect scenes in the life of Isis . . . and many of the attributes of Isis, the God-mother, the mother of Horus . . . are identical with those of Mary the Mother of Christ.

Isis often wears a regal headdress that symbolizes her name as meaning "throne" or "queen." Erich Neumann writes about Isis as "throne":

> As mother and earth woman, the Great Mother is the "throne" pure and simple, and, characteristically, the woman's motherliness resides not only in the womb but also in the seated woman's broad expanse of thigh, her lap on which the newborn child sits enthroned. To be taken on the lap is, like being taken to the breast, a symbolic expression for adoption of the child, and also for the man, by the Feminine. It is no accident that the greatest Mother Goddess of the early cults was named Isis, the "seat," "the throne," the symbol of which she bears on her head; and the king who "takes possession" of the earth, the Mother Goddess, does so by sitting on her in the literal sense of the word.

The twelfth-century renaissance was especially conscious of the role of "throne" and the goddess. In Latin the word for "throne" is "cathedra." The medieval church gave birth to cathedrals — over 125 were built the size of Chartres — and every single one was dedicated to Mary, with such titles as Notre Dame de Chartres, Notre Dame de Lyons, Notre Dame de Paris, and so on. Over 375 other churches the size of these cathedrals were built dedicated to Mary also. In many of these cathedrals a statue of the Black Madonna can be found even to this day. A cathedral by definition meant the *throne where the goddess sits ruling the universe with compassion and justice for the poor.*

The Black Madonna calls us to a renaissance of culture, religion, and the city. Anthropocentrism, clericalism, and sexism have co-opted the invention of the cathedral to mean the "place where the bishop has his (usually his) throne." This is false. The cathedral is designed to be the center of the city. It brings the goddess to the center of the city to bring the city alive with goddess energies and values. Cities were birthed in the twelfth century with the breakup of the land-based economic, religious, and political feudal system. The youth fled to the cities, where religion reinvented itself separately from the monastic establishment that had ruled for eight centuries; where education invented itself in the form of universities that were separate from the rural monastic educational system; where worship reinvented itself in each city's cathedral as separate from the monastic liturgical practice in the countryside.

Today, for the first time in human history, more than 50 percent of humans are living in cities; by 2015, over two-thirds of humans — a great proportion of them young people — will be living in cities. The Black Madonna and the "throne as goddess" motif contribute to the resurrection of our cities. They give us a center, a cosmic center, a synthesis and unity and a life-energy by which we can redeem our cities and take them back from lifelessness and thanatos. Artists gather in a city. Celebration and ritual happen in a city. Nature and human nature congregate in a city. No wonder Meister Eckhart and other medieval mystics celebrated the *human soul as city and the city as soul*. It is the task of a renaissance to bring soul back to city. We might even define renaissance as a "rebirth of *cities* based on a spiritual initiative."

Part of a renaissance is a reinvention of education and art. The goddess also ruled at the university — she was "Queen of the sciences" and "mistress of all the arts and sciences" who was "afraid of none of them, and did nothing, ever, to stunt any of them," as Henry Adams wrote. All learning was to culminate in her. She was about wisdom not just knowledge. The renaissance that the Madonna represented was both religious and educational.

Often the headdress of Isis depicts the full moon between curved horns, and it has the shape of the musical instrument that the Egyptians played in her honor, called the sistrum. Plutarch stated that the purpose of the sistrum, which is a kind of rattle, was that "all things in existence need to be shaken, or rattled about . . . to be agitated when they grow drowsy and torpid." The Black Madonna *shakes things up*.

Is this not an archetype for our times? Is she not a forebearer of a renaissance, one who comes to give new birth to a civilization, a birth based on a new sense of spirituality and cosmology and learning — a learning that reawakens us to our place in the universe? How will work in the world become wise, as opposed to exploitive, without wisdom? How will the human soul move from knowledge to wisdom without the kind of effort the goddess can bring? How will a renaissance happen without a balance of male/female, heart/head, body/spirit truly occurring at all levels of education, from kindergarten to university? What role will art play when the artist too lets go of the internalized oppression of the modern era and recommits himself or herself to serving the community and to serving the larger community of ecological sustainability?

Black and Green: A Twenty-First-Century Marriage

Isn't it clear, having considered these dimensions of the Black Madonna, that a marriage of the Green Man and the Black Madonna would truly constitute a *marriage of the century* — the twenty-first century? A truly Sacred Union?

When the Divine Feminine and the Sacred Masculine nurture and sustain one another, a new era, one that draws from the wisdom of ancient eras, might truly emerge. It is a marriage to work and pray for.

Why would the Green Man and the Black Madonna represent so vital a family at this time in history? First, because it is colorful. Races and ethnicities are intermingling much more than ever before, and we are all becoming people of color. Caucasians are becoming fewer, while mixed and other races expand. So the honoring of the Black Madonna and Dark Madonnas, whether Guadalupe or Pele, is of great significance in our time. An honoring of darkness is long overdue.

Another historical reason for honoring the Black Madonna is that we all come from Africa. No matter what we look like today, we are branches of the same ancestral tree. Ours is a time for recognizing that all humans are kin; we are one tribe, one race, the human race. Our ancestors, our mothers and fathers, were all African. The Black Madonna reminds us of this important fact, our common ancestry, our common lineage, our common tribe, a single race. Here all racism ceases; it shuts its ugly mouth; it gets out of our confused and degraded brains; and it exits our institutions and ideologies once and for all. Unity becomes the bedrock for diversity. The unity comes first. Our origins matter. They count. Recently we were teaching a group of inner-city teenagers these lessons, and one yelled out, "You mean Eve was black?" He got it. "In the beginning" we were all black. That is the Black Madonna's message for our time.

A Black Madonna consorting with a Green Man makes for a colorful courtship. The green and the black; the bright and the dark; the motherly solitude of blackness and the fecund potency of greenness marrying. Imagine that! A Sacred Marriage indeed: the Defender of Mother Earth marrying the Origin of Our Species.

What other meanings does a marriage of the green and the black have? Darkness depicts *depth*, and the Green Man, as all living things, shoots its roots into the darkness from which it derives its nourishment and sustenance. Without the black, green withers and dies. It must live connected to the depths in order to survive. Green needs black. And green provides black with color and conspicuousness; it brings the darkness up to the surface, where others can see it and admire its handiwork. It is a channel by which the beauty of the black becomes more visible. Green spreads. The planet turned green when foliage took over. It made black less lonely, more a contributor to diversity and the thrill of colors.

My experience with the Black Madonna is also that she is a bit of a trickster. Her logic is not the logic of the daytime or the logic of Aristotle and patriarchal clarity. It is more the logic of paradox, humor, foolishness, surprise, and the unconscious. To respect her is to respect this other kind of logic. She is not for the literal-minded, which may be one reason why she is so unhonored by exclusively left-brain thinkers, whether fundamentalists or liberals. Her sense of time is not that of our clock time. Like indigenous people, for her, time waits and gestates, time comes to fruition when it is ready. She operates on her own time, but she does operate.

Green Man is already a marriage — that of Nature and the Human. He brings out our inherent love of nature, which goes back as far as humans go back but that the modern age sidetracked with its anthropocentrism and idolatry of the human. The Green Man marries heaven (sun, clouds, water) and earth (roots, soil, subsoil). Together, the Green Man and the Black Madonna represent a deep marriage of the masculine and the feminine, of light (photosynthesis) and dark.

YIN AND YANG:
SACRED MARRIAGE OF BALANCE AND HARMONY

The ancient Chinese symbol of Yin and Yang, two nestled half-moons of black and white within a circle, represents the entire universe and the basic dynamic it contains: Yang (sunlight) and Yin (moonlight) are separate but dynamically related, and together they maintain balance and harmony. As Allen Tsai writes, "Yang is like man. Yin is like woman. Yang wouldn't grow without Yin. Yin couldn't give birth without Yang. Yin is born (begins) at Summer Solstice and Yang is born (begins) at Winter Solstice." This dynamic of Yin/Yang, Feminine/Masculine, represents a balance of oppositional energies that underlies everything: the cycles of the sun, the four seasons, the yearly calendar, medicine and healing, and much more. The key to harmony is not rest, or stasis, but keeping the tension alive and balanced. This could be called the Sacred Marriage of Opposites. As Richard Hooker puts it:

> The yin and yang represent all the opposite principles one finds in the universe.... Each of these opposites produce the other: Heaven creates the ideas of things under yang, the earth produces their material forms under yin, and vice versa; creation occurs under the principle of yang, the completion of the created thing occurs under yin, and vice

versa, and so on. This production of yin from yang and yang from yin occurs cyclically and constantly, so that no one principle continually dominates the other or determines the other.... All conditions are subject to change into their opposites.

Hooker draws some meanings from this philosophy of Yin and Yang:

First that all phenomena change into their opposites in an eternal cycle of reversal. Second, since the one principle produces the other, all phenomena have within them the seeds of their opposite state, that is sickness has the seeds of health, health contains the seeds of sickness, wealth contains the seeds of poverty, etc. Third, even though an opposite may not be seen to be present, since one principle produces the other, no phenomenon is completely devoid of its opposite state.

Yin and Yang describes a relationship of complementary opposites rather than absolutes. They describe a *process*. Too much of either Yin or Yang leads to a dangerous imbalance. And isn't every successful marriage a dynamic balance of give and take?

In the *Gospel of Thomas*, an ancient collection of the sayings of Jesus, there is a saying that is thoroughly grounded in Yin/Yang dialectics. Jesus says:

When and if you make all twos into one:
if you make the side you show
like the side you hide, and
the side inside like the side outside
and your higher side like your lower one
with the result that you make
the man and woman in you as one
so that there is nothing more to
become either male or female;
when you find what really sees —
eyes in the place of your physical eye —
and you find what really grasps,
and stands, and walks;
when you make your self-image
the original image of humanity;
then you will be entering
the original guiding power,
the king- and queendom
of the Holy One.

The fact that Jesus himself is understood very early as an incarnation of Wisdom (who is feminine) is another echo in early Christianity of the awareness of the Yin/Yang dialectic, of the sacred marriage honored within the Christ. Jesus becomes a model for other men to emulate, for he brings both the sword (the masculine) and compassion (the feminine or womb energy).

Drawing from the Taoist tradition of Yin and Yang in his study on *The Return of the Mother*, Andrew Harvey celebrates the Sacred Marriage in the following manner: "This 'keeping of the One so as to remain in harmony' is the essence of the path of the sacred feminine, the clue to the sacred marriage, the fusion of masculine and feminine in the dark silent depths of the psyche to produce the child." The uniting of the sacred opposites brings much that is new, much that is fresh. "The Christian alchemists tell us that when in our being we have completed the sacred marriage of opposites, of the male and the female, the sun and the moon, the dark and the light, the conscious and the unconscious, we become a sacred androgyne child, free of reason's madness and the ego's frivolous gloom, free of all conscious and unconscious. Barriers and definitions, mysterious and complete as reality itself, at one with its mystery in the ground of our perfected being."

In this union there is also a communion of heaven and earth, of old and young, of new and old. Here the Christ or Buddha nature is restored. Harvey writes, "To be one in this glorious sense is to be in heaven here, to be one with the Tao, to possess the Grail, to be in union with the Mother. Lewis Thompson wrote: 'The ever new, magical universe is continually reborn in the child. Only the grownup was banished from Eden. The child eats of the Tree of Life. For him or her, the laws of the universe are magical. This childhood and this magic, the Christ restores.'"

Recognizing and respecting the Divine Feminine is not the same as putting the Feminine on a pedestal — which is another way patriarchy keeps the feminine separate from itself, either raising it up or putting it down. Rather, Yin/Yang recognizes that the Feminine is inseparable from the Masculine; they are companions in each moment, in oneself and in all beings. Harvey puts it this way: "The patriarchal vision of the Mother exalts and transcendalizes the feminine from a secret fear of its power, and tries, whether consciously or unconsciously, to distance the demands of its sacred tenderness, urgent clarity, and passion for justice by mythologizing and distancing it. The tendency of modern matriarchal revivals of the Mother, on the other hand, insists excessively on the Mother as *only* immanent. The full glory of the Mother

is that she is at once both transcendent *and* immanent, the source of love and
love-in-action."

Put another way, the marriage of Yin/Yang means the Divine Mother takes
on characteristics of the Sacred Father (action and strong protection), while the
Sacred Father takes on characteristics of the Divine Mother (compassion and
intimate caring). A true marriage indeed, one in which the children prosper.
From the healthy union of masculine and feminine is born a living child. A
mystic child. One in love with the universe, in love with life.

Harvey sees this child in the following way:

> The child, in fact, becomes the mother of a stream of sacred works.
> Only the divine child can be at once reposed and fecund, because in
> its own intimate being, the child unites Shiva and Shakti, male and
> female, silence and force, and is then released to dance for God, in
> God, as a part of God.
>
> This understanding of the divine child is essential for the trans-
> formation through the sacred feminine now, . . . as we face the end of
> nature. I believe that all the religious systems, including the systems
> of initiation by masters and avatars, have failed us, because they have
> all prevented us from a direct, ecstatic, complete relationship with the
> Divine Mother that transcends all creeds and religions and so from a
> direct birthing of the divine child with us.

Celtic scholar Dolores Whelan points out that in the Celtic mythology there
is a special primacy given the feminine and "the feminine is understood as the
ground of being." In today's anthropocentric culture, we are so cut off from
the Divine Feminine we barely consider what the term "ground of being" might
even mean. But in Celtic lore myths abound about the sovereignty of the land

> where the feminine is understood as a personification of the fertility
> of the land and is expressed in the form of a goddess. When a king is
> inaugurated, he must ritually marry the local goddess representing the
> sovereignty of the land. If his rule is just the land will bring forth its
> bounty and the king will be deemed successful. But this requires that
> he is in right relationship with the feminine, the goddess of the land.
> His success is dependant upon his ability to be in right relationship
> with the feminine.

A ritual known as *Bainis Ri* celebrated the sacred wedding of the king and
the goddess of the land. This marriage represented the union "of the worlds of

the human, the natural world and the unseen world." A sacred marriage indeed!

I recently asked a wise psychologist to explain to me Carl Jung's theories on the Sacred Marriage. His answer was very liberating and allowed me to proceed with my own thoughts in this chapter. He said, "Every time I read Jung on this subject, I find him totally confused and confusing." My experience exactly! My feeling is that Jung was, deep down, a neo-Platonist and a chauvinistic Swiss patriarch, and for all of his talk and theorizing about animus/anima and male/female, he never quite got it. The "it" being the need to balance dialectically the supposed "opposites" of Yin/Yang, the masculine/feminine tension. The "it" being the Sacred Marriages we have celebrated in this chapter — the various weddings of the Divine Feminine and the Divine Masculine: of Father Sky and Mother Earth; of the Green Man and the Black Madonna; and of Yin and Yang. But there are many more marriages than these. Once one unleashes the memory of Sacred Marriages, one lets flow many holy unions.

OTHER SACRED UNIONS $\boxed{12}$

THE MASCULINE AND THE FEMININE are not the only pair of opposites that can be united in Sacred Marriage. The dialectic principle of balance and harmony we discussed with Yin and Yang can be applied to many areas of thought and society. Here are some other Sacred Marriages, some subtle and some not so subtle, that deserve our urgent attention and efforts at union and communion.

DUALISM AND NONDUALISM:
FROM PISCEAN TO AQUARIAN CONSCIOUSNESS

Using the ancient astrological signs, we might say we are moving from the Age of Pisces to the Age of Aquarius. Pisces, symbolized by two fish swimming in opposite directions, represents dualism, or separation. The past two thousand years have witnessed many dualisms or separations, just as the two thousand years before the Age of Pisces witnessed many expressions of the Age of the Ram: the Bible's Old Testament is filled with stories of sacrificial offerings of lambs and rams, such as the Jewish practice in the Bible of celebrating Passover by killing a lamb and the important story of Isaac killing the ram in place of his son.

The early Christians were very aware of astrological metaphors — their primary symbol was that of the fish (Pisces), the new astrological moment in history: IXTHOS, the Greek word for "fish," became an acronym for "Jesus Christ

Son of God." This symbol was carved and scratched on many walls in the catacombs where Christians hid to perform their memory rituals and to bury their dead. Jesus's many references to making "fishers of men," to immersing people into the *waters* of baptism like fish — this symbolism was not lost on the first Christians. In addition, the death of Jesus at Passover time meant that his memory was archetypally honored as the "last lamb slain" in the Age of the Ram. With his death the new age of Pisces began. No more need for animal sacrifice.

Today, we are asked to sacrifice our attachment to the Age of Pisces, the age of dualisms, of either/ors, of what might be called the age of conflicting marriages. Today, we must balance dualism with nondualism: recognizing the deep meaning of marriage as a reunion of the Divine Feminine and the Sacred Masculine that merges both, so they become "Mother-Father Earth," as the therapist I quoted in chapter 11 said.

In contrast to the Age of Pisces, Aquarius, from the Latin *aqua* for *water*, symbolizes a commingling and a coming together. In the great sea, the great Mother, in the womb, all things are in union. It is a fine metaphor therefore for marriage, particularly with the Divine. The fish is in no way separate from the water but breathes it in and exhales it. The fish is in the water, and the water in the fish. This is a fine metaphor for *panentheism*, as I have written over the years: God in us and us in God. The Age of Aquarius is an age of mysticism, therefore, of God in all beings and all beings in God — and of our greater awareness and practice of this deep reality.

Look around today at what is happening within our species throughout the world and at what is happening on this endangered planet that we call home, our Mother Earth. It is often called "globalization," and like everything human, it casts a shadow; it has a very dangerous side. But it is also, in its deepest sense, a commingling, a *mixing*, a series of many marriages. It is affecting deeply our collective consciousness and our way of seeing the world — especially for the younger generation, who are not married or beholden to the previous Age of Pisces but who have been born in and into the Age of Aquarius.

KJ: MERGING EAST AND WEST, BODY AND SOUL

KJ is a thirty-one-year-old gay man who is himself a *mix*, a marriage of many sorts. He was born and raised in Vietnam; one of his parents is Thai and the other Vietnamese. One side of his family is Catholic, and the other side is part Buddhist and part "ancestor worshippers," reflecting the indigenous and tribal ancestry of Thailand. He came to America when he was sixteen, and thus is both Asian-educated and American-educated. He is now an American citizen, and he considers himself both Buddhist (more as he gets older) and Christian (less so as institutionalized Christianity becomes more homophobic).

KJ graduated from college as a computer programmer, but he soon found he was not happy doing that. "It was not me," he says. He then moved from mind work to bodywork and now earns his living as a masseur. But he is more than that, for though he is reluctant to use the word, he is also a healer. Working with the body as he does, KJ is a midwife of the marriage of soul and body, of matter and spirit. He also marries in himself peace (the personal fruits of spirituality) with moral outrage (the fire of the prophet).

I also find in KJ, as I do in many of his generation, a marriage of young and old. That is, he combines the knowledge and hope of youth with the experience and wisdom of elders. Here is a portion of my interview with him, which focuses on the many Sacred Marriages KJ embodies.

FOX: Briefly tell us your story.

KJ: I grew up in Vietnam in a family that was both Catholic and Buddhist and was nonjudgmental. We celebrated all the holidays — Christian and Buddhist. In our culture you don't separate Catholic holidays and Buddhist holidays — you know who you are, but when it is time to celebrate, you learn to live together. Not "my religion and my God are better than yours."

As for my bodywork, it started out with my meeting a man in Thailand who was doing bodywork, and he said, "You should do bodywork," and I responded, "Huh?" But two years later, I did not know what I wanted to do, and I thought of him, having seen him only once. I called him up and he said, "I've been waiting for you to call." So he gave me my first teachings on bodywork, and then I went to school to study bodywork. I just got hooked on it. I don't know what it is. . . . It is very spiritual. I'm at peace spending an hour or ninety minutes alone in a room with a person — that is my favorite time of the day because my mind gets to be set free from everything. At that moment I don't know anyone else but the person in front of me and myself. It seems like there is no time in that place.

FOX: That feeds into my next question. What is your understanding of spirituality? You have just said it is your feeling of being at peace, of your mind ceasing from other things, and of having no sense of time and space. Can you elaborate?

KJ: Yes. Regarding space, when you are there, you don't know what will come to you or where you will travel to on that journey, those sixty or ninety minutes. You don't know. You don't know what your client is going to see next or where he or she will travel to. You don't really know. And spending that time with a person's energy, you are both going to travel to a special place, and what you get out of it will not be the same. You might see your God and he or she might see their guru — you don't know. So you may never meet in the same space, but when it is over and done, you know you both get to that destination without meeting each other.

To me that is the beauty of it. I don't have to be at the same place you are, but at the end of the journey we can say, "Oh, yes, I was there." And also we allow one to be in touch with one's inner feelings, one's subconscious level that brings one to awareness of one's body and of alignment with the universe.

FOX: Do you think this happens to many bodyworkers, or do you think this is kind of unusual?

KJ: I think it should. It should happen to all bodyworkers. Because anyone really working from deep in their heart and with a good intention, you should get there. Because to me a bodyworker is not just only a physical worker. A mental space and psychic relaxation is one aspect, but deeper than that is your spirit and your soul, so there can be both. For me a goal to achieve as a bodyworker is to get you out of your physical state and physical body at the moment, to get you out of that to take you to a different place. At that place you have no worries, no thoughts, and no fear of anything. It's just you in that space and me.

FOX: Was this part of your training and included in your training as a bodyworker?

KJ: First of all, the training is more on the physical aspects; the spiritual aspect depends on the instructor. A lot of instructors are spiritual to begin with because they love what they do and they don't do it for the money. They do it because they enjoy doing it, and they talk about how they do it, and they hope that you can attain what they do and you can see what they see. It is up to the practitioner to decide what they want to do and how far they want to go in the spiritual connection. They can explain it to you, but if you don't have that intention and you don't have the connection, you don't have to do anything. It is up to you how far you want to go and what you want to get out of it. It doesn't come naturally; you have to apply yourself to get there. When you get there, it comes naturally. And then you don't know what the next level is. You really don't know. It gradually grows in you. Then also the person you work with, the client or guest, they also take you and open you up and take you to the next level and introduce you to everything. We all have our own background, but when you get to that spiritual level, you just flow with that person, and where you want to go and how you want to go you don't know. I just let it be and go with the flow.

FOX: Have you had experiences of healings both physical, emotional, and spiritual while doing bodywork?

KJ: I never thought of myself as a healer. I never thought of myself saying: "I'm going to do this for you and make you feel better and reconcile the difficulties in your life." I never had that intention of saying: "Hey, today I'm going to take you on a journey to see your God." I don't have that intention, I never thought of that. I am just surprised and shocked because people tell me, "Oh my God, you are such a healer. You take me so that I see things. How do you do it?" I say, "I didn't do anything. You are the one who did it. I'm just there to help you to open the door; I'm just a person with a car, offering transportation to help you to get there, but to open that magical door is up to you. How you want to open it is up to you, not to me." I never think of myself as a healer and am flattered and surprised and in shock from time to time when people say it. The only intention I know is that I want to make a difference. I want to change your life mentally and physically in a very good way so that now you will be in tune with your body and your spirit. And without any intention to be a healer. When I think about a healer, I blush, that is just too much, too kind to say those things to me. I never think of it that way.

FOX: Do you think there is a difference between male spirituality and female spirituality?

KJ: To me there is no difference. Male and female spirituality are the same thing. Either you feel God or you don't feel God. If you feel God, it doesn't matter what religion you are in. There can only be one God. At the core of it I don't see any differences, but in terms of men and women, yes. They see things differently, especially in this society, when men are brought up not to express their emotions. "Men don't cry." It can mold us to become emotionless. Numb, numbness with God. Men repress that and are afraid we will become vulnerable. On the other hand, women and little girls are happy to cry: "It's okay for you to cry because you are a girl." And so they become more sensitive; they are more in tune with their body.

When men are attuned with their body, they say, "Oh, yes, they touch their feminine side." This is not a good thing to say about a man. It's okay to say it about women — it means they are sexy and attractive. But not for a man to be in touch with his feminine side. This makes a big difference. What I am saying applies to Western society. But in Indonesia, for example, in Bali, there is a very spiritual dance in which the woman's role is always played by a male. The male learns women's movements and trains for years to learn this and become very feminine in his movements, and society considers this a very high art and a way to connect to God. They don't put it down; they worship that. They don't talk about "gay or straight" or "butch or feminine." They don't have that. So it depends on your upbringing. But in America, yes, for most people they make a difference between male and female.

FOX: Do you think spirituality is different for a homosexual man and a heterosexual man?

KJ: For the most part, in this society there is. Judging from my work, more gay men talk about their feelings and their emotions. They allow themselves to go out and experience new things because they are more sensitive and they are more aware of sensitivity. They also experience more criticism from their peers because they may act feminine. So we are quite aware of that, and most gay men tend to be more on the creative side and more artistic and because of that we let our imaginations go wild. So it is easier for us to be in tune with our emotions and feelings than heterosexuals.

But with all that, still most gay men don't open ourselves up freely like women do. We don't. Because the gay community says, "Here is a sexy boy who has to have a beautiful body." Sexy in a somewhat macho way; you cannot be Nellie and macho at the same time. Either you are Nellie or you are butch and rugged. Gay men are better than heterosexual men insofar as they can express themselves more freely, but women are more in tune because from day one as a little child they were brought up that way.

FOX: How about the difference between East and West? You mentioned some differences already. You are living in a Western culture but you grew up in an Eastern culture. Do you think that Westerners are more dualistic and separate more the body and the soul and that the East has a more relaxed integration of spirit and body?

KJ: In the West it seems that people talk about a separate body and soul and they separate it. If I step outside of my body, they find it amazing. Some don't even know this is possible. In the East people don't talk about body and soul, and they don't find it amazing because in the East they are all brought up that way. In the East people are marinated from the time they open their eyes that there is no separation. It is a way of life; they don't question it. Because of that it may lead to overly superstitious attitudes. In the end it is a spiritual thing. When I was young I read a lot of literature from the age of eight on, and Eastern writers talk about how when people sleep their soul steps outside their body. That is a very Buddhist thing to say. As a kid you see that and don't question. You see someone else seeing it, you don't question it; it is a way of life and quite normal. It's okay. We don't discuss it. We don't even know how to explain it. They know in their heart about body and soul. No explanation. But here people will find a way to define it. In the West we put a value on it, and we want a logical explanation for everything. In the East we don't do that. Some things don't make sense. But they just do it anyway.

FOX: More a sense of mystery?

KJ: Yes. A way of life over thousands of years, just the way it is. Religion there is much more powerful than in the West, I think. They don't brainwash you and get involved in politics. They just say, "Here I am. I am here to open my arms for you." They don't recruit you, brainwash you, or manipulate you. They don't talk about "evil" but about what you are supposed to do to become a better person. They don't say, "This is an evil thing you must not do." If you go to church here, they talk about the devil, and they build on fear and manipulate your way of thinking. "If you don't do this, you are not a good person." If you want to be a politician, you have to belong to a religion like this. Religion is always part of any election in America. If you are a spiritual person, you don't really want politics. In the West, you get involved in politics.

FOX: Is the West more materialistic? Science is often reductionistic.

KJ: The West has been industrial for years. We get not only what we need but also what we want. In the East it is less so. People of the younger generation behave more like that — they want the same things the West wants. But in the East, even though one does not have it, they will be okay and will make the best of what they have and will share. Among the younger generation and upper class in the East, now there is more involvement in doing things to help others, reaching out to the unfortunate, like missionaries. This is a new trend among younger people. There is something Western about it.

FOX: When did you arrive in America?

KJ: At sixteen. I grew up in both places. I don't know what my religion is. At a younger age, I thought it was cool and fun and awesome to be Catholic, but as I get older and living in America I am afraid to be Catholic or Christian because they do so much judgment. They attack other religions. Deep in my heart I don't believe in that. People manipulate Christianity and make it worse. But the core of religions, I think, is the same.

As I get older I like the Buddhist philosophy because it is an open policy; you can make your own judgments and come and go as you please, and they don't judge you. It fits into my lifestyle because it is spiritual. Christianity has judgment, that homosexuality is a sin, for example, and all gay men should die — I don't agree with that. God is Creator of all. Why did God create gay men? We are all children of God. Why did God create me as a gay man, so I can be abused and humiliated by others? What's my purpose? Why be told it is sinful to be gay and you go to hell? Then God is an evil person. That is my logic and I question that. Buddhism does not have that.

FOX: The Bible says "God is love," not that God is "heterosexual love." But you would think it did from what some Christians preach.

KJ: If that's the case, then God is as evil as the devil. Why did he create me?

FOX: Many theologians are fighting that homophobia.

KJ: But those who preach homophobia are the most powerful and political and run the country.

FOX: And the loudest!

KJ: You never hear that with Buddhists, who rarely talk about sexuality.

FOX: You are thirty-one. Do you think there is a deep interest among young people in spirituality?

KJ: In the East, always. My personal experience is that in the East that question doesn't exist. People never question that, so to me that means in Asia it's okay to make the assumption that everyone is spiritual. How much, I don't know. Their parents don't impose it, saying, "You have to believe this. . . ." No, you don't have to talk about it; not in school either. School doesn't teach or discuss religion. Just in the West. They don't dispute or debate religions; here they do. While growing up in the East, I went to Catholic school, but I was not

Catholic and never accepted it. When they celebrated their holidays I participated and I was treated just like the others. They knew I wasn't Catholic but
they didn't care.

Here in America, you ask: "Do you believe in God?" In the East, no one
asks that question. In the poorer and less-developed countries, the only thing
that keeps people going is hope. Hope is connected to religion. That keeps them
going. I think that is true everywhere. When there is no food to eat, we ask religion for a miracle. In Asia they turn to religion for life to be better. Super-
stition is close to that kind of religion.

FOX: In the younger generation there is more mixing going on with globalization and so on. Do you think the younger generation is less dualistic and
grasps the power of what you are doing as a bodyworker, for example, more
easily?

KJ: Definitely. I see a lot of changes. Teenagers and young adults think with
more understanding about religion. They are more free-spirited, and they will
try new things and are not afraid of trying. While our parents can be so rigid.
But with the Internet that allows many to be exposed to new things, and also
with the economy of Asia now improving and the technology, it becomes part
of the spiritual world. Music, games, they all contain philosophy in them. Cultural exchanges also. Kids are smarter than the older generation; they are more
mature and more sophisticated. Global warming, becoming vegans, all that
brings awareness. The younger generation see their parents, and they search for
their own spiritual path, whether by yoga or meditation, which is a beginning
that will take them to the next level. Eastern philosophy of life has become more
and more accepted by a lot of people in the metropolitan areas and in big cities.

FOX: More mature and more sophisticated includes regarding spirituality? They
more readily recognize a distinction between religion and spirituality, church
and spirituality?

KJ: Yes they do. There's another thing. They are more open-minded and are
open to different religions. This does not mean they betray their own religion,
but their parents and grandparents said they could not do that. A free spirit
feels differently.

FOX: What about sexuality and spirituality? Is there a connection? Sexuality
can be a spiritual practice, right?

KJ: There is definitely a connection. Being Buddhist, sex is almost a forbidden subject, but in all the Eastern philosophies there is a connection. For me, sexuality and spirituality are connected, they go hand in hand. As I become more spiritual I become more open about my sexuality. And I accept it and the differences and let go of sexual hang-ups, and I can see things in myself and others much easier. As a Buddhist it is a major thing that I can now talk about sex without blushing. Deep down we all want to talk about it. Most of my family is Buddhist now, and we can talk about sex, so it is no longer a taboo subject. Both West and East, the younger generation today can be more open talking about sex. It is no longer a hidden subject.

FOX: Anything you want to add?

KJ: To sum it up, bodywork can be very spiritual. It is up to the worker how he or she approaches it. No boundaries at all. Apart from me, I don't know what will happen next. How far can I go or help others to get there? I don't know. It's kind of mysterious to me and I think it always will be. And I like that because I think that's the way it should be.

FOX: Otherwise you would be bored!

KJ: Exactly.

FOX: What spiritual practice do you do besides the bodywork itself?

KJ: I don't go to temple that often; I don't talk about it that often at all. I seldom talk about spiritual things, but the thing is, my way of life, the way I live my life, the way I conduct my business and my day is always very spiritual. I conduct my life with kindness. I believe in cause and effect and karma. I don't think about the karma; I can do it in a natural way without thinking. I do it without thinking; it's a way of life. It's no longer religion or "spiritual." It is integrated, and that's the only way I know, unquestionably and undeniably, to do it this way.

FOX: How long has it been this way for you?

KJ: I guess all my life. It's not this or that. It's just the way it is. If I face something new, I probably for that moment question myself, Is that the right way or wrong way? Do I believe or not? I answer those questions and the next thing I know it becomes part of me. Like a second skin. You don't think. For me the spiritual part is connected to the other parts. It's the way it is. Some people say, "Don't question God." I don't question my spirituality anymore. I don't.

A MYSTIC UNION: HUMANS AND THE DIVINE

The consciousness of mysticism is on the rise. Mysticism is about our experiential union with the Divine. The rediscovery in the West of the role that the wisdom tradition played in the life of the historical Jesus, and the rediscovery of the Creation Spirituality tradition and its great Earth-based mystics, bring back to life theological terms like Deification, Divinization, Panentheism, Mysticism, Godhead — all terms that are kosher and orthodox but were practically banished or, even worse, wrongly understood for centuries. Great saints like Hildegard of Bingen, Thomas Aquinas, Meister Eckhart, Julian of Norwich, Nicolas of Cusa, and others have sung of these realities. Now people are looking for themselves, even if seminary training has in no way caught up to the reality on the road. The rediscovery of the Kabbalah and the Jewish renewal movement in Judaism have done the same. Many people think they have to go East to experience mysticism, when in fact the West carries within itself stunning examples of our marriage with the divine. Consider the following statements from Western saints.

Hildegard of Bingen: "Limitless love, from the depths to the stars: flooding all, loving all, it is the royal kiss of peace."

Thomas Aquinas: "God has become human so that humans might become divine."

Mechtild of Magdeburg: "I who am divine am truly in you . . . and you are in Me."

Meister Eckhart: "Isness is God."

Meister Eckhart: "What good is it to me if Mary gave birth to the Son of God 1400 years ago and I do not give birth to the son of God in me?"

Julian of Norwich: "We are in God and God, whom we do not see, is in us."

Nicolas of Cusa: "Divinity is the enfolding of the universe, and the universe is the unfolding of divinity."

ECUMENISM: MARRYING PROTESTANT AND CATHOLIC

The ecumenical movement that began in the early twentieth century among Protestant denominations, and that fifty years later came to fruition at the Second Vatican Council in its expression of ecumenism between Catholics and Protestants, is another Sacred Marriage that needed to happen and needs to deepen. A Christianity that ignores the *protesting principle* of Protestantism is not an authentic Christianity, for it ignores the prophetic dimension of spirituality. At the same time, a Christianity that ignores the catholic or universal experience of the Oneness of God, that is the tasting of God *in all things* or *the mystical dimension of reality*, is not authentic either. A marriage of the two principles is essential, the mystical and the prophetic, the local and the universal.

Whether any of today's particular expressions of "church" need remain to give form to community and worship remains to be seen. New forms are certainly needed to carry the new wine of this marriage into the new millennium. And these new forms should carry it ever so *lightly*, with as little bureaucratic and instructional baggage as is possible, thus lightening the load of ecclesial burdens.

THE MONK IN THE CITY:
MIXING LAY AND MONASTIC PRACTICES

There is a great mixing of monastic and lay practice going on in the world today. Over the years, I have met many, many young people who in a previous time would have been monks or nuns but who are not drawn to live in monasteries. Instead, they live very much "in the world," working jobs, engaged in commerce, experiencing relationships, raising families. KJ is one of those people who pursues spiritual, monastic practices in the context of everyday life. Though KJ never considered a monastic life, he had, as he alludes, some interesting encounters with Buddhist monks who intuited his spiritual gifts. Once, when he was ten years old, he was visiting a Buddhist temple and a monk came up to him and said, "Some day you will be a healer." Another time, in his twenties, he arrived late at a Buddhist monastic ceremony, and after the service a monk said to him: "I smelled you when you came in. You have a special role to play as a healer." But even today, after embracing his spiritual gifts, KJ does not want to become a monk. Like most of us, he prefers the struggle to make a living and to live out relationships in the world.

Another good example is a man, whom I've known for twenty years, who was raised in a pious Catholic family in the Midwest and whose brother is a priest. However, he now lives in an off-the-grid eco-village in North Carolina, which is a monastery of the future, without formal and instructional vows. The village attracts bright young people as well as middle-agers, who live a variety of lifestyles, but together everyone is committed to a life built on sustainable, renewable energy that supports, rather than damages, the Earth.

The late monk Bede Griffiths said to me before he died, "The future of monasticism is not with monks. It is with laypeople." This *mixing*, this Sacred Marriage of monk and lay, is an increasing reality. Consider the great Eastern monks of our time, such as the Dalai Lama and Thich Nhat Hanh, who have felt drawn to serve laypeople and to "boil down" monastic practices so that everyone can learn to meditate and find peace within, but without abandoning everyday life. Think of the dispersion of yoga practices and other forms of meditation that many Hindu monks have shared with the West through ashrams, retreat centers, and yoga schools. I have visited youth-initiated ecumenical monasteries in Ireland that seem to me to be expressions of this same marriage of lay and monastic.

I see these movements as one more example of the move from the Age of Pisces — when monks were clearly defined and separated from lay people — to the Age of Aquarius, when monks live all around us and even within all of us. A Sacred Marriage indeed!

PATIENCE AND IMPATIENCE:
THE MARRIAGE OF EAST AND WEST

Years ago I was giving a weekend workshop near Santa Monica, California, and the organizers put me up overnight in a beautiful private home overlooking the beach. It was a Buddhist home with many graceful Buddha statues. I was alone that night, but I was told that a group might arrive early in the morning to chant. And chant they did. It was a wonderful way to wake up in the morning, to the sounds of hearts and minds calling on breath and spirit to start the day.

During the night I had a powerful dream about Buddha and Jesus. What I learned from the dream was this: the West needs the East and the East needs the West. I realized that Buddha lived a full life, dying at about age eighty-three, having been a husband, father, prince, pauper, teacher, and enlightened one. He lived through all of life's stages. And he taught the kind of serene inner peace that we all yearn to learn.

Jesus's story was very different. He was never a prince, never comfortable. From the time he went away as an adolescent into the desert to learn from John the Baptist and his followers, he was a marked man. After John's beheading by the Roman Empire, Jesus knew life was short and precarious. He was on the lam most of his teaching years. He distilled the best of his Jewish ancestry, combining both the nature-based mysticism of the Wisdom tradition and the prophetic impatience of the prophetic traditions. The Jewish prophets said a loud "No!" to injustice. They believed that individual enlightenment or salvation is not the whole story about life: All are saved or none are saved. Justice matters. Compassion and justice go together.

I see a Sacred Marriage of Buddha and Christ beginning to happen in this new century. East and West: Buddha's holy patience and serenity and Jesus's holy impatience and passion for justice. *We need both. We need this Sacred Marriage.* Every individual and every community needs both holy patience and holy impatience. Gandhi himself, representing the ancient Eastern wisdom of Hinduism, said that he learned to say "No!" from the West. In Gandhi's eyes, Hinduism was overly patient, for instance, with allowing the continued impoverishment of the "untouchables." "Next incarnation they will do better" was the shibboleth. "No!" said Gandhi. Justice needs to happen swifter. Gandhi represents a marriage of East and West. So does Martin Luther King Jr., who was a disciple of both Gandhi and Jesus, and whose spirit-filled activism filled the streets with marchers demanding equal rights and an end to racial injustice right now.

Father Bede Griffiths was an English Benedictine monk who lived and worked in an ashram in southern India for fifty years, and he wrote a book called *The Marriage of East and West*. In it, he writes about "the Vedic Revelation" of Hinduism and "the Judaic Revelation" of the Hebrew Bible, as well as "the Christian Revelation," which he sees as "the Rebirth of the Myth." He says:

> The ideas of Western science and democracy have penetrated to every part of the world — they are marks of the growth of humanity to a greater maturity, to a greater realization of what it means to be human.... But the limitations of Western science and democracy have become more and more evident. The disastrous effects of Western industrialism, physical, social and psychological, polluting the world and threatening to destroy it, are only too evident.

What is also evident to Griffiths is the overmasculinity of Western culture and religion.

> At the [sixteenth-century] renaissance the dominant, aggressive, masculine, rationalist mind of the West took charge, so that Europe remains today in a state of imbalance. The balance can only be restored when a meeting takes place between East and West.... This meeting must take place at the deepest level of the human consciousness. It is

an encounter ultimately between the two fundamental dimensions of human nature: the male and the female — the masculine, rational, active, dominating power of the mind, and the feminine, intuitive, passive and receptive power. Of course, these two dimensions exist in every human being and in every people and race. But for the past two thousand years, coming to a climax in the present century, the masculine, rational mind has gradually come to dominate Western Europe and has now spread its influence all over the world.

For Griffiths the Sacred Marriage of East and West is equivalent or parallel to the Sacred Marriage of the Masculine and the Feminine. The West represents the masculine, the East the feminine.

> The Western world... has now to rediscover the power of the feminine, intuitive mind, which has largely shaped the cultures of Asia and Africa and of tribal people everywhere. This is a problem not only of the world as a whole, but also of religion. ... All the Christian churches, Eastern and Western, have to turn to the religions of the East, to Hinduism, Buddhism, Taoism and the subtle blend of all these in Oriental culture, and to the deep intuitions of tribal religion in Africa and elsewhere, if they are to recover their balance and evolve an authentic form of religion which will answer to the needs of the modern world.

Thus the marriage of East and West is also a marriage of Science and Intuition. And it begins in ourselves, within each individual. To embrace intuition means being comfortable with darkness, for "intuition belongs not to the sunlit surface of the mind, but to the night and the darkness, to the moonlit world of dreams and images, before they emerge into rational consciousness." Intuition precedes intellect and the very "source of intuition" derives from "the experience of the body, the senses, the feelings, the imagination." All these precognitive experiences marry and interact together, for "there is no such thing as a mere sensation, a mere feeling, a mere thought. Every sensation, every feeling, every imagination affects my mind, modifies my being. I live and act as a whole." And how big are we? How does our "whole" interact with other "wholes"? "The self is not the little conscious ego, constructing its logical systems and building its rational world. The self plunges deep into the past of humanity and of the whole creation. I bear within my mind, my memory in the deep sense, the whole world." The self, therefore, is cosmic in size. In East and West, psyche and cosmos also marry.

How do we develop our intuition? "Intuition cannot be produced. It has to be allowed to happen. But that is just what the rational mind cannot endure. It wants to control everything. It is not prepared to be silent, to be still, to allow things to happen.... There is an activity of the mind which is grasping, achieving, dominating, but there is also an activity which is receptive, attentive, open to others." Intuition, as Griffiths sees it, "exists at every level of our being"; it suffuses our body. "The idea of 'thinking with the blood' is not an illusion. There is a very profound self-awareness at this deepest level of our being. Tribal people, especially in Africa, always tend to think with the blood, expressing themselves in the beat of drums and the movements of the dance." Of course this is integral to the wisdom of indigenous peoples everywhere — to pray by dancing, to pray with one's feet. For Griffiths, "bodily instinct" is a real and authentic kind of knowing:

> It finds expression not in abstract concepts but in concrete gestures, in images and symbols in dance and song, in ritual sacrifice, in prayer and ecstasy.... People who habitually go barefoot and expose their bodies to the sun, as they do in many parts of Asia and Africa, have an intuitive awareness of the powers, the *sakti* in Hindu terms, in the earth, in the air, in the water and in the fire of the sun. They experience these forces of nature acting upon them and have an instinctive knowledge of the hidden powers of nature.

And this way lies wisdom that is greater than knowledge, which can be a distraction and even an illusion. "It is the great illusion of the Western world that knowledge consists in abstract thought and that an illiterate person is ignorant. In reality many illiterate people possess a wisdom which is totally beyond the reach of Western man. Ramakrishna, the Hindu saint, who more than anyone else was responsible for the renewal of Hinduism in the last century, was an illiterate Brahmin, who spoke from the depths of an intuitive wisdom." We might add that Jesus, too, was illiterate.

Griffiths calls therefore for a Sacred Marriage as we are calling for: "What we have to seek is the 'marriage' of reason and intuition, of the male and the female, then only shall we discover a human technology corresponding with man's deepest needs."

NEW CEREMONIES: INDIGENOUS AND POSTMODERN

Postmodern, Western culture has so much to learn from indigenous peoples. They are wise in many ways that the modern world has shunned, particularly in regards to ritual and ceremony, to rites of passage, and to alternative ways for dealing with grief and celebration. Many people I know have profited profoundly from sweat lodges and vision quests, from Sundances and ceremonial chants. Jung said he never worked with a North American at the level of spirituality when he did not find an Indian inside. We have more indigenous blood and soul in us, more hunter-gatherer, than we might think. We can and need to respect and nourish this, within each of us individually and within our culture.

It is not enough to ask forgiveness of indigenous peoples for the way the modern world has treated them. We must also ask them to teach us. It is not that we do not have something to teach them also; it is about mutual respect, openness, and sharing. For most of American (and Western) history, this mutuality has been absent, and the continent's indigenous cultures have represented a shadow side of Western culture. To propose a Sacred Marriage between indigenous and modern cultures does not mean a domination of one over the other — it does not mean that the West destroys or steals indigenous ways, nor that indigenous ways should replace Western ones. It is about listening and paying attention to and learning from one another to create a whole culture, one that looks to the future while remaining grounded in its ancestors.

When I attended the funeral of my Lakota friend Buck Ghosthorse (whose life and teaching I discuss in chapter 5), a special happening occurred. I was honored to be asked to speak at his funeral, and it was arranged that I would speak last. But as the other elders spoke before me, and I realized my time was close, I grew concerned. Why? Because I'm no good at funerals. I cry easily. Not so much out of sadness as out of a sense of beauty. There is something whole and complete about a person's life when death puts a period to it. I find it very moving.

I said to myself, "I sure don't want to cry in front of these five hundred Indians. What to do?" Then I realized the rain was falling gently from the sky, and I said, "Good, Father Sky is crying. I don't have to. And the Earth can absorb my grief as I stand on her." And so it was. When I stood up and spoke, I had a powerful experience I have never had before — I felt my words were not coming from my mouth but directly from my chest. I was talking directly from my heart, and Father Sky from above and Mother Earth from below were holding me.

This was one more special gift that Native people have given to me through their dances, sweats, vision quests, ceremonies, teaching, laughing, and

just plain company. I will always be grateful for this marriage of indigenous and
Western ways in my life.

A WHOLE NEW MIND:
MERGING LEFT AND RIGHT BRAINS

Another Sacred Marriage being called for in our time is the marriage of our left
and right brains, or what author Daniel H. Pink in his book *A Whole New
Mind* calls "L-Directed Thinking" and "R-Directed Thinking." L-Directed
Thinking is an "attitude to life that is characteristic of the left hemisphere
of the brain — sequential, literal, functional, textual, and analytic." When
schools and politicians seek to improve education by demanding more exams,
they are exhibiting L-Directed Thinking. Computer programmers must rely
on L-Directed Thinking. It is very masculine, and it defines our information
age, but it is inadequate by itself.

In contrast, R-Directed Thinking is "an attitude to life that is characteristic of the right hemisphere of the brain — simultaneous, metaphorical, aesthetic, contextual, and synthetic. Underemphasized in the information age,
exemplified by creators and caregivers, shortchanged by organizations, and neglected in schools," it is the thinking of the future.

Pink does not call for a replacement of L-Directed Thinking but for a new
balance, a *new marriage* of both — especially because R-Directed Thinking has
been underappreciated and undervalued compared to L-Directed Thinking.
"But this is changing," Pink writes. "The R-Directed aptitudes so often dis-
dained and dismissed — artistry, empathy, taking the long view, pursuing the
transcendent — will increasingly determine who soars and who stumbles."
Many of the characteristics of R-Directed Thinking he identifies as more
feminine. Psychologist Frances Vaughan, in her book *Awakening Intuition*,
makes a similar point when she says, "If we're only intuitive, we're likely to be
dreamers. If we're only rational, we may find life to be disillusioning and dispir-
iting. But if we combine both faculties within ourselves, we can live as effective visionaries in the world."

This Sacred Marriage will result in a "whole new mind," one that responds
more effectively to the challenges and opportunities of our age, such as new
modes of communication, the computer and the Internet, globalization, the urge
for transcendence and the rise of women's consciousness. Pink recognizes three
stages in recent human brain development, which correspond to the evolution

of our work worlds over the past 150 years : In the Industrial Age, the lead character was "the mass production worker, whose cardinal traits were physical
strength and personal fortitude." Next, in the "Information Age," the central
figure was the "knowledge worker, whose defining characteristic was proficiency
in L-Directed Thinking." Today, Pink says we are entering the "Conceptual
Age," and its principal workers will be "the *creator* and the *empathizer*, whose
distinctive ability is mastery of R-Directed Thinking." The Creator and the
Empathizer correspond strikingly to the Blue Man, who brings consciousness
and creativity and is the man of compassion. But they also represent a Sacred
Marriage, since "the female brain is predominantly hard-wired for empathy.
The male brain is predominately hard-wired for understanding and building
systems." Of course, we were hunter-gatherers for 90 percent of human history, and I suspect during this period all humans, male and female, relied heavily on their intuitions, including as a way to communicate with animals and
plants. Pink seems to agree, observing, "back on the savanna, our cave-person
ancestors weren't taking SATs or plugging numbers into spreadsheets. But they
were telling stories, demonstrating empathy, and designing innovations. These
abilities have always comprised part of what it means to be human. But after
a few generations in the Information Age these muscles have atrophied. The
challenge is to work them back into shape." Agricultural workers combined
physical strength with intuition.

Interestingly, Pink feels computers are what will push us from L-Brain
Thinking to R-Brain Thinking: when it comes to "rule-based logic, calculation
and sequential thinking — computers are simply better, faster, and stronger.
What's more, computers don't fatigue. . . . Last century, machines proved they
could replace human backs. This century new technologies are proving they
can replace human left brains. As the scut work gets off-loaded, engineers and
programmers will have to master different aptitudes, relying more on creativity than competence, more on tacit knowledge than technical manuals and
more on fashioning the big picture than sweating the details."

Pink believes that the very prosperity that L-Directed Thinking has provided has ironically lessened the significance of material goods in favor of "more
R-Directed sensibilities — beauty, spirituality, emotion. For business, it's no
longer enough to create a product that's reasonably priced and adequately functional. It must also be beautiful, unique, and meaningful, abiding what author
Virginia Postrel calls 'the aesthetic imperative.'" Pink points to several interesting statistics to show how this is already transforming the work world. He

says in the United States today the number of graphic designers has increased tenfold in ten years, and they outnumber chemical engineers by four to one. "More Americans today work in arts, entertainment, and design than work as lawyers, accountants, and auditors." While the Harvard MBS program admits 10 percent of its applicants, the UCLA fine arts graduate school admits only 3 percent of its applicants. The number of jobs in the caring professions, such as counseling, nursing, and hands-on health assistance, is "surging." Nursing will account for more new jobs over the next decade than any other profession; an additional one million nurses will be needed. Apparently, compassion has a future.

If we can balance our left- and right-brain ways of knowing, it will mean the emergence of more balanced men and women. The Sacred Marriage of the mind produces concrete results. According to Pink, "great minds are androgynous" and a "psychologically androgynous person in effect doubles his or her repertoire of responses and can interact with the world in terms of a much richer and varied spectrum of opportunities." This androgynous way of thinking actually balances our internal masculine/feminine dynamic. "When tests of masculinity/femininity are given to young people, over and over one finds that creative and talented girls are more dominant and tougher than other girls, and creative boys are more sensitive and less aggressive than their male peers."

The importance of seeking and achieving an androgynous inner nature is underscored by Carl Jung, as well as by Robert Bly and Marion Woodman in their retelling of the story of "The Maiden King." Bly and Woodman write about the tradition of the alchemical "inner marriage," in which the union of the bride and her lover represents an internalization of masculine and feminine energies and ways of thought. Woodman points out that when we are young, if we are male, we project onto our partner our femininity, and if we are female, we project our masculinity. "As life continues, however, we begin to realize we cannot enter an outer relationship unless we are coming from our own inner marriage.... Until the inner Bride and Bridegroom creatively love each other, the outer relationship is starving, becoming a substitute that may collapse into crippling codependence. In the new paradigm, we are sooner or later pushed toward our own maturity — the androgyne."

This process of bringing the two together in oneself is not easy. It "demands hard work in bringing to union a well-differentiated femininity and an equally well-differentiated masculinity in an inner marriage in subtle body.... To embrace the androgyne as a symbol of the inner marriage, as the God/Goddess within, requires a long, painful process of differentiation." But it does occur, and it is the signal achievement of spiritual maturity, as the ancient symbols of Shiva and Shakti, and of yin and yang, attest. The Sacred Marriage of our left and right brains is another way of saying we seek the masculine indwelling in the feminine and the feminine indwelling in the masculine.

A GAY AND STRAIGHT WEDDING

The objection to homosexuals being allowed to act as homosexuals, fall in love as homosexuals, and make love as homosexuals, has depended on the well-worn shibboleth that "homosexuality is unnatural." If one operates exclusively from one's own experience and perspective, then a heterosexual might well say, "homosexuality is unnatural." But what heterosexuals ought to say is that "homosexuality is unnatural for me. I don't need it. I get aroused and excited and fall in love with people of the opposite sex."

That is the whole point. Turn it around and you will grasp something of the confusion and hurt of the homosexual. To the homosexual as an individual, "heterosexuality is unnatural." The homosexual is not aroused and does not fall in love with people of the opposite sex, but with people of his or her own sex.

The entire debate revolves around the issue of *what is natural? Who says what is natural or unnatural?* Obviously, this last question is a very political one, for it is about power, the power to declare this or that version of marriage "natural" or not. The theological importance of the issue is underscored by Thomas Aquinas who wrote in the thirteenth century, "A mistake about creation results in a mistake about God." As KJ says, if homosexuality exists, God must have created it. The question easily becomes a political one because a minority (homosexual) can readily be subjugated by a majority (heterosexual).

As for religion, the Bible says, "God is love." It does not say, "God is heterosexual love." A religion based on love respects and honors the diverse forms of love that God has established. The heart of the Sacred Marriage of gay and straight is a respect for God's love in whatever forms it's expressed.

The fact is, homosexuality has always been and thus is likely to always be an aspect of humanity and the natural world. It is not new and it is not exclusive to humans. Questions about what makes an appropriate marriage and an appropriate family are social and political questions, and the answers can and do change.

How do we know humans are not the only creatures who experience homosexuality? Science has proven it. Studies have found that over 464 species — including dolphins, geese, flamingos, dogs, cats, birds, and more — have homosexual populations. Further, among humans, studies have found that on average 8 to 10 percent of all human populations across all societies worldwide are homosexual. Created by God, confirmed by science: Homosexuality is part of nature, and by extension, it is also natural.

Accepting and respecting this is the first aspect of the Sacred Marriage of Gay and Straight, which is also a celebratory embrace of nature's diversity. It asks us to stretch and expand our imaginations so they match the creativity and diversity of the world itself. This marriage is about lifting judgments about right and wrong and accepting what is. Nature is biased toward creativity; it surprises, and it does not make everything the same. Isn't it amazing that nature ensures that heterosexuals give birth to so many homosexual children? Apparently, when it comes to sexual preference, nature prefers to have a significant minority population who prefer sex with their own sex than with the opposite sex. The "marriage" of which I speak is simply that of the sexual majority (heterosexuals) accepting and befriending the sexual minority (homosexuals). Studies show that young people today are less threatened by gay and lesbian differences. Probably this has a lot to do with gays and lesbians coming out more publicly since the brave political battles their ancestors fought to achieve equality and acceptance two generations ago. Some 80 percent of people under thirty are in favor of full gay and lesbian rights.

One might say the Sacred Marriage of Gay and Straight is about the acceptance of all difference. This "marriage" is about opening up the definition of one's family or tribe. It is about seeing that the world teems with *many tribes, many colors, many varieties*. Vive la différence! Let differences reign. Variety makes for wonder, laughter, creativity, and health. So this marriage means defining "family" in part by variety, which keeps us from getting stuck in sameness and becoming culturally arrogant. It is also the Sacred Marriage of the Majority and the Minority, since the "marriage" of gays and straights symbolizes the willingness of the straight majority (for straights will always be a majority) to acknowledge and celebrate the gay minority. It recognizes that gays, and all minority populations, join the majority as citizens, lovers, parents, humans.

The Sacred Marriage of Gay and Straight also directly addresses our notions of gender and sex. Homosexuals reverse, confuse, and play with gender polarity. It is true that many homosexual men are more in touch with their feelings, their creativity, and their spiritual awareness — their feminine side — than heterosexual men in general. Many homosexual women are more in touch with their masculine side than heterosexual women. But gay men can also be macho, and lesbians can be fem, and transgender people mix and match gender in every conceivable way — and through all this gay populations demonstrate the *relativity* of male and female gender stereotypes. They show that gender identity is not static, uniform, or dependent on one's body. Embracing this as a principle opens the door for everyone to play with gender roles within themselves, and to express their own unique sexual identity in all its individuality, humor, and diversity. The marriage of gay and straight is a reminder not to take gender literally.

Finally, within the gift of truly accepting gay love as equal to heterosexual love is the realization that, no matter what St. Augustine thought, sex does not have to be procreative in the literal sense. Gender aside, the only real difference between gay sex and heterosexual sex is that the former does not and cannot create a baby. And surely, considering the current population explosion, which poses serious threats to the environment and our own sustainability on the planet, all sex shouldn't be procreative. The world hardly needs the huge influx of children that would mean. No, the Sacred Marriage of Gay and Straight embraces love for love's sake. It embraces the sexual expression of love as reason enough for sex. Sex is not just for begetting children. Sex can be fun and an end in itself. Like prayer is. "Without a why," as Meister Eckhart put it. In this marriage, gays can teach straights to have more fun with sex, to play with their gender roles, to get lost in it, and therefore to bring mysticism into it. Doesn't the Bible have a whole book about that — the Song of Songs — which celebrates human love in itself (not to create children) as the presence of God, the return of Paradise, a hint of heaven on earth?

Here lies a deep and real "Sacred Marriage" — the solidarity that gay and straight can make happen when they join common cause for justice's sake, when they let go of their fears and biases to recognize the *deep union* that they already share as human beings. This "sacred marriage" is beginning to manifest itself on our planet in a special way today thanks to the courage of gay and lesbian people asserting their true selves in the face of much opposition. And the courage of political and judicial leaders to understand the justice issues that are at stake. Now gays and straights together can make common cause for economic, political, racial, and gender justice.

YOUNG AND OLD: SHARING WISDOM

Peter Kingsley tells the story of how in ancient Greece the *kouros* or "young man" was considered very special. When the goddess encountered Parmeneides, she first calls him *kouros*. Kingsley comments: "In terms of physical age it could mean someone under thirty. But in practice the word had a far wider meaning. A *kouros* was the man of any age who still saw life as a challenge, who faced it with the whole of vigour and passion, who hadn't yet stood back to make way for his sons. The word indicated the quality of a man, not how old he was." So the quality of *kouros* is something the young teach the old. In addition, for the Greeks, the quality of *kouros* was closely connected to initiation — he "stands at the border line between the world of the human and the world of the divine; has access to them both." The great lawgivers of Crete were understood to have had their laws revealed to them "in a cave, through the ritual practice of incubation."

There is a parallel tradition in Persia where a *fata* indicates a young man under thirty but also applies, Kingsley writes, to a "man of any age who's gone beyond time, who through the intensity of longing has made the initiatory journey outside of time and space and come to the heart of reality; who's found what never ages or dies." The Sufis of Persia teach that this mixture of the young and old is necessary because the world could not survive without these "young men." They are the prophets, and there is never a time when they do not exist some place on Earth. "They have the responsibility of making the hero's journey into another world, to the source of light in the darkness and bringing back the timeless knowledge that they find there. Without this knowledge or guidance, people would be totally deaf and blind. They'd be completely lost in their own confusion."

In contrast, Robert Bly makes a very important observation about youth/ elder relationships in our culture:

> There is evidence from many cultures that an opening toward spirituality arrives around fifteen or sixteen. What happens? In India the outer world "responds." So to speak. A child in an Indian village or city sees on the street constant religious processions. . . . A kind of madness of religious feeling helps the adolescent whose spiritual chakra has just opened feel at home.
>
> But in our culture, the adolescent does not see ecstatic religious

singers on the street. What he or she does see is posters advertising sexual energy.... The spiritual opening, having received almost no response, closes again. "Something marvelous is about to happen." But it doesn't.... What arrives is disappointment.... Adolescents in all societies, we suspect, feel the disappointed emptiness; but in our culture, it's as if adolescents are *sold* this emptiness.

Bly is telling us that the elders are failing the young and even taking advantage of them in our culture. We need a new relationship with more direct communication, more give and take. I have written before about *adultism*, which is the sorry state of adults having repressed their child inside and this repression arising as projection onto the young. I believe that goes on a lot in our culture. I think Woodman is observing the same thing when she observes that "most young men in our culture [have] no spiritual heritage into which his elders are going to welcome him." Spirituality is lacking as a conscious awareness in most men. This is one profound reason why men need to be more at home with their child inside — which of course is the mystic inside who wants to "play in the universe." If adults were in touch with that deep reality, the young would be more at home with adults. Men would have more of substance to pass on to the young men.

Here is how Woodman puts it: "The adult fully and consciously awake is at one with the child fully and unconsciously asleep.... They depend upon each other, their dependence uniting rather than separating the two realms — the unconscious and consciousness, sleep and awareness." This, too, is the Blue Man awakening: more expansions of consciousness, more swinging between states of young and old, awake and asleep, conscious and unconscious, dreams and reality. Indeed, Woodman talks of how dreams often tell about the birth of a divine Child and "the dreamer is astonished by its beauty, and its capacity to talk with the wisdom of an elder.... The old life dies; a new life is born. The soul is finding a new world."

Sometimes we are taught that the elders hold all the knowledge or wisdom in a community. But today I feel a new balance, a new marriage, is required that recognizes the wisdom emerging from the young. After all, the scriptures say that "out of the mouth of babes will come wisdom," and in the ancient Rule of St. Benedict that has furnished the basis of monastic discipline for sixteen thousand years, Benedict proclaimed that when there is an important issue for the community to decide, the first one to hear from ought to be the youngest in the community. In fact, our society is hard on both the elders *and* the young. When one is neglected, the other is as well, for there exists a certain natural and organic link between the stages and ages of grandfathers and grandchildren. Our culture has unnaturally severed that link in many ways. What we need today is *intergenerational wisdom*. For that to occur, the young must be listened to anew. Adultism must be addressed. The adult must rediscover the "puer" or "puella," the divine child inside. This means that the mystic, the Christ or divine youth in us all, must be reawakened. Then the old no longer resent the young, who are recognized and understood. Together, young and old can make a sacred journey, and in this way unite in a Sacred Marriage.

THE ULTIMATE HOLY MATRIMONY: SPIRIT AND SOUL

Spirit and soul are not the same thing. In Latin, "spirit" (*spiritus*) is masculine and "soul" (*anima*) is feminine. An awakened soul seeks spirit, but an asleep soul may distort spirit, so that spirit is all "sky" energy with no "earth" energy. This leads to the Icarus story, in which the young male is drawn to the sky and the sun and the yang energy without being grounded enough to know his limits. The sacred marriage of the alchemists, called the "conjunctio" or "coitus," refers to the union of our divine spirit with the soul and also with the body. The purpose of the union is to bring spirit, soul, and body together rather than to allow them to separate. It takes work. The union is often depicted in alchemical drawings as the marriage of King and Queen or of man and wife.

In our culture, dominated as it has been by an excessive patriarchy, we have to work hard to bring soul and spirit together again. Spirit has for too long been "on its own" — its energy has not served the soul or the feminine or the Earth but other gods, whether gods of war, of mammon, of power for power's sake. A distorted spirit, which ignores the soul, leads to violence, in which energy, time, talent, and treasure are put into the so-called "spirit work" of corporate and national expansion. This is not real spirit work. To bring soul in is to bring other animals into our consciousness and awareness (the word "animal" comes from *anima* or "soul"). It means bringing the plant world in, since plants too have souls. Our distortion of spirit has led to an unprecedented destruction of plants and animals and soul.

The "holy marriage," or *hieros gamos*, includes an intimate union of opposites. It is represented symbolically in the Jewish traditions as a Temple where

Yahweh, the unseen Holy One, consummates a marriage with Shekinah, his feminine bride. The search for the lost bridegroom that the lover undertakes in the Song of Songs tells that story also. The responsive Bride and the active Spirit produce a child, the Christ child in the Christian story, who will go about doing God's work on Earth. The Divine Child is not dead. Only in need of new parents, ones who are open to a new balance and a new wedding of the soul and spirit, Feminine and Masculine.

CONCLUSION: REAL MEN ARE
BEARERS OF THE SACRED MASCULINE

WHAT I HAVE WRITTEN about the Sacred Masculine in this book is not new. Father Sky, the Green Man, the Spiritual Warrior, the hunter-gatherer; honoring our bodies, celebrating sexuality, elders and youth communicating well; the Blue Man and the Fatherly and Grandfatherly Hearts — these are all teachings from our ancestors. If we've forgotten or neglected the ways of being these metaphors and archetypes represent, that says more about us and our modern world than it does about these archetypes and their importance. These metaphors *appear* to be new because something happened about eight thousand years ago that distorted manhood. Men went a little crazy. Taming the horse. Inventing agriculture. Professional armies. War. It sucked in our souls and imaginations as well as our wealth. Empires became the name of the game. The survival of the fittest.

Certainly, as we look at the state of the world, it would be demoralizing and even despairing to say that this is the best human beings can do. The ongoing prevalence of war, the persistence of discrimination and intolerance, and the worsening ecological destruction of the planet (now going by the popular name "global warming") are not things to praise. Healing them would seem to require new strategies, new approaches, new conceptions, since our current ones have been inadequate. However, I believe deeply that we don't just need something "new" but something very old, something essential that we've lost track of. We will begin the real healing of our communities and world when we renew and recover our conception of the Sacred Masculine and embody it in each of our individual lives.

The Divine Feminine, the goddess, the Divine Mother — for several decades now, she has been stirring and awakening and returning with force in our day. Bravo! Alleluia! But her return requires that men too awaken — and the healthy man in every woman. *Together* we can rise and reinvent the Sacred Marriage of Yin and Yang for a crowded, fast-communicating, postmodern world. We do that not by ignoring the wisdom of the premoderns, but by honoring that wisdom and bringing it along and applying it to our world. Are we not Cain's sons and daughters? How much, besides replacing Cain's rock with an atomic bomb, has really changed in human nature?

Can human beings change? Can men change? What defines a "real man"? In this conclusion, I will look at how a healthy masculinity can reflect the *best* in us and truly serve our communities when it incorporates and embodies all ten aspects of the Sacred Masculine.

PLAYING WITH ARCHETYPES

As I've said, the ten archetypes in this book are metaphors. They are useful ways to embody and conceptualize ideas or ways of being. And they are meant to be playful. We should take them up in our imaginations and in our lives and adapt them to fit. Connect them, combine them, mix them. In that spirit, here are some ways to play with these ideas, and I invite readers to take this further.

Consider, for example, the obvious relationships between Father Sky and the Blue Man. Sky is blue like the Blue Man, who is cosmic. Consciousness and creativity often come "from above" and "out of the blue," and the Blue Man's compassion is the "imitation of God." As we alluded to earlier, one role of the Green Man is as a prophet, which is also the realm of the Spiritual Warrior, and both certainly merge when we focus our attention on the eco-peril challenging our world. Fully ingesting the Green Man means being serious about the prophetic role in one's life, and there is no prophet who is not a warrior, and no authentic warrior who is not a prophet. Do you respond to Icarus and Daedalus? They certainly need lessons about the Fatherly Heart — clearly Daedalus, murderer of his nephew, is deficient in his heart-attitudes toward the younger generation. If this changed during Daedalus's exile with his son, he didn't change enough, for he failed to communicate effectively about life and death issues with Icarus. Both suffered. Both could have profited from an Earth Father, or Fatherly Heart, connection. Indeed, would this have tempered Icarus's relationship to Father Sky?

Hunter-gatherers — which includes all of us — are also warriors, and at this time we all should be hunting and gathering whatever we can find that awakens the Green Man and provides for green sustainability of the Earth. As we hunt for mates and for lovers, we also ask how the Fatherly Heart enters into the equation. And as we develop into more effective Lovers and ravishers (and ravishees), we also nurture our amazing bodies and our profound gratitude for our bodies. We realize our bodies are Temples, the creation of our fourteen-billion-year universe. In them, our lovemaking turns cosmic, just as the food and drink we take in is harvested from the cosmos: a meal of sunlight and water, earth and air, ancestor and space dust, bringing life to lungs and stomach and mouth and feet.

With our Grandfatherly Heart, we accept death and open to the wisdom of youth. Wherever we are in our adventurous journey, we are held in the combined embrace of Father and Grandfather Sky — whenever we welcome a newborn baby, care for it, share wisdom, and learn from the wisdom of the newborn, letting it touch the whole family. As elders, we gather and share all our learning. One can hardly be an elder without having acknowledged one's "amazing body" and subsequently having cared wisely for it. One can hardly come to elderhood without tasting warriorhood personally, without hunting and gathering, without meeting Blue and Green Men, Father Sky and our Earth Father. We cannot become an elder without being married many times, uniting in Sacred Marriages with all aspects of the Divine Feminine, dancing within ourselves with all the sacred opposites we named in the previous chapters. What healthy masculine has not danced with the healthy feminine in his life? Indeed, a healthy masculine manifests itself through the interconnections of Sacred Marriage, of which there are an infinite variety, and always more to come.

FALSE MASCULINITY: REAL MEN EAT BEEF

Society is continually trying to define for us what "real men" do, what "real men" are. Most often, these definitions do not serve or benefit men or communities or the sacred; they serve corporations or politics. For instance, consider the ad that has appeared frequently over the past decade that declares "Real Men Eat Beef." No doubt, this is paid for by the cattle growers association, but just because we know that this is a manipulative corporate message doesn't make it less effective. Like many ads, it distills a particular philosophy into a succinct message. The essential word is "real." To say "men eat beef" would be to state an unremarkable fact, and it wouldn't sell many steaks. Rather, a particular kind of man eats beef, a *real* man as opposed to, presumably, an "unreal" man. What makes a man "unreal"? By implication, femininity. Thus, not eating beef brands one as "feminine," and the ad further implies that any man who displays or honors feminine attributes — emotional openness or creativity, perhaps — would not eat beef and therefore is not a "real man." Beef is for *manly men*, for solely masculine men. And if you are a real man, then you'll eat beef. You know who you are, and the rest fail the beef test.

But do you know who you are? Are you a real man? The ad appeals to a man's self-doubt. It appeals to his shame. After all, who wants to be an unreal man or an effeminate man or a gay man or a less-than-manly man? The ad plays on any fear we might have about the Divine Feminine, either inside or out-side us, and it would have us question the quality of our own masculinity should we embrace the feminine. Do we really cut the mustard? How manly am I? If I'm not sure, should I eat more beef to make up for it? The ad appeals to the doubt in every man (and there is no human who does not wrestle with doubt) about whether he is acceptably masculine. It is a clever ad for it hits men where they are vulnerable — where shame creeps in.

The ad spreads three lies. The first, the one that's easiest to see and dismiss, is that a real man proves his manhood by eating lots of beef. A man might be-lieve he was displaying his manliness through prodigious beef eating, but who would believe their masculinity depended on eating beef? There's almost a winking irony to this simplistic, reductionist equation, as if it said: of course, real men do what they want, but what they want is beef.

The second lie is the ad's distraction. It would make eating beef an ex-pression of self, making beef necessary to one's identity, rather than having us consider whether it's an important food for one's physical health or the health of society. As your doctor will tell you, eating too much beef can kill you. Men who eat too much beef frequently die of cardiac arrest. In addition, the beef industry is incredibly polluting, the treatment of cattle is frequently inhumane, and as a source of nutrition for humans, cattle are a terribly inefficient use of resources (considering how much grain, water, and soil must be used to grow cattle). Also, the methane released by cattle farting is considered a factor in global warming, since methane is the most dangerous of all hot-house gasses. If a "real man" is also a man who cares for his own health and the health of society and the planet, then a "real man" doesn't become addicted to beef; he eats it in moderation, if at all. And if beef isn't necessary to be a man, and it's potentially unhealthy to self and environment, *why* eat it at all? I stopped eating beef about eighteen years ago, after reading books by Jeremy Rifkin and John Robbins (*Beyond Beef* and *Diet for a New America*, respectively), and I hardly miss it. And, last time I checked, I was still a "real man." (As are Rifkin and Robbins.)

What is not being said is that it takes a man who hates the planet or who does not respect his amazing body to succumb to eating beef in excess. A real man *thinks*. He reads and studies in addition to eating. It is part of being a hunter-gatherer. A real man hunts for the facts.

The third lie is the most insidious. It is the proposal that only masculinity makes a man. This feeds male fear of the Divine Feminine, for it makes any closeness with the feminine a threat to our status as men. It may be silly to equate this with beef eating, yet it's often an unquestioned assumption that any definition of maleness must reject the "feminine," including such attributes as compassion, creativity, receptivity, compromise, and generativity. Indeed, *false masculinity* is almost always defined by its rejection of the feminine.

How much advertising is spent on selling us false and illusory images of masculinity that both appeal to shame in us *and* spread illusions about what masculinity *really means*? One is reminded of the swagger and outdoors appeal of the classic "Marlboro Man" that lured generations of young men into a dangerous and addictive smoking habit. The facts are as follows: the very actor who played the rough-and-tumble, macho "Marlboro Man" in the ads died painfully and prematurely of lung cancer. So much for "real men" illusions. Every man needs to *take back* his understanding of what it is to be male and to be authentically masculine.

For a very real example of this same illusory sales pitch, consider the neoconservative slogan that arose soon after the start of the current Iraq War: "Anyone can go to Baghdad. Real men go to Tehran." In other words, "real men" don't fight "easy" wars (as the Iraq War was supposed to be at the time, a "cakewalk," but that was nearly a hundred thousand lives and a trillion dollars ago). No, real men prefer the worst, deadliest wars possible. What does this imply about the soldiers who were then fighting and dying in Iraq? That their manliness somehow did not measure up to those soldiers who would prefer a war with Iran? Of course, the real targets of this slogan were not the soldiers fighting in Iraq, but the US politicians and citizens in America. In this equation, the entire nation's masculinity was being called into question if it did not embrace a second full-scale military assault on the Middle East.

Here again, the distracting lie is that war is necessary to define and prove one's identity, one's maleness, never mind questions of policy or cause, never mind how much death and destruction result. War proves you're a man, and if you don't go to war, and go to war with *this* country, then you are not a man. This call to *false masculinity* lurks behind much war-mongering and war-making; it plays on fear and shame in men, bullying them to fight in order to prove their "masculinity." In fact, "real men" define themselves by what they do to avoid war (using negotiation and diplomacy), and when that fails, they define themselves by their reasoning and conduct: engaging in war for clear self-protection, as a last result, and as much as possible protecting and ensuring civilian lives.

The men, the elected officials, who instigated the Iraq War, and who then said "real men go to Tehran," have failed these tests of "manhood" on every count. They went to war on false pretenses, leading to the deaths of tens of thousands of civilians, the decimation of a country, and the unraveling of an entire society. By their terms, then, "real men" are dangerous and deadly men with a callous disregard for others. If this is true, who would ever want to be a "real man"?

Real men try diplomacy. Real men check their reptilian, fight-or-flight brains at the door; they think and don't just act or react. Those who say that "real men go to Tehran" are in fact revealing their lack of manliness, their lack of a wise and grandfatherly heart. They spurn the Blue Man within in their efforts to spew venom and war. They repeat the mistakes of Daedalus — their envy and hatred for the young is obvious as they send them to their deaths.

WHAT MAKES MEN "REAL"

As a way to counter these caricatures of "real men," here is a list of what actual men do who embody the Sacred Masculine we've discussed in this book.

Real men work to save the planet, and like any prophet, take the attacks that standing up for a moral cause invariably brings about.

Real men love the Sky. They are curious and eager to learn about the new cosmology, and they share their excitement with others, especially the young.

Real men meditate. They are not afraid to look *inside* and see the vastness that is there.

Real men awaken their mammalian brain to remain connected to their compassion, rather than let the win/lose mentality of the reptilian brain take over.

Real men treat youth with respect. Real men sport a Fatherly Heart.

Real men love their bodies. They work to keep them healthy, honoring their Temple with good food and cleansing exercise. They stand up to the ways and poisons of corporate food and corporate agriculture that fill our bodies and those of our children with toxic sugars and chemicals (such as hydrogenated oils).

Real men enjoy sex and taste the delights of ravisher and ravishee.

Real men are not homophobic (or heterophobic). They acknowledge and respect the diversity of creation, which includes sexual diversity.

Real men seek to expand their consciousness. They get to know the Blue Man inside, increase their powers of imagination and creativity, and exhibit compassion.

Real men listen to music and are unafraid to follow the inner journeys of joy and grief, celebration and community, surprise and elegance that it inspires.

Real men are warriors, not soldiers. They learn to battle (jihad) with oneself first, to overcome the temptations of power for power's sake, greed, power-over, and power-under. They seek power-with (compassion).

Real men wage peace, not war. Real men know that peace is harder to wage than war, and that waging peace begins in one's own heart.

Real men enter war reluctantly, as a last resort.

Real men send young men to war reluctantly, as a last resort.

Real men practice solitude.

Real men are not afraid of the "dark night of the soul." They do not run from it but know that darkness has important things to teach them.

Real men criticize institutions (including religious ones) that wage lies and wars that poison the true meaning of justice and religion.

Real men defend what they cherish, including space, children, grandchildren, Earth, and all her marvelous creatures.

Real men communicate with younger and older generations, and they listen as deeply as they teach.

Real men use all the brains God has given them — the intellectual and rational brain *and* the intuitive and mystical brain.

Real men remain curious and alive and are always learning, and they hunt for ways to heal and preserve what is good and beautiful.

Real men have inclusive families. They expand the Fatherly Heart to take in and welcome all people.

Real men are fathers to the young. They embrace their children *and* other children, and they remember the "extended family" of tribal memory.

Real men, when they become elders, *refire*. They don't retire. They join forces with the youngest generation.

Real men respect women. They respect the women in their lives and the women's movement's fight for justice and gender equality for all women.

Real men befriend other men.

Real men do not shame themselves or other men about their masculinity.

Real men channel their aggression in ways that do not harm themselves or others.

Real men stand up to addictions that dictate to their soul, and they do the inner work necessary to detox inside.

Real men experience their emotions. They don't run from their feelings.

Real men honor the passages of life with meaningful rituals.

Real men are generous, not hoarding.

Real men embrace the Divine Feminine in themselves. They know all humans are a Sacred Marriage of masculine and feminine, and they commit to knowing and nurturing this balance for a lifetime.

This list speaks not just about what real men *do* but about what real men *are at the level of our beings.* As Meister Eckhart put it seven centuries ago, "Worry less about what you do and more about who you are: For if you are just, your ways will be just, and if you are joyful, your ways will be joyful." True action comes from authentic being. A real man explores being and not just actions. A real man *acts* from his being, not from a mere action/reaction reptilian response. The archetypes presented in this book all speak to our *beings* as well as to our actions. That is their power. That is why archetypes shake us up. They transform us. They turn things inside out. Being makes a difference, it arouses imagination, and spreads itself into activity. We spread new seeds everywhere, some of which, as Jesus observed, fall on rock or on hard ground and do not take root. But some fall on fertile soil and do indeed take root.

An example of something *real men* are doing in our time to tame the reptilian brain in business can be found in networking groups with an ecological and community conscience, such as Businesses for Social Responsibility, Co-op, America's Green Business Network, and the Social Venture Network. The most recent effort is the B Corporation Movement. Companies in this movement "are stewards of the whole, not just stewards of maximizing shareholder wealth," says Jan Coen Gilbert, a Stanford business school graduate and entrepreneur who cofounded the B Corporation Movement. "We are witnessing the birth of a new sector of the economy between the private sector and the nonprofit sector. Our grandchildren will be talking about this new sector the way we talk about the nonprofit sector." He foresees it accounting for 5 to 10 percent of GDP. It will attract capital and thus grow even larger.

Men are seed-carriers. We carry and create seeds, lots of them, an abundance of seeds. A man manufactures 15 billion sperm cells each month, and one ejaculation releases 400 million of them. But sperm is also a metaphor. Are we spreading the seeds of new and healthy life? Are we, metaphorically speaking, fertilizing with the feminine, creating children, and nurturing, protecting, and providing for our communities? That is what real men do.

DEALING WITH SHAME AND AGGRESSION

Throughout this book, we have seen the twin themes of Shame and Aggression raise their heads. If in fact these ten archetypes offer significant and profound insight into masculinity, it stands to reason that they should also offer insight into these twin issues of maleness. Dr. John Conger insists that we need to acknowledge that we are both images of God *and* images of apes, and if true, this makes a good moment to reflect explicitly on how the ten archetypes offer insight about shame and aggression, those shadow sides that we inherit from our earlier primate brothers and sisters.

Father Sky

It is significant to recognize that if shame is "not belonging," then not belonging to the sky and to the greater universe may actually form the basis of all shame. It is the shame of shames. Such ignorance, such not belonging, is dangerous. If we are alienated from the cosmos, where will we ever find belonging? We could wander forever through life's infinite shopping mall and never find the consumer items that help us belong.

Regarding aggression, we should be aware that if we feel shame from a sense of not belonging to the universe, we may well be profoundly pissed off without even knowing where that anger and alienation is coming from. A cosmos that is denied will be a cosmos that will bite us in the backside. Furthermore, our cosmic-size anger and our cosmic-size grief will find *no healthy outlet* if we only live in a human-made world of cosmetology, instead of a grand cosmology. When we learn about Father Sky, we learn that there is a place that can absorb and recycle our anger and grief. Take them to the sky.

The Green Man

If shame is "not belonging," then to be cut off from plants, animals, and the Earth is profoundly shaming. We are subconsciously ashamed to be living lives of hollow anthropocentrism, lives passed in front of television sets instead of face to face with creation itself. Nature and creation with all their majesty, their wonder, and their beauty satisfies. As for aggression, we may well find that we take our anger out on others — kicking the dog around or the trees or the polar bears — simply because we are cut off from all our relations. This is what "sports" like dog fighting are about: we can't find enough outlets for our aggression in our regular lives, so we take it out on Mother Earth and her creatures.

One indigenous ritual for dealing with anger goes like this: Dig a hole in the earth. Find a rock and ask it if it will play the role you are going to ask of it. Put your anger into the rock and wrap it in a cloth that means something to you and bury the rock in the hole and cover it with dirt. In this way Mother Earth, who is bountiful and generous, not unlike Father Sky, absorbs one's anger and keeps it where it will not harm others. Thank Mother Earth and Gaia for her generosity. This is the way of a Green Man. He knows that loving is not only giving but also asking.

Icarus and Daedalus

How ashamed was Daedalus over killing his nephew (or at least over being caught for killing his nephew)? He was sent into exile, the ultimate shame, to live on an island with his son. Did Daedalus want to redeem himself when he constructed wings so he and his son could escape? Clearly, shame plays a central role in this story. Due to Daedalus's inability to control his anger, he shamed not just himself but his son with exile. Icarus, innocent of any crime, then paid the ultimate price due to his father's lack of protection and communication. When Icarus died, Daedalus continued his escape but then hung up his wings forever, unable to bear having saved himself but not his son. Here, then, is a perfect metaphor for shame: to vow never to fly again.

The spur to the story is anger. Daedalus was angry and envious of his nephew, so angry that he murdered him. Envy and anger often go together and lead to murderous thoughts. However, Daedalus also used his anger to feed his imagination; he did not collapse in despair but worked toward a solution. He constructed a labyrinth to please the king, and conspired to escape the island with the aid of his own miraculous invention: wings. He turned his anger to creativity. Do we?

Hunter-Gatherer

Shame is a constant issue for the hunter-gatherer: his efforts are in service of the tribal community, and they provide his sense of belonging, but if he suffers defeat or fails that community (and thus becomes cut off from it), then he has failed in his essential reason for being. In the extreme, defeat in battle meant being cannibalized by the victor (or perhaps killed by one's prey). We typically think of cannibalism in terms of the victor, but what of the ones who are eaten? Metaphorically speaking, might masochism come into play here? A hunter-gatherer, filled with shame, might feel he "deserves to be eaten," and thus find defeat, and fail his tribe, over and over again. The Garden of Eden story seems to echo this notion of "shame" after the sin of Adam and Eve. To live in the Garden of Eden is to live without shame, prior to shame itself. Redemption means, then, a life without shame.

Aggression is clearly not lacking in the hunter-gatherer either. Aggression is even necessary: it takes aggression to hunt the animals that are key to survival, and it takes aggression to protect one's tribe from other tribes who might attack or encroach on one's territory. However, it is a keen and sharp and focused aggression. It is not aggression for aggression's sake but aggression for survival's sake. The hunter-gatherer can be seen, then, as one model for how to channel and focus aggression in the appropriate ways and contexts. Aggression can be useful, but it also must be contained and limited, or it becomes self-defeating and self-destructive. A hunter-gatherer who cannot control his own aggression becomes hurtful of the tribe he's meant to serve.

The Spiritual Warrior

If *shame* is not belonging, the true spiritual warrior voluntarily risks not belonging in order to stand up for what matters and to challenge his own community. As

Jesus observed, "a prophet is without honor in his own country." Indeed, sometimes it is the ostracization of society, or the betrayals of others, that spurs the warrior's courage to stand up and speak out and stand out. The spiritual warrior, then, refuses to internalize shame, though he often arouses shaming in others. However, a spiritual warrior does belong — he belongs to an exceptional line of ancestors — all those moral heroes we praise for their generosity and sacrifice on behalf of justice, such as Jesus and Gandhi, Malcolm X and Martin Luther King Jr., Isaiah, and Muhammad.

Like the hunter-gatherer, the spiritual warrior uses anger and aggression and contains it at the same time. Anger becomes moral outrage within his own heart, and this fuels his actions. However, unlike the hunter-gatherer, these actions are not themselves violent or aggressive or deadly. The spiritual warrior seeks to change others, not defeat them, and so his decision making is rational and compassionate, seeking effective results, not just a discharge for personal anger. Effective results are ones that do not perpetuate harm but end the cycle of violence or of revenge. I have been struck by how many men I know who have been able to recycle their anger by learning what we call "martial arts," but which Professor Pitt prefers calling "healing arts." They are preventive medicine for anger, keeping it from being projected onto others. They heal the practitioner and the community. Do not underestimate the power of "martial" or "healing arts" to assist warriors to learn deep discipline for their aggression.

The Lover

Ever since Adam and Eve donned fig leafs, shame has been associated with our bodies, or at least it has been by Christianity. It did not help that Augustine, deeply affected by both Manichaeism (a philosophy that considered all matter evil) and dualistic Neo-Platonism (Augustine defined "spirit" as "whatever is not matter"), equated sexuality with original sin. For Augustine, sex is itself shameful and all lovemaking is at least a venial sin. Why? Because one loses control. I find this more than odd, since I think all mystical experience is about losing control, "getting lost in the temple" of the universe — or in the case of two lovers, in two universes. Patriarchal religion frequently seems to make it a moral imperative to render sex a shameful and guilt-ridden act, rather than a natural and ecstatic and indeed sacred exchange of love.

At the extreme, when anger overwhelms sexuality, it becomes rape. Rape is about anger, not sex. It is using sex to display one's aggression in order to dominate, or have power-over, another. Rape is not sex gone bad; it is aggression gone bad. Often, sexual anger is rooted in sexual shame, though aggression that leads to hurtful sexuality also creates shame. This can become a toxic loop. Healing this begins with an acceptance of one's sexual self and an approach to sex that sees it as a context for bonding; then, belonging and playful spontaneity can get richly expressed in sexual love. Sex itself can involve aggression, but this needs to be contained in healthy compassion, mutual respect, and a sense of play.

Our Cosmic Body

Sexual shame is connected to bodily shame, which is encouraged by religious beliefs that separate divine Spirit from sinful matter (as Augustine above). Many of us carry some shame about our bodies. This is the driving force behind the advertising industry, which plays on bodily shame: if only we use this product, wear these clothes, drive this car, we too will be beautiful and acceptable, "part of the crowd." If our bodies do not match the idealized type — we are not buffed up or are considered overweight or underweight — we often feel ostracized and not belonging to the group. Also, shame itself, of any kind, gets expressed with our bodies — we blush, we perspire, we fidget, we look down, we hunch over and shrink up. We also sometimes starve ourselves (become anorexic or bulimic) when we feel ashamed. Because of this, knowing and feeling that our bodies are already amazing, caring and honoring our bodies, is powerful medicine for all the diseases of shame.

Just like sexual shame can result in sexual anger, so bodily shame can evolve into bodily anger, which is typically directed at oneself. This anger often results in depression; couch potato-itis and acedia, the lack of energy to begin new things, may not be laziness so much as repressed anger. We pile body armor on top of body armor. Taking drugs and overindulging in alcohol or sugary, fatty foods are other ways we try to mollify our anger and maybe even keep it from harming others. We try to eat or drink or drug ourselves into peace of mind. But ultimately our body pays the price. The ultimate expression of aggression to our bodies is suicide, and men are sadly accomplished at achieving that result once we put our minds to it. Suicide is often described as a "way out" (of one's crippling shame), and one might ask a disturbing question: Is it possible that as a culture, even as a species, we are engaging in *subtle* forms of suicide? Through human-caused ecological devastation, global warming, traffic in nuclear weapons, and war, we hurt the planet's body? Are these events fueled by aggression and thanatos, hatred of body and hatred of life itself, which begins with shame over our own bodies?

The Blue Man

Recall that both for Swami Muktananda and Hildegard of Bingen, the Blue Man appeared while in deep meditation. The Blue Man is *anything but shameful.* Shame ceases with an awareness of the Blue Man. The Blue Man reminds us of our intrinsic worth, our intrinsic divinity, our intrinsic Christ-likeness. The Blue Man calls for our fullest consciousness and our fullest powers of healing and compassion. The Blue Man steers our hands to work for others to relieve their suffering and to celebrate the joy of living. The Blue Man also overcomes the fear of death, including the fear of not belonging or the "little death" that being exiled from our community may bring about. The Blue Man thus builds courage, enabling our larger and expanding heart to do its God-like work in the world. The Blue Man replaces shame with dignity and nobility.

Similarly, anger and aggression seem diverted by the Blue Man. Thich Nhat Hanh, among many other meditators, tells us how simply breathing in peace and breathing out peace in a conscious way can calm us down and neutralize anger and aggression. Scientific studies corroborate this point. Those who can learn to control their breath by paying attention and breathing deeply and steer-ing it in peaceful directions move beyond being run by their anger. Short breaths accompany anger. Clearly then, our breath is deeper than our anger. Anger depends on breath and cannot operate without it. So getting to the breath and deepening it pulls the rug from underneath our anger. No wonder the word "breath" and the word "spirit" are the same words in most languages of the world, including biblical languages. Breath is spirit and spirit is breath. Both are invisible. But both count. Anger can be neutralized by both.

Earth Father, or the Fatherly Heart

A healthy Earth Father has taken in the lessons of the Green Man and the Blue Man, of Father Sky and the spiritual warrior. To the extent that he has done so, he has healed shame with strength and compassion. Nevertheless, we have to ask: What role does shame play in fathering? How much *shame* do fathers rain on their children? How often is shame used as a motivating factor when fathers discipline their sons? How many sons are ashamed of fathers who may be absent or not caring or not providing or not modeling healthy manhood? As with Icarus and Daedalus, a father's shame can infiltrate and harm his re-lationship with his son; thus, to be a healthy role model and parent, a father must deal with and heal his own shame first.

Rites of passage strike at the heart of shame: they are the ways the tribe's fathers initiate the boys into manhood, that is to say, into *belonging to the tribe called men*. Fathers heal shame in sons by creating this sense of belonging. But when we lack rites of passage, for our sons or ourselves, we feed shame. Sons will act out their nonbelonging, which often happens in gangs. These are places where one who is ashamed can *seem* to belong with other men, but lacking the compassionate guidance of elders, these young men create their own often deadly rites of passage. Violence and prison become tests of manhood, but they are self-destructive and harmful to the community. A truly Fatherly Heart has dealt with shame and models ways his sons may do so.

Anger too plays its role in fatherhood, as many of us know. An Earth Father has learned to recycle his aggression, to recognize and process his own anger, so that it is not expressed toward or taken out on his children. An Earth Father does not take his anger out on himself either, by drinking or drugs or depression, for then true fatherhood goes lacking. It limps. A truly Fatherly Heart encourages healthy expressions of anger, teaching sons how to steer it appropriately, such as with martial arts. I know one father of two teenage boys who took martial arts classes with his sons because he wanted them to find their anger in their bodies and learn how to process it. Sports is another way to learn to deal with anger in appropriate ways, as are other forms of meditation.

I know of a father whose teenage daughter was acting up, being angry and exasperating around the house one rainy day. They lived on an Indian reservation, and the father instructed his daughter to get a blanket and an apple. He drove her to a deserted space, told her to leave the car with the apple and blanket and said, "Until you can learn to live with yourself, you are not fit to live with others." She was so angry she threw the apple down the canyon. As the day went on and she felt hungry, she went hunting for the apple. The blanket came in handy, too. When, after a long day *alone*, her father came to pick her up, she had changed. Solitude had taught her something about righting her anger. A truly Fatherly Heart offers his sons and daughters alternatives to acting out of anger, and he models the healthy use of anger. He does not dismiss all anger as negative, but teaches how anger can serve, how anger is a fuel that teaches us perseverance and strength when we are journeying on difficult paths.

Grandfather Sky, or the Grandfatherly Heart

To one degree or another, shame may stay with us throughout our life. Part of growing older, part of the lesson of Grandfather Sky, is how to put shame in perspective. Shame is grounded in our individual ego; our sense of belonging, or not belonging, is experienced very personally. When elders learn to let go of shame and "mellow" in old age, it's often because their perspective shifts: they see that we belong first of all to the universe and only secondarily to human communities, and if we are sometimes "on the outs" with a human community, we still always belong in the universe. We may also let go of the need to "belong" in certain ways (such as needing to be leaders), but be happy to belong in any role. We have the perspective to look back on those times in life when we were banished, and felt shame, and see that often, in retrospect, these led to our proudest moments. The elder has learned that shame is limited by one's attachment to one's individual ego. Grandfather Sky knows you can't please everyone, and that it is more important to be at home in one's own heart than with many strangers.

The Grandfatherly Heart has learned how to deal with anger in similar fashion, how to steer it and use it in positive ways, and how to recognize it in young people. Grandfather Sky knows anger is often a sign of grief and that it's important grief work to let that anger out in healthy ways. Another reason why young people should be around older people and not just around people their own age is that elders have, hopefully, learned to laugh at life's disappointments and to take difficulties and conflict in stride, rather than to lash out or seek revenge. The wider perspective of Grandfather Sky helps elders feel and release all strong emotion — even anger. They breathe deep and melt both shame and anger. This becomes an important lesson that we can model with others.

Our Sacred Marriages

Clearly, one does not want to bring shame to any union, coupling, or marriage. One wants to leave shame outside. After all, every marriage is a *new belonging*, a new tribe or couple is being celebrated, a new family started. Almost by definition, a marriage involves one's best self. If a man feels shame about his masculinity, then an equal relationship with the feminine cannot come to pass. So all the lessons of shame we have discussed here come to a kind of culmination when any marriage — however we define it — takes place.

The same holds for anger. Marriage itself symbolizes a healthy union of equals, free of shame and anger. It's also true that close and dialectical relationships will themselves provide moments of anger. These need to be dealt with in a healthy, appropriate manner, which isn't possible when we bring old angers and old aggressions to the union. In fact, the Sacred Marriages we've discussed are doorways for resolving and cleansing ourselves of old hurts and old angers so they do not raise their heads in new relationships and our actual marriages. Father Sky and Mother Earth, Green Man and Black Madonna, Yin and Yang: these creative couples embody relationships free of anger and shame. Can East and West, Protestant and Catholic, L-Directed Thinking and R-Directed Thinking, young and old, gay and straight ever relate authentically if anger or shame are dragged in from past experiences?

A Sacred Marriage of any kind requires inner work; at the heart of that inner work for men, as we have seen, is dealing with anger and shame. The work is never done. But it is important that it be conscious and it be engaged in. This is the true meaning of *jihad* and of spiritual athleticism: to work on oneself. As the Sufi mystic Hafiz puts it, "The warriors tame the beasts in their past so that the night's hoofs can no longer break the jeweled vision in the heart." When we marry, we want to share that jeweled vision. Nothing less. That is what makes the marriages we have considered *sacred marriages*.

Using Archetypes to Heal

The fact that shame and aggression permeate so much of our culture's understanding of masculinity, and their influence is so pervasive in society, is proof positive that we need these strong and healthy ten metaphors or archetypes to turn things around. With shame and aggression comes a loss of joy — both within the individual and within the culture. For a shamed man is not eliciting or spreading joy; more often he is spreading aggression and shame. Nor is this discouraged; it is encouraged widely, even generously, in a culture that opts for shame over blessing and aggression over inner peace. We are missing a profound joy when we feel we do not belong to the Sky or to the Earth and its creatures; to ancestral lines of hunters or to a noble clan of warriors; to a family and healthy adult/child relationships; to a healthy sexual relationship and to the beauty and health of one's own body; to an expanding consciousness and creativity that engage one's God-like powers of compassion and justice; or to a circle of elders who support one another and serve the young.

Anger and aggression mount when the cosmos is missing and there is no sky to absorb our anger and recycle it — when we cannot relate to the earth and invite it to absorb our anger and grief and engage our lower chakras. This sets up a sequence of denial and pretense and passive-aggression because we are busy pretending we do not carry anger inside us. When moral outrage is denied, grieving is short-changed, and vice versa. If we bottle up anger, it works like a pressure cooker on the stove, cooking a dangerous stew that can explode into violence at any time. We come to desire war as a release, and real warrior-hood gets overtaken by soldierhood. Anger takes over the body, creating all kinds of armor and rigidity; it takes over the mind, leading to the armored rigidity and compulsive control of fascism and fundamentalism. Misdirected aggression gets taken out on those who are "weaker," those who are "other": on women, children, other races, the land, and other creatures. Sexuality becomes a conquest, not a creative expression of playful sharing. Generativity and imagination dry up. When all this occurs, then suicide, homicide, and even genocide become commonplace.

Real men deal with their own wounded masculinity, with their male issues of shame and aggression. They take in the archetypes named in this book and ask: How am I doing? Which of these speaks deepest to me? Where am I strongest? Where am I most lacking? To belong again is the great healing. It puts shame to flight and with it a great deal of frustration and anger: to belong to the universe again (Father Sky); to belong to the Earth and its varied creatures again (the Green Man); to belong to community again (hunter-gatherers); to belong to a tribe of courageous people defending Earth, women and children (spiritual warriors); to belong to one's sons and daughters in active listening and communication (Icarus and Daedalus); to belong to our own divine and joyful sexuality (the lover); to belong to our holy and amazing bodies (our temple); to belong to our capacity for expanded consciousness (the Blue Man); to belong to our fatherly selves (Earth Father); and to our elder and grandfatherly selves (Grandfather Sky). All this makes real the development of men and of masculinity. It puts shame, anger, and misplaced aggression to flight. It results in peace, an inner peace that gets projected onto our institutions, politics, and religions.

REAL MEN MAKE CHOICES

Life is a series of choices. As the Jewish scriptures promise, "I put before you life and death, *choose* life." An ethical and moral life is a life of many choices. When men make conscious choices, moral behavior follows, and then they become "real men." We might play with this profound teaching in the following manner:

I put before you life and death. Choose life.

I put before you biophilia (love of life) and necrophilia (love of death). Choose biophilia.

I put before you community and genocide. Choose community.

I put before you Father Sky and shopping malls. Choose Father Sky.

I put before you the Green Man and a degraded earth. Choose the Green Man.

I put before you fatherhood that listens to and teaches children and fatherhood that ignores and orders children. Choose fatherhood that listens and teaches.

I put before you a hunter-gatherer's curiosity and courage and incurious, depressive couch potato-itis. Choose curiosity and courage.

I put before you a spiritual warrior and a warring soldier. Choose the spiritual warrior.

I put before you the gift of sexuality and the degradation of the sexual. Choose the gift of sexuality.

I put before you a healthy and amazing body and a neglected body. Choose a healthy and amazing body.

I put before you a compassionate expanded consciousness and a fearful egocentric consciousness. Choose a compassionate expanded consciousness.

I put before you a fatherly heart and a cold, distant, revengeful heart. Choose the fatherly heart.

I put before you an engaged grandfatherly heart and a detached "retired" heart. Choose the engaged grandfatherly heart.

THE GREAT SECRET

The Great Secret of masculinity is this: with a little bit of effort, men can learn to steer their testosterone to serve the mammalian brain rather than the reptilian brain. In doing so men heed the advice of some of the wisest, most beautiful, and most courageous men who have ever lived — authentic warriors and elders like Buddha, Jesus, Isaiah, Muhammad, Kabir, Meister Eckhart, Lao Tsu, Black Elk, Aquinas, Martin Luther King Jr., Gandhi, Howard Thurman, the Dalai Lama, Thich Nhat Hanh, and more.

What is that advice and what is the Great Secret? That we are — men and women alike — capable of compassion. That to the extent that we practice compassion with ourselves, the Earth, and all creation, we are part divine.

When we serve the mammalian (compassionate) brain, then all our ways change. Compassion changes everything. Nonviolence changes everything.

That every man has two hemispheres of the brain and a heart and a connection to the universe becomes a reality. Real men are birthed and reborn, and they birth other real boys who become men. And women develop their healthy masculine sides, liberated from the distorted and poisonous masculine.

Men must take compassion to heart; to work; to relationships; to citizenship; to politics; to economics; to business; to religion. When we finally do that we will live the essential teachings of Buddha, Jesus, Muhammad, and others. Those who have taken these teachings to heart and put them into practice we call "saints." They are far too rare. "Saint" is the real name for "hero," as in a "hero's journey." A saint is someone living out his fullest self. A saint is not so removed from us: a saint's journey has its ups and downs, and a saint is not perfectly innocent or untainted by anger, shame, aggression, or "sin." A saint is someone who brings forth one's full heart to the journey called life, who lives not only for himself but for others. A saint tastes magnanimity (a great soul) and spreads it. A saint grows his soul, even in the midst of suffering and disappointment. A saint soars and knows the thrill of soaring yet remains grounded in community and earthiness. A saint wrestles with all the archetypes in this book and forgets none. Like Jacob of old, the saint wrestles with the angels, and he wakes up both wounded and visited by the Holy One and the holy wrestlers, our ancestors, who have gone before us. A saint does not settle for pettiness or smallness of soul but invests in the expanding universe, the true Father Sky energy, to match his expanding heart and soul.

Today the Sacred Masculine is poised and ready to return. So much in our lives and culture gives evidence that we are at a cusp, at a tipping point and a turning point — including the disasters that stare us in the face daily. Are we up to it? Can we let go of the Distorted Masculine in order to entertain the Sacred Masculine? Time is not on our side. But our ancestors are. They and creation itself are cheering for us to make the right decision. To be *real men* to ourselves and our children and generations to come.

APPENDIX A: EXERCISES FOR DEVELOPING THE TEN ARCHETYPES

JUST AS WE WORK OUT OR EXERCISE to make our bodies stronger, so some working out and exercising may prove necessary to deepen the ten archetypes named in this book in order that the Sacred Masculine can find a home in us. Following are some suggested exercises. I encourage you to add to them by developing your own.

CHAPTER 1:
EXERCISES TO DEEPEN OUR SENSE OF FATHER SKY

1. Take a camping trip or otherwise get out on a starry night in a place (usually out of the city) where you can see the sky. Lie down. Drink it in. Have a friend or child with you. What are you learning, seeing, feeling, connecting with?
2. Visit a planetarium. Check out some corner of the sky. Who, what are you seeing? How does it make you feel?
3. Invest in a telescope. Look in it regularly. Invite others. What are you feeling, seeing, learning?
4. Visit the website www.google.com/sky. Check out the universe. How big is it? How big are you?
5. Read *View from the Center of the Universe* and look at the DVD of the same title. How does it move you, change you, give you a new sense of belonging?

6. Mentor young people on the new cosmology. Create rituals together celebrating it and feel its truths pass through your body in dancing its wonders.

7. Take the new cosmology to work. To your church or synagogue or mosque. To your neighbors. Show the DVD above and discuss it.

8. Take my book, *Sins of the Spirit, Blessings of the Flesh*, and read and discuss chapters 1 and 2, "Redeeming the Word 'Flesh'" and "Universe Flesh." Practice awe daily.

9. Explore ancient cosmology and creation stories from various cultures. How do they relate to today's cosmology story from science? How alike? How different?

10. If you are a Christian, what do you know about the tradition of the Cosmic Christ? If a Buddhist, study Buddha Nature as it relates to the Universe. If a Jew, the tradition of the "glory" of God.

CHAPTER 2: TASKS TO DEEPEN
YOUR CONNECTION WITH THE GREEN MAN

1. At home, are you recycling trash and garbage? Have you changed to low-energy lightbulbs? Have you insulated your home, including windows and attic? Do you garden and teach your kids to garden? Have you installed solar energy or wind energy, and do you encourage your elected representatives to support them?

2. Regarding transportation, what are you doing to use less or no fossil fuels? Do you have a hybrid car? Do you bicycle as much as possible? Do you walk regularly? Do you carpool? Do you use public transportation? Do you cajole your elected representatives to make all of this easier? And automobile manufacturers?

3. In your churches, do you recognize Christ as a Green Man if you are a Christian? If not, why not? Do you recognize the green imperative as that of the prophets and a deep tradition of the Sabbath in Judaism if you are Jewish or Christian or Muslim? What do your spiritual teachers teach about God's love of creation? Have you done the research? If not, why not? If a preacher, do you preach about the Green Man?

4. Study creation spirituality and its rich history of green mystics and prophets: from Jesus to Hildegard of Bingen, from the Celts to Thomas Aquinas, Francis of Assisi, Meister Eckhart, Mechtild of Magdeburg,

Nicolas of Cusa, and more from the Middle Ages, as well as Rachel Carson, Wendell Berry, Thomas Berry, and more in our time.

5. What about your diet — are you eating too much meat, too much beef? (Cow farting produces methane, which is terrible for the environment.)

6. At work, what are you doing in the workplace to live less by unclean fuels and more by clean and renewable fuels? Lightbulbs? Carpooling? Public transportation? Bicycling to work?

7. What about your political participation? Do you or do you not demand of your representatives local, state and national, that they be green? Have you done enough? What about the media — do you write letters to editors, call in to radio programs, express your moral outrage at human arrogance and anthropocentrism that is killing the planet not only for our children but for all the other species as well? Are you demanding that your country live up to the highest standards of the Bali precepts?

8. Are you making rituals that celebrate the wonders of the planet but also that allow you to grieve the loss that we are all experiencing?

9. How many trees have you planted lately? Why not organize others, especially the young, to plant trees, plant trees, plant trees.

10. Study the lives and writings of John Muir and other mystic prophets, spiritual warriors on behalf of the Earth.

11. What contemporary "Green Men" leaders speak to you and challenge you? Are you becoming a leader in your work world as well?

CHAPTER 3: WAYS TO LEARN LESSONS
FROM ICARUS AND DAEDALUS

1. Did your father help put wings on you as a youth? How? How not? Have you forgiven him? Have you praised him?

2. What instructions assisted this putting on of wings?

3. How did it go? Did you fly? Did you find your mystical/prophetic self at an early age? Alone or with a mentor?

4. Did you crash? If so, what have you learned from your crashes?

5. What about your mother: Did she assist you in soaring with wings? Or was she more an earth-bound influence?

6. How do putting on of wings and touching Father Sky connect for you?

7. How have you learned to ground yourself so that reaching for the sky does not result in crashing?

8. What stories of others have you observed or heard about that include these themes of soaring, crashing, and miscommunicating?

9. How have communications been between you and your father? How much interfering did your father do regarding your love life or your work?

10. Are there signs of Germont/Alfredo relationships in your own father/son relationship? What price have you paid for these? Has there been reconciliation?

11. Will you relate to your sons differently? How will you do that? How will you not behave like a "rash old fool"?

12. How much time do you spend with the young? What young music and languages are you learning and encouraging?

13. How are you teaching the young and how are they teaching you?

CHAPTER 4: WAYS TO EXAMINE
THE HUNTER-GATHERER INSTINCTS IN US TODAY

1. How do you deal with your anger and aggression? What works? What does not work?

2. The next time your reptilian brain kicks in, try another approach than just kicking back — try breathing deeply and reciting a mantra like "He is my brother, he is my brother, he is my brother," or "Love my enemy, love my enemy, love my enemy."

3. List areas where your hunter-gatherer instincts are alive and well and being practiced. Take my list from this chapter and check them out — how many are you engaged in? Do you recognize and agree that these represent hunting and gathering? Add some of your own to that list.

4. Shame: How is it a part of your life? What are you most ashamed of? Where does this shame originate? How are you dealing with it? Are you de-shaming yourself? What is most holding you back? What is most effective in this detox effort?

5. "Nothing great happens without anger," said Thomas Aquinas. How are you using your anger for good causes? How are you directing your anger into healthy relating and healthy work and healthy struggle?

6. Are you afraid of your anger? Do you keep it down and hidden . . . until it boils up and over in inappropriate ways? What groups can you join to help you deal honestly with your anger?

7. How does creativity play a role in steering your anger into directions that are positive and not harmful to others? Have you dealt with your passive-aggression? How? Do you assist others to deal with theirs? How?

8. Carl Jung once said: Scratch a sentimentalist and you find violence. Are you a sentimentalist? How is a sentimentalist different from being a person of deep feelings? (Hint: Anne Douglas says sentimentalism is "rancid political consciousness." It is the repression of justice and the struggle for justice.) Are you in touch with your deep feelings? How? If not, why not?

CHAPTER 5: WAYS TO BRING
THE WARRIOR ALIVE IN YOURSELF

1. What inner work are you doing? Around joy? Around grief? Around creativity? Around moral outrage?

2. What cares and concerns are you standing up for and being heard about? What is holding you back?

3. Have you found your voice? How? If not, what is inhibiting you?

4. Have you confused "soldier" and "warrior" in the past? Are you over it now? Do you see our culture and the media confusing the two? If so, what are you doing about setting them straight?

5. How are you encouraging young men to be warriors and not just soldiers?

6. I have listed brief stories of several warriors whom I admire. What warriors do you admire? List them. What do they teach you?

7. Do you recognize the prophets as warriors? What do they teach you? Do you recognize Jesus as warrior — what does he teach you? Do you recognize Gandhi and Martin Luther King Jr. and Malcolm X as warriors — what do they teach you?

8. How have you learned courage (a big heart)?

9. When was the last time you stood up and stood out and took a stand? What was the cause? How did it make you feel? Was there a reality of solidarity in the experience? What price did you pay for this action? Would you do it again?

10. Who are your enemies (not personal but as carriers of principles you cannot go along with)? Are you proud of the enemies you have made? Have you thanked them lately for making you strong and clarifying your values?

11. What do your enemies teach you and bring alive in you that is positive?

12. Ulysses and Don Quixote are discussed in this chapter. Do you identify with one or both of them? How or how not?

13. Are you living out the Four Paths that develop a warrior? Which are your strongest? Which do you need to develop more deeply?

CHAPTER 6: HOW WE CAN KEEP OUR SEXUALITY ALIVE, DEEP, AND UNPREDICTABLE — THAT IS, SPIRITUAL

1. How have your experiences of the "joy of sex" evolved in the last five years? Ten years? Twenty years?

2. When you hear about the temples of the East as well as Chartres Cathedral in the West that celebrate the sexual and the divine together, how does that make you feel? Did you get these same messages from the church or from the synagogue?

3. Is linking Sexuality and Spirituality difficult for you? Is it a big jump? If so, why is that? What can you do about it? Maybe you have misdefined spirituality.

4. Is accepting diversity in sexuality difficult for you? Is accepting the reality of homosexuality in about 10 percent of the human population a problem for you? If so, why is that? What are you doing about it?

5. Do you have gay and lesbian friends? Coworkers? Relatives? If you are gay or lesbian, do you have straight friends, coworkers, and relatives you hang out with?

6. Go to the Bible and read the "Song of Songs." Read parts of it with your spouse or lover.

7. How are you practicing sexuality as a *metaphor* and not just as a literal experience?

8. Have you experienced sexuality as a mystical experience, an experience of awe and beauty that carried you to faraway places? How did this change you?

9. How are you teaching sexuality to the younger generation?

10. Take a workshop in Tantric sex. It may change your life. Your marriage. Your relationship.

11. Are you getting your church community to move beyond sexuality as a moral problem and an antipleasure ideology to sexuality as mystical experience? How are you doing this? What success are you having?

CHAPTER 7: HOW TO REDISCOVER CARE
AND APPRECIATION FOR OUR BODIES

1. What kind of bodily exercise are you currently engaged in? Do you walk? Work out? Swim? Run? Hike? Climb? Play sports?

2. Do you have out-of-body experiences when doing these things? Do you have unitive or mystical experiences while doing them? Do they take you to another zone? How much fun is that? How healing is that?

3. What kind of bodily exercises or sports did you engage in in the past? What did these do for you personally and spiritually? Do you miss them? Are you nostalgic for them?

4. Read chapters four and five of *Sins of the Spirit, Blessings of the Flesh* and meditate on the sacredness of "Human Flesh" and also on your seven chakras. What are the implications of this attitude toward the body and this recognition of its specialness?

5. What are your eating habits? How have they changed? Are you alert to too much sugar, to hydrogenated oils, to too much fat, to too much red meat? Are you keeping your body in decent shape and loving it that way? If not, why not? If not, what are you taking out on your body — what anger, what issues, what relationships? Can you let them go?

6. What about your drinking habits? Have you experienced alcoholism in your life or have those who are near to you? Do you attend AA or other programs for those afflicted by eating or drinking disorders? What have you derived from those meetings? Are you learning to love your body anew?

7. Breathing exercises. Do you do them? Meditation? Mantras? Breath work? What are the results? How have your practices evolved?

8. What is beautiful in women you admire? In men you admire? How do you share in that beauty?

9. Do you bring body to prayer and to church or synagogue or mosque? Have you done sweat lodges? Sundances? Raves? Other sacred dancing? If not, why not? Do you encourage the young to do so? Do you talk to them about their experience of linking dance and trance?

10. All life is impermanent. Meditate on death — when the body you now dwell in (and beyond) will no longer exist. Can this help you to appreciate your body more and cherish it more while you are together? The bodies of others you love or appreciate will also some day pass

away. Does that awaken your sense of beauty in the present moment? And gratitude?

11. Is the whole human enterprise a quest for immortality, as Otto Rank proposes? What are the implications of this? Have you worked through your fear of death? How are beauty and death allied?

12. What are the implications of the teaching of today's science that matter and light are the same thing?

13. Do you love sports? Do you love to play them? Which ones? When? How has this relationship evolved? What delight and learning do you derive from sports you play or have played?

14. Do you love watching others play sports? Live? On TV? What delight and learning do you derive from watching others play sports? How much watching do you do? Is it excessive? If so, can you cut back? Have you turned from an athlete to a couch potato or do you know others who have? How can you get over this addiction?

15. Is your body welcomed at work? How is it involved? Or not involved? How is it honored and treated at work? If badly, how can you improve the situation?

16. John Conger guides us in four ways to get in touch with our bodies. Have you tried them? With what results? If not, it is not too late to try them now.

CHAPTER 8: PRACTICES FOR BRINGING THE BLUE MAN MORE FULLY ALIVE

1. Both Swami Muktananda and Hildegard of Bingen experienced the Blue Man while meditating. Do you meditate? If not, why not?

2. Have you encountered the Blue Man yet? Have you asked for his coming to you? If he has come, what lessons has he passed on to you? How do they compare to those of Muktananda and Hildegard?

3. How much has your consciousness expanded in the past year? Five years? Ten Years? Twenty years? In what areas and arenas has it expanded? In what areas does it still need to expand?

4. How can our previous discussion of Father Sky (after all, the sky is blue) contribute to your expansion of consciousness and a fuller awareness of the Blue Man?

5. What groups or communities are you connected to that truly challenge

or support your expansion of consciousness? How do your enemies as well as your allies assist this expansion?

6. What books or music or physical endeavors assist this expansion?

7. Is Creativity a priority in your life? How many ways are you creative each day? At home? At work? In relationships? In parenting? In your citizenship? If creativity is not a priority, why is that? What are you doing to change that?

8. What experiences of art do you enjoy and participate in? What would you like to participate in? What is holding you back? When will you "make the move"?

9. List creative people you admire. What can you learn from them?

10. Do you agree with Navajo painter and healer David Palladin that "if you can talk, you are an artist"? In what ways are you an artist regarding yourself, your family, your work, your God?

11. Is Compassion truly the goal of all consciousness and creativity? Compassion is about living a life of authentic interconnectivity, thus following the laws or habits of a universe that is interconnective. How are we doing? What is holding us back? Does the Blue Man call us to make a leap of compassion in this time? How is it going?

CHAPTER 9: WAYS TO DEVELOP
MORE FULLY OUR FATHERLY HEARTS

1. What is the best thing about being a father?

2. What is the most difficult thing about being a father?

3. How are you a father to kids other than your own?

4. Have you adopted children? Become a mentor or big brother to children?

5. In what ways does your job impact children? How often do you reflect on this and bring these values to your professional and work decision-making?

6. I list nine attributes of the Fatherly Heart. Which ones most strike you and do you practice? Add other attributes that you can name.

7. Which of the songs about Father speak deepest to you?

8. As a son, how do you rate your father? His strengths? His weaknesses and mistakes?

9. Do you have unresolved issues with your father? Have you written him a letter (whether alive or dead) to resolve issues and to thank him?

10. How are you or will you be a different father from your father? Are you so sure? How will you try to imitate what your father did or was?

11. What alternative "fathers" did you have in your life? How did they impact you? Have you written them a "thank you" (whether alive or dead)? Don't you think you should?

CHAPTER 10: LESSONS FOR DEVELOPING THE GRANDFATHERLY AND ELDER HEART

1. Name some elders you admire. What do they teach you? Why do you admire them so? Have you thanked them?

2. What do the young teach you? Why do you need them as much as they need you?

3. Retirement vs. Refirement. Comment on the difference. What fires you up in your older years?

4. How are you staying or intending to stay physically, mentally, intellectually, and spiritually alive and vigorous in your later years? Are you establishing habits now that will carry on then?

5. What are your plans for Refirement time?

6. Your experience of being a grandfather — what makes it great? What are you learning? How is it changing you? How are you sharing this with others?

7. What young people are you connecting to and learning from and teaching or mentoring?

8. Your legacy: What do you want to leave behind? How do you want to be remembered (if at all)?

9. If you have money or assets to leave behind, have you chosen well the groups or movements that can use your assistance so you do not leave it up to lawyers, accountants, or family members alone to make such decisions on your behalf? Are you following your values, are you supporting the "new shoots" and not just the old, tired institutions?

10. Death. What is its meaning to you?

11. Resurrection, Reincarnation, Regeneration: Do you believe in one or more of these? What does it mean to you? How does this understanding affect your daily living and outlook on life?

12. Meister Eckhart said his soul was as young as the day it was created
    — and younger. Are you of the same ilk? How young is your soul?
    What keeps it young and makes it young?
13. Any regrets or requests for forgiveness to receive or give before you exit?
    If so, why put it off?
14. Any thank-yous that you have not yet bestowed before you exit? If so,
    why put it off?

APPENDIX B: A THOUGHT
ON RITES OF PASSAGE

IT IS CUSTOMARY IN OUR CULTURE to say that "getting a driver's license" is our rite of passage. Or "graduation from high school (or college)" is our rite of passage. Or "getting commissioned in the army" is our rite of passage. I do not deny that achievements like driving a car, attaining an education, or undergoing military training are *kinds* of rite of passage — as are marriage, becoming a parent, passing through midlife crisis, becoming an elder, becoming a grandparent, retirement, and more.

But, and I cannot stress this enough, these do not substitute in any way for the rite of passage that our culture is most lacking in, which is that passage from boyhood to manhood, from girlhood to womanhood. Why is this so? Because the so-called rites of passage of driving, graduating, or getting through training are *achievements* of the individual. But a true rite of passage from childhood to adulthood is decidedly *not an achievement of the individual*. It is an achievement of nature. Nature brings us to that turning point in our lives when boys start shaving and girls start menstruating. This is not a personal achievement. It is not a feather in one's cap for accomplishing something. It is something that *happens to us* — and by "us" I do not mean just the individual. I mean the entire culture. All of us, fathers and mothers, grandparents, and all citizens are impacted by the coming of age of the next generation, by their having the physical capacity to reproduce our species and keep the entire ancestral caravan moving along.

That is what is at stake in a rite of passage — not that an individual youth has accomplished something, but that Nature has accomplished something in our youth that is not about ego but is about the entire tribe, the entire community, the future. And this is why a certain severity accompanies traditional rites of passage — there is a fierce responsibility for adults to carry on the struggles of our tribe, and this responsibility takes on a new dimension at puberty.

How does our culture measure up to this requirement of rites of passage? Not very well. The Christian tradition talks of "confirmation" and the Jewish tradition offers "bar mitzvah" and "bat mitzvah," but it is my experience that for the most part these ceremonies lack the bodily depth and fierceness that true rites of passage entail. They are often quite forgettable. There are tribes in Africa, for example, whose rite of passage includes circumcision. Why? In order that a young man learn early that being an adult includes pain and sacrifice. The same message is carried in a Native American Sundance. Sacrifice is one's gift to the people. It is part of being a man. It is part of being a human. It is part of being a contributor to the community.

In our culture of confirmation and bar mitzvah, adults tend to lavish the youth with gifts. That carries the danger of rendering the youth still more dependent and more the center of attention rather than challenging him or her to the adventure and generosity that true adulthood and true citizenship in the community is about. It holds the power to deceive the youth into still more ego-centeredness and anthropocentrism and even consumeritis.

I believe it is a mark of our anthropocentric culture that we imagine a rite of passage derives from our accomplishments. Not so! A rite of passage derives from Nature's accomplishments. That is why it requires authentic ritual that marries macrocosm (cosmos and Father Sky) with microcosm (human). That is why it requires ceremony that is both beautiful and effective in connecting the human and the rest of nature. It may require, especially for the males, some severity. That is why it makes a difference in the self-awareness and other-awareness of the youth. It opens them from "me" to "we." If not, it fails us. And youth who are not undergoing authentic rites of passage will indulge in silly efforts of their own, usually destructive ones, to make up for this lack. Lurking behind this failure there will be an intense anger, hostility, and even grief on the part of the budding adult. For the true entrance into the community has never been accomplished.

This failure to offer meaningful rites of passage falls on the shoulders of the adults. It is the adult's responsibility, it is the elder's responsibility, to offer meaningful rites of passage to the youth.

ENDNOTES

PREFACE: WHY "HIDDEN"?

ix   *"various kinds of silences"*: Aquinas in Matthew Fox, *Sheer Joy: Conversations with Thomas Aquinas on Creation Spirituality* (San Francisco: HarperSanFrancisco, 1992), 195.

ix   *Norman Lloyd is a cameraman who spent four years*: Edward Guthmann, "Vietnam Vets Vent Anguish," *San Francisco Chronicle*, November 12, 2007, E5.

x   *"The deep ecology of Tom Berry"*: cited by University of Bath professor Peter Reason in "Transforming Education," a talk given in London, England, September 15, 2007, at the "Earth Is Community" Conference honoring Thomas Berry.

xi   *"most young men in our culture"*: Robert Bly and Marion Woodman, *The Maiden King: The Reunion of Masculine and Feminine* (New York: Henry Holt and Company, 1998), 181.

xiv   *"Not a single email, phone call or letter about the column"*: Joan Ryan, "Sorting out Puzzle of Male Suicide," *San Francisco Chronicle*, January 26, 2006.

INTRODUCTION:
IN SEARCH OF THE SACRED MASCULINE

xx   *"Many of us were looking to the Great Mother"*: Joseph Jastrab, *Sacred Manhood, Sacred Earth* (New York: HarperPerennial, 1994), xxvii.

xxi   *"the metaphors you live by — whether, say, you think"*: Daniel H. Pink, *A Whole New Mind: Moving from the Information Age to the Conceptual Age* (New York: Riverhead Books, 2005), 135f.

xxi   *"Whenever we recognize ourselves in a myth"*: Jean Shinoda Bolen, *Gods in Everyman: A New Psychology of Men's Lives & Loves* (New York: Harper & Row, 1989), 303.

xxi   *"in the great world of metaphor, both masculine and feminine"*: Bly and Woodman, *The Maiden King*, xvii.

xxii   *"with its overemphasis on sports and financial success"*: ibid.

xxii   *"Metaphor is more easily experienced unconsciously"*: ibid., 119f.

xxiii   *"mental reframings of reality itself"*: Joel R. Primack and Nancy Ellen Abrams, *The View from the Center of the Universe* (New York: Riverhead Books, 2006), 243.

xxiv   *"is an energy field, like that of a magnet"*: Bly and Woodman, *The Maiden King*, 150.

xxiv   *"in the inner world, doing is becoming"*: Bolen, *Gods in Everyman*, 303.

xxiv   *"an archetype will reappear in a new form"*: William Anderson and Clive Hicks, *Green Man: The Archetype of Our Oneness with the Earth* (San Francisco: HarperCollins, 1990), 25.

CHAPTER 1: FATHER SKY

3   *"What a catastrophe, what a maiming of life"*: Jastrab, *Sacred Manhood*, 32.

4   *"invade the earth, energize it and make it sacred"*: Eckhart in Matthew Fox, *Meditations with Meister Eckhart* (Santa Fe: Bear & Company, 1983), 70.

4   *Among the Aboriginals of Australia in the Dieri country*: E. O. James, *Primitive Ritual and Belief* (London: Melhuen Company, 1917), 103f.

5   *The southeastern tribes of Australia believe in supernatural*: Mircea Eliade, *Australian Religions* (Ithaca, NY: Cornell University Press, 1973), 3f.

5   *Another Australian tribe, the Wiimbaio*: ibid., 4f.

6   *The Australian Murinbata tribe of western Arnhem Land*: ibid., 39.

6   *"the greater gods are almost always 'heavenly.'"*: Tony Swain and Gary Trompf, *The Religions of Oceania* (London: Routledge, 1995), 126f.

6   *"The heavenly part of the universe is the home"*: John Mbiti, *Introduction to African Religions* (Chicago: Heinemann Education Publishers, 1991), 35f.

7   *"The mythology of the sky gods (Uranus, Cronus, and Zeus)"*: Bolen, *Gods in Everyman*, 296.

7   *"Those who first looked up to the heavens"*: Aristotle in James Miller, *Measures of Wisdom: The Cosmic Dance in Classical and Christian Antiquity* (Toronto: University of Toronto Press, 1986), 55.

8   *Barbara Ehrenreich talks about "an epidemic of depression"*: Barbara Ehrenreich, *Dancing in the Streets* (New York: Metropolitan Books, 2006), 129, 137f.

9   *"If God had formed us of the stuff of the sun"*: Calvin in Matthew Fox, *Sins of the Spirit, Blessings of the Flesh: Lessons for Transforming Evil in Soul and Society* (New York: Harmony Books, 1999), 145f.

9   *"That Man is the product of causes which had no prevision"*: Russell in Primack and Abrams, *The View from the Center of the Universe*, 273.

10   *this mind-set "reinforces our collective irresponsibility"*: ibid., 242.

11   *"Just as intelligent life on Earth is acquiring"*: ibid., 151, 117f.

11   *the size of a thing "is not arbitrary but crucial"*: ibid., 156, 161, 176.

11   *"Creatures much smaller than we are could not"*: ibid., 174f.

12   By the *"interplay of the complexity of our brains"*: ibid, 175.

12   *Our species only evolved to its present state*: ibid., 130.

12   *Furthermore, we live in a most interesting corner*: ibid., 182.

12   *In its beginning "there was — and almost everywhere else there still is"*: ibid., 193.

12   *"If space time had been perfectly smooth"*: ibid., 202.

13   *Actually, what we now call "dark matter" is in fact not dark*: ibid., 102.

13   *"We are no longer lost; we have discovered"*: ibid., 120.

13   *"I still hanker for the original world"*: Scott Russell Sanders, *Hunting for Hope: A Father's Journeys* (Boston: Beacon Press, 1998), 138.

13   *He believes that "our deepest religious urge"*: ibid., 54, 39f.

14   *"with every breath, we inhale millions of molecules"*: Ackerman in Fox, *Sins of the Spirit*, 79.

15   *"The evolution of life cannot be explained without geology"*: Primack and Abrams, *The View from the Center of the Universe*, 219.

16   *"Jupiter's gravity has helped protect Earth from being hit"*: ibid., 210.

17   *"We will recover our sense of wonder and our sense"*: Thomas Berry, *The Great Work* (New York: Bell Tower, 1999), 49.

18   *"In many ways the young everywhere have more in common"*: Primack and Abrams, *The View from the Center of the Universe*, 252f.

18   *"I was totally blown away by how many stars"*: Deborah Gage, "Microsoft Star Gazing," *San Francisco Chronicle*, May 13, 2008, A-1. See also www.worldwidetelescope.org.

CHAPTER 2: THE GREEN MAN

20   *He points out that "trees are the most successful life forms"*: Fred Hageneder, *The Spirit of Trees: Science, Symbiosis, and Inspiration* (New York: Continuum, 2001), 15.

20   *"Light courses through its structure"*: ibid., 45.

21   *Trees are like "cosmic antennae" and radiation*: ibid., 47.

21   *"fire became the driving force in the development"*: ibid., 63.

21   *"Almost everywhere in the world the beginnings"*: ibid., 64f, 75.

22   *"I am the vine; you are the branches"*: John 15.5, 16.

24   *As Anderson points out, beginning in the late twelfth century*: Anderson and Hicks, *Green Man*, 85.

24   *"From this time onwards a new spirit entered Western art"*: ibid.

24   *The oak, as Robert Bly explains, was tied "firmly to religious ritual"*: Woodman and Bly, *The Maiden King*, 91f, 216.

25   *Adams felt it "expressed an intensity of conviction never again reached"*: R. P. Blackmur, *Henry Adams* (New York: Harcourt Brace Jovanovich, 1980), 189, 203f.

25   *Adams asks the following question of the modern era*: ibid., 204.

26   *the Green Man symbolizes above all "irrepressible life"*: Anderson and Hicks, *Green Man*, 14.

26   *"I am the thought of all plants"*: ibid., 12f.

26   *The Green Man is a composite image, and this "composite of leaves"*: ibid., 14.

27   *Anderson believes that it was "extraordinary that the Great Mother"*: ibid., 67.

27   *He is "the cosmic man or intelligence"*: ibid., 111.

28   *Sir James Frazer observes that "the killing of the tree spirit"*: ibid., 31.

28   *Anderson talks of the Christ on the abbey church of St. Pierre*: ibid., 61.

29   *"in its most general sense, the symbolism of the tree"*: J. E. Cirlot, *A Dictionary of Symbols* (New York: Philosophical Library, 1962), 328.

29   *Psychologist Eugene Monick points out that the "axis mundi"*: Eugene Monick, *Phallos: Sacred Images of the Masculine* (Toronto: Inner City Books, 1987), 76.

29   *"the ancient image needed by men today"*: ibid.

29   *"the whole life-effort of man [is] to get his life"*: Lawrence in Jastrab, *Sacred Manhood*, 93.

30   *"Earth as a planet is integrated into the cosmos"*: Primack and Abrams, *The View from the Center of the Universe*, 240.

30   *Black Virgins also emerged "contemporary with the revival"*: Anderson and Hicks, *Green Man*, 68.

30   *"In their portrayals of the Green Man as a benign"*: ibid., 88.

31   *"We paint what we suffer and what we feel"*: Jacob Bayhham, "Burma Artists Hide in Shadow of their Sad Work," *San Francisco Chronicle*, April 9, 2008, A-13.

32   *The report says: "The United States possesses abundant wind"*: H. Josef Hebert, "Use of Wind Energy Expected to Grow Dramatically," AP, May 12, 2008.

32   *"generations of modern men have grown alienated"*: Jastrab, *Sacred Manhood*, 32.

CHAPTER 3: ICARUS AND DAEDALUS

35   *"Young people do start out with imagination"*: Bly and Woodman, *The Maiden King*, 152, 202.

37   *Symbolist Cirlot writes that "every winged being"*: J. E. Cirlot, *A Dictionary of Symbols*, 25.

37   *French writer Gaston Bachelard puts it this way: "Of all metaphors"*: ibid., 104.

38   *As psychologist John Conger points out, "his dreams were inflated"*: John P. Conger, *The Body in Recovery: Somatic Psychotherapy and the Self* (Berkeley: Frog Ltd., 1994), 72.

41   *Adultism, as I have discussed elsewhere*: See Matthew Fox, *The Coming of the Cosmic Christ* (San Francisco: Harper & Row, 1988), 181-85.

CHAPTER 4: HUNTER-GATHERERS

44   *Diamond writes, "Until the end of the last Ice Age"*: Jared Diamond, *Guns, Germs, and Steel: The Fates of Human Societies* (New York: W. W. Norton, 1997), 16, 86.

44   *"My own impression, from having divided my life"*: ibid., 18.

45   *As Barbara Ehrenreich observes in* Dancing in the Streets: Ehrenreich, *Dancing in the Streets*, 1, 9, 13.

45   *"Go back ten thousand years and you will find"*: ibid., 21f.

46   *"Like primates in the wild today, early humans"*: ibid., 28f.

46   *Aldous Huxley comments, "Ritual dances provide a religious"*: Huxley in Ehrenreich, *Dancing in the Streets*, 33.

46   *They were an "original affluent society"*: Marshall Sahlins, "Notes on the Original Affluent Society," at the Man the Hunter Conference, 1966.

46   *"They impressed me as being on the average"*: Diamond, *Guns, Germs, and Steel*, 20.

47   *Studies indicate that they were and are "walking encyclopedias"*: ibid., 143.

47   *Diamond concludes: "In mental ability New Guineans"*: ibid., 21.

48   *"As a result, one acre can feed many more"*: ibid., 88.

48   *"Most peasant farmers and herders, who constitute"*: ibid., 105.

49   *As Diamond points out, "there was often not even a conscious choice"*: ibid., 105f.

49   *"Even in the cases of the most rapid independent development"*: ibid., 107.

49   *Social hierarchy went "hand in hand with militarism and war"*: Ehrenreich, *Dancing in the Streets*, 44.

50   *"Germs thus played decisive roles"*: Diamond, *Guns, Germs, and Steel*, 92.

52   *A recent study was done in Oakland*: Meredith May, "Deadly Legacy: Many Young Black Men in Oakland Are Killing and Dying for Respect," *San Francisco Chronicle*, December 9, 2007, A-1, A-12.

61   *Thomas Aquinas observed back in the Middle Ages that the "lover"*: Aquinas in Fox, *Sheer Joy*, 78.

61   *One excellent example is Nobel-winning physicist Steve Chu*: Rick DelVecchio, "As Warnings Grow More Dire, Nobelist Emerges as Leader," *San Francisco Chronicle*, March 5, 2007, A-1, A-8.

62   *a journalist wrote, "As the hunt progressed"*: John Johnson Jr., "Spacecraft sends pictures that hint of seas on Titan," *San Francisco Chronicle*, March 14, 2007, p. A-9. Italics mine.

62   *As reported by the* Norfolk Virginian-Pilot, *Pentagon auditors*: "Profit Upon Profit," in "Editorials," *Toledo Blade*, March 1, 2007.

63   *a recent report described how AIDS researchers have "successfully mapped"*: Saben Rusell, "Vulnerable Spot on HIV Could Lead to a Vaccine," *San Francisco Chronicle*, February 15, 2007, A-19.

63   *Louis J. Ignarro, from the University of California at Los Angeles School of Medicine, writes that*: Louis J. Ignarro, "Nobel Prize Winner's Breakthrough—Prevent Heart Attack and Stroke With Nitric Oxide," in *Treasury of Health Secrets* (Des Moines: Bottom Line Books, 2004), 485. See also Louis Ignarro, *No More Heart Disease* (New York: St Martins Press, 2005).

66   *Ehrenreich believes that "for most people in the world today"*: Ehrenreich, *Dancing in the Streets*, 225, 230, 232f.

67   *Jared Diamond in his studies of hunter-gatherers points out*: Diamond, *Guns, Germs and Steel*, 108.

74   *Scott Sanders observes the connection between consumerism and our hunting-gathering ancestors when he writes*: Sanders, *Hunting for Hope*, 129f, 131, 135.

CHAPTER 5: SPIRITUAL WARRIORS

77 It is *"the task of moving modern industrial civilization"*: Thomas Berry, *The Great Work*, 7.

78 *"There's a difference between being a soldier and being a warrior"*: Jastrab, *Sacred Manhood*, 19.

78 The Sufi mystic Hafiz knew the difference between soldier and warrior: Hafiz in Matthew Fox, *One River, Many Wells: Wisdom Springing from Global Faiths* (New York: Jeremy P. Tarcher/Putnam, 2000), 415.

89 *About this period, he said, "I was not happy about the workings"*: Bhante in Greg Lynn Weaver, "In the Footsteps of the Buddha: 108 Year Old Monk is Still on the Path," *Holistic Health Journal* (Autumn 1997), 30-35.

94 *what Howard Thurman called "the literal substance of oneself"*: Fox, *One River, Many Wells*, 15.

96 *"The power and allure of evil and the cold reality"*: Chris Hedges, "The Christian Right and the Rise of American Fascism," www.theocracywatch.org, November 15, 2004, 2.

97 *"This image of Christ as warrior is appealing"*: ibid., 9.

98 *"The cult of masculinity pervades the ideology"*: ibid., 9, 12.

102 *"a troubling notion for many of us — the possibility"*: Jastrab, *Sacred Manhood*, 108.

CHAPTER 6:
MASCULINE SEXUALITY, NUMINOUS SEXUALITY

105 *Dr. Gunther Weil has put it this way: "Our Western institutional religious tradition"*: Weil in Mantak Chia and Michael Winn, *Taoist Secrets of Love: Cultivating Male Sexual Energy* (Santa Fe: Aurora Press, 1984), xi.

106 *Toaist master Mantak Chia makes the astute observation that*: ibid., 51f, 66, 49.

106 *"This image is so powerful, so charged with life-force"*: Robert Moore and Douglas Gillette, *King, Warrior, Magician, Lover: Rediscovering the Archetypes of the Mature Masculine* (San Francisco: HarperSanFrancisco, 1990), 119.

107 *the meaning of sexuality is "to reveal to human beings"*: Monick, *Phallos*, 24, 27.

107 *In Mali, Africa, there are houses built for Muslim religious leaders*: Jean-Louis Bourgeois, et al., *Spectacular Vernacular: The Adobe Tradition* (New York: An Aperture Book, 1996), 70.

107 *Eliade points out that "except in the modern world"*: Eugene Monick, *Castration and Male Rage: The Phallic Wound* (Toronto: Inner City Books, 1991), 17.

108 *"many people feeling sexual frustration turn to food"*: Chia and Winn, *Taoist Secrets of Love*, 17f.

108 *"as Ranke-Heinemann writes, that 'the locus par excellence'"*: Riane Eisler, *Sacred Pleasure: Sex, Myth and the Politics of the Body — New Paths to Power and Love* (San Francisco: HarperSanFrancisco, 1995), 204, 205, 206.

108 *"associated with the sacred, with religious rites"*: ibid., 58f.

108 *"Religious authorities taught men that the bodily"*: ibid., 222, 228.

109 *Eugene Monick believes that "a man's spirit is his phallic energy"*: Monick, *Castration and Male Rage*, 121.

109 *The dominator mentality has led to another sexual metaphor*: David Deida, *The Way of the Superior Man* (Boulder, CO: Sounds True, 2004), 4, 4f.

112 *David Deida observes that a man's relationship to the beauty*: ibid., 155.

112 *Spiritual traditions the world over have testified*: Fox, *One River, Many Wells*, chapter 15.

112 *"A man's attraction to women must be converted"*: Deida, *The Way of the Superior Man*, 155.

112 *"In your worship of women, never forget that they die"*: ibid., 155–57.

113 *Deida puts it this way: "Desire can be a doorway"*: ibid., 158.

113 *Deida wisely encourages us to "feel lust"*: ibid., 148, 148f.

114 *"a mature relationship with Eros is fundamental"*: Jastrab, *Sacred Manhood*, 63. Italics his.

114 *In a lifetime, "the normal male ejaculates enough semen"*: Chia and Winn, *Taoist Secrets of Love*, 17f.

117 *"Natural wisdom tells a male"*: Monick, *Castration and Male Rage*, 95.

121 *They should read scientists who have studied creation and have found*: See Bruce Bagmihl, *Biological Exuberance: Animal Homosexuality and Natural Diversity* (New York: Stonewall Inn Editions, 1999).

122 *David Deida observes that "the gay and lesbian community"*: Deida, *The Way of the Superior Man*, 4f.

123 *Lame Deer, a Lakota shaman, says such a person "has a gift of prophecy"*: Walter L. Williams, *Spirit and the Flesh* (Boston: Beacon Press, 1992), 42, 213.

123 *"People who don't respect their Indian traditions criticize"*: ibid., 217.

125 *Poet Gary Snyder defines the sacred this way: "Sacred refers"*: Gary Snyder, *The Practice of the Wild* (Berkeley: North Point Press, 1990), 94.

CHAPTER 7: OUR COSMIC AND ANIMAL BODIES

127 *"To darkness are they doomed who worship only"*: John P. Conger, *Jung & Reich: The Body as Shadow* (Berkeley: North Atlantic Books, 2005), 1.

127 *Science has now demonstrated that our bodies*: See Brian Swimme and Thomas Berry, *The Universe Story* (San Francisco: HarperSanFrancisco, 1992).

128 *As naturalist Diane Ackerman says, "With every breath we inhale millions of molecules"*: Fox, *Sins of the Spirit*, 79.

129 *As Wyller puts it: "With the development of the human brain"*: ibid., 89.

129 *"the cheapest foods are the worst for you" says Dr. Marks*: Kevin Feking, "U.S. Continues to Crush Records in Obesity Rates," *San Francisco Chronicle*, August 28, 2007, A8.

130 *"The victory of an overrationalized life is promoted at the expense"*: Conger, *Jung & Reich*, 108.

130   *"The body is the original animal condition"*: ibid., xixf.

130   *"Unfortunately, in the unfolding drama of Western culture"*: ibid., 31.

131   *"psychology has been in danger of becoming body-phobic"*: ibid., xix.

131   *Carl Jung put it this way: "It has forever been the aspiration of mankind"*: ibid.

131   *"Much of the world we have made starves our senses"*: Sanders, *Hunting for Hope*, 53.

133   *"Our bodies are wild"*: Snyder, *The Practice of the Wild*, 16.

133   *"We are wild. Through our bodies, through the ever-flowing"*: Sanders, *Hunting for Hope*, 48.

134   *"In the center of the castle of Brahman, our own body"*: Fox, *One River, Many Wells*, 155.

134   *"The heart is a sanctuary at the center of which there is a little place"*: ibid.

134   *Julian writes that the human soul is a "beautiful city"*: Brendan Doyle, *Meditations with Julian of Norwich* (Santa Fe: Bear & Co., 1983), 114, 95, 97.

135   *"Our bodies are bright like Blake's tiger"*: Sanders, *Hunting for Hope*, 57, 44.

137   *As Gary Snyder says, "Everyone who ever lived took the lives of other animals"*: Snyder, *The Practice of the Wild*, 184f.

138   *"A subsistence economy is a Sacramental economy"*: ibid., 185.

144   *"Being ungrounded in this world is dangerous"*: Conger, *The Body in Recovery*, 61, 63f.

144   *Conger writers, "Boundaries give us protection"*: ibid., 75.

145   *Social space is one thing, and intimate space is another*: ibid., 77f, 79.

145   *"Over time, our full breath has been reduced"*: ibid., 82.

147   *"The deficits of feeling face us with a humanity"*: ibid., 147f, 156.

147   *They provide the "opportunity to become kinesthetically and psychologically"*: ibid., 156, 161.

147   *As Jung put it, "The difference we make between the psyche and the body"*: ibid., 211.

150   *As Conger puts it: "We have a baby body, a child body"*: ibid., 212.

150   *"Do not disdain your body"*: Sue Woodruff, *Meditations with Mechtild of Magdeburg* (Santa Fe: Bear & Co., 1982), 42.

151   *By defining our bodies as specially organized* light: Quotes in Fox, *One River, Many Wells*, 61.

CHAPTER 8: THE BLUE MAN

153   *He prayed: "O mother Guru! O father Guru!"*: Swami Muktananda, *Play of Consciousness: A Spiritual Autobiography* (South Fallsburg, NY: SYDA Foundation, 1994), 189.

153   *"The egg grew and grew until it had assumed"*: ibid., 190f.

154   *"The Blue Person, who grants the realization"*: ibid., 193.

154   *Swami Kripananda has called the Blue Pearl a "scintillating blue dot"*: ibid., 115.

154   *"This Supreme Being appears to be different"*: ibid.

155   *"I saw a very bright light, and inside it there was a person"*: Bruce Hozeski, trans., *Hildegard of Bingen's Scivias* (Santa Fe: Bear & Co., 1986), 87.

155   *"God's own great work and most precious pearl"*: ibid., 89.

155   *Christ is "the son of justice having the lightning"*: Matthew Fox, *Illuminations of Hildegard of Bingen* (Santa Fe: Bear & Co., 1985), 37. For more on this vision, see page 35ff.

156 *She speaks of how human hands offer the "tangibleness"*: Hozeski, *Hildegard of Bingen's Scivias*, 90.

156 *"A word has sound so that it may be heard"*: ibid., 91.

157 *the throne of god, according to Ezekiel*: Ezekiel 1.26.

158 *Christ is a "light of lights"*: See John 1.4-5, 9; 8.12; 9.5.

158 *"Once I had seen that sphere of unmanifest Light"*: Muktananda, *Play of Consciousness*, 198.

158 *"The rapture of bliss was steadily increasing"*: ibid., 199.

158 *"Every day my conviction became stronger"*: ibid., 199f.

158 *"As I gazed at the tiny Blue Pearl"*: ibid., 205.

159 *"Chiti" is the power of universal consciousness*: ibid., 28.

159 *Just like Wisdom herself, who in the Western Scriptures "plays everywhere"*: Proverbs 8.

159 *"As I passed inside the Blue Pearl, I once again saw"*: Muktananda, *Play of Consciousness*, 206f.

159 *"I see first the blue light and then the person"*: ibid., 207.

160 *"While the universe celebrates itself in every mode of being"*: Berry, *The Great Work*, 19.

161 *yet lacks "any color, any shape, or any form"*: Swami Muktananda, *From the Finite to the Infinite* (South Fallsburg, NY: SYDA Foundation, 1994), 491.

161 *"The blue light is in everyone's heart"*: ibid., 491, 493.

161 *"The light of this Pearl is so brilliant"*: ibid., 493, 494, 495.

162 *"In reality the universe is a divine sport"*: Muktananda, *The Play of Consciousness*, 210f.

163 *"Shiva can create only when He is united"*: Swami Kripananda, *The Sacred Power: A Seeker's Guide to Kundalini* (South Fallsburg, NY: SYDA Foundation, 1995), 14.

163 *"found a tiny cavern inside lined with glittering quartz"*: Jastrab, *Sacred Manhood*, xxii.

164 *"the purpose of sexual desire is creation"*: Deida, *The Way of the Superior Man*, 148.

165 *the Chandogya Upanishads say: "Where there is creating, there is progress"*: Fox, *One River, Many Wells*, 245.

165 *"Art is the only language wild enough"*: Jastrab, *Sacred Manhood*, 169.

166 *The Dalai Lama teaches that "we can reject everything else"*: Fox, *One River, Many Wells*, 377.

166 *"Be you compassionate as your Creator"*: Luke 6.36.

166 *"The presence of God is felt"*: Fox, *One River, Many Wells*, 389.

167 *In an article entitled "Zen and the Art of Lawyering"*: Heidi Benson, "Zen and the Art of Lawyering: Legal Eagles Find Meditation a Stress Solution," *San Francisco Chronicle*, July 30, 2007.

169 *"It is amazing what the power of compassion in action"*: Letter to author, December 12, 2007. For more about Bernard's work go to www.ewb-usa.org. See also the article on him in *Time* magazine: http://www.time.com/time/magazine/article/0,9171,1689197,00.html.

169 *Thomas Aquinas teaches that "God is supremely joyful"*: Fox, *Sheer Joy*, 119, 120.

170 *"Grandfather fire is the original light"*: Primack and Abrams, *The View from the Center of the Universe*, 34.

CHAPTER 9: EARTH FATHER

173 *we live with a "popular belief that in almost all primates"*: Jeffrey Moussaieff Masson, *The Evolution of Fatherhood* (New York: Ballantine Books, 1999), 1, 5.

174 *animal parents "do all they can to secure"*: ibid., 7f., 16f., 35.

174 *Masson recognizes wolves as "magnificent fathers"*: ibid., 40f.

174 *For the dog, "we are the pack"*: ibid., 45.

175 *Masson has found that generally speaking, "among mammals, fatherhood"*: ibid., 53, 55.

175 *Masson believes that "it is a good thing for human fathers"*: ibid., 76f.

176 *"As each new generation of men become fathers"*: Bolen, *Gods in Everyman*, 296.

176 *"The earth father takes on the job of providing"*: ibid., 296, 297.

176 *"Fathers the world over, rich and poor alike, are increasingly"*: Robert M. Franklin, *Crisis in the Village: Restoring Hope in African American Communities* (Minneapolis: Fortress Press, 2007), 97f.

177 *healing the fatherhood crisis today requires "expanding job placement services"*: ibid., 99.

177 *Our society is, he says, "losing the art of intimacy"*: ibid., 101.

177 *"Nothing will change so long as we wait for the absent fathers"*: Bly and Woodman, *The Maiden King*, 146.

178 *"If you ask your earthly father"*: John Dominic Crossan, *The Essential Jesus: Original Sayings and Earliest Images* (San Francisco: HarperSanFrancisco, 1994), 115.

178 *Robert Bly says that "an 'unconscious father' is a force for tyranny"*: Bly and Woodman, *The Maiden King*, 27.

178 *"The old petrifying mother is like a great lizard"*: ibid., 28.

179 *"The hero — by definition solitary — is thus the pinnacle"*: Gordon Wheeler and Daniel E. Jones, "Finding Our Sons: A Male-Male Gestalt," in Robert G. Lee and Gordon Wheeler, eds., *The Voice of Shame: Silence and Connection in Psychotherapy* (San Francisco: Jossey-Bass, 1996), 92, 93.

179 *which invariably "implies a relationship of need or dependency"*: ibid., 86, 65, 83, 67.

180 *"The Nazis," he said, "were not going to return with swastikas and brown shirts"*: Chris Hedges, "The Christian Right and the Rise of American Fascism." Interview on "Democracy Now," February 19, 2007.

180 *Robert Bly believes that a good father helps "wean each person"*: Bly and Woodman, *The Maiden King*, 46.

183 *"For far too long our concept of God has suffered"*: Essay by Matt Henry, "A Songwriter's Reflections," sent to author March 2007. Audio versions of Matt's songs are available at www.paintedguitar.com/paternalheart.html.

183 *"Often our trust is not full"*: Doyle, *Meditations with Julian of Norwich*, 67.

184 *"Nothing people ever do is as appropriate"*: Fox, *Meditations with Meister Eckhart*, 82.

186 *St. Paul notes that the whole creation has been "groaning in labor pains"*: Romans 8.22.

186 *"God's self-knowledge, which from eternity"*: Matthew Fox, *Passion for Creation: The Earth-Honoring Spirituality of Meister Eckhart* (Rochester, VT: Inner Traditions, 2000), 93.

187   *Leonardo Boff fondly calls God a "motherly Father and a fatherly Mother"*: Leonardo Boff, *Holy Trinity, Perfect Community* (Maryknoll, NY: Orbis Books, 2000), 72.

187   *the* vav *and the* heh *"represent the male and female forces"*: Aryeh Kaplan, *Jewish Meditation: A Practical Guide* (New York: Schocken Books, 1985), 154.

187   *The Kabbalists would likewise call it Boundless*: Daniel C. Matt, *The Essential Kabbalah: The Heart of Jewish Mysticism* (San Francisco: HarperSanFrancisco, 1996), 67.

188   *"The Tao is like an empty bowl"*: John C. H. Wu, trans., *Tao Teh Ching* (Boston: Shambhala Publications, 1989), 9.

188   *Or, as Eckhart says, "What is created flows out"*: Fox, *Meditations with Meister Eckhart*, 57.

188   *Theologian Jürgen Moltmann contends that God's creativity derives from*: Jürgen Moltmann, *God in Creation* (Minneapolis: Fortress Press, 1993), 75-77.

190   *As the divine has bestowed on us the "dignity of causality"*: Fox, *Sheer Joy*, 128.

192   *"A mentor does not have to be a Mother Teresa"*: Meredith May, "A Plague of Killing: Filling a Void," *San Francisco Chronicle*, December 10, 2007, A10.

192   *Ankara, Turkey, has been hit by a drought so fierce*: See Tom Engelhardt, "How Dry We Are: A Question No One Wants to Raise About Drought," November 11, 2007, www.tomdispatch.com. See http://www.tomdispatch.com/post/print/174863/Tomgram%253A%2520%2520As%2520.

193   *As Marion Woodman puts it, "A flawed solar myth"*: Bly and Woodman, *The Maiden King*, 138.

193   *"The transformation of* Homo sapiens *into* Homo consumerus *takes place"*: Troy Jollimore, "Hey, Kids! Madison Avenue Wants You! A Review of *Consumed: How Markets Corrupt Children, Infantilize Adults, and Swallow Citizens Whole*," *San Francisco Chronicle*, April 1, 2007, M1, M3.

194   *"Our economy rewards competition rather than cooperation"*: Sanders, *Hunting for Hope*, 72.

194   *"You're so worried about the fate of the earth"*: ibid., 10, 1f.

194   *"Of all the enemies to public liberty war is, perhaps, the most to be dreaded"*: James Madison, "Political Observations," April 20, 1795, in *Letters and Other Writings of James Madison*, vol. 4 (1865), 491.

196   *Masson reports that he has "never spoken to a father of grown children"*: Sanders, *Hunting for Hope*, 202, 203, 207.

196   *Scott Sanders reports that "I cannot turn off my fathering mind"*: ibid., 14, 209, 208.

CHAPTER 10: GRANDFATHER SKY

200   *"Eye-opening research… found the happiest Americans are the oldest"*: Lindsey Tanner, "Despite Myth, Old Age Is the Happiest Time," AP, April 18, 2008.

201   *he found he was being "initiated as an elder"*: Zalman Schachter-Shalomi, *From Ageing to Sage-ing: A Profound New Vision of Growing Older* (New York: Warner Books, 1995), 2f.

201   *Schachter calls this saging, a "new model of late-life development"*: ibid., 5, 7, 50, 15.

203   *As John Weir Perry puts it, "In our later years, we feel connected to the world"*: ibid., 149f.

204   *The Sufi mystic Hafiz declares, "God has written a thousand promises"*: Fox, *One River,
      Many Wells*, 335.

204   *"Thus we are, we are mortal"*: ibid., 338.

205   *"Native Americans think of their elders as wisdomkeepers"*: Schachter-Shalomi, *From
      Age-ing to Sage-ing*, 52f., 53.

206   *"the decline of vigor in old age is largely"*: ibid., 265.

207   *As Schachter points out, "beginning with the Industrial Revolution, mentoring"*: ibid., 191.

207   *A particularly poignant story was recently told of actor Ed Harris*: Jesse Hamlin, "They're
      in the Big Leagues Now," *San Francisco Chronicle*, April 25, 2008, E1, E6.

209   *True elder mentoring, in Schachter's eyes, requires five elements*: Schachter-Shalomi,
      From Age-ing to Sage-ing, 200-203.

217   *Native American Chief Seattle, who was an amazingly beautiful man and that great
      farewell speech*: See Matthew Fox, *A Spirituality Named Compassion* (Rochester, VT:
      Inner Traditions, 1999), 164f.

CHAPTER 11:
THE SACRED MARRIAGE OF MASCULINE AND FEMININE

221   *Taoist teacher Mantak Chia says, "within every moment"*: Chia, *Taoist Secrets of Love*, 57f.

222   *"a balanced union of female and male"*: Riane Eisler, *Sacred Pleasure*, 144.

222   *He writes, "A castrated man cannot enter into the* hieros gamos*"*: Monick, *Castration
      and Male Rage*, 77, 17.

225   *Thomas Berry puts it this way: "A younger generation is growing up"*: Thomas Berry, *The
      Great Work*, 200.

225   *David Suzuki, in an appropriately titled book* The Sacred Balance: David Suzuki, *The
      Sacred Balance: Rediscovering Our Place in Nature* (Vancouver: Greystone Books,
      2002), 84.

228   *"Your depression is connected to your insolence"*: Bly and Woodman, *The Maiden King*, 76.

231   *the dark feminine who exercises "tough mother love that challenges"*: Dolores Whelan,
      Ever Ancient, Ever New: Celtic Spirituality in the 21ˢᵗ Century (Blackrock: Dublin, Ire-
      land: The Columbia Press, 2006), 75.

232   *the African goddess Isis "prevailed through the force of love"*: Lucia Chiavola Birnbaum,
      Dark Mother: African Origins and Godmothers (New York: Authors Choice Press,
      2001), 20.

232   *"The next step toward religious understanding"*: ibid., 26f.

232   *"The Black Madonna is the embodiment of the Divine Feminine"*: Jennifer Zazo, ex-
      cerpt from Curatorial Statement of The Black Madonna Exhibition, August 2, 2007.
      See http://www.theblackmadonnaexhibition.com.

232   *"In the dreams of contemporary men and women, there is appearing"*: Bly and Wood-
      man, *The Maiden King*, 146f.

233   *In a previous study I listed a number of reasons*: See Fred Gustafson, ed., *The Moonlit
      Path: Reflections on the Dark Feminine* (Berwick, ME: Nicolas-Hays, 2003).

233   *Meister Eckhart observes that "the ground of the soul"*: Fox, *Meditations with Meister Eckhart*, 42.

233   *Andrew Harvey puts it this way: "The Black Madonna is the transcendent Kali-Mother"*: Andrew Harvey, *The Return of the Mother* (Berkeley: Frog Ltd., 1995), 371.

233   *Eckhart calls God's darkness a "superessential darkness"*: Fox, *Meditations with Meister Eckhart*, 43.

234   *The Black Madonna calls us down to honor our lower chakras*: See Fox, *Sins of the Spirit*, 94-116, 167-327.

235   *Andrew Harvey says, "The Black Madonna is also the Queen of Nature"*: Harvey, *The Return of the Mother*, 371.

236   *Meister Eckhart says, "All the names we give to God"*: Fox, *Meditations with Meister Eckhart*, 42.

237   *"an immense force of protection, an immense alchemical power"*: Harvey, *The Return of the Mother*, 372.

237   *Andrew Harvey says, she is "queen of the underworld"*: ibid., 372f.

238   *"I have exhaled a perfume like cinnamon and acacia"*: Ecclesiastes 24.15, 19-22.

239   *"Compassion means justice"*: Fox, *Meditations with Meister Eckhart*, 103.

239   *"has routed the proud of heart. He has pulled down princes"*: Luke 1.51–53.

239   *"The convulsive hold which Mary to this day"*: Blackmur, *Henry Adams*, 203.

239   *"I am Nature, the universal Mother"*: Eloise McKinney-Johnson, "Egypt's Isis: The Original Black Madonna," *Journal of African Civilizations* (April 1984), 66.

240   *"O child of God and Mother of things"*: M. D. Chenu, *Nature, Man and Society in the Twelfth Century* (Chicago: University of Chicago Press, 1968), 19.

240   *the Thet "knot" is an important symbol of Isis*: McKinney-Johnson, "Egypt's Isis," 71.

240   *"The pictures and sculptures wherein she is represented"*: ibid., 67.

241   *"As mother and earth woman, the Great Mother is the 'throne'"*: ibid., 68.

242   *she was "Queen of the sciences" and "mistress of all the arts and sciences"*: Blackmur, *Henry Adams*, 206.

242   *"all things in existence need to be shaken"*: McKinney-Johnson, "Egypt's Isis," 71.

243   *An honoring of darkness is long overdue*: See Eulalio R. Baltazar, *The Dark Center: A Process Theology of Blackness* (New York: Paulist Press, 1973).

244   *"The yin and yang represent all the opposite principles"*: Richard Hooker, "Chinese Philosophy: Yin and Yang," July 27, 2007. http://www.wsu.edu:8080/~dee/CHPHIL/YINYANG.HTM.

245   *"When and if you make all twos into one"*: Neil Douglas Klotz, *The Genesis Meditations: A Shared Practice of Peace for Christians, Jews, and Muslims* (Wheaton, IL: Quest Books, 2003), 221.

246   *"This 'keeping of the One so as to remain in harmony' is the essence"*: Harvey, *The Return of the Mother*, 312, 90.

246   *Harvey writes, "To be one in this glorious sense is to be in heaven"*: ibid., 90.

246   *"The patriarchal vision of the Mother exalts and transcendalizes"*: ibid., 359.

247   *"The child, in fact, becomes the mother of a stream of sacred"*: ibid., 91.

247 *"where the feminine is understood as a personification"*: Whelan, *Ever Ancient, Ever New,* 35f.

247 *This marriage represented the union "of the worlds of the human"*: ibid., 58.

CHAPTER 12: OTHER SACRED UNIONS

262 *"The ideas of Western science and democracy have penetrated to every part"*: Bede Griffiths, *The Marriage of East and West* (Tucson, AZ: Medio Media Publishing, 2003), 151f., 152, 153.

263 *"intuition belongs not to the sunlit surface of the mind"*: ibid., 155f.

263 *"Intuition cannot be produced"*: ibid., 157, 158f.

264 *"It finds expression not in abstract concepts"*: ibid., 158f.

264 *"It is the great illusion of the Western world"*: ibid., 159.

264 *"What we have to seek is the 'marriage' of reason and intuition"*: ibid., 160.

266 *Daniel H. Pink in his book* A Whole New Mind *calls "L-Directed Thinking" and "R-Directed Thinking"*: Pink, *A Whole New Mind,* 26.

266 *"But this is changing," Pink writes*: ibid., 27.

266 *"If we're only intuitive, we're likely to be dreamers"*: Schachter-Shalomi, *From Age-ing to Sage-ing,* 43.

267 *the lead character was "the mass production worker"*: Pink, *A Whole New Mind,* 48f, 166, 67. Italics his.

267 *when it comes to "rule-based logic, calculation and sequential thinking"*: ibid., 43f.

267 *material goods in favor of "more R-Directed sensibilities"*: ibid., 33, 59, 164.

268 *According to Pink, "great minds are androgynous"*: ibid., 132.

268 *"As life continues, however, we begin to realize"*: Bly and Woodman, *The Maiden King,* 224.

268 *It "demands hard work in bringing to union"*: ibid., 221f.

272 *Kingsley comments: "In terms of physical age it could mean"*: Peter Kingsley, *In the Dark Places of Wisdom* (Inverness, CA: The Golden Sufi Center, 2004), 71f.

272 *Kingsley writes, to a "man of any age who's gone beyond time"*: ibid., 217f.

272 *"There is evidence from many cultures"*: Bly and Woodman, *The Maiden King,* 21f.

273 *when she observes that "most young men in our culture"*: ibid., 181.

273 *Here is how Woodman puts it: "The adult fully and consciously awake"*: ibid., 118, 157.

CONCLUSION:
REAL MEN ARE BEARERS OF THE SACRED MASCULINE

284 *"Worry less about what you do and more about who you are"*: Fox, *Meditations with Meister Eckhart,* 97.

285 *Companies in this movement "are stewards of the whole"*: Ilana DeBare, "For Philanthropy, B Is Letter Perfect," *San Francisco Chronicle,* May 18, 2008, C1, C5.

293 *As the Sufi mystic Hafiz puts it, "The warriors tame the beasts in their past"*: Fox, *One River, Many Wells,* 416.

ACKNOWLEDGMENTS

I WISH TO ACKNOWLEDGE THE MANY CONTRIBUTORS, silent and not so silent, to these pages — men and women who have taught me and challenged me over the years. In addition to those to whom I have dedicated the book, allow me to thank all those authors I invoke in my footnotes for teaching me by way of their thoughts and wonderful language. A camaraderie of thinkers continually feeds me good and nourishing intellectual food. Each chapter has focused in a special manner on a particular theme, and within each I have drawn in a special way from a few of those thinkers, whether they are Anderson and Hicks on the Green Man, or Primack and Abrams on Father Sky, or Chia and Deida on Sexuality, or Diamond and Ehrenreich on Hunter-Gatherers, or Masson and Sanders on Fatherhood, or Muktananda on the Blue Man, or Rabbi Schachtner on the Grandfather Heart and eldership.

I also give special thanks to those men who came out of the closet to speak their hearts on masculine spirituality through interviews, including K J, Professor Pitt, John Conger, Jim Miller, Mark Nicholson, and Christian de la Huerta.

I want to acknowledge the groundbreaking work of Robert Bly, Joseph Jastrab, and others in the first generation of male liberationists who began this work with dedication and commitment and on whose shoulders I precariously balance. And I thank Jim Roberts and Brother Joseph Kilikevice for their inspired work with men.

I want to thank my editor at New World Library, Jason Gardner, and also editor Jeff Campbell. Thanks also to my book agent, Ned Leavitt. A special thanks to Fred Gustafson for letting me adapt my article on the Black Madonna from his fine book *The Moonlit Path*. And to Dr. Clarissa Pinkola Estés, Aaron Stern, Philip Harmonn, Marvin Anderson, and Lama Tsomo for their encouragement along the way. And Dennis Edwards, Mel Bricker, and Debra Martin for their assistance in upholding my daily responsibilities, and Tom Christian for his research assistance. I am also grateful to the Academy for the Love of Learning for their support and encouragement, and to Debra Martin for introducing me to the Blue Pearl and the Blue Man.

PERMISSION ACKNOWLEDGMENTS

Grateful acknowledgment is made to the authors and publishers for the use of the following material. Every effort has been made to contact rights holders of quoted material. If notified, the publishers of this book will be pleased to rectify an omission in future editions.

Pages 181–82: "Father Earth," copyright © 1970 by Clarissa Pinkola Estés, used by permission of Clarissa Pinkola Estés, excerpted from *La Pasionaria*. For permissions requests: projectscreener@aol.com.

Pages 182–91: Matt Henry's essay and lyrics to "Matter of Time" and "While You Let Me" by Matt Henry, used by permission of Matt Henry.

INDEX

ABOUT THE AUTHOR

MATTHEW FOX WAS A MEMBER of the Dominican Order for thirty-four years. He holds a doctorate (received summa cum laude) in the History and Theology of Spirituality from the Institut Catholique de Paris. Seeking to establish a pedagogy that was friendly to learning spirituality, he established the Institute in Culture and Creation Spirituality, which operated for seven years at Mundelein College in Chicago and twelve years at Holy Names College in Oakland, California. For ten of those years at Holy Names College, Cardinal Ratzinger (now Pope Benedict XVI), as the Catholic Church's chief inquisitor and head of the Congregation of Doctrine and Faith, tried to shut the program down. Ratzinger silenced Fox for one year in 1988 and forced him to step down as director. Three years later he expelled Fox from the order and aborted the program. Rather than disband his amazing ecumenical faculty, Fox started the University of Creation Spirituality in Oakland, where he was president for nine years.

He is currently a scholar in residence with the Academy for the Love of Learning in Santa Fe, New Mexico. He is working with others to create a new educational experience for inner-city youth called YELLAWE (Youth and Elder Learning Laboratory for Ancestral Wisdom Education). He lectures, teaches, writes, and serves as president of the nonprofit he created in 1984, Friends of Creation Spirituality. He is the author of twenty-eight books and lives in Oakland, California. His website is www.matthewfox.org.